The Tragedy of Religious Freedom

The Tragedy of
Religious Freedom

Marc O. DeGirolami

Harvard University Press

Cambridge, Massachusetts · London, England

2013

Library of Congress Cataloging-in-Publication Data

DeGirolami, Marc O.
The tragedy of religious freedom / Marc O. DeGirolami.
pages cm
Includes bibliographical references and index.
ISBN 978-0-674-07266-4 (alk. paper)
1. Freedom of religion—United States.   I. Title.
KF4783.D44 2013
342.7308'52—dc23   2012045931

For Lisa and Thomas,

and for my father

Contents

Conflict is perpetual: why then should we be deceived?
Stuart Hampshire, 1999

What has been missing in recent generations from the debate between positivists and legal naturalists is recognition of the normative significance of the historical dimension of law.
Harold J. Berman, 2005

Introduction

S cholars of the law confront a predicament. To theorize about the
law—to organize one's ideas into generalities that capture real legal
phenomena—is the peak of scholarly achievement. And with good reason, for when legal theory explains the world of law without distortion
or caricature, when it reflects crisply the legal world's infinite variety in
subtle and elegant abstraction, it offers incomparable illumination. At its
best, legal theory is a wonder, a pathway to wisdom. The trouble is that
legal theory's ambition to evaluate and pass judgment can suffocate its
capacity to explain and understand. At its worst—when it is puffed up
with pride—legal theorizing tends toward legal dogmatizing.

In few areas is this propensity more pronounced than in the legal
theory of religious liberty. The reasons are many but may be distilled to
a single, fundamental incongruity. Legal theory seeks to fix crystalline
conceptual categories, the better to praise or condemn the law's coercive
demands. Legal theory is embarrassed by incoherence. It desperately
wants to sort out and weigh up. Its critical eye is perpetually trained not
only on the rules imposed by the law, but also, and inevitably, on the
social and cultural objects of those impositions. But the social practice of
religious liberty is resistant to legal theory's self-assured, single-minded
drive to evaluate, justify, and adjudge.

For some time, and increasingly in recent years, scholars of religious liberty have criticized both the direction and coherence of the law.[1] It is no exaggeration to say that *Employment Division v. Smith*,[2] the Supreme Court's most important religious liberty decision of the last two decades, is commonly viewed by scholars as one of the great disasters of the law of church and state.[3] The doctrine encrusting the constitutional proscription against government "establishment" of religion fares little better by their lights.[4] Disaffection for their own field, one might say, is unique in uniting them.

Yet the root of their displeasure is not, as many thinkers insist, in the failure of courts to discover and apply the true or best principles of religious liberty. Neither, as claim others, does it lie in the refusal to accept the skeptical conclusion that the quest for theory is in vain because "principles" of religious liberty, timeless or otherwise, are academic phantoms. One or the other of these positions has informed more than a generation of academic writing about religious liberty, as scholar upon scholar either champions some principle of legal theory or rebels against the lot of them. In their enthusiasm to expound and justify their prescriptions for constitutional policy, many scholars have swept past the predicament of legal theory—that theory is both necessary and dangerously apt to distort the complexity of the world that it strives to understand.

In contrast with both positions, this book claims that the true impediment faced by those who study the law of religious liberty has been the failure to attend sufficiently to the predicament of legal theory. Any legal theory that reduces religious liberty to a set of supreme principles, let alone a single all-powerful imperative, is demanding far too much. Such theories are poorly equipped to understand and manage the untidy welter of values that are encompassed in the social and legal practice of religious liberty. Yet neither is skepticism the answer. Legal theory is inescapable if the values that characterize the sundry ideas of religious liberty are capable of sustained and insightful reflection. Theory is the academic's highest art: "To comprehend and contrast and classify and arrange," Isaiah Berlin once observed, "to see in patterns of lesser or greater complexity, is not a peculiar kind of thinking, it is thinking itself."[5]

Tragedy and History

This book defends a conception of religious liberty that avoids the twin dangers of reliance on reductive and systematic justifications, on the one hand, and thoroughgoing skepticism about the possibility of theorizing, on the other. The best theory of religious liberty will be flexible enough to acknowledge its own limits in the face of the frequently conflicting goods of religious liberty, even as it seeks to understand them. It will reflect a pluralistic perspective on the law of church and state that embraces the contingency and conditionality, but also the context independence, of the multitude of values of religious liberty. It will proceed with caution on the delicate terrain that is its subject. And, of greatest practical importance, it will offer an approach to conflict resolution that is neither a systematic decision procedure nor an ad hoc all-things-considered pragmatism, but instead reflects a particular cast of mind or disposition—a quality more than a theory.

The approach is called the method of tragedy and history, and it consists of five central theses. First, the clash of values of religious liberty—that the values which swirl around the conflicts of religious liberty are incompatible and incommensurable. Second, the inadequacy of skepticism—that notwithstanding the perpetual clash of values, a hard skepticism about the possibility of a principled approach to religious liberty under the Constitution is unavailing. Third, loss, sacrifice, and the disposition of custom—that the disposition or quality which issues from the clash of values of religious liberty is keenly attuned to the losses and sacrifices entailed in legal decision making, as well as the role that habit and custom play in the formation of conceptions of religious liberty. Fourth, the need for modest movement—that because of the tragic conflicts which attend many religious liberty cases, the best approach to these issues is gradualist and incremental. And fifth, the conciliations of history—that in light of tragic conflict, courts should use doctrinal and social history as guides to legal change.

A brief word about my use of the terms *comedy* and *tragedy*. A comedy moves from sorrow to joy. Its aim is to take an existing chaos and to order it through and through—to give it a satisfying and intimately worked-out architecture. In a comedy, everything falls into its proper, collision-less place—a place in which a problem that at first seemed intractable has been fully worked out, completely resolved, with the result that the human condition has progressed and been improved.[6] Consider, in this vein, Dante Alighieri's *Divine Comedy*. Attention is seldom paid to the choice of the term *comedy*—Dante's own[7]—but it is an enlightening designation. When Dante ascends to the Empyrean, the perfection of God's triune universe—*Inferno, Purgatorio, Paradiso*—is at last revealed to him in its fully systematized splendor.[8] What begins in the anguish of a dark and tangled forest[9] ends in the contented, childlike comfort of divinely illuminated grace and understanding.[10]

A tragedy, by contrast, proceeds not from joy to sorrow, but from struggle to unresolved struggle. Aristotle discusses tragedy in some detail in his *Poetics*,[11] but in this context the meaning is perhaps closer to the sensibility evoked by the philosopher Martha Nussbaum in her study of Greek tragedy:

> That I am an agent, but also a plant; that much that I did not make goes towards making me whatever I shall be praised or blamed for being; that I must constantly choose among competing and apparently incommensurable goods and that circumstances may force me to a position in which I cannot help being false to something or doing some wrong. . . .[12]

Tragedy is a study in opposition; comedy in consilience. Whatever leads the tragic hero to choose one course of action, elevating one conception of the good, also does irreparable damage to other viable conceptions and ultimately to his own ethical worldview. The roads not taken are also permanently closed down. In certain conflicts, though each opposing force may be itself ethically justified, "each can establish the true and positive content of its own aim and character only by denying and infringing the equally justified power of the other."[13] Tragedy arises when, as in law, there is partial order and partial disorder. And one feels tragedy's sting in the effort to make a single and perfectly harmonious whole—a comedy—of ineluctably clashing ideals.

These classical, literary, and philosophical meanings of comedy and tragedy are suggestive of this book's purposes. The first three theses of the method of tragedy and history are tragic inasmuch as they challenge the reigning academic orthodoxy that it is theory's role to provide fully systematic and ever-improving—that is, comic—resolutions to legal dilemmas. The avatar of comic legal theory is the famous legal and political philosopher Ronald Dworkin, who has explained its core creed:

> It is in the nature of legal interpretation—not just but particularly constitutional interpretation—to aim at happy endings. There is no alternative, except aiming at unhappy ones. . . . Telling it how it is means, up to a point, telling it how it should be. . . . That is a noble faith, and only optimism can redeem it.[14]

Most recently, Dworkin has mounted a thoroughgoing defense of the "hedgehog's" approach to political theory—the view that all political and legal value is monistic,[15] that value pluralism is deeply in error, and that "[t]he truth about living well and being good and what is wonderful is not only coherent but mutually supporting."[16]

Comic theorists of religious liberty take the view that legal theory's fundamental aim is to order the law so as to lend it both a clean predictability and a satisfying coherence.[17] For constitutional disputes in the area of religious liberty, comic theories hold out the promise that they can justify, in a rigorously systematic way, specific outcomes in line with their monistic premises. They also, at times, ignore or marginalize loss, regret, and the paradoxes of lived experience—the natural residue of each decided case.

Thus, on a comic view, if a group of Native Americans objects to the government's plan to build a road straight through its sacred lands, but it cannot translate its complaint into the language of "noncoercion," then there simply is no constitutional religious liberty interest at stake; that the result risks destroying the religion itself is, even if undesirable, irrelevant.[18] If Amish parents maintain that their children ought to be exempted from two years of high school education, and the state objects, some comic theorists of religious liberty argue that the only acceptable criterion by which to assess the validity of the respective positions is egalitarian;[19] anything else would be constitutionally inconsequential. If a religious organization claims that it ought to be permitted the freedom to appoint an all-male clergy, that claim is rejected by the comic theorist as obviously in violation of antidiscrimination laws that are facially formally neutral. So powerful is the hold of comedy on the imagination of legal thinkers that even those writers who have called attention to the conflicting values of religious liberty inevitably revert to prescribing an answer that champions a small set of principles—a solution that is held out as somehow optimal or at least a distinctive progress beyond the previous state of affairs. Even for them, conflict is never truly foundational; it is an obstacle to be observed and tacitly circumnavigated.

The virtue of comic theory is that it brings the intellectual and psychological comforts of clarity, elegance, and system where an intolerable confusion is felt to reign.[20] No one would deny that comic theory provides simple and easily applied rules. But it does so at considerable cost. Where there is an irreconcilable clash of values of religious liberty, comic theories of religious liberty resolve it by flattening out the conflicts until they are coherent but often unrecognizable.

The tragic theses of the method of tragedy and history reject this view. In its place, they offer this conjecture: it is of the essence of the plural values contained in ideas of religious liberty—and of what we prize in them—that they resist the incursion and domination of other rival values. Each value struggles in perpetuity to avoid absorption and subordination by the others.[21] And this means that decision making in this area can never be fully systematized, and that it will be forever burdened by tragic outcomes, results that sacrifice important values whose loss cannot be compensated by the triumph of others. An aversion to the conceits of systematization and an embrace of the inevitability of tragic loss and sacrifice, therefore, must represent the cornerstone of any viable approach to religious liberty. The clash of values is not merely an impediment to be pointed out and bypassed. It is a permanent fixture of the human condition, made manifest with singular acuity in these First Amendment conflicts. It results both from the limits of human reasoning and from the conflict of human interests and aspirations.

The tragic theorist holds that the intellectual surrender required of the commitment to religious liberty demands the abandonment of the comic conviction that a single, integrated answer may be found to the question of why it is that religious belief and practice have value and ought to be protected by law. It requires this relinquishment because the collisions of the values of religious liberty are foundational and constitutive features of our own lives. It is because the conflicts of religious liberty reflect a fundamental and often irreconcilable pluralism, rather than merely the appearance of conflict which judges, lawyers, and all manner of public intellectuals ought under ideal circumstances to resolve, that the tragic reconciliations of the past deserve particular regard.

It is here that the last two theses of the method of tragedy and history enter the scene. These theses are historically oriented in that they counsel a reticent yet still fully engaged role for both lawyers and courts that emphasizes doctrinal and social history as the benchmark of argument (for lawyers) and judgment (for courts). The first of the historic theses prescribes a modest and ascetic approach to doctrinal change. The second emphasizes the importance of existing legal doctrine and the nation's social history of engagement with questions of religious liberty in negotiating the tragedies of conflict.

A critic could not be faulted for pointing out that legal doctrine and American history may be vague, ambiguous, or unsatisfying guides. Legal doctrines may be unsettled. They may conflict. Or they may reflect outdated and otherwise unattractive values and practices. And the same may be said for the social traditions of the American nation as they have developed through time. Nevertheless, the historical theses of the tragic-historic method make the case that doctrinal and social traditions offer points of reference against which the tragedies of the conflicts of religious liberty may be managed. Only thus can the predicament of legal theory be competently managed.

The use of doctrinal and social history as a benchmark—a beacon—in managing conflict also renders the historical theses harmonious with the tragic theses. The answers offered by the historical theses do not purport to resolve the conflicts described by the tragic theses. That is an impossibility which comic legal theory only appears to accomplish by a beguiling but ultimately misleading appeal to system. Instead, doctrinal and social history offer a modality of conflict resolution that may not exacerbate the conflicts of religious liberty by indulging in legal theory's excesses.

In negotiating the conflicts of values, the method of tragedy and history is guided by the power of the past—that is, by the belief that the force of social history and legal precedent is useful because it represents the collected wisdom of the past in managing the tragedies of the present. However he decides—whether for the church or the state—the tragic-historic judge will ensure that his opinion presents as thorough an accounting of the rival claims as can be accommodated. Just in virtue of presenting that account, he will affect the development of the law, for legal dicta—the nonbinding reflections that season judicial opinions—often influence future cases. And he will face backward—toward the litigants, the doctrine, and the history that precedes them—for guidance in moving forward.

In what follows, the method of tragedy and history will be explained, compared with other influential theories of religious liberty, tested in several concrete contexts, and defended against various criticisms. Taken altogether, the method of tragedy and history responds to the single greatest challenge posed by the religion clauses: how to account for the plurality of ideas about religious liberty—which is directly influenced by the plurality of ideas about religion itself—and the state's proper relationship to them.

While a detailed exposition of the tragic-historic method is pursued in later chapters, it may be helpful to preview three overarching commitments evinced by its theses when considered synthetically. These might be summarized as suggesting a tertium quid—a third thing—for legal theory: neither a monistic reduction nor a skeptical resignation, but a new possibility.

First, it is a strength of the tragic-historic method that it can accommodate the reasonable views of competing approaches while rejecting their more implausibly ambitious claims. In this way, it strikes a middle course between the prevailing monistic and thickly skeptical theories of religious liberty, a position that the intellectual historian Arthur Lovejoy once acutely described as "the delicate and difficult art" of theory, in which "since no fixed and comprehensive rule can be laid down for it, we shall doubtless never attain perfection."[22]

What is reasonable in the monistic accounts of religious liberty is the conviction that certain values or principles are important and ought to influence decision making. What is unreasonable is the inflation of those values or principles to inviolable status. What is reasonable in the skeptical accounts of religious liberty is the disavowal of theories that aspire to fully systematic constitutional resolutions without tragic remainder. What is unreasonable are the further conclusions that there are no context-independent values of religious liberty, that judges and lawyers have no more (and perhaps much less) to say about religious liberty than anyone else, that the best that can be done is an intuitive, commonsensical "muddling through" unguided by any larger view, and that the category "religion" is incapable of any constitutional protection because it is merely the figment of the scholar's imagination or the object of the intellectual colonist's hegemony. The method of tragedy and history steers a path between these two poles, taking what is best from each and leaving the rest.

Second, in traveling this middle road, the method of tragedy and history also suggests a different answer to the question of what role public intellectuals ought to play. Both monists and skeptics believe that theory is and must be meant to solve the conflicts of religious liberty by recourse to an interpretive rule or doctrine that provides a clear-cut and general decision procedure across an entire swath of cases. Monistic theorists are sanguine about this role for theory. Skeptics are not. But both subscribe to the same fundamental view of legal theory's purposes. Likewise, it is a common view of the judicial role that judges are not following the Constitution—are not faithful to it—unless they can formulate principles applicable across discrete categories of constitutional dispute.[23] If they cannot do so, the argument goes, then decision-making authority ought to lie elsewhere.

The method of tragedy and history differs on all counts. It does not agree that constitutional fidelity and the rule of law are damaged when judges are forthright in confronting the clashing values that underwrite so many religious liberty cases. It does not count the widely decried "inconsistency" of the law of church and state as a flaw or an impediment to a properly functioning legal system. Certainly it does not expect or hope that intellectual energy, powerful and elegant as it may be, will ever solve this state of affairs.

To the contrary, the method of tragedy and history holds that it is exactly the theoretical unruliness of the multiple values of religious liberty that counsels a different role for legal theory—one that is guided by modest movement (the fourth thesis) shaped by doctrinal and social history (the fifth). The fundamental reason that the tragic-historic method prizes legal and social traditions—rather than a single value such as autonomy, neutrality, or equality—is that by attending to traditions and historical contingencies, ordinary citizens who give thought to these issues will better understand the reasons that the law has developed as it has, with all of the contours, blemishes, warts, and disfigurations that attend a real, lived, historically inflected experience.

People are born into families, which are in turn parts of economic, ethnic, cultural, racial, regional, intellectual, and religious communities. The languages that they learn to speak; the educations that they receive from parents, schools, and teachers; the influences on their reading habits, their cultural predilections, their friendships, their animosities, their career ambitions, their leisure pursuits; the ways in which they learn to express themselves and their emotions, and to understand what is permitted and forbidden; their fears and hopes—all of these and thousands of like qualities are learned not autonomously, not neutrally, and certainly not equally, but historically. They are learned by participating (cognizantly or not) in the traditions that prevail in particular and local social milieus.

No one denies that people may reject aspects of their histories, and the tragic-historic method is not wedded to all histories indiscriminately. Indeed, idolizing the abstract idea of "history," like "tradition," borders on incoherence. But the claims of history and tradition are not defeated simply by pointing out that they may be repudiated. Those who reject their histories choose others. It is to these social histories—ones that are especially powerful and various in the area of religious belief and practice—and the ways in which legal precedent has grappled with the conflicts among them that public intellectuals should give their sustained attention. Fortunately, there is a rich Anglo-American legal tradition that is oriented in precisely this historical direction—the tradition of the common law.

The third general quality that characterizes the tragic-historic method is its own conflicting internal structure—its diffident openness. The method of tragedy and history aspires to something other than the usual liberal value of tolerance. It challenges its audience—judges, common lawyers, and the ordinary citizens to whom it is addressed—to open themselves to the full range of values of religious liberty, if only to arrive at a more complete understanding of the conflicts that must be decided and the sacrifices and tragic losses that ensue as the law develops.[24] At the same time, in defending modest legal movements, it demands that changes in constitutional practices be effected gradually and cautiously. This presumptive resistance to doctrinal change is necessary for the crucial reason that the rule of law requires that certain formal values— predictability, stability, and equality of application—be respected. But diffidence is also necessary as the best way to manage the competing claims of the rival values of religious liberty while remaining as receptive to them as possible.

Plan of the Book

The book is divided into three parts. Part One describes the central problem that the method of tragedy and history confronts: the current orthodoxy of comic legal theory. It argues that comic legal theory is inadequate because of its core methodological commitments. Chapter 1 presents and critiques the work of several influential and important comic monistic theorists whose work reduces the idea of religious liberty to a single value, equality or neutrality. Skeptical theorists, those who believe that comic legal theory has nothing to offer the law of religious liberty, as well as others who recognize value conflict but nevertheless ultimately rely on a small number of principles, are considered in Chapter 2. The error of the skeptics is the leap from the justified rejection of comic legal theory to the unjustified view that there can be no constitutional theory of religious liberty at all. In all, Part One illustrates the common difficulty faced by today's scholars of religious liberty: a tendency either toward monism or skepticism.

Part Two presents the method of tragedy and history. Chapters 3, 4, and 5 diagnose the predicament of legal theory and explain the tragic theses. Chapters 6 and 7—the historic theses—offer a way forward. It is important to emphasize that the prescriptions offered are not meant to resolve once and for all the clashes described in the first three theses. They are instead an attempt to grapple with the intractable difficulties of conflict in the law of religious liberty in a more honest, realistic, and ultimately more intellectually satisfying fashion than other theories have thus far achieved.

The tragic-historic method is tested in Part Three against several categories of cases, and its value as an approach to conflict resolution is explained and assessed. Chapter 8 considers the special challenge that is posed by the *Smith* case, which held that a single value—formal neutrality—constitutes the sum and substance of religious free exercise under the Constitution. Chapter 9 applies the tragic-historic method to several discrete free exercise disputes, and Chapter 10 does the same for the establishment of religion. Chapter 11 examines various conceptual objections. In specific, it responds to criticisms that the tragic-historic method is overly "negative" in either of two senses—that it is too soft-edged and particularistic to be consistent with the rule of law or that it takes an overly pessimistic view of the meliorative power of legal theory. And, finally, it addresses the important objection that the tragic-historic method demands an inappropriately muscular role for the judiciary.

It is well to conclude this introduction on a reticent note. This book's project is a limited one. It focuses on the challenges of religious freedom in the courts and under the Constitution. But primary responsibility to manage the tragic conflicts of religious liberty rests outside the courts—in other institutions, private as much as public. And if the approach explained in this book is appealing, it will not be because it presents an abstraction that purports to approximate perfection or the world as it ought to be—not because it spins the ball of legal theory faster and more cleverly than its rivals. To the contrary, the method of tragedy and history is worth considering precisely because the possibility of theory is always fragile. It strains to take within its compass the broadest range of values of religious liberty so as to do the least damage to them when conflicts are decided in favor of some and against others. In so doing, the tragic-historic method suggests that legal theory's fundamental aims and limits may be altogether different from what is commonly supposed.

PART I

Religious Liberty and
the Comedy of Legal Theory

This part explores some of the most prominent contemporary accounts of religious liberty. Chapter 1 considers monistic theories, and Chapter 2 reflects on skeptical approaches, including the views of several theorists whom I call quasi tragedians. The purpose of this canvas is to identify and probe what this book claims is legal theory's shared defect—a tendency to detour past the predicament of legal theory when it addresses the reasons for valuing religious liberty. Those already familiar with the accounts discussed may be forgiven for their impatience, but as Sir James Fitzjames Stephen once said of the views of John Stuart Mill, "in stating the grounds of one's dissent from widespread and influential opinions, it is absolutely necessary to take some definite statement of those opinions as a starting point, and it is natural to take the ablest, the most reasonable, and the clearest."[1]

The common characteristic shared by all of these theories, both monistic and skeptical, is their "comic" quality. They are comic inasmuch as they take it as foundational that it is legal theory's purpose to provide systematic and fully worked-out solutions to the problems of religious liberty by recourse to a single overarching value or principle,

sometimes without adequately acknowledging tragic loss.[2] The difference between monistic comic theories and skeptical comic theories is
that the former see this aim as desirable, while the latter see it as delu-
sional. Yet the two comic approaches do not differ on the fundamental
point that legal theory's essential purpose is to effect systematic improvements and progress to the human condition, manifested through our collective legal healthfulness, our Constitution.

The skeptical comic theories have therefore appropriately been called
"anti-theories,"[3] which suggests that their progenitors, too, work within
the same general presuppositions about the purpose of legal theory
espoused by their more sanguine colleagues. The skeptical theorists take
themselves to augur the end of legal theory, given their own assumptions
that legal theory is and must be a comic enterprise. Though the skeptics
perform a valuable service in criticizing comic legal theory, their account
of religious liberty is incomplete and ultimately unsatisfying as well.

The preference for comic theory may be understandable, and it is certainly true that order and clarity which does not sacrifice real complexity
is both elegant and intellectually satisfying.[4] But is the law of religious
liberty ultimately incapable of full systematization? Are the conflicts of
religious liberty unmanageable without the recognition that whatever
path ultimately is chosen often will result in sacrifice and tragic loss of
something truly valuable? This part explores these issues.

CHAPTER 1

The Monists

T his chapter examines the two dominant schools of comic thought about religious liberty under the Constitution: *egalitarianism* and *neutralism*. Each school takes a single value—equality or neutrality—to be the single value of religious liberty. The scholars considered are among the most important, thoughtful, and influential writers on these subjects, but my hope is that by emphasizing the common weakness in their theories—the lack of proper appreciation for the predicament of legal theory—I will have set the board for Part Two's exposition of the method of tragedy and history.

Egalitarianism

The first category of comic theory takes equality to be the single master value of religious liberty. Since the idea of equality, in all of its historical and cultural variety, is unmanageably large, it will help to narrow it. Scholars that champion equality argue for (1) an intrinsically valuable egalitarianism that is (2) distributive in nature.[1] In its relationship to religious liberty, the view is that the government must distribute and guarantee equally the good of free religious belief and practice.

Comic egalitarians thus value the equal distribution of a kind of mild autonomy within a limited range of religious choice, which entails valuing that autonomy as well.[2] Yet they do not generally prize other values of religious liberty, or if they do they are prepared to dispense with them should they conflict—as they frequently do—with distributive egalitarianism. The crucial problem for comic egalitarian conceptions of religious liberty is that they are unable to systematize or specify in a satisfying way what makes religious liberty valuable for those who cherish it and how it relates to any particular wider context that brings out its value.

The past decade has witnessed the flowering of comic egalitarian theories of religious liberty. The eminent philosopher Martha Nussbaum, for example, has argued that the single value of religious liberty "holding all the key concepts together is the idea of equality, understood as nondomination or nonsubordination," epitomized in the principle of "equal respect."[3] Nussbaum's approach subordinates every other principle to equality. Thus, "conscience"—"the faculty in human beings with which they search for life's ultimate meaning"[4]—is described as being without value if it is not equally distributed.[5] "Accommodation"—"giving religious people a 'break' in some area, for reasons of conscience"[6]—is a valuable practice only if it "seems required by equality."[7] "[L]iberty" "is only fair if it is truly equal liberty" and is worth protecting only insofar as it enables individuals to satisfy the needs of their "consciences" equally.[8] "Separation of church and state" is valuable only insofar as it serves the principle of equal respect.[9] "Equality," in sum, "provides an orienting account" of religious liberty, and "we make progress" by demanding that policies be justified by recourse to an overarching egalitarianism.[10]

But the most sophisticated egalitarian statement of religious liberty belongs to Christopher Eisgruber and Lawrence Sager (E&S) in their important book, *Religious Freedom and the Constitution.*[11] E&S dub their account "Equal Liberty," and it consists in the view that "the Constitution expresses special concern for religion because and to the extent that religious difference inspires inequality in stature and reward."[12] For E&S religious liberty is valuable inasmuch as it is a "protection against discrimination"[13] when religion's function of facilitating "free speech, personal autonomy, associative freedom, and private property" is implicated.[14] Moreover, the distributional or "fairness" component of equality is the authors' chief concern.[15] Religious liberty under the Constitution is not implicated "[i]n the absence of a convincing equality-based claim."[16]

In the free exercise context, E&S decry broad rights of religious exemption:[17] if exemptions from generally applicable laws are permissible, it is because of the particular cultural "vulnerab[ility] to deep and undeserved disadvantage" of the group seeking them.[18] They see no constitutionally relevant difference between religion and other claims of conscience, and they deny that religion ought to be accorded any pride of place. Discrimination, religious or otherwise, is the touchstone.[19]

On the establishment front, E&S claim that religion is not "an anomaly" deserving "exotic constitutional treatment."[20] Instead, all disputes are examined through a distributive egalitarian lens: when the issue is state funding of religious institutions, "the government [must] distribute its resources fairly";[21] when the issue is the propriety of religious displays or symbols on government property, the question is whether the meaning of the display suggests "disparagement" of other views;[22] and when the issue is the role of religion in public education, E&S are not troubled by religion's exclusion. Since no public school demands meditations in which students are compelled to affirm that "there is no transcendental being to thank or blame for our success or failure," the converse—a religious prayer, acknowledgment, or expression of gratitude—is unnecessary to equalize any disparagement of religion.[23]

When the government displays objects with religious associations, or when it decides on official policies as to religion, or when it makes curricular choices about religion's place in public education, E&S claim that the nature of these decisions should be judged by their "social meaning"—"the meaning that a competent member of the community would attach."[24] This "social meaning" test is the gauge of disparagement, and it bears a strong resemblance to the Supreme Court's endorsement test—the view that these sorts of activities are unconstitutional if they send a message to nonadherents that they are second-class citizens or "outsiders" and to adherents that they are preferred or "insiders."[25]

Suppose, for example, that a town wished to display both a crèche at Christmas on municipal property and Fra Angelico's *The Annunciation* in an exhibition at the local museum.[26] For E&S, "[t]he social meaning of the crèche includes disparagement of those who do not embrace Christianity as their religious belief," while the display of *The Annunciation* "would properly be understood as an instance of framing rather than embracing the religious content of the painting."[27] Government may "mention" religion but not "use" it; religion may be deployed by the government to serve nonreligious ends but not to sponsor religion.[28] Thus, E&S claim that the display of *The Annunciation* is no more disparaging than the use of the words *San* or *Saint* in the names of the cities "San Antonio" or "Saint Paul" because in both cases religion is merely mentioned.[29] The social meaning of references to religion is to be judged neither, in the authors' view, by those "thin-skinned" people who may object on antireligious grounds to religiously themed Italian Renaissance paintings nor by the "singularly obtuse" who are blind to overt government sponsorship, but instead by "objective" persons.[30]

There are several difficulties with these claims—problems that highlight the fundamental weaknesses of comic theories of religious liberty generally and usefully contrast with a tragic approach. I raise four here.

First, to the extent that the social meaning of a religious display, or a religious practice in a public context, or a decision to include religious learning in the public school curriculum, can be objectively ascertained, the ease and practicability of doing so will often be a matter of fine degree. It may be simple enough to say that confessional Bible readings in public schools are unconstitutional. It is much more difficult to determine whether the inclusion of gospel music or a Negro spiritual at a graduation ceremony or winter concert is an objectionable disparagement;[31] or whether a music class that examines the text of the *Stabat Mater* and its interpretation by various classical masters fails the test; or whether a prayer to open a legislative session or a Thanksgiving proclamation in which God is mentioned violates the Constitution; or, indeed, what precisely it is about artistic masterpieces with religious themes that the government deems of value.[32]

The study and celebration of Fra Angelico's painting is qualitatively different from the use of the name "San Antonio." To understand well what is worthwhile about *The Annunciation*—why, indeed, it is cherished and admired for its "extraordinary artistic force"[33]—demands some knowledge of and appreciation for the religious tradition from which the artist drew and took inspiration.[34] It is of course true that one need not be a Christian to appreciate Fra Angelico's aesthetic use of color, positioning, and so on. Yet it is often problematic, if not impossible, to disaggregate the religious from the aesthetic: what one responds to in Fra Angelico—or in Dante, or in Bach, and so on—is in part the beauty (or horror) of the representation *of religion*, just as the beliefs, images, and practices of religious traditions inspired these and scores of other artists, writers, and thinkers. The same cannot be said for the rote use of the name "San Francisco," or "Saint Bernard" when referring to the lovable dog, or "Saint Elmo's Fire" when describing the twentysomething self-discovery film of the mid-1980s. Justice Douglas once referred to the interconnections of religion and culture as revealing "certain shadings," and they cast penumbras more extensive than theorists of the religion clauses are wont to acknowledge.[35] E&S fall victim to this very difficulty.

Indeed, it is exactly because of these nuances and so many others in the historical and cultural valences of religion that the meaning of a religious display, or of a curricular program of study and reflection about religion, or of a graduation or legislative prayer, will often be much more difficult to assess than is possible with a rough-hewn dichotomous test of "sponsorship" or "disparagement."[36] E&S would reject as "craven"— and in clear violation of their social meaning test—a holiday display by a municipality in which secular symbols exist alongside a crèche or other religious symbols.[37] They seem sure—or at least "pretty confident"— that the secular elements of such a display are a "fig leaf" to conceal religious disparagement.[38]

What gives them such confidence? It is their comic monistic methodology. By boiling down all Establishment Clause concerns to a single value—disparagement—and fixing the social meaning that they would attach, all establishment cases may be systematized along an orderly spectrum of permissibility. Thus, the interest of a municipality in acknowledging the holidays celebrated by its citizens, or the interest of those citizens in seeing their tradition fleetingly honored, or the civic esprit and uplift such symbols can elicit—all seem relegated to the "craven" category.[39] These values are excluded exactly because they do not fit within the overarching egalitarian commitment to nondisparagement.

The authors do point out that their nondisparagement model does not imply that religious displays are "somehow banished material," because they "can imagine displays that include a crèche and avoid the problem of endorsement."[40] If, for example, a town included a crèche in a display whose theme was "When the Spirit Moves Us" and included a range of spiritual commitments, "including, possibly, music and art," that would satisfy them.[41]

Yet this move provokes a second criticism: why should this arrangement be acceptable to them when the motley display of symbols in *Lynch v. Donnelly*—"a Santa Claus house, reindeer pulling Santa's sleigh, candy-striped poles, a Christmas tree, carolers, cut-out figures representing such characters as a clown, an elephant, a teddy bear, hundreds of colored lights, a large banner that reads 'SEASONS GREETINGS,' and [a] crèche"[42]—so plainly is not? In both, after all, there is the potential for disparagement, as the spiritual commitments of some will be slighted and the social meaning may be felt by reasonable observers to imply government favoritism. One possibility is that in *Lynch* the display was erected during the Christmas season, thus increasing the disparagement quotient that the objective observer would perceive.[43] Another might be that the *Lynch* display lacked sufficient secular symbols to escape condemnation as "fig-leafery."[44] A third might be that it did not contain enough non-Christian (that is, minority) religious symbols. A fourth might be the lack of an "immediately recognizable" aesthetic or thematic coherence,[45] or perhaps the absence of an adequate number of musical or artistic components (notwithstanding the *Lynch* display's inclusion of "carolers"). The authors do not provide clear answers to the question of what exactly it is about displays with religious content that would satisfy or violate the master value of nondisparagement.

Yet if E&S can imagine a religious display that might pass their test, why are they so ready to ascribe disparaging motivations in the cases involving real people where these issues were actually confronted? The authors' protests that they could, if pressed, conjure up fictional religious displays that might pass their social meaning test are reminiscent of Justice Souter's dissenting views in a recent Ten Commandments case.[46] Justice Souter was likewise confident that a Ten Commandments display in a park near the Texas State Capitol—one among a pastiche of seventeen other monuments[47]—was plainly unconstitutional because the Ten Commandments represented a "manifestly religious purpose" to anyone observing it.[48] He distinguished this amalgam from what one might see hanging in the National Gallery—Giotto's *Madonna*, for example, next to other masterpieces with nonreligious subjects—on the basis that:

> 17 monuments with no common appearance, history, or esthetic role scattered over 22 acres is not a museum, and anyone strolling around the lawn would surely take each memorial on its own terms without any dawning sense that some purpose held the miscellany together more coherently than fortuity and the edge of the grass.[49]

Yet it is difficult to discern anything more than Justice Souter's personal aesthetic sensibilities at work here. In his view, any sensible observer ought to be able to distinguish between a disparaging and "manifestly religious" display[50] and a nondisparaging, aesthetically cohesive museum exhibition.[51]

Interestingly, E&S disagree with Justice Souter's conclusion that the Ten Commandments display in *Van Orden v. Perry* was unconstitutional, observing that "many people would be upset by its removal" and asking "is it really so much to put up with?"[52] Perhaps its removal would indeed be upsetting, and perhaps its display is in fact unobjectionable to some, but *if* that is true, the reasons have little to do with E&S's master value of nondisparagement. To the contrary, whatever the reasons may be, they depend on the suppressed reality that any comic monistic theory of religious liberty is compelled to deny: that there are legitimate concerns other than the chosen value lurking within these disputes—concerns that cannot be systematically arranged or rank ordered by recourse to any single metric.

A third objection involves the stability of the concept of nondisparagement. Suppose a municipality honors a religious minority—its burgeoning Sikh population, for example—by displaying a sign with the five "Ks" of Sikhism during a Sikh holiday.[53] For E&S, the town's Christian majority would have no cause to complain; and even if other religious minorities might have such cause, the town could mollify their grievances by honoring their traditions in turn. But when Christmas comes, why should it not be disparaging to the town's Christians to see their own tradition studiously ignored?[54]

It might be that E&S are relying on a finer distinction—something like the difference between undifferentiated disgruntlement or frustration and a sense of political exclusion.[55] We ought to be especially sensitive, the argument might go, to disparagements that convey messages of lesser status or political alienation, but the display of minority religious symbols does not convey that message to the religious majority. Yet even if it were possible to distinguish cleanly between these two senses of disparagement, it would be entirely reasonable for a member of the religious majority to feel at least a limited sense of political exclusion or alienation under the Sikh-honoring scenario.

It is true that Christianity represents a national majority religious tradition, but there are large and well-populated pockets of the United States where Christians constitute either an outright minority or a rapidly decreasing majority. In *Skoros v. City of New York*,[56] for example, a federal appellate court upheld the New York City Department of Education's holiday display policy, which permitted display of a menorah at Chanukah and a star and crescent at Ramadan but not a crèche or nativity scene at Christmas.[57] The court held that the plaintiff could not reasonably believe that her own tradition was being excluded and that other traditions were being endorsed, because the policy's aim was to promote "understanding and respect" for religious difference.[58] Yet even so, it is difficult to understand why the court could not accept that a reasonable observer living in New York City might feel politically alienated by the policy: it does not take too vivid an imagination to believe that, for example, an Evangelical Christian living in Brooklyn might feel exactly that sense of exclusion.[59] In any event, *Skoros* raises the issue of which political community—national or local—ought to matter for purposes of assessing disparagement.

It is not clear how Equal Liberty would deal with these problems, in part because one can discern at least two clashing values of antidisparagement in operation, both of which the authors seem at various points to espouse. E&S might be concerned solely with disparagement of minorities (bracketing for the moment the issue of who exactly constitutes the minority); in fact, this seems to be the view entailed by their emphasis on "vulnerability."[60] If so, the first and second town displays would be constitutional while the third acknowledging the majority holiday would not. Yet only someone obdurately indisposed to acknowledge the sensibilities of the majority would fail to appreciate the (reasonable, objective) sense of denigration that the exclusion of its religious symbols would likely represent, particularly in light of the prior recognition of the town's minorities.[61] Justice Kennedy once criticized just this lopsided quality of the Supreme Court's endorsement test—its systematic and structural devaluation of the sentiments of the majority—in a decision holding the holiday display of a crèche on the steps of a Pittsburgh county courthouse unconstitutional:

> If there be such a person as the "reasonable observer," I am quite certain that he or she will take away a salient message from our holding in these cases: the Supreme Court of the United States has concluded that the First Amendment creates classes of religions based on the relative numbers of their adherents. Those religions enjoying the largest following must be consigned to the status of least-favored faiths so as to avoid any possible risk of offending members of minority religions.[62]

Alternatively, E&S might prefer a more formal principle: not to allow the third display, after finding the first two acceptable, would disparage the majority. There are moments when they seem to endorse this position, as when they would permit a religious prayer in public school only if there is a comparable atheistic affirmation and in their general approval of *Employment Division v. Smith*'s rule that there is no right to a religious exemption from neutral laws of general applicability.[63] But this formal conception of disparagement itself breaks up into fragments on closer inspection. The type of formal equality that would permit a religious prayer only in response to an atheistic affirmation ignores the qualitative difference between silence and affirmation.[64] E&S are admirably sensitive to the increased likelihood of disparagement to minorities when "sectarian" references are made by school officials. But they are rather tone-deaf to the objection that, for many, the exclusion of a religious prayer at a public school graduation, for example, is *itself* a disparagement; it is a tacit affirmation of religion's nonnecessity, unimportance, and inappropriateness. For these people (who may themselves constitute a minority), a public school need not affirm an atheist view explicitly to disparage religion; religion's omission is affirmation enough. There are, in sum, rival "equalities" at work within the fabric of E&S's commitment to non-disparagement—clashing values masked by their comic monistic methodology.[65]

Finally, and moving to the free exercise realm, at times E&S themselves defect from their commitment to Equal Liberty. In discussing the reasons that the Catholic Church ought to be permitted to retain its tradition of an all-male priesthood (or, in the legal argot, to discriminate in hiring on the basis of sex), for example, E&S claim that the values of autonomy and freedom of association demand that "churches should be free from state interference in their choice of clergy."[66] Yet E&S's principle of nondiscrimination is not capable of preserving this doctrine—indeed, it seems committed to denying it.[67] There is also a sense in which equality or a concern for discrimination simply is a weak or at least incomplete explanation for the value of religious liberty. The reason, for example, that public schools ought not to pronounce themselves on the truth of any religious position derives not solely, or even primarily, from a concern about discrimination, but from the historical recognition that governments are notoriously poor and unreliable arbiters.[68]

The authors sometimes assert that religions exhibit unique features—they embody a person's "expansive webs of belief and conduct"; they "insist on the unique truths of their beliefs"; they "assign powerful and pervasive judgments of identity and stature to the status of being in or out" of the religious tradition.[69] But these statements about religion in turn demand something more substantial than a norm of nondiscrimination or nondisparagement. Special significance ought to entail special concern.[70] Likewise, the authors concede that they would impose "unique prohibitions" on religion "that have no secular analogues,"[71] most especially in the areas of religion in public schools and government funding of voucher programs.[72] But then neither a formal nor a minority-oriented nondiscrimination principle suffices to ground their own substantive views of religious liberty, since religion again seems to be singled out as a unique phenomenon.

E&S at one point acknowledge the tension among values when religiously motivated conduct and "other legitimate public values and purposes" conflict.[73] Yet with Nussbaum, they insist that "it is a sign of America's progress" that ever-greater numbers of citizens adhere to a conception of religious liberty that emphasizes equality as the cardinal value.[74] They believe that any differential treatment between the values of religious liberty and "roughly comparable secularly grounded interests" denotes a violation of their egalitarian principle.[75] While these rivalrous values need not be precisely scalable, "Equal Liberty *does* depend on our ability to see these interests as sufficiently comparable to indict a government that accommodates one and flatly rebuffs the other."[76]

It may be that these last points represent the clearest statement of a comic methodology, and the most salient way in which a tragic approach differs from it. To suggest that the disputes in all religious liberty conflicts ought to be systematized into a scheme of roughly comparable values using an egalitarian gauge is mistaken. In fact, these disputes implicate too many values that clash—and whose resolution too often requires the sacrifice of values that invariably leaves tragic residue— to be resolved by the claim that the values in competition are roughly equivalent. For each conflict in this area, there is a multiplicity of real microconflicts of values that are flattened out, if not misunderstood and mischaracterized, by the insistence that the only proper way to understand them is as manifestations of discrimination or disparagement. A tragic approach would reject the argument that the reasons for protecting religious liberty are exhausted by distributive egalitarianism. Comic egalitarians seem committed to the notion that the more undeviatingly we adhere to their approach, the more "progress" we, as a society, make. Not so for the tragedian: whatever "progress" may mean, it will not be achieved by ever-stricter allegiance to comic legal theory.

Neutralism

The political value of neutrality, conceptualized at the highest level of generality, prizes the state's noninvolvement or noninterference with religious beliefs and practices. The philosopher Charles Larmore has written that the "central idea of the modern liberal state" is that "the state should be neutral. . . . [It] should not seek to promote any particular conception of the good life . . . because it is supposedly a *truer* conception."[77] There is overlap between certain conceptions of neutrality and equality. For example, one might characterize the holding in *Smith* in terms of neutrality: a law that is not designed intentionally to interfere with a person's religious beliefs is presumptively valid because neutral on its face—it represents a "hands-off" approach to religious matters.[78] Or one might frame *Smith* in terms of equality: since the religion clauses champion sameness of treatment as an aspiration, no one should, for religious reasons, be allowed to violate laws of equal application. Nevertheless, theories of neutrality may be distinguished from egalitarian theories on the basis that the former assume that the crucial value is the state's noninvolvement or noninterference[79]—a negative value—while the latter emphasize the positive good of achieving a state of affairs in which equality is maximized.

The Supreme Court's religion clause jurisprudence of the last generation gradually has replaced church-state separationism with a neutrality model.[80] The free exercise shift occurred suddenly, though not without warning,[81] in the *Smith* decision. The establishment shift has been no less definite, particularly in the realm of government funding of religious institutions.[82]

Unlike the comic egalitarian accounts examined earlier, the two neutrality accounts considered here are widely disparate. But what unites them with the egalitarians is a common comic monistic commitment— the view that religious liberty may be reduced to a single value and systematized by recourse to that value.

Douglas Laycock, perhaps the foremost scholar of American religious liberty, has long defended the view that the state must "minimize the extent to which it either encourages or discourages religious belief or disbelief, practice or nonpractice, observance or nonobservance,"[83] leaving religion "as wholly to private choice as anything can be."[84] Laycock distinguishes two core meanings of neutrality: "formal" and "substantive."[85] While substantive neutrality requires neutral incentives with respect to engaging in or refraining from religious activities, formal neutrality requires neutral categories: a law is formally neutral "if religious and secular examples of the same phenomenon are treated exactly the same."[86]

Consider, for example, the case of children and the sacramental consumption of Communion wine. It is formally neutral to prohibit children from all alcohol consumption in public, including the sipping of Communion wine.[87] But an exemption from an alcohol consumption ban for underage Communion wine sipping would be substantively neutral because, on the one hand, providing the exemption would not encourage anyone to convert to Catholicism, while, on the other, punishing parents or priests for permitting underage Communion wine sipping creates powerful disincentives to practice Catholicism.[88]

Substantive neutrality, Laycock claims, can "reconcile" all the tensions that inhere in the totality of other values of religious liberty.[89] These include a small number of more or less identical values that might go under the general label of autonomy.[90] Substantive neutrality also reconciles the separation of church and state with the voluntaristic, or choice-centric, value.[91] Laycock's view, in sum, bears a strong structural resemblance to the comic egalitarian position. The master value—the value that provides, as Nussbaum had it, an "orienting account"[92]—is substantive neutrality. But Laycock recognizes that substantive neutrality must be neutral about *something*, and that something is variously called individual autonomy, choice,[93] voluntarism, the separation of church and state, or liberty.[94]

It is something of a terminological conundrum that a theory that goes by the name of "neutrality" plainly requires special—and so nonneutral—treatment of religion.[95] Indeed, while Laycock's view that religion deserves special constitutional solicitude may be appealing (as it often is), it is not neutral.[96] In the free exercise context, substantive neutrality resonates much more with the pre-*Smith* framework of interest balancing than it does with *Smith*'s ostensibly harder rule, and Laycock has been highly critical of *Smith* and supportive of the statutory regime that Congress passed to rectify it.[97]

If one were to take this voluntaristic view of neutrality as the single "reconciling" principle or value of religious liberty, it is worthwhile to consider what would thereby be sacrificed. At the very least, an overriding concern with substantive neutrality would exclude the value of formal neutrality; neutrality as to religious incentives is not the same as—indeed, it is often in direct conflict with—neutrality as to categories.

One can appreciate the quality of the sacrifice in the example of conscientious objection to military service. The issue is that the state may grant an exemption to those that object to military service, and many of these exemptions are justified as accommodations to the free exercise of religion.[98] The question is then whether nonreligious objectors to military service (secular pacifists) ought to receive an exemption, just as do religious objectors.[99] In a famous case, for example, Elliott Welsh explained his request for a statutory exemption from military service by stating that his pacifism was founded in "our failure to recognize the political, social, and economic realities of the world [in which] we, as a nation, fail our responsibility as a nation."[100] What does substantive neutrality counsel in the case of the nonreligious conscientious objector?

One prominent advocate of substantive neutrality, Michael McConnell, resolves this problem by excluding the secular conscientious objector from the ambit of protection by drawing a line between theistic belief and unbelief.[101] Laycock criticizes this position as taking too absolute a view on the derivation of moral convictions.[102] It moreover reduces the category "religion" to a single quality—theistically derived moral conviction—without explaining why other beliefs and practices commonly encompassed within the idea of "religion" ought not to qualify. And excluding the secular, nontheistic objector from the zone of protection creates an incentive toward theism, an incentive that substantive neutrality is designed to avoid.

But Laycock's own solution to the problem of the secular conscientious objector runs into difficulties as well. Religious liberty, he claims, should protect "obligations that transcend . . . self-interest and . . . personal preferences" and which a person feels so powerfully that he is compelled to obey.[103] But the problems of ambiguity and vagueness with this view—at one time championed by the theologian Paul Tillich as that which a person deems an "ultimate concern"[104]—are well rehearsed.[105] Principal among them is that this functionalist standard threatens to remove any feasible distinctions between the religious and the nonreligious. If anything that one deems an "ultimate" or "transcendent" concern is religious, the category ceases to retain much meaning. Laycock's standard encompasses a vast—seemingly limitless—array of beliefs and practices.[106] Recognizing that judges will inevitably be faced with serious line-drawing difficulties, Laycock retreats, arguing that the "scope of protection for religions inside the Clauses . . . should not be changed, lest the core of religious liberty be determined by anomalous cases at the margin."[107]

One can certainly sympathize with this concession: Laycock is (admirably) interested in retaining what religious liberty already exists and is entrenched as a matter of common practice and cultural tradition. But this unsatisfying resolution—one demanded by substantive neutrality—is one of Laycock's own making. Either he defines "religion" so broadly as to include any consideration of "transcendent" concern, in the process excluding much that is indisputably religious in nature,[108] or he accepts a regime of arbitrary distinctions. If he chooses the latter route, the difference between substantive neutrality and formal neutrality is thrown into the highest relief, and formal neutrality is, plainly, sacrificed.

There are other problems with substantive neutrality which suggest that it cannot be the value of religious liberty by which all others may be reconciled and properly ordered. One need not go quite so far as to argue that "the quest for neutrality, despite its understandable appeal and the tenacity with which it has been pursued, is an attempt to grasp an illusion,"[109] to sense that substantive neutrality may be only one feature, one consideration, affecting the resolution of religious liberty disputes.

Substantive neutrality might be interpreted in two different ways: (1) neutrality as to government aims or purposes to influence religious choices; or (2) the avoidance and/or rectification of unintended government influence.[110] It is relatively uncontroversial that the government in general should not aim to influence religious choices directly.[111] But Laycock and other advocates of substantive neutrality clearly mean something more muscular than neutrality as to government purposes: his own paradigm example of underage sacramental alcohol consumption might well not survive a neutrality-as-to-aims analysis, since it is entirely plausible that the government would prohibit the practice for public safety reasons alone.

Once one sees that neutrality as to unintended influence is the real benchmark of substantive neutrality, it becomes much more difficult to argue that substantive neutrality can bear the weight that Laycock lays on it. It is surely the case that the government is justified in passing many laws that unintentionally influence religious choices. It is justified in requiring that all children attend school; in banning certain narcotics categorically; in deciding where and how to build its highways and infrastructure; in declaring national holidays and weekly days of rest; and in countless other ways that can and do substantially influence religious choices. Thus, Laycock's seemingly more modest aspiration to offer substantive neutrality as a "reconciling" or "unifying" principle—rather than a master value—of religious liberty is ultimately unsatisfying because of its decidedly comic monistic quality. Government noninfluence as to unintended effects is at most one consideration—one factor—in the play of clashing values, and it does not reconcile the others to itself.[112]

What of formal neutrality? Formal neutrality, we have said, is neutrality as to categories, and a formally neutral approach may be either permissive (constitutionally sufficient) or mandatory (constitutionally compelled). And formal neutrality receives an impassioned defense by Marci Hamilton in her book, *God vs. the Gavel: Religion and the Rule of Law*.[113] Indeed, Hamilton goes so far as to suggest that any singling out of religion for accommodation is objectionable if the social harm resulting from that accommodation is more than "de minimis."[114] "De minimis" is not a very high burden; depending on its specification, Hamilton's approach begins to look like mandatory formal neutrality.[115]

For example, Hamilton describes in vivid detail the conflicts that arise when religiously inclined landowners seek to use their property in ways that threaten the character of residential communities.[116] A religious person wishes to expand his home to accommodate greater numbers of worshipers; there ensues a considerable increase in traffic and commerce;[117] a once-a-week house of worship is transformed into a "multiple-use social center";[118] the homeless arrive, seeking food, shelter, and spiritual guidance, and the neighborhood begins to deteriorate.[119] The result of the inevitable legal entanglements is a concomitant ill will among neighbors.[120]

Hamilton places the blame for these and other problems of what she sees as overzealous accommodation in Congress's reaction to the *Smith* decision in the form of two statutes: the Religious Freedom Restoration Act (RFRA) and the Religious Land Use and Institutionalized Persons Act (RLUIPA). RLUIPA reinstated the interest-balancing approach to land use and prison disputes implicating religious liberty: if the state passes a land use law that imposes a "substantial burden" on the religious use of property, the state must demonstrate that the law serves a compelling state interest.[121] Hamilton argues that the land use provisions of RLUIPA are an unwise repudiation of the constitutional principle enunciated by *Smith*, and that "RLUIPA has turned neighbor against neighbor and is one of the most religiously divisive laws ever enacted in the United States."[122] RLUIPA's "primary problem," in Hamilton's view, is that it creates "two classes of citizens" and that it is "fundamentally unfair" because it requires accommodations unless the government can offer a compelling interest to defeat them.[123] And it is "unfair," Hamilton writes, because religious groups ought to follow "generally applicable, neutral laws" just like everyone else.[124] The value of formal neutrality is a "gut instinct for Americans"[125] which is violated by any special religious accommodations.

It bears reflection whether the antagonisms that Hamilton identifies were simmering all the while. "[D]ivisive religious discord" about the proper use of land is a product of conflicting interests and beliefs about what is worthwhile or valuable.[126] That strife may indeed be driven in part (just as it is reflected in part) by the evolving nature of religious practice in America and its incompatibility with rival interests and values: traditional notions of home ownership, the desire for a certain neighborhood character, the concern to keep property values as high as possible, and the efforts of a municipality to control geographic expansion. And it is also true that RLUIPA *might* have given religious organizations a structural advantage that they previously did not enjoy.[127]

But Hamilton has hardly stated a persuasive case for enshrining a comic monistic principle of formal neutrality by demanding that any deviation from it must be justified by a demonstration that the harm to others would be "de minimis." Providing an attractive haven for the homeless and encouraging the establishment of institutions that will see to their physical and spiritual needs, as well as to the needs of countless other believers, may well displease neighboring landowners. They will be disturbed by the tumult, the noise, and the inconvenience. They will be despondent about the losses in their property values, and they may even feel that they are being constructively evicted. But for Congress to decide that the values cherished by the landowners ought to be sacrificed to serve the values of the religious organization and its adherents is not necessarily a craven capitulation to "special interest[s]."[128] To make a choice about where the public good lies in a particular dispute is precisely to decide that one way of life—or at least one value or set of values—ought to be protected to the detriment of other clashing values.

Hamilton might reply that the choices reflected in RLUIPA not only elevate one type of substantive value (religious liberty) over others ("the emotional, economic, and even spiritual value that American families invest in their homes"[129]), but also violate formal neutrality or, as Hamilton puts it, "fair dealing" by creating "two classes of citizens."[130]

Yet there is nothing objectionable about recognizing that formal neutrality is one among many values that must be considered in the resolution of these disputes. Indeed, it was Laycock's failure to account for formal neutrality—his assertion that substantive neutrality could function as the "reconciling" value of religious liberty—that rendered his approach unpersuasive. Hamilton makes a similar mistake. In considering the growing tensions between historic preservation and religious liberty, she writes:

> This is a story repeated frequently—the religious institution sees no moral or social problem with treating historical properties as throwaways and treats those who do place value in historical preservation as enemies of the good. Good government would inject the idea of the public good into this competition of interests and find means of serving everyone's interest. The best result in every land use dispute is the win-win result.[131]

This statement goes to the heart of Hamilton's profound confusion about the quality of religious liberty disputes. She is oblivious to the reality that these conflicts present dilemmas in which the "win-win result" is not only unfeasible, but incoherent. If a church is not able to sell a historically important property and if it is prevented by the municipality from using its own land as it sees fit, then the values that it cherishes—nothing less than its religious liberty—will have been sacrificed for the sake of promoting the value of historic architectural preservation or economic prosperity.

A government, just inasmuch as it wishes to be a "[g]ood government," ought not to hide behind the self-deluding lie that its resolution of this dispute or any other will result in a "win-win" outcome for everyone involved. It will not. To the contrary: the good government is the one that acknowledges frankly—and without dissimulation and the reflexive use of vague bromides such as "the public good"[132]—the reality that it is faced in common experience with equally and irreconcilably ultimate values. The vindication of some demands the destruction of others. One of these values, but *only* one, is the value of formal neutrality. But elevating formal neutrality to the status of a comic supervalue would do irreparable violence to the values of religious liberty as they are instantiated in countless beliefs and practices.[133]

CHAPTER 2

The Skeptics

Thus far, I have focused on theories that advocate a monistic value of constitutional religious liberty and claim that all clashing interests in the conflicts of religious liberty can and should be systematized by reference to the premeditated value. But some scholars are skeptical about this view of the religion clauses.

The rejection of comic monism has given rise to two distinctive varieties of skepticism. The first variety—"strong skepticism"—includes writers who doubt that there are any values of religious liberty at all, or at least any values that might be protected and enforced constitutionally. Scholars of this powerfully skeptical cast of mind sometimes go so far as to suggest that the protean quality and tortuous history of the category "religion" has become unstable or conceptually vapid—so much so as to render the protection of religious liberty entirely meaningless, unmanageable, and "impossible."[1] The second variety comprises the "quasi tragedians"—scholars who acknowledge the plurality of values of religious liberty, but who ultimately rely on a small number of values to resolve those disputes and hold out their resolutions as universally optimal.

The fundamental reason that skepticism is unpersuasive is that it ignores the reality that the values identified by the comic monists discussed in Chapter 1 (but also numerous others that often do not figure in the standard accounts) are real, actually valuable, and worthy of constitutional protection. The skeptics recognize, rightly, that the comic monistic approach to religious liberty fails to explain the nature and range of the values of religious liberty. But they then conclude that there are no principles or values of religious liberty, and that there *can be* no such principles or values as a matter of logical coherence.

The strong skeptics fail to consider an intermediate possibility: that there exist many clashing values of religious liberty (though not a limitless number) and that negotiating their perpetual conflict is the manner in which the contours of the constitutional right to religious liberty become known and developed. It is through the negotiation of these conflicts—and the consequent development of the common law of religious liberty—that legal change in the protection of religious liberty occurs over time.

The quasi tragedians are different. With the strong skeptics, they, too, are properly attuned to the reality of multiple and conflicting values of religious liberty. Yet unlike the strong skeptics, the quasi tragedians often sidestep or avoid the implications of pluralism by relying on the selfsame values championed by the monists in Chapter 1—equality, neutrality, and even, most recently, religious truth.

Strong Skepticism

The leading strong skeptical view belongs to one of the most penetrating and thoughtful scholars of law and religion writing today—Steven Douglas Smith. In his book, *Foreordained Failure: The Quest for a Constitutional Principle of Religious Liberty*,[2] Smith argues that:

> [T]here is no single or self-subsisting "principle" of religious freedom; there is only a host of individuals with a host of different opinions and notions about how much and what kind of scope government ought to give to the exercise of religious beliefs and practices.[3]

Yet this pluralism need not mean, Smith at that time insisted, that certain ideas or conceptions of religious liberty could not be more or less appealing or defensible. It only means that devising a single principle of religious liberty was an academic phantom. Smith's was one of the first and keenest critiques of the monistic impulse in contemporary theorizing about the religion clauses. This feature of Smith's account is very much in sympathy with the views advanced in Part Two of this book.

Yet it is in his tentative prescription in *Foreordained Failure* that one begins to detect divergences from the tragic approach. Having concluded, plausibly, that there is no single or unitary principle of religious liberty, Smith goes on to argue that religious liberty is ungovernable by any theory and is instead an entirely "prudential" matter. That is, that the best—the most reliable, the most sensible, the most practical—resolution to conflict is through the exercise of "gut feeling," "muddling through," or "ad hoc" pragmatic judgments, rather than by recourse to a grand and inviolable principle.[4]

It is in this sense that Smith and other strong skeptics are ultimately in some sense still comic theorists: just like the monists, the skeptics believe that the ultimate aim of any theory—just inasmuch as it *is* a theory—must be a full systematization of the social and legal practice of religious liberty by recourse to a principle or value. In contrast with the monists, skeptics like Smith reject this role for theory, and in so doing they also sometimes make the claim that principles or values of religious liberty have no use at all in thinking about the prudential practice of religious liberty.

One can see this clearly in the contrast that Smith draws between "principled" and "prudential" accounts: the former founder because they inevitably must rest on "background beliefs about religion, government, society, and human psychology."[5] Since any theory of religious liberty will be persuasive only insofar as its background premises are persuasive, no theory of religious liberty can achieve what it purports to accomplish—to "reconcile or to mediate among competing religious and secular positions within a society"—in a satisfying way because the basis of any theory of religious liberty must always depend on a contested position.[6] Theories of religious liberty do not stand neutrally above or outside of disputes about background suppositions; they are neck-deep in them. They cannot help but afford their own background views a "preferred position."[7]

Thus, in order to choose among "Catholic and Protestant and Deweyan and Marxist theories of religious freedom," we would need first to decide which among the underlying commitments of these "faiths" was most attractive. But this seems to defeat the very purpose of a theory of religious liberty—to avoid making pronouncements about which conception of the good life is truer or more plausible.[8] Having abandoned both principle and theory for prudence, Smith concludes not only that judges and legal theorists are no more capable than anyone else of engaging in prudential thought, but also that continuing to permit judges to strike down democratically elected laws becomes far less legitimate than it might be under a regime of principle.[9]

Skepticism about the power of theory to make any sense of religious liberty becomes harder-edged and more thoroughgoing in Smith's later work.[10] The values of equality and neutrality are now dismissed; indeed, they are sometimes described as both useless and empty.[11] Similarly, the value of autonomy is claimed to border on incoherence, and its power to provide an anchor for understanding religious liberty is questioned.[12] "Theory"—the activity of generating "an internally consistent set of principles capable of generating answers to questions of religious freedom"—is rejected.[13] Smith says that his approach "lowers rather than raises the stakes of religious freedom controversies" not only by abandoning the pretense that there is a correct constitutional test deducible from a single principle, but also by insisting that judges and constitutional scholars should play a comparatively peripheral and modest role.[14]

The skepticism grounding his prudentialism drives Smith to embrace the virtue of "tolerance" over the reign of principle.[15] Tolerance implies "self-restraint toward what we believe to be without social value"; therefore, tolerance is not "acceptance in the strong sense of approval or endorsement" nor does it demand that all objectionable ideas must be allowed.[16] Tolerance can be "sympathetic" and "respectful" to different views and values, but it is a highly limited concept that always maintains a definite distance between one's own views and opinions and the views to be tolerated.[17] Tolerance is possible because one can, on the one hand, be committed to one's own view of the truth and, on the other, acknowledge one's own fallibility in making those commitments and respectfully admit that others, too, have made parallel commitments in good faith. Since there is no principle that can explain the practice of tolerance, the best that can be hoped for is a "modus vivendi," a "messy" political compromise.[18]

If comic monistic theorists too often ignore the predicament of legal theory, skeptics sometimes may think too much about it. The emphasis on prudential tolerance can tend toward something like a declinist view of religious liberty. Indeed, Smith has recently suggested that we have reached "the twilight of religious freedom"[19] because of the predicament in which legal theory finds itself:

> We carry on an inherited discourse that no longer draws sustenance from the secular premises on which it attempts to operate. . . .
>
> Moreover, it is not obvious just what else [we] could do. The discourse of religious freedom will no doubt continue, for a time anyway, but pending some new (or perhaps renewed?) illumination, the discourse will be stumbling along in the dusk.[20]

The nostalgic and disconsolate quality of these comments, evocative of the closing remarks of the moral philosopher Alasdair MacIntyre in his influential work, *After Virtue*,[21] suggests one probable consequence of adopting a prudential approach and abandoning the theoretical enterprise entirely—a tendency toward thick skepticism about the possibility that intellectual energy can help us to conceive of a remotely satisfying account of religious liberty.

Dissolving Religion

Strong skepticism about the possibility of a theory of religious liberty comes from other, and quite different, scholarly quarters as well. Where Smith claims that the very idea of religious liberty depends on long discredited theological assumptions, various religious studies scholars have argued along a parallel track that the distinct category of "religion," and by implication "religious liberty," is an anachronism or worse.

One early, provocative critique of this kind originated with the influential anthropologist Talal Asad. Asad pointed out that there simply is no "universal definition of religion" not only because of its culturally contingent qualities, but, more importantly, because any "definition is itself the historical product of discursive processes."[22] The category "religion" was devised as an idiosyncratically Christian political effort to achieve coherence among a motley collection of entirely disparate beliefs and practices. And what was true for religion itself was true for religious liberty. The idea of religious tolerance developed by John Locke[23]—which was profoundly influential on the American founding generation in its construction of the Bill of Rights[24]—was not motivated by liberal concessions to disadvantaged minorities but was instead a "political means to the formation of strong state power that emerged from the sectarian wars of the sixteenth and seventeenth centuries."[25] Early Americans were in the hegemonic business of forming a nation, and religious liberty was one instrument through which a new kind of modern heresy—the heresy against the now omnicompetent state—could be squelched more effectively than by outright persecution.

In a related vein, the historian of religion, Jonathan Z. Smith, has written that:

> Religion is solely the creation of the scholar's study. It is created for the scholar's analytic purposes by his imaginative acts of comparison and generalization. Religion has no independent existence apart from the academy.[26]

If religion is in fact the scholar's invention—useful, perhaps at one time, as an instrument for ordering academic activities or for making sense of a sphere of learning and experience—then the category can and ought to be discarded as an organizing concept if it has outlived its academic utility. If there is no cogent meaning that can be given to the category of religion today, then religious liberty likewise ceases to be a meaningful political and legal concept. It needs to be reimagined to suit contemporary needs or abandoned.[27]

An even more radical version of the critique from religious studies may be seen in the claims that the standard list of "world religions" is merely indicative of the ways in which Euro-centric culture and identity established and propagated itself "as a harbinger of universal history, as a prototype of unity amid plurality."[28] The idea of religious traditions themselves as originally conceived is, in Tomoko Masuzawa's critical reconstruction, a "totalizing," "othering," and "suprahistorical" "category and a conceptual framework initially developed in the European

academy" to assess the "social, cultural, and political practices observ-
able among the inhabitants of regions elsewhere in the world."[29] This
more nastily colonial version of the critique is similarly echoed in the
cynical observation that "ecumenical liberal theology has been disguised
(though not very well) in the so-called scientific study of religion,"[30] and
it is the responsibility of intellectuals to engage in the "exorcism of an
undead Christian absolutism."[31]

It is not surprising that these critiques have been relatively slow to
affect law and legal scholarship.[32] There are several reasons for their lack
of influence. First, lawyers and law professors universally pay close heed
to text. Even those lawyers who believe that the interpretation of text can
change and who prefer some variety of an evolving "living constitutionalism"[33] to the methodology of originalism agree that attention to text is
an important part of discerning legal meaning. There is little debate that
the text of the First Amendment specifically mentions the establishment
and free exercise of "religion." To accept the critique of the religious
studies scholars would be to take the extraordinary act of reading the
religion clauses out of the Constitution—dispensing with the written
text entirely as passé, antiquated, or even politically illegitimate. There
is no provision of the Bill of Rights that has yet suffered this fate.[34]

Second, dispensing with religious liberty would present the problem
of what to do with precedent. A battalion of cases interpreting the religion
clauses of the Constitution now exists as part of our legal heritage and
tradition. Discarding the term *religion* leaves hundreds of cases purportedly about religious liberty in a kind of no-man's-land. It would be as if a
theorist or public intellectual one day decided that there actually were no
such things as buses or subways, and as a result the government felt that it
could no longer provide public transportation. This may not seem a serious loss to those who are consumed with the quest to explode or dissolve
purportedly outdated conceptual relics, but many people rely on the law
to shape and structure their activities, and the loss of an entire body of
law—and therefore of legal protection—governing what is still for many a
vital part of life would represent a deeply unsettling development.

Third, and most important, the critique of Asad and others illustrates
the gulf between the disciplines of law and religious studies. The legal
enterprise is primarily concerned with managing existing social projects,

interactions, and arrangements. It is therefore dependent on the particular history of this country—its culture, traditions, customs, and common patterns of behavior—taking what exists in society and controlling,
arranging, and regularizing it according to legal forms. Legal scholars
likewise give sustained attention to this function of the law. When legal
scholars and courts are faced with the difficulty of "defining" religion,
for example, and of determining how capacious the category ought to
be, they are not generally guided by the substantive[35] or functionalist
frameworks[36] that have so deeply influenced religious studies scholars,
but instead by historical and culturally contingent settlements that can
be analogized to present legal problems.[37] The academic study of religion, by contrast, is not concerned with maintaining an existing formal
mechanism of organization. To the contrary, the critique of the category
of "religion" demonstrates a contrary interest: to dismantle and dissolve
those customary structures.[38]

Notwithstanding the considerable distance between the disciplines of
law and religious studies, the critique of the religious studies scholars
has begun to take root among legal academics, most especially in the
work of Winnifred Fallers Sullivan. Sullivan argues that the idea of religious liberty is "impossible" because the government is simply unable
to enforce "laws granting persons rights that are defined with respect to
their religious beliefs" without slighting and misunderstanding the ways
in which the pluralistic, lived religions of the United States and the world
are actually practiced, confessed, and experienced.[39] The Free Exercise
Clause represents the "betrayal at the heart of laws guaranteeing religious freedom" inasmuch as it reflects an "essentialized" understanding of religion's meaning, which privileges the known and ostracizes the
unknown.[40] The Establishment Clause is in need of a "requiem" because
"[d]isestablishment is coming to mean less privatized pluralism through
the separation of religion(s) from public life and more a permeable and
inclusive public accommodation of the religiousness of all Americans."[41]
"Religion," she claims, "is being naturalized,"[42] and its naturalization
consists in the pruning away of antiquated or customary assumptions
about its very nature, as well as the state's relationship to it.

Someday, an enterprising scholar of the history of ideas might remark
on the irony that writers like Steven Smith and Winnifred Sullivan,

working from entirely different traditions and ideological perspectives, seem to converge in the same place. In fact, the prudential tolerance that Smith advocates moves the discourse of religious liberty in a direction that he might well disapprove—not backward with MacIntyre in search of a renewed founding-era illumination,[43] but forward with Sullivan and the critical religious studies scholars toward a more robustly subjectivist vision in which pluralism is seen as an insurmountable impediment to (rather than a necessary feature of) the continued existence of constitutional religious liberty. The strongly skeptical quality of both approaches tends toward the view that there can no longer be any values or principles of religious liberty at all.

There is, indeed, an underlying thematic unity in the various staunchly skeptical treatments of religious liberty. Conservatives and radicals unite in the view that the protection of religious liberty is an anachronism, whether beneficent or malign, whose justifications are the vestiges of a lost world that can no longer serve to ground what was historically one of the foremost civil rights—indeed, the "first freedom."[44]

Skepticism and Tragedy Contrasted

At first blush, it may seem that one way to describe a tragic approach is as a theory of what scholars such as Steven Smith and, to a lesser extent, Winnifred Sullivan have been up to in developing their skeptical accounts. It is certainly true that a tragedian shares the skeptic's doubts that a single value or set of internally coherent values of religious liberty can completely explain or systematize the disputes of religious liberty, let alone resolve them. And it is also the case that skeptics effectively criticize other theories of religious liberty that do not account for regret as to the considerable losses entailed by comic monism.

Yet the appearance of explanatory congruence is dispelled when one considers the reasons that the tragedian rejects comic accounts of religious liberty. He does not do so because the activity of constitutional theorizing and the search for principles that should guide decision making are inherently flawed or incoherent enterprises, or because an entirely prudential approach unguided by any larger orientation or direction is the best we can do, or because it is theory's Sisyphean task to overcome the "daunting obstacles" of religious pluralism,[45] or (least of all) because "religion" as a category is a conceptually incoherent relic of colonial Western civilization that must be "naturalized," forsaking its constitutional status in the process. The tragedian does not reject the effort to understand religious liberty disputes in terms of the values or principles that are being brought to bear, and he does not repudiate the attempt to explain those disputes by recourse to theory.

To the contrary, the tragic approach takes those values and principles seriously by postulating a theory—an account; a view; or, even more accurately, an orientation, ethic, or quality—of the religion clauses that reflects the true nature of those conflicts and the values underwriting them. Thomas Berg once wrote the following about the skepticism of antitheoretical accounts:

> The claims of the anti-theorists are largely driven, and justifiably so, by skepticism about prevalent theories that equate religious freedom with highly secularized government and thus seek to privatize and marginalize religion. But the anti-theorists wrongly jump to the conclusion that no viable theoretical approach is available.[46]

By contrast, as will be seen in later, the tragedian does offer an explanation for the conflicts of religious liberty, but it is a different genre of theory than the sort that the skeptics so ably attack. The values of religious liberty identified by the scholars considered in Chapter 1—as well as many others that do not generally appear in influential academic accounts—are true and actual values, all of them indisputably "first-order principles" of religious liberty,[47] though they may and often do manifest themselves differently in specific historical and social contexts. But because these values often clash, because they cannot be decisively systematized through a comic methodology, and because decision making in this area often results in sacrifices that cannot be compensated for, the tragedian counsels a certain mood or disposition when confronted with the conflicts of religious liberty. That disposition, as will be seen, is reflected in the final two, practical theses of the method of tragedy and history—an attitude that inclines toward gradualist adjudication and that is guided by both doctrinal and social history.

These last points gesture toward another important distinction between a strongly skeptical position and the method of tragedy and history. Because skeptical accounts sometimes assume that a kind of commonsensical "muddling through" is the best that is possible,[48] they reach the view that neither scholars nor judges should have very much to say about religious liberty—or at least that they should not have any more to say than legislators and ordinary citizens. In fact, for reasons of epistemic competence as well as democratic legitimacy, skeptical approaches generally conceive a highly limited and constrained role for the judiciary and an expanded role for the legislature.[49]

The tragedian takes a different view. He holds that both judges and scholars are ideally suited to appreciate the ways in which the law of religious liberty has developed, since they have been trained in the analysis of legal doctrine and are expert in evaluating what would represent meaningful deviations and shifts in existing custom and common legal practice. Moreover, given their own internal norms, judges are the group of state actors most likely to accept the fact of precedent as itself a compelling guide for judicial decision making, something that, as will be seen, is stressed by the fifth thesis of the method of tragedy and history.[50] Because of their relative insulation from political pressure, judges are institutionally equipped both to adopt the philosophical posture of a tragic approach and to take cognizance of existing social patterns in rendering their decisions. The judiciary, in this way, follows the political process, but at a significant remove, one that allows it to proceed cautiously, incrementally, and always with an eye trained on the tragic quality of the conflicts adjudicated and the ways in which those conflicts were negotiated by judges in the past.

A final difference between a skeptical and tragic outlook concerns the ideal of tolerance itself. Notwithstanding the critique of the religious studies scholars discussed earlier, tolerance is a venerable idea that has represented a kind of paradigm position for liberal states confronted with religious difference,[51] and there is much to commend it. An approach of prudential toleration as to questions of religious liberty is concerned with achieving a modus vivendi whereby a dominant group—and for legal purposes, this will mean the state—"puts up with" religious pluralism within side-constraints that often depend on some articulation of cognizable harm, because that type of approach is the best that can be hoped for or expected from the political process.[52]

A tragic approach again differs. It begins not with an aspiration to "put up with" religious pluralism, but instead with the recognition that pluralism is the inevitable and intractable state of affairs that religious liberty addresses. The tragedian counsels not the "getting over" of a "problem" but rather that judges should make explicit the impossibility of complete systematization of the values of religious liberty and the inescapability of tragic sacrifice and loss that decision making must entail. Judges must enter the fray because they are most capable of adopting an appropriate posture toward these conflicts in deciding them. The tragic approach distrusts an overreliance on democracy to resolve the disputes of religious liberty after a fashion that will reflect a tragic sensibility. Perhaps most importantly, it sees a different role for theory than the systematic resolution of problems, a role that the skeptics so effectively criticize. A tragic theory aims at understanding rather than resolving with finality. It accepts the reality of the conflict of values as a feature—the defining feature—of many of these cases. The tragic judge uses theory—theory properly conceived—to explain the nature of the dispute as well as what has been gained and lost when the case is decided.

Quasi Tragedians

The other category of skeptical thought is quite different. It is neither fully skeptical nor fully monistic, and for that reason it is both difficult to categorize and useful as a transition to the method of tragedy and history. It is a family of hybrid or mixed theories, each member of which partakes of selected portions of monistic and skeptical approaches.[53] Like some of the strong skeptics, theorists in this group begin promisingly with the recognition that there are many values of religious liberty and that they cannot be reduced to a single concern or unitary principle without serious cost. Thus, for example, Steven Shiffrin argues that the religion clauses are underwritten by multiple and often conflicting values, and that there is "no single determining principle that resolves" the conflicts of religious liberty.[54] Quasi-tragic accounts represent an advance over monistic egalitarian and neutralist approaches in their pluralistic view of religious liberty.

Yet what makes these theories quasi-tragic—and in the end akin to comic monistic approaches—is that even though they acknowledge legitimate conflicting concerns, ultimately they rely on a small number of values to resolve the conflicts of religious liberty. Moreover, like other comic approaches, quasi-tragic theories hold out these resolutions as somehow optimal or ideal for all discrete categories of legal conflict. In this sense, they are not truly or completely tragic because they do not take conflict to be foundational; instead, the clash of values of religious liberty is often noticed and then sidestepped or tacitly avoided.

The quintessentially quasi-tragic approach to religious liberty is Kent Greenawalt's "contextualism,"[55] a theory in great sympathy with the view offered in this book. The difference, however, is that contextualism in the final analysis gives categorical and systematic primacy to a very small number of values.

At the opening of his monumental study, Greenawalt encapsulates his overarching approach in three ideas: the irreducibility of values, the nonformulaic quality of religious liberty, and the utility of particularistic assessment.[56] These three ideas are summed up in the metaphor of "bottom-up" theorizing.[57] Greenawalt is skeptical about theories that posit a master value of religious liberty because "almost inevitably they omit too much or provide an overarching value that is so inclusive it yields little help in resolving practical problems."[58]

From these broad-brush observations, it appears that contextualism has much in common with a tragic approach. Yet an important clue to the crucial difference can be found in a single word that recurs in his discussion: *fairness*.[59] Fairness is the value constant that makes theoretical sense of the contextualist approach. Yet for all its prominence, the idea of fairness is never discussed in detail. Often fairness is teamed closely with equality: is it fair to treat Saturday worshipers as "relevantly equal or unequal to workers who want to spend Saturdays with their families,"[60] or for a religious organization to discriminate in the hiring of clerics on the basis of gender?[61] In fact, fairness often seems synonymous with equality for Greenawalt.[62] At other times, however, Greenawalt seems to associate fairness with the idea of neutrality, disputing the claim that neutrality is empty and linking neutrality to separationist concerns.[63]

The difficulty is that Greenawalt claims that it is precisely a defining feature of his approach *not* to select a single value such as fairness as the monistic value of religious liberty. Yet he relies on the concept of fairness to convey an allegiance to equality and neutrality interpreted as a type of institutional autonomy or separation. And these two values play a paramount role in his approach. Greenawalt's contextualism therefore represents a considerable improvement over comic monistic theories of religious liberty inasmuch as it rejects single value reductions. Yet in place of a single value, Greenawalt substitutes two in the establishment context, with a special emphasis on the value of equality. Thus, while his analysis of Establishment Clause conflicts is indeed nuanced in its attempt to wrestle honestly with the conflicts between these two values, it does not go nearly far enough in perceiving the number of clashing values in these disputes.[64]

The contrast with a fully tragic position is especially sharp in the establishment context, principally because for Greenawalt fairness—in the form of the two values of equality and separationist neutrality—predominates. For example, in his discussion of the constitutionality of the phrase "under God" in the Pledge of Allegiance, Greenawalt is particularly—one might even say exclusively—troubled by egalitarian concerns:

> [T]he words "under God" taken literally have religious significance. . . . These words trouble some of the small percentage of young people who do not believe in a single God. My already strong intuition that this must be so was confirmed by an atheist student in a seminar describing how uncomfortable, how much an outsider he felt, when the Pledge was recited at his school.[65]

While it is indeed implausible to claim that the phrase "under God" does not have religious significance (a position at one time taken by Justice O'Connor[66]), and while Greenawalt allows that not all religious endorsements are serious enough to be constitutionally objectionable, he is too dismissive of the view that some people, very much including some school-age students, might want "under God" included because it is an acknowledgment of the country's religious heritage, a sign of respect for that heritage, and a way to achieve, in a small and ephemeral way, a unity of feeling and sympathy with other students.[67] Moreover, in the context of what is undeniably a civic exercise (both the Pledge itself and the enterprise of public education generally), the statement that the nation is "under God" sounds in the language of patriotism—though it is difficult to separate cleanly just where the civic begins and the religious ends, or to distinguish how strongly each student reciting the Pledge may have sensed the respective patriotic and religious inflections.[68] It is of course true that not all students will feel either patriotic or religious; Greenawalt's atheist student did not. But the fact that every student will not approve does not mean that the interests of those who do approve and are edified by the practice are illicit or improper.

Similarly, Greenawalt's emphasis on "the inclusiveness of the view that is endorsed" is further evidence of the centrality of equality in his scheme.[69] Equality is so important that the only justification for not striking down the phrase "under God" that Greenawalt can accept is:

> the widespread outrage and antagonism toward the Court, as well as a corrective amendment, which would be likely to be generated by a decision striking down "under God" in the Pledge for schoolchildren.[70]

Strikingly absent from this assessment is any consideration of historical practice and tradition. This is especially surprising in light of the fact that Greenawalt is keenly aware of the arguments to be made in favor of the value of historical practice, settled expectations, and predictable outcomes—indeed, he even lists historical traditions as a way to reconcile conflicting values.[71] Why then do these considerations play little role in his ultimate resolution?

The answer lies in his quasi-tragic commitments. For Greenawalt, even as he carefully identifies competing values, equality is generally the value that is ultimately given overriding weight. More than this, Greenawalt hopes and expects that the competing values of historical acknowledgment that attend mild endorsements will be sloughed off with the passage of time.[72]

This puts contextualism squarely at odds with a tragic position. For Greenawalt, as for the comic egalitarians, a regime in which nonendorsement is given fullest and most unwavering expression would be ideal; yet his is a quasi-tragic position inasmuch as it grudgingly acknowledges that given the history of the nation, such a regime is not currently politically feasible (though in time, it hopefully will be). Nevertheless, the cognitive perceptions of nonadherents—of religious "outsiders"—are the supreme consideration.[73] A fully tragic position, by contrast, would be more sensitive to competing values, including the power of the claims of historical practice, precedent, and tradition.[74]

Another area that illustrates the distinction between a quasi-tragic and fully tragic approach involves the question of government aid to religious schools, though here it is the value of neutrality that becomes predominant for the quasi tragedian. The most important recent case in this area is *Zelman v. Simmons-Harris*, where the Supreme Court held that the First Amendment permitted the city of Cleveland to include religious schools in its school-choice voucher program.[75] Under the program, a student could remain in Cleveland's dismally performing public school system and receive an amount of money for additional tutoring, or the student could attend a private school with a portion of the tuition paid by the state.[76] The program was challenged on the ground that many of the eligible private schools were also parochial schools and the use of public funds to pay for education at a religious school was alleged to violate the Establishment Clause. The Supreme Court upheld the program on a neutrality rationale: the program was an example of "true private choice" and therefore formally neutral because it attributed all decision making to the individual family rather than the government.[77]

Greenawalt believes that both *Zelman* and vouchers generally are "regrettable."[78] Now the value of neutrality takes center stage, but it is neither the formal nor the substantive neutrality of the comic neutralists.[79] Instead, his principal concern is with separationist or institutional neutrality—that there are simply some realms into which neither the state nor the church ought to enter.[80] Government does not act neutrally if it sets up programs whose inevitable effect will be to favor religious educational providers "to the near exclusion of nonreligious providers,"[81] echoing the concern of the second prong of the establishment test announced in *Lemon v. Kurtzman*, which asks whether the challenged law or practice has the primary effect of advancing or inhibiting religion.[82]

And yet missing from this assessment is the reality that without a voucher program, the government's financing decisions with respect to education themselves have an asymmetric—and decidedly nonneutral— impact on parents' educational choices. All public school spending goes to nonreligious institutions, thereby diminishing school choice.[83] The difficulty is precisely a tragic one: the values of separationist neutrality and equality of impact clash, as do two different valences of differential impact—the differential impact implicated by a voucher program like Cleveland's, and the differential impact that attends the larger general structure of the government's educational financing. The former is decisive for Greenawalt—sufficient of itself to oppose the Cleveland voucher program. From a fully tragic perspective, by contrast, it would be a factor to be considered, but not necessarily a decisive one.[84]

In sum, Greenawaltian contextualism, while approaching a tragic view, ultimately does not go far enough. It recognizes the complex tangle of the clash of values that constitutes the core of religious liberty disputes; but it does not permit that welter as much space to breathe, or as much power to affect the possible range of outcomes, as would a fully tragic perspective. Quasi-tragic theories of religious liberty in the end often give overpowering weight to concerns of equality and neutrality. In this, they resemble comic egalitarian and neutralist approaches. Both the comic monists and the quasi tragedians deny that conflict is a truly foundational and unavoidable feature of the law of religious liberty. The monists do so explicitly; the quasi tragedians covertly. But both, in the end, are insufficiently attentive to the predicament of legal theory—its limitations and inadequacies in the face of complexity.

There are other important quasi-tragic theories: Steven Shiffrin's "7 & 7" account, for example, which identifies seven values of free exercise and a corresponding (and perhaps slightly too convenient) seven values of establishment,[85] and Paul Horwitz's constitutional "agnosticism."[86]

Horwitz's approach is particularly powerful and elegant. Like other quasi tragedians, Horwitz is cognizant that there are many values of religious liberty that no theory is entirely capable of systematizing.[87] He advocates an "agnostic" orientation to the issue of whether a religious claim is "true"—a posture of provisional indecision on the merits, coupled with a commitment to genuine inquiry and engagement with the truth claims of religion. He claims that agnosticism does greater justice to the range of conflicting values of religious liberty than do monistic theories.[88] Yet Horwitz also seems certain that the issue of religious truth is exceptionally important, and that the state ought to be an empathetic conversation partner with the claimant about the nature and quality of the beliefs in issue.[89] The state should treat "the needs of religious believers . . . not just as a matter of individual conscience, but potentially as a matter of absolute truth."[90]

Historically there have been excellent reasons to be chary of government efforts to delve too deeply into the truth claims of religion; indeed, one reason that conceptions of religious liberty arose in liberal democratic states was that the state had routinely demonstrated that it was not in the least competent to take imaginatively empathetic leaps into the truth claims of religion that would bind the rest of us. If the separation of church and state continues to be a viable conception of religious liberty,[91] it surely must be because the state is notoriously ill suited to inquire into religious truth. Yet Horwitz writes:

> Separationism, for instance, can be seen as an approach that seeks to dig a trench between government and private religious choice, or that views religion as either beyond the competence of the state or so divisive a subject that it should be set aside from issues of democratic governance. But these justifications either depend on questions that cannot be answered absent a judgment about religious truth . . . or make an ultimately fruitless effort to avoid them altogether.[92]

It is religious "truth" and its discovery, Horwitz seems to say, that can explain or make sense of an institutional commitment to separate church from state. And so what begins as an entirely proper recognition of the plural and irreconcilable values of religious liberty becomes a view in which truth-seeking and truth-finding assume primacy.

Setting aside the point that not all conceptions of separationism need adopt the metaphor of a moat protecting both citadel and besiegers, it is not clear why separation as a practical strategy recommended by long and blood-soaked historical experience need engage with religious truth. A presumption in favor of separation or, in the Supreme Court's locution, against "excessive entanglement" between church and state might be justified for largely pragmatic and historical reasons.[93] That historical settlement, as well as the values underwriting it, does not depend on our present sense of the extent to which any specific religious claims are or might be true.[94] Even if we could be sure that the specific claims of any religious tradition were true, or probably true, or even generally true, there would still be important reasons for the state to maintain its institutional separation from the religion professing those beliefs.[95]

Horwitz's claim that the value of truth-seeking can make holistic sense of the conflicts of values of religious liberty overstates the extent to which the search for truth is prized in the law. Truth-seeking is certainly one value among many pursued by our legal system. Others include affording adequate process, enabling people to have their grievances heard and adjudicated, and achieving finality with respect to any dispute. And there are many occasions where the value of truth-seeking is systematically sacrificed in the law. In criminal law, courts exclude evidence that has been collected in violation of the Fourth Amendment as "fruit of the poisonous tree,"[96] even if it is probative of the truth. Likewise, the law contains many testimonial privileges—among them spousal privileges,[97] priest–penitent privileges,[98] and the constitutional privilege against self-incrimination[99]—that obstruct the search for truth in a legal proceeding. And the doctrine of so-called "actual innocence" throws up procedural obstacles to overturn the criminal convictions of those who claim to have unearthed fresh evidence of their innocence.[100]

Horwitz is right that attention to religious truth has not figured prominently, if at all, as a cognizable value of religious liberty; he is also right that truth-seeking is an important function of legal process. Yet he claims too much in arguing that the search for religious truth should assume a central or dominant place in the negotiation of values of religious liberty. In this, he follows in the footsteps of other quasi tragedians who, though noting the plural and clashing quality of these disputes and the values that they instantiate, nevertheless fall back on one principle or aim as singularly important in achieving satisfactory resolutions. These approaches are not tragic through and through.

PART II

Tragedy and History

This part introduces and explains the five theses of the method of tragedy and history. The first three theses describe the conditions of theorizing about religious liberty—the tragic component of tragic-historic method[1]—while the last two respond to those conditions.

As was discussed in earlier chapters, my use of the term *tragic* draws on classical and literary understandings, though it does not track those meanings precisely. A tragic perspective denies that fully systematic answers to the conflicts of religious liberty are possible. It also emphasizes an acute sense of the losses and costs that adjudication invariably entails, and it seeks to make those losses and costs explicit in judicial opinions.

The final two theses respond to the tragic theses, pointing toward an approach that best accommodates the predicaments of tragic judgment by emphasizing incremental adjudication that relies on legal and social history for guidance. That approach is described as "historical," and, as with "tragedy," the term requires some initial explanation.

To call an approach historical might evoke the idea of "historicism" in philosophy, the most famous example of which is late eighteenth-century to mid-nineteenth-century German historicism, which was not so much a theory or doctrine as "a programme . . . [with] a simple but ambitious goal: to legitimate history as a science. The historicists wanted history to enjoy the same status and prestige as the natural sciences; but they claimed that it had its own goals, methods, and standards of knowledge, which were unlike those of the natural sciences."[2] German historicism's aim was to vindicate the belief in "the autonomy of historical knowledge" as well as "the autonomy of the historical world"—that "everything that happens in history must be explained within history and according to specifically historical methods."[3]

While there are sympathies between the historical theses of the tragic-historic method and this important philosophical program—most notably (1) the idea that human values and institutions exist only within history, and the consequent caution against the proclivity to generalize, if not to "eternalize," the values of religious liberty; and (2) the view that "history has its own standards and methods of knowledge"[4]—there may be significant differences as well.[5] In any event, the method of tragedy and history does not call for a revival of German historicism or its application to the law of religious liberty.

Closer to the method of tragedy and history is the late nineteenth-century and early twentieth-century English and American "historical" jurisprudential school. The central premise of the historical approach was that a proper explanation of law and legal systems demands not the distillation of abstract values or principles, but attention to the history of the society in which law is situated.[6] Judges, for the historical school, infuse the law with this historical sensibility. Historical jurisprudent James Coolidge Carter, for example, remarked that judges are "both by appointment and tradition the experts in ascertaining the customs of life," emphasizing the gradualist process of change that is effected by the common law method and the need for judges to refer both to precedent and social custom.[7]

The historical component of the method of tragedy and history shares several commitments with this jurisprudential view, but there are differences as well, one of which is that the historical view described here is dependent on the tragic theses.[8] It is the conflicts of religious liberty described in the tragic theses that both stimulate law's change *and* insist on its gradualism and historicity. The historical posture adopted by the method of tragedy and history insists that legal change is itself a seemingly internally clashing concept, combining alteration with sameness: for "if there were no alteration there would be an unbroken sameness; if there were no remaining the same there would be the recollection of that which had unaccountably gone and the observation of that which had unaccountably appeared."[9] Legal change in the area of religious liberty comes about by holding together these complementary but conflicting and oppositional ideas and by managing the perpetual struggle between identity and difference through the constraining method of the common law.

CHAPTER 3

The Clash of Values of Religious Liberty

We have seen that from the comic standpoint, the idea of religious liberty is greatly, and misleadingly, simplified. Comic theorists emphasize familiar justifications for religious liberty—equality, or neutrality, or the separation of church and state, or individual autonomy and choice, or the necessity of avoiding political division or strife,[1] or the futility of compelling belief[2]—that appear to explain fully the state's commitment to religious freedom.

But comic explanations offer only weak protection for religious liberty because they say nothing about what religious freedom is valuable for[3]—about the multiplicity of ways in which that freedom could be interpreted, valued, and exercised, whether by the state, an individual, a religious institution, or a cultural community.[4] And they mistakenly suggest that there are only two parties who have roles to play, the individual and the state—the believer always seeking greater freedom, the state intent on curbing it within limits deemed to be acceptable, safe, or socially sanitary.[5]

Spheres of Variation

We require a richer sense of religious liberty and the implications that its variety will have for law. Something must be known about the particular context in which claims for and against religious liberty are asserted, understood, and evaluated.[6] Attention must be paid to the predicament of legal theory—that theory, while inevitable and important, can distort and misunderstand the legal world that it aspires to explain. Few of these questions can be explored without first acknowledging that conceptions of religious liberty are cultural constructs. What is deemed valuable about the freedom to believe in and practice religion, and the state's relationship to that freedom, will vary between and among cultural communities and individuals through time.

The Native American whose religious rituals include the smoking of peyote will value a conception of religious liberty in which he is at liberty to do so. He will reject as illegitimate any conception of religious liberty that does not recognize peyote smoking as sufficiently important to permit it.[7] But more than this, he will value the freedom to smoke peyote for its moral significance, for what the ritual expresses about his way of life, and for the type of person that he imagines and hopes himself to be.[8] It is this sense of moral significance, and not a set of abstract and cold propositions, which gives texture to the system of ethical and cultural beliefs of which it forms a part—a lived experience and moral tradition.

The freedom of the Roman Catholic to take a sip of wine as part of the sacrament of Communion bears a resemblance, as a detached propositional feature of a conception of religious liberty, to the Native American's conception, but the significance of the freedoms within the respective ways of life of which the ritual is only one part are entirely different. In order to understand why the freedom is valued—what moral shape it takes within the larger set of customs of which it forms a part—more must be known about that broader context. Liberal democratic states, on the other hand, have no cultural attachment either to peyote smoking or wine sipping and may not value a conception of religious liberty in which these practices are permitted. And that, too, is in part because peyote smoking or the consumption of alcohol has no moral significance for them. It expresses and represents nothing of intrinsic value.[9] These variations and countless others in the values of religious liberty evince, as James Madison famously put it, nothing less than "[a] zeal for different opinions concerning religion" itself.[10]

The variations take shape within three distinct spheres. First, there is interreligious variation. The Roman Catholic idea of religious liberty is not the same as the Protestant, the Jewish, the Muslim, the Native American, or the Sikh idea of religious liberty. To be free to believe in and practice any of these faiths is to enjoy the liberty to adhere to, confess, and act in accordance with their respective complex of beliefs and traditions, each one of which has had much to say about the justification and scope of religious liberty.

Second, there is intrareligious variation, itself divisible into two subgroups: (1) variation within traditions about the scope of acceptable dissent; and (2) variation within traditions about the scope of freedom from state intrusion. As an example of the first subgroup, among Roman Catholics, there are those who believe that the Magisterium's interpretations and pronouncements ought nearly always to be obeyed. For these believers, to be a Catholic means to enjoy religious liberty as a corollary to those limits.[11] Others whose idea of Catholicism is more expansive will have different ideas about the scope of their religious liberty *as Catholics*.[12] And a vast and shifting middle ground exists between these two poles; some Catholics may give the Church's teachings presumptive force on most matters, others only on crucial matters,[13] others still may give no deference but may extend a conversational respect,[14] and so on.

As an example of the second subgroup, freedom from government intrusion, some Muslims argue that the idea of religious freedom extends only to Muslims and the "People of the Book," while others take a broader view.[15] Those Muslims who oppose a broader idea of religious liberty sometimes do so on theological grounds: they support their view with reference to the Muslim prohibitions on polytheism, apostasy, blasphemy, and, ultimately, to a religion whose "founding principle is the unity of God."[16] Yet even for those Muslims of less restrictive inclinations, the question of the law's general applicability is contested, since for Muslims the state exists to enforce Islamic law on those within it.[17] Of course, intrareligious variation is not without limits: too radical a departure will mark a break from the religious tradition.

Third, there is temporal variation. Even among members of the same religious community, the values of religious liberty may change over time. And these changes need not be unidirectional: religious communities may revive older understandings of religious liberty; and religious liberty may not necessarily increase as religious belief and practice become more individualistic.[18] Even across a fairly limited time frame, what religious liberty demands is often the subject of disagreement.

For a non-Muslim residing in a Muslim country, and at one time the beneficiary of a certain type of contractual protection by the state in exchange for paying a tax, there was disagreement through time about the kind of behavior that would breach the agreement and whether that behavior was properly considered part of the non-Muslim's religious liberty.[19] Certain communities of American Baptists of the late eighteenth century had a specific idea of religious liberty that nineteenth- or twentieth-century Baptists are unlikely to share, since their respective ideas of religious liberty took shape in response to unique historical concerns.[20] Catholic ideas about the value of religious liberty—whether it is best characterized as an intrinsic[21] or instrumental good[22]—witnessed substantial changes in the twentieth century.

All of these variations reinforce the notion that conceptions of religious liberty are fluid, culturally contingent, perpetually developing, and highly protean.

Conflict

So far so good. By isolating these spheres, we have begun to probe the nature and depth of the challenge that religious pluralism poses to the theoretical enterprise. But we now must address the issue of conflict.

Difficulties arise whenever these multifarious and shifting ideas of religious liberty conflict with other values either internal or external to them, so that a decision must be made in favor of some and against others. The values of religious liberty intersect and compete with others that are constitutive of the particular sociocultural conditions. Piety, asceticism, charity, devotion, sacrifice, self-control, fidelity, tolerance, equality, human dignity, temperance, patience, the autonomy of conscience, and obedience form only a partial list of values that have at various moments shaped specific ideas and traditions of religious liberty. Many of these same values—in addition to others such as patriotism, law-abidingness, and the formal values associated with the rule of law—have in different ways shaped civic, familial, professional, and other associations and institutions. In this way the state, too, develops its own understandings of religious liberty, which vary in ways that mimic religious pluralism within any of the three spheres.[23]

Conflicts occur not only among different types of values, as when a Native American's piety, instantiated in his ritualistic peyote smoking, conflicts with the state's interest in law-abidingness, reflected in its laws against drug use, but also among different values of the same type, as when the Roman Catholic idea of human equality (and what it means for religious liberty) conflicts with the idea of human equality contained in Title VII of the Civil Rights Act[24] (and what *that* means for religious liberty).[25] Equal treatment demands the absence of unjust discrimination, but what counts as unjust discrimination is open to an array of conflicting interpretations, religious and otherwise, that can clash within the same community.[26] These intersecting conflicts are experienced in two ways.

First, individuals or institutions that exist simultaneously within more than one particular cultural community must be judges as between competing claims. These "one-person conflicts," in Bernard Williams's phrase, often are expressions of larger conflicts within a person or an institution.[27] Does the Roman Catholic American citizen believe that his freedom—or his church's freedom—to discriminate in hiring or in ordaining priests should supersede or yield to his belief in human equality as that ideal has been interpreted in contemporary American law and culture? Does the Native American who is also a U.S. citizen believe that his spiritual need to smoke peyote should supersede or yield to the state's antidrug laws, where he holds an allegiance to both cultural communities? Likewise, how do the Roman Catholic and Native American Churches negotiate these conflicts as institutions, situated as they are within multiple communities?

It is also true that a person's values as judged from within a *single* tradition often conflict, as the demands of liberty and equality may conflict within the tradition of liberal democracy.[28] Even more problematically, and as we saw in Chapter 1, equality itself "breaks down on analysis into rival equalities, such as equality of opportunity and equality of outcome,"[29] presenting a conflict of goods within a single value. Resolving these conflicts often is a matter of an individual or institutional self-examination for their compatibility with particular ways of life to which the individual or institution is committed.[30] Some values may have greater power than others; some may be so vital that they generally will prevail over all others; many more will carry far less categorical force.

Second, the intersections may be experienced as "third-person conflicts." Third-person conflicts arise where one must judge as between the conflicting requirements of entirely disparate cultures.[31] The question now is how a third person who is charged by law with deciding those conflicts does so. The third person—a judge—carries into the conflict her own personal and institutional commitments and obligations, and she decides the conflict by engaging in measurements guided by one or more "covering values."[32] The more seriously the judge takes the vast scope and variety of the values of religious liberty, the greater the range of covering values.

The First Thesis of the Method of Tragedy and History

The crucial difficulty for resolving both one-person and third-person conflicts is that the conflicting values—whether between different types of values or between different values of the same type—often exhibit two key features: *they are incompatible and they are incommensurable.* This is the first thesis of the method of tragedy and history.

Incompatible values are at least partially mutually exclusive because of qualities intrinsic to the values themselves: to choose one necessarily means not to choose the other. A decision in favor of the government's right to build a road straight through sacred Native American land is a choice between values that are partially incompatible: economic efficiency and industrial progress over piety, privacy, and silence.[33] Conflict between the state's antidrug laws and the claims of a Native American who seeks to smoke peyote for ritual purposes pits the partially incompatible values of law-abidingness against the perception of a transcendent truth.[34]

Incommensurability, by contrast, is the idea that there is no unifying metric by which to compare choices and the values underlying them.[35] No single scale of worth can be used to compare incommensurable values, because it cannot be said that one of the values is superior to the other or that they are equal.[36] Incommensurability therefore might mean one of three things: (1) that it is meaningless to compare such values;[37] (2)

that it is pointless or silly to compare such values;[38] or (3) that it is inappropriate to compare such values.[39] The first thesis holds that incommensurable values in the realm of religious liberty disputes are those that are inappropriate or invalid to compare, where the judgment as between alternatives not only is mistaken but also grossly inapt.[40]

The First Thesis and Religious Liberty

For religious liberty conflicts, values may be incompatible but commensurable: a church whose highest value, racial purity, is manifested in the exclusion of all racial minorities, holds values that are incompatible with a polity whose highest value is racial harmony, but it is likely that the respective values can be gauged and measured along a single metric or covering value: racial inclusiveness or tolerance.[41] Or some values of religious liberty may be incommensurable but compatible: what is valuable in the practice of Christian penance is incommensurable, but not necessarily incompatible, with what is valuable in the practice of Buddhist meditation. One might realize the values in both of these practices if one's conception of the good were capacious enough (difficult though this may be), even if one would readily admit that there is no universal scale of assessment according to which one could rank or measure the respective worth of penance and meditation without fundamentally misunderstanding and distorting what is valuable in each practice.

It is only when the values of religious liberty, or other values with which those may conflict, are both incompatible and incommensurable that conflicts become problematic. These special kinds of opposing values are related "in being both valued, in its being totally or proportionally impossible to realize them together, and in there being no basis on which their intrinsic merits could be compared" without misunderstanding the core of what renders them valuable.[42] And both one- and third-person religious liberty conflicts are likely to be common where one or more of three conditions applies:

- where a person or people are committed to a value within any single tradition (equality, for example, in a liberal democratic tradition), which fragments into multiple incompatible and incommensurable goods (equality of opportunity, distributive equality, and government neutrality, for example); or

- where a person or people are committed to a single tradition that prizes distinct incompatible and incommensurable values, like equality and liberty, or the rule of law and the authority of conscience; or
- where a person or people are committed to multiple traditions (Roman Catholicism and liberal democracy, for example), each of which contains values that are incompatible and incommensurable.

We now have a complete picture of the conflicts often at issue in religious liberty disputes, as well as an account of how and why those conflicts arise. The conflicts:

1. are either among values of religious liberty or between those values and other values external to them, which are
2. incompatible,
3. incommensurable, and
4. third-person conflicts in a legal dispute.

As we will see, many religious liberty cases take precisely this form. Requirements 1 and 4 are always satisfied: church–state conflicts pit certain values of religious liberty against others in a third-person conflict. But it is worth pausing over two well-known Supreme Court church–state decisions to highlight the incompatible and incommensurable nature of the values at stake.

The First Thesis and the Free Exercise of Religion

The relationship of the first thesis and the constitutional right to the free exercise of religion is perhaps nowhere more powerfully in evidence than in the famous case of *Wisconsin v. Yoder*.[43] The State of Wisconsin charged members of the Old Order Amish and the Conservative Amish Mennonite Church with disobeying Wisconsin's compulsory school-attendance law, which required that all children attend public or private school until the age of sixteen.[44] The Yoders and two other parents had withdrawn their children from school at ages fifteen, fifteen, and fourteen, respectively, and they argued that the compulsory attendance rule violated their religious liberty.[45] The Amish[46] claimed that "their children's attendance at high school, public or private, was contrary to the Amish religion and way of life";[47] their children's continued school attendance would, in their view, "endanger their own salvation and that of their children."[48] Relying on the corroborating testimony of experts and various secondary sources, the Court characterized the core claims of the Amish as "a fundamental belief that salvation requires life in a church community separate and apart from the world and worldly influence" and "devotion to a life in harmony with nature and the soil . . . to make their living by farming or closely related activities."[49] Chief Justice Burger, writing for the Court, then offered this summary of the conflict of values in the respective ways of life of the Amish and the state:

> The high school tends to emphasize intellectual and scientific accomplishments, self-distinction, competitiveness, worldly success, and social life with other students. Amish society emphasizes informal learning-through-doing; a life of "goodness," rather than a life of intellect; wisdom, rather than technical knowledge, community welfare, rather than competition; and separation from, rather than integration with, contemporary worldly society.[50]

The incompatibility of the respective values together with the physical and emotional distance from the Amish way of life that would result from additional years in school (precisely at a time when physical and emotional proximity was most important in forming lasting connections to the Amish community)[51] combined to form a powerful free exercise challenge to the state law.[52]

It was also important to the Court that the Amish way of life was conducive to a productive, "law-abiding, and generally self-sufficient existence."[53] According to an expert credited by the Court, the learning of specific skills and practices emphasized by the Amish educational system—skills that were "directly relevant to their adult roles"—prepared Amish children for productive adult lives in a fashion "perhaps superior to ordinary high school education."[54]

Both the Court and the dissent understood the values and obligations reflected in the state law, as well as the multiplicity of ways in which that set of commitments might conflict with others. The government's duty to ensure that all of its citizens are sufficiently educated to meet the vocational needs of a career may conflict with parents' rights to provide their children with an education of their choosing, provided that it also "prepare[s] [them] for additional obligations."[55] The government's interest in creating opportunities and exposing its budding citizens to the "unparalleled progress in human knowledge"[56] and the "new and amazing world of diversity"[57]—to opportunities to be "a pianist or an astronaut or an oceanographer"[58]—may conflict with the parents' and the local community's interests in fostering in children a respect for and attachment to local customs, traditions, and practices.[59] The government's interest in cultivating an inquisitive, questioning, and critical sensibility[60] so that a child may be better equipped to participate as a citizen in democratic government may conflict with the parents' or the community's interest in cultivating an intuitive decency,[61] learned not by developing the skills of intellectual inquiry and deft argumentation, but by observing and modeling the habits and manners of admired fellows or teachers committed to a particular way of life (much as courage, perseverance, and effort may be learned by modeling the behavior of participants in an athletic contest). The government's interest in developing a materialistic or consumerist ethos in children, as well as, perhaps more benignly, simply in cultivating their tastes and sensitivities[62]—so that children might eventually have enhanced experiences both as producers and consumers in the dominant sociocultural milieu[63]—may conflict with the parents' or the community's interest in developing in children the sense that a materialistic or even an excessively aesthetic outlook can be damaging to one's spiritual and psychological well-being.[64] And then there are the interests of the child, which are in the process of developing and may partake of all of these conflicting commitments in unpredictable ways.[65]

It is easy—all too easy—to see these conflicts as simply between two different ways of life, the Amish and the state's, though it is certainly accurate to characterize the conflicts as between alternative cultures engaged in making claims on the loyalties of the Amish children—as a "soul-making competition" where the contestants are rival traditions.[66] Yet all of these conflicts just as plausibly may be characterized as examples where a *single* tradition—and here I mean at least a liberal democratic tradition, but perhaps the Amish tradition as well[67]—is committed to multiple values that are partially incompatible and incommensurable.

The value of a thorough basic education against the value of parental control over the direction of one's children's upbringing. The value of cultivating independence of mind and a critical, intellectual inquisitiveness against the value of a deep-rooted, intuitive goodness or decency. The value of a certain connection, of greater or lesser degree, to the socioeconomic and cultural structures of the dominant society against the value of a certain connection, of greater or lesser degree, to natural or local community structures of spiritual meaning and worth. And the value of equality as to educational resources and opportunities for all children against the value of parental and familial nurturance, which must of necessity be partial and unequal.[68]

These conflicts are irreconcilable. But more than this, they are problematic because they represent tensions between values to which members of liberal societies are *also* committed in varying degrees, tensions that cannot be resolved by any single, overarching standard of worth without grave risk of misunderstanding and mischaracterization. Those who are not committed to the Amish way of life may be able not only to tolerate,[69] but also to understand, if they have ears to hear it,[70] the language in which the Amish dissent was expressed: as a call for the value of a parent's shaping the direction of a child's education, the value of local cultural and familial traditions, the value of a life unencumbered and undefined by the trappings and easy comforts of modern life,[71] and so on.

These values may resonate generally because they are themselves part of the welter of value structures of citizens of liberal societies. To be sure, the emphases and specific manifestations of the values may be different, but the values are recognizable nevertheless. The point is not merely, or even primarily, that one can predict that parents ordinarily will do a better job than the state at raising their own children. It is instead that the state ought to accord parents a wide range of choice in this area because it recognizes that permitting a degree of parental control over a child's upbringing is itself intrinsically good. It is a good to be exercised wisely and lovingly, to be sure,[72] but parental nurturance is a value *even if* (as is likely) the direction of that upbringing will bring it into tension, if not conflict, with a number of fundamental civic judgments reflecting values to which citizens of liberal societies are also deeply committed. Thus, when political theorist Stephen Macedo writes that "perhaps we may tolerate the Amish but we should not (at least in important respects) celebrate them" because they are not "good liberal citizens,"[73] he takes a regrettably parsimonious view of what liberal citizens might actually value—and even celebrate. Liberal men and women, just in virtue of their liberality, are broadly, variously, incompatibly, and incommensurably committed.

Finally, it is important to see that the conflicts of religious liberty in *Yoder* also involve the incompatible and incommensurable valences of at least one *single value,* equality, within a single tradition, liberalism. In an early appearance of the value of formal neutrality that eventually won the day in *Employment Division v. Smith,*[74] the state argued that the compulsory education law "applies uniformly to all citizens of the State and does not, on its face, discriminate against religions or a particular religion."[75] That position was rejected by Chief Justice Burger as an overly rigid understanding of neutrality because a "regulation neutral on its face may, in its application, nonetheless offend the constitutional requirement for government neutrality if it unduly burdens the free exercise of religion."[76] While the Court also recognized that an exemption from generally applicable laws can be viewed as a type of favoritism, and therefore as implicating establishmentarian (and egalitarian) concerns, it believed itself to be successfully negotiating this "tightrope."[77] Nevertheless, the Court emphasized the law-abiding and socially productive qualities of the Amish in justifying the exemption, tacitly suggesting that another less law-abiding religious community might not receive the same favorable treatment. And it asserted that claims of exemption rooted in a secular basis would not have received similar treatment: "Thoreau's choice was philosophical and personal rather than religious, and such belief does not rise to the demands of the Religion Clauses."[78]

It is this multiplicity of conflicting meanings of equality which suffuse *Yoder* and give it the appearance of being unprincipled or internally inconsistent that has been a source of intense debate and disagreement. The trouble, as Steven Smith has noted, is that a large swath of scholars agree with the result but remain wholly dissatisfied with *Yoder*'s reasoning.[79]

The discomfort derives from scholars' yearning for the consolations of comic monism. They search for a single principle—a master value of free exercise—by which they can solve the puzzle of the *Yoder* conflicts and systematically organize all other cases like it. One of these critic-supporters is legal scholar Laura Underkuffler, who believes that "equality is an indispensable principle for the interpretation of the Religion Clauses."[80] Yet after stating this principle, Underkuffler reasonably acknowledges that there may be disagreement about what the principle actually demands.[81] To the challenge that granting exemptions from generally applicable laws to a religious group is an offense against at least one core conception of equality, Underkuffler responds that the exemption actually serves or fosters equality because:

> *if* we define religion broadly, as the protection of individual conscience—*if* we understand religion to be rooted in the ability, and responsibility, of individuals to act as moral agents—then we can justify the special protection of religion as a substantive value choice.[82]

Underkuffler recognizes that not everyone who favors an egalitarian vision of religious liberty will be satisfied with this position, because in the end the state is making a certain type of value judgment that may displease those who disagree. But she believes that this is the best that can be done: at least, this type of privileging of individual conscience is egalitarian in spirit. Each individual is equally protected, as a reflective entity seeking "personal moral awareness."[83]

It is no small token of Underkuffler's discomfort with *Yoder* that in an essay devoted to *Yoder*, discussion of the case occurs only twice: at the very beginning of the essay and when Underkuffler criticizes the majority for its "failure . . . to acknowledge the validity of the equality challenge in . . . the *Yoder* decision and others like it."[84] Yet to be embarrassed by the outcome in *Yoder* is natural enough if one is looking for a monistic solution to the case, let alone to systematize all "others like it" according to that principle. The distress is powerful enough that Underkuffler verges on acknowledging that the competing understandings of equality are not capable of reconciliation. An equality that emphasizes differential impact as opposed to differential treatment will only be convincing to those egalitarians who agree that "by 'equality before the law' we mean not only the law's terms, but also its differential impact."[85] An equality that emphasizes the importance of protecting individual conscience as opposed to a more procedural equal treatment will only be convincing to those egalitarians who agree that "equality before the law" means not only the law's terms, but also the capacity for equal "individual moral agency."[86]

But the predicament is actually much worse than this. If one examines the claims advanced in *Yoder*, it becomes clear that to the extent the Amish were making religious liberty claims grounded in the value of equality at all, those claims had little, if anything, to do with the right to "individual moral agency" in matters of conscience. They involved the (equal) right of a parent to nurture and guide a child's upbringing; the (equal) right of a community to choose a way of life that seemed best to it;[87] the (equal) right to elect a communal life set apart from the cultural structures of meaning and value of the dominant society—the equal right, in short, to group or institutional dissent from prevailing sociocultural orthodoxy. One might say that the Amish were seeking religious liberty *to be liberated from* the demand that they develop and exercise "individual moral agency." And all of these claims flowed from the requirements of the Amish way of life.

"But," will interject the comic egalitarian, "how is it possible to generalize these claims by recourse to the idea of equality, so that we can organize all future cases like *Yoder* by reference to that principle?" The answer is that, often enough, it is not possible. Sacrifices to values will be necessary. Yet this failure does not mean that "unprincipled" constitutional decision making is all that remains. It means instead that there is a complex of conflicting and incommensurable values—an interminable clash—that swirls around the idea of religious liberty and that will take very different shape and carry different inflections depending on the particulars of the claims being asserted. It is these qualities of the conflicts in *Yoder*—and so many cases like it—that explain the uneasiness that afflicts many scholars. In the realm of religious liberty conflicts, we care about too many values that refuse to be arranged neatly according to a premeditated order or scale of worth not to elicit a sense of discomfiture that something of value will have been lost to view, misunderstood, or sacrificed.

The First Thesis and the Establishment of Religion

Many cases involving the establishment of religion illustrate the first thesis of the method of tragedy and history, but one that does so particularly well is *Lee v. Weisman*,[88] which dealt with the constitutionality of "nonsectarian" prayers at public school graduation ceremonies.[89]

A Rhode Island public school regularly invited members of the clergy to deliver invocations and benedictions at graduation; on each occasion, school officials provided the speaker with a set of guidelines recommending that whatever prayer was chosen be "nonsectarian," "inclusive," and "sensitive."[90] Rabbi Leslie Gutterman, the school's selection for the middle school graduation in 1989, gave an invocation that was civic in emphasis but also overtly monotheistic.[91]

In finding the school's practice unconstitutional, Justice Kennedy's opinion for the Court held that the value of religious liberty at issue was noncoercion, which was especially salient in middle school.[92] Though students were not compelled to attend their graduations, Justice Kennedy found that "in our society and in our culture high school graduation is one of life's most significant occasions," rendering the graduation ceremony effectively compulsory.[93] The peer pressure on dissenting students to stand and participate in the religious exercise was the type of psychological coercion forbidden by the Establishment Clause.[94]

But the four Justices joining the Court's opinion made clear that they did not believe coercion to be the operative value of disestablishment. Justice Souter championed the type of neutrality that may accommodate religion only if it "lift[s] a discernible burden on the free exercise of religion,"[95] while Justice Blackmun preferred the value of nonendorsement.[96] In explaining the value of neutrality as the cornerstone of religious liberty, Justice Souter argued that nonpreferential establishments were no less objectionable than establishments of particular religions.[97] He also claimed that the value of graduation prayers for those supporting them was precisely what the Establishment Clause forbids: government endorsement of the superiority of one religion over all others.[98]

The conflict in *Lee* is best characterized as one within differing conceptions of religious liberty, but if what Justice Souter says is correct, then the first thesis of the tragic-historic method may not apply at all, because the conflicting values—neutrality and sponsorship—would be incompatible but commensurable. The dispute would then turn on whether religious sponsorship or religious neutrality, as Justice Souter describes these terms, is more consistent with the state's conception of religious liberty. Religious neutrality seems clearly to prevail—it is the only option consistent with the Constitution.

In fact, however, Justice Souter may have misunderstood the values of religious liberty of those supporting the graduation prayers. Kent Greenawalt's disagreement with Justice Souter on this point provides a better entrée to understanding the conflict:

> I do not think [sponsorship] fairly captures why many people want prayers at a graduation. Rather, they want, as members of a group participating in an event of deep significance in the lives of graduates and their parents, to acknowledge God and seek God's blessing.[99]

While Greenawalt ultimately sides with the *Lee* majority, it is this more subtle appreciation of the values in conflict that leads him to acknowledge that something of worth and importance is thereby lost.[100]

What is lost are several values of religious liberty. First, there is value in the acknowledgment of God at a moment when such recognition may be particularly meaningful. But this acknowledgment is not an expression of religious superiority or dominance; to the contrary, it is an expression of gratitude and humility.[101] It is part of the conception of religious liberty of those supporting inclusion of the prayers to be free to acknowledge and thank God in a ceremony that marks a major moment of achievement and transition.[102]

The freedom *to express religious gratitude in a public forum*, then, is an additional value of religious liberty.[103] Constitutional scholars Ira Lupu and Robert Tuttle have identified three ways in which it might be thought valuable that the government acknowledge religion: acknowledgment as "historical accuracy, reverence, and cultural recognition."[104] Lupu and Tuttle claim that the last of these, "cultural recognition," permits the state to "acknowledge the important role of religion within the social and political community," provided that the acknowledgment has a secular purpose.[105] Acknowledgment as cultural recognition is distinguishable from government sponsorship because the government is responding to the social or cultural experiences and preferences of the populace and is also able to offer a secular purpose for the acknowledgment.[106]

It is here that an argument in Justice Scalia's dissent in *Lee* supplies a possible secular link—that public prayers represent a tradition of unifying tolerance and cordial goodwill among those of different faiths.[107] Just as the government is permitted to consider and acknowledge the religious preferences of the majority in selecting a uniform day of rest (because it is beneficial and useful for the civic polity, as a community, to enjoy such a day), so is it permissible for the government to acknowledge the religious preferences of the majority by including a prayer in what is an otherwise secular ceremony (because prayers on certain kinds of public occasions have traditionally represented and reflected a tolerant and convivial civic spirit).[108]

The concept of cultural acknowledgment gestures in the direction of yet another value of religious liberty—one that has been called "religion as public resource"[109] or alternatively "religion as public utility."[110] Through time and customary use, the beliefs and practices of religious communities can become important and valuable cultural artifacts for the public at large. The "fruits of faith"—not only music, art, literature, and architecture, but also the uses of religion in political discourse, symbolism, and iconography—are felt to belong to communities constituted by believers and nonbelievers alike.[111]

One might question whether this type of public use of religion qualifies as a "religious" liberty interest at all, since at least some of those who value religion as a public resource or utility might do so for reasons unrelated to their own religious convictions. They may enjoy a cathedral's frescoes on a purely aesthetic level, or they may appreciate the elegant poetic economy of a psalm, the rhetorical pungency of a sermon, or the complex polyphonies of a Bach oratorio.

Yet setting aside the thorny question of what qualifies as "religious," it is at least equally likely that some people who are religious do find religious value in the public enjoyment of religious resources. And it is not implausible to suppose that at least some people with different or no religious backgrounds or commitments might find spiritual comfort, inspiration, or a more generalized sense of belonging and camaraderie in the use of religious resources on occasions of great moment.[112] As was seen in Chapter 1, it is exceedingly difficult to maintain the conceptual purity of the categories of aesthetic appreciation, spiritual uplift, and religious inspiration, as feelings in each of these domains are actually experienced.

It is, of course, true that Deborah Weisman did not feel this way about the invocation and benediction at her graduation. But it may also have been true that many of the assembled students—including those who either were not religious or who belonged to religious traditions that do not acknowledge the God of Judaism and Christianity—did experience this kind of psychological ownership of religion as public utility during the graduation invocation and benediction.

Religion as cultural acknowledgment and public utility explains—in a way that is at least partially incompatible and incommensurable with Justice Kennedy's master value of noncoercion, or with Justice Souter's master value of neutrality—the continuing practice of legislative prayers,[113] the invocation of God at the opening of the Supreme Court's own sessions,[114] and the display of religious symbols on government property during the holiday season.[115] While it may be true that some religious beliefs are profoundly personal, it is also sometimes the case that religious liberty demands that religion be self-consciously public.

The point, however, is not to endorse in an unqualified way the dissenting view in *Lee*. Indeed, Justice Kennedy's view that the value of noncoercion prohibits graduation prayers and Justice Souter's view that the state ought to remain neutral in all but limited circumstances are both compelling. Yet there is no denying that the values of cultural acknowledgment, religious gratitude, and religion as public utility are incompatible with Justice Souter's neutrality plus accommodation-to-lift-burden value or with Justice Kennedy's noncoercion value. The difficulty is that both Justices believe that they have discovered the single value of the Establishment Clause. Justice Souter goes so far as to claim that government can "take religion into account" *only* when laws of general application impose a discernible burden on religious belief or practice; otherwise, it must maintain an Olympian neutrality.[116]

Even more unfortunate is that Justice Souter misunderstands the values of religious liberty advocated by the public school, thereby giving them an appearance of commensurability with his own monistic value. He observes that "[r]eligious students cannot complain that omitting prayers from their graduation ceremony would, in any realistic sense, burden their spiritual callings" because those students could "express their religious feelings . . . before and after the ceremony" or "organize a privately sponsored" ceremony.[117]

Viewed in this light, the conflicting values of religious liberty are incommensurable but compatible: the students could express their religious sentiments before or after the ceremony, and the ceremony itself could exclude those sentiments. Justice Souter's suspicion, however, is that the values are commensurable but incompatible, because the public school and the prayers' supporters seek to sponsor one religious view in a public, governmental context—exactly what the Constitution prohibits.

But in reality, the conflicting values are incommensurable as well as incompatible, because those supporting the inclusion of the graduation prayers might well have been seeking government's cultural acknowledgment of religion, the opportunity to express gratitude to God on an important public occasion, and the enjoyment of religion as a public resource. They will not be satisfied with Justice Souter's "privately sponsored" ceremony—not because they want the state to crown their religion king, but because (1) events of great sociocultural significance seem irreparably diminished in their eyes without a public religious acknowledgment; and (2) certain religious rituals and practices are public, civic resources, and they value the freedom to partake of and enjoy those resources in a community of their fellows. And yet it is also no less true that including the prayers will damage the religious liberty of dissenters like Deborah Weisman—either because they will feel coerced to participate in a religious practice or because they will believe that the state is endorsing a religious view that they reject. They will sense that the state is imposing on them a change—an unwanted, unlooked for alteration to the structures of meaning and moral traditions that have been formative for them and to which they are attached. Future chapters will offer a view about how best to negotiate the clash of values in cases like *Lee v. Weisman*.[118] The aim of the first thesis is to illustrate that however cases of this kind should be decided, it is *not* by recourse to a monistic value of religious liberty.

The clash of the values of religious liberty is a pervasive feature of the law of church and state, one that can be masked and exacerbated by the inability of those charged to resolve third-person conflicts to understand the multilayered character of the values at issue. Too often, the subtleties of the rivalrous values are ignored or suppressed in order that they might be either justified or condemned within the bounds of a rigid theoretical frame that misunderstands the reality and omnipresence of conflict. The first thesis of the method of tragedy and history remedies this distortion—and it begins to align the orbits of legal theory and the world that it aspires to explain.

CHAPTER 4

The Inadequacy of Skepticism

In rejecting the comic monistic view of religious liberty, the first tragic thesis entails at least the view that the values of religious liberty cannot be reduced to a single, all-powerful principle, imperative, or set of principles. One might wonder whether it also necessarily entails the proposition that all conceivable values of religious liberty are relative—that is, the denial that any value has salience or application outside of a given context, and a resulting strong skepticism about the existence of any context-independent principles or values of religious liberty. An absolute skepticism posits that because "no theory of religious liberty will satisfy everyone," "there can be no satisfactory theory of religious liberty at all."[1]

As we saw in Chapter 2, some theorists of religious liberty seem at times to verge on this position.[2] But strong skepticism is not necessarily entailed by the rejection of comic monism. Indeed, the method of tragedy and history denies an assumption common to both strong skepticism and monism—namely, that only those approaches that posit comic monistic values count as theories. Legal theories sometimes describe the nature of the law, sometimes provide explanations of legal doctrine, and sometimes suggest a practical course of action for adjudicators. As to all of these functions, legal theories often differ in approach and method.[3]

Contrary to both the monistic and skeptical alternatives, the method of tragedy and history adopts a middle view that "values can be conditional and still have a context-independent rational and moral authority."[4] The second thesis of the tragic-historic method suggests that conflicts about what are the true values of religious liberty *ultimately derive from* the irresolvable conflicts among the multiplicity of context-independent values of religious liberty. In mediating the conflicts of religious liberty, any limiting principle on the range of acceptable values must therefore refrain from enshrining a rigid rule or principle. It must proceed modestly and gradually, opening up the jurisprudence of religious liberty to more values than do comic monistic accounts, but not admitting a limitless number.

Easy Cases

The argument for the context independence of plural values begins with the simplest case, the fact that many basic prohibitions on conduct inimical to human well-being are common to nearly all cultural communities. Explicit or implicit regulations dealing with the killing or physical mistreatment of other human beings, sexual behavior, the fair distribution of economic resources, the punishment of criminal transgressions, and a host of duties toward family members and friends—these are only a small number of injunctions that, while given unique content and shape in particular moralities, constitute the subject matter of what is regulated universally.[5] Courses of conduct that violate particular rules in these domains are inevitably condemned as "inexcusably unjust, or dishonest, or humiliating, or treacherous, or cruel, or ungenerous, or harsh," even though the specific conduct rejected may vary between and within cultural communities.[6]

The explanation for this commonality cannot be distilled, however, to a single principle, purpose, value, or theoretical dictum that transcends cultural contingency. Its pluralism instead reflects the reality of certain values that take form in particular, multifarious, independently coherent ways of life.[7] The term *way of life* is intentionally imprecise because it is "marked out by many details of style and manner . . . which a group of people of similar dispositions in a similar social situation may share,"[8] and it is structured by countless customs, traditions, and rituals of behavior and practice that are deemed worthwhile.

Yet if this pluralistic commonality of injunctions among ways of life does exist, and if these domains of moral concern can be understood and recognized even by those who may not subscribe to all of the specific prohibitions and injunctions, is there not some quality of objectivity or context independence about these moral prescriptions, speaking to a kind of core commonality amid difference? It is at any rate exceedingly difficult to distinguish those values that are held for conventionalist as compared with realist reasons, so perhaps the question does not demand a definite answer.[9] The point is merely that categorical prohibitions which cut across different conventional systems exist and bear a degree of resemblance.[10]

Moreover, if these first and relatively uncontroversial points are accepted, they might be extended to an intermediate or secondary range —a range somewhere between, on the one hand, the absolute injunctions just described and, on the other, social graces or manners. Stuart Hampshire raises the example of codes of honor in two distinct societies. Notwithstanding the differences between the two in substance, both codes may nevertheless be recognized as codes of honor, "and dishonour incurred in the breach of different disciplines is in each case recognizably dishonour, in virtue of the type of behaviour, and the way of life, that has been betrayed."[11] These are values whose identity will depend to a far greater degree on cultural variability than do the absolute, or "primary," injunctions.[12] Nevertheless, secondary values, like the absolute prohibitions, are not relative if by that one means that their value is strictly relative to the society in which they are measured.[13]

The Abstract and the Particular

It is possible to decide in advance whether a value—even a secondary value like the injunction to behave honorably—is good in the abstract, without being able to decide in advance whether it is powerful enough in a specific situation to defeat another conflicting value.[14] Yet it is only in the value's embodiment in a particular, real-world struggle that one can make judgments about how strong it is by comparison with another value.

For example, as an abstract matter one might plausibly claim that equality, law-abidingness, autonomy, the authority of conscience, and tolerance are values of religious liberty that are intrinsically worthwhile for human beings. And one might also argue that each of these ought to have salience and force in some particular legal cases, as and if they apply. Yet one might also refrain from making judgments in advance about which value ought to prevail when they conflict.

Likewise, it is possible to say that a conception of equality as formal nondiscrimination and a very different conception of equality as the elimination of differential impact are both valuable in the abstract, and that both ought, on relevant occasions, to be applicable to a specific conflict of religious liberty, *without* pronouncing in advance which of these competitor conceptions of equality ought always to predominate.[15]

The reason to refrain from absolute and abstracted judgments about which value should take precedence over the others is that different people will reasonably judge differently—that is, "reason" will admit a plurality of responses—and we do not want to cut off the possibility that a value which has salience in one case will have less (or none) in another.[16] It may not be necessary to go so far as to say that "[w]hile some ways of life can be ruled out as violating minimum standards of humanity, *most* cannot."[17] But at least the range of possibilities, in the area of religious liberty, is considerably broader than what comic monism allows, and it often demands case-sensitive assessments that hold together a plethora of clashing values. And yet the range is not unlimited and the pattern of decision making need not be incoherent.

Consider the following story.[18] After college, William has opportunities to go to graduate school in English literature at a rural university distant from his family or to begin a job as an investment consultant at a firm in a large metropolis near his family. He chooses graduate school: although he could use the money from the investment position and he had entertained thoughts about becoming a businessman, and although he would prefer to live close to his family and in a large city, he had dreamed of becoming an English literature scholar and believes that an academic career will make his parents more proud. At graduate school, William marries Daphne, a journalism student. Daphne receives a job offer in New York City for a leading newspaper. William has not yet finished his graduate studies, but he has been thinking about leaving graduate school with a master's degree and attending law school. Even though William deeply regrets not completing his PhD, the couple decides that in light of the importance of the position to Daphne's career, their desire to be together, and William's budding interest in law school, as well as the prospect of living in a big city, they will move. In New York, they have two children and William attends law school. Daphne is now offered a prestigious position in Switzerland with an international newspaper. In light of the substantial disruption to the children of such a move, the stability of Daphne's position at the New York newspaper, the significant change of lifestyle that a move abroad would demand, the fact that William is still in school and had previously left school in part to advance Daphne's career, their desire not to splinter the family unit, and the distance from their extended families—and notwithstanding that William and Daphne love European culture and are avid hikers for whom life near the Swiss Alps would be attractive—Daphne declines the offer. Upon graduating from law school, William is offered a clerkship in Washington, DC, with an important judge. Despite the disruption to their family life (and because their children are young), and even though the salary of the clerkship is comparatively small, William accepts.

William and Daphne have now made a number of choices about their lives but there was no decisive principle or value that controlled these choices. The same considerations recurred, but at each point of decision the couple emphasized a different set of them, and past choices informed present ones. Their choices assumed, as it were, a narrative form or shape.[19] Reasons that contributed to their decision making at one point were deemed less important at another point. If the couple had been asked to list all of the motivating considerations in the abstract, they might have identified career advancement, the unity of the family, disruption to the children, the value in completing projects under way, parental pride, the pursuit of hobbies and other interests, proximity to extended family, job security, financial considerations, cultural familiarity, the excitement of lifestyle changes, and the choices that had been made in the past. But the specific judgments reached were governed neither by any one of these considerations nor by another master value. Factors that were powerful in one context—the age of the children and their ability to adjust to new circumstances, for example—lost some or all of their power in another. The choices were made case by case, but this does not mean that they were incoherent or unpredictable. This story is an analogy for the method of tragedy and history.

The method can also draw an analogy from philosophical moral particularism. Moral particularism holds that the possibility of moral thought does not depend on the existence of a suitable supply of moral principles or values.[20] The sharp point in particularism is not merely that context matters[21] (of course it does), but that reasons or values which are salient features in some specific cases may not be so in others, and that reasons or values do not have constant—let alone categorical—weight.[22]

Moral particularism is a plausible way to understand some issues about the salience of particular values in law. Even the intentional inflic-tion of pain on a human being (if anything is a moral absolute, surely it is this) is often assessed in particularistic fashion in legal contexts: it is sometimes regarded as an evil (in the law of intentional infliction of emo-tional distress, among other contexts),[23] and at other times as an instru-mental and even intrinsic good (for example, in certain conceptions of retributivist thought in punishment theory).[24] Moral particularists are value pluralists, seeing moral judgment as the capacity to discern among values in conflict.[25]

The analogy to moral particularism is more suggestive than direct, and certain ambitious forms of particularism are not well suited to law.[26] But neither are legal decisions and the reasons that a judge adduces in favor of reaching a specific outcome entirely different from particular-istic thought in other contexts.[27] Just as in those contexts, values do not retain a uniform polarity either across diverse domains of conflict or from case to case within the same domain.[28] They vary.[29]

Whatever the power of these analogies, however, legal decisions in constitutional cases are not ordinary or moral choices, principally because legal decisions are far more constrained by past precedents and authoritative materials.[30] We do not expect as much consistency or pre-dictability in ethical or personal choices as we do from a legal system; in law, the choices of the past may bind those of the future.[31] Indeed, the past figures prominently in the method of tragedy and history's fourth and fifth theses.[32]

The absence of a controlling value across categories of cases, or across cases within the same category, does not stand in the way of past decisions providing substantial guidance to future litigants and judges. The method of tragedy and history is happy to grant—indeed, it is dependent on granting—that authoritative materials, past legal practices (in case law, for example), and the legally relevant values in those practices can and should inform future legal decisions. What it resists is the view that we can predict precisely what difference some legally salient value in one context will or ought to make in the resolution of future cases.[33] Coherence in legal decision making comes not from allegiance to an external overarching principle or value but instead from the expression of patterns internal to the social practices and traditions of legal judgment.[34]

Delimiting the Range: From Easy to Hard Cases

The distinction between agreeing on the importance of abstract values like liberty or equality and declining to decide conclusively how their clash ought to be negotiated in future controversies still leaves an important objection. Even if the relevant values in any given domain of legal dispute are broader than comic monists claim, and even if the method of their resolution ought often to be particularistic, can the tragic-historic theorist offer *any* limitations *ex ante* on the types of values courts might appropriately countenance? Such limitations might discipline ad hoc decisionmaking, rein in lawlessness, and help judges facing a host of clashing values in a First Amendment dispute. After all, if we take the clash of values identified in Chapter 3 seriously, do we not then leave judges in a paralysis of options, since no value can be ruled out of bounds, and any outcome is as good as any other?

There is no denying that this is a difficult issue, and there are several delimiting possibilities. Ultimately, however, since the very point of a tragic-historic approach is to expand the range of values that are constitutionally salient and to examine situations of conflict in particularistic fashion, the issue of delimitation cannot be answered by a quick and easy rule.

The first possibility is to require *a minimum of experiential significance.* What matters is that a crucial range of experientially significant value clashes exists. Nothing is gained by including values subject to only small or minor incursions, incursions that are not experienced as significant by anyone involved in the conflict.

Suppose a person wishes both to eat an ice-cream cone and to attend his child's college graduation, but he cannot do both simultaneously because food is prohibited inside the building where the ceremony is being held. The values underwriting these activities are therefore conflicting. They may also be incommensurable, but one type of competing value—the pleasure derived from eating the ice cream—is so experientially insignificant as to be outweighed by the other values—the joy and parental pride of seeing a child graduate from college.[35] To be sure, the objection remains that for some people, eating ice cream is the ne plus ultra—the ultimate pleasure—and that it is therefore wrong and unfair to exclude the values of ice-cream consumption from the experientially significant range.[36] But for most people, as a matter of common experience and insight, the value of attending the graduation seems clearly to be the only clashing value whose loss will be experienced as important.

To make the point more stark, it is one thing to choose between obeying a criminal law and engaging in a ritual on which one believes that salvation depends, and it is another thing to choose between obeying a criminal law and chewing gum. The line is of course indistinct, but requiring some experiential significance will eliminate trivial or extremely insubstantial values from the range.

The second limiting possibility is to include only those values that are *morally salient or morally powerful* as within the relevant clashing range. There are certain moral outlooks that are not reasonable choices for us today: "The life of a Bronze Age chief or a medieval samurai are not real options for us,"[37] because the ways of life in which those values figure are no longer morally acceptable. They are outmoded, not only historically, but also morally, even as individual features of those ways of life might nevertheless offer insight or illumination for features of our moral life today. Andrew Koppelman makes a similar point in defense of what he calls "baselines" in his theory of neutrality. The state need not be neutral between *all* competing conceptions of the good—it need not adopt any "super-baseline" to justify the baselines that it adopts in evaluating government neutrality as to religion—because some conceptions of the good are excluded by the relevant social practices:[38] that "[l]aws against murder contradict the religious beliefs of Aztecs" is no reason to reject them today, because the moral life of an Aztec warrior is simply no longer a live option.[39]

The morally salient limitation might also be useful in a slightly more difficult case—for example, in making the choice between becoming a productive and engaged member of society or becoming an isolated and indolent heroin addict. The experiential limitation might not be effective to eliminate the values attending the latter option, as a person could experience the values associated with heroin addiction as powerful, perhaps even supremely powerful.

Yet if one were to limit the range to morally powerful or salient values, one could more easily eliminate the value of heroin addiction. There is a difference between a choice between clashing values each of which represents a genuine moral conviction and one that does not.[40] It is difficult to see how whatever values are instantiated in a life of withdrawn heroin addiction represent a genuine moral conviction about that way of life. "We want ultimately to ask," as Martha Nussbaum points out, "whether among these cases there are some in which not just contentment, but ethical goodness itself, is affected."[41] Another way to put the point is that we are interested in value clashes in which both experiential and moral significance play a role.

A more difficult borderline case would be the choice between the self-abnegating reclusive life of a monk and a life of sexual adventurism and self-affirming excitement. Assuming that these ways of life were incommensurable, the experientially significant limitation on the relevant range of values might again not be especially helpful: Don Juan[42] and Madame Bovary[43] felt a powerful attraction to and desire for the ways of life that they chose, ones whose values we can certainly understand, if not embrace. The difficulty with the morally salient limitation applied in this context is that it would be a mischaracterization to describe *all* instances of, for example, adultery as morally insignificant or utterly devoid of ethical content. Alongside license and lazy pleasure-seeking, there may be a quest for freedom, emotional connection, self-definition, and perhaps even emancipation.

In hard cases of this kind, it would be foolish as well as futile to attempt to draw any kind of sharp or fixed line of demarcation between "moral" and "nonmoral" cases of conflict. Much will depend on intu-itions shaped by historical and cultural circumstances about the par-ticulars of the conflict at issue.[44] What one is likely to find is not a rigid division between the moral and the nonmoral, but a range in which some claims will carry greater moral power than others. In any event, in hard cases the tragic theorist would not be too quick to dissolve the clashing values in play. Indeed, one would hardly need a tragic approach at all if one were interested in clean, abstract, and hard-edged divisions of this kind.[45] The point is not to cut off values prematurely, even if they can eventually be subordinated in the specific event of conflict: "[w]e do not want to rule out or to obscure this possibility. We want to look and see."[46]

The third limiting possibility is specific to the constitutional law of religious liberty. It derives from the text of the First Amendment and the interpretation of the right to religious liberty in this country over time. Certain kinds of values are—even if both experientially and morally sig-nificant—ruled out by the religion clauses and by their gradual elucida-tion. In the language of moral particularism, these values might be called invariant legal reasons.[47]

If, for example, the United States Congress passed a law declaring Christianity to be the official national religion, or establishing a "Church of the United States of America," that law would be unconstitutional for textual reasons alone. That is, even if both experientially significant and morally salient values could be adduced to support the law,[48] the clear constitutional proscription on any federal law "respecting an establish-ment of religion" rules out this legislation.[49] Likewise, a law imposing an onerous tax exclusively on a single religious institution, or compelling people to attend church services, would certainly be unconstitutional, even if there were both experientially and morally significant values supporting these laws, because they would violate the constitutional command against laws "prohibiting the free exercise" of religion. The valuation of a particular practice for experiential or moral reasons is not the same thing as the valuation of it as a manifestation of a conception of religious liberty under the Constitution.

To recapitulate, these three principles—experiential significance, moral significance, and constitutional significance—represent useful limitations on the range of values in religious liberty conflicts. The tragic-historic judge guided by these limitations will still exercise considerable discretion, but the range of values is hardly boundless and the range of outcomes is hardly unpredictable.

The Second Thesis and the Law of Religious Liberty

How might the second thesis of the tragic-historic method apply specifically to the clash of values of religious liberty? As an initial matter, something far less potent than full-blown skepticism accurately describes the nature of the various conflicts among values. Returning briefly to *Wisconsin v. Yoder*,[50] the values of parental control over a child's upbringing, attachment to nature and to local traditions and associations, equality of educational opportunity, equality of educational access, an intuitive decency, a commitment to the cultural traditions of one's community, critical curiosity about education and the possibilities of life, and others are all (1) worthwhile values that conduce in different ways to human well-being; and (2) values that ought to have roles to play—that ought to be considered and accounted for—whatever the ultimate resolution of the conflict between the State of Wisconsin and the Amish may be. Moreover, the values (1) are experientially significant; (2) reflect real or genuine moral commitments; and (3) are well within the limitations imposed by the text of the First Amendment and represent part of a long-standing cultural and customary understanding about the nature of religious liberty under the Constitution.

To say this is already *both to include* a multiplicity of values as real and important *and to exclude* many other possible values as experientially insignificant, not morally salient, or otherwise not in keeping with the text and traditions of American religious liberty.

Had the Amish claimed, to take two extreme examples, that an exemption for their children from two years of public school education was necessary because those two years were better spent indoctrinating them to pursue a life of violent crime or compelling them to live in a commune in complete isolation from their friends and family, those types of activities, even if subjectively deemed valuable by the Amish, would be rightly excluded from the range of values that are both worthwhile and have legitimate roles to play in the resolution of the dispute. Social threats, especially grave ones, are reasonably countenanced by the state when it receives demands for religious exemptions.

Likewise, in *Lee v. Weisman*,[51] if the school had offered as a reason for the graduation prayer the value of communicating to all students that the Christian or Jewish God was the most important of all religious deities, and that they should all prostrate themselves before and worship Him, that is a value which has no proper role to play in the resolution of religious liberty disputes. There are many other similar sorts of values that, because of experiential, moral, or textual and customary insignificance, simply would not count for judges charged with deciding the disputes of religious liberty.

In offering these examples, I am alive to the criticism that these are easy cases, and that more difficult examples might better challenge the second thesis. I address some of those challenges in future chapters. The point here is more limited—to dispel the argument that the clash of values of religious liberty implies that there are *no possible* delimiting principles on the exercise of discretion in deciding conflicts, and that this is a recipe for descent into a completely arbitrary legal world.

What has been said is at least sufficient as an argument against an entirely "unprincipled" approach to religious liberty, one that takes a radically skeptical view about the existence of *any* principles or values of religious liberty by which we can address the conflicts of religious liberty. The position described by Christopher Eisgruber and Lawrence Sager as the strongest form of skepticism—that because "no theory of religious liberty will satisfy everyone," "there can be no satisfactory theory of religious liberty at all"[52]—is false. The values underwriting the conflicts of religious liberty are not entirely context dependent, because many are easily excludable as irrelevant or inappropriate while many others are not. One might go further than this: certain values of religious liberty—liberty itself, in all of its multifarious and conflicting dimensions, might be one of these—will always be among the values that will have a role to play.

The second thesis of the method of tragedy and history posits that just as monistic approaches were inadequate methodologically, so, too, are strong skeptical accounts. It distinguishes the method of tragedy and history from that strong skepticism. Skepticism is inadequate because even if certain types of values ought to be excluded as either irrelevant or not worthwhile, and even if certain values such as equality or liberty will frequently have a role to play (and both of these propositions tell against the radically skeptical view), there nevertheless will often remain a substantial plurality of contingent, though context-independent, incompatible, and incommensurable values swirling within the particular conflict (which tells against monistic accounts). That was the case for both *Yoder* and *Lee*, and it is the prevailing condition in many other cases.

CHAPTER 5

Loss, Sacrifice, and the Disposition of Custom

S omeone as yet unconvinced by the first two theses of the method of tragedy and history might wonder what reasons or evidence support the claims, first, that the values of religious liberty clash and, second, that skeptical accounts of religious liberty are inadequate. Or, to come at it from the other direction, someone persuaded by the first and second theses might wonder what follows from them for conflict resolution in the realm of religious liberty. The third thesis grapples with these questions.

Loss

One answer is that it is a basic fact of our experience that we feel a sense of *loss* when we are compelled to decide either between clashing values of religious liberty or between those values and other clashing external values. Drawing on the discussion in Chapter 4, we might call this *the answer from loss*: the fact that one experiences a sense of loss or regret when one clashing value has been chosen over another. Michael Stocker once observed that "there is a remainder of wrongness, within and despite the rightness of the right act."[1] This does not mean that the choice we make is somehow unwarranted or wrong, or that we should not make it. It may well remain the right choice. But there is a difference between thinking that, under certain circumstances, an act must be done and thinking that the situation admits of one and only one clear choice.[2]

Moreover, the sense of loss involved is different from empathy for the loser,[3] or the wish that one did not have to choose sides, or even a feeling of obligation to treat the losing side with respect. The specific sense of loss here concerns not a feeling, or an emotion, or a duty, but a belief: the belief (irrespective of whether or not one is gloomy or distraught about it) that true and important values have been lost by the necessity to make a choice, that the choice made lacks the values of the unchosen alternative, and that the choice made may also contain disvalue.[4] It is this belief about what the chosen option lacks and what the unchosen option did not lack that connects this component of the third thesis to the method of tragedy and history.[5]

Because we often do experience this sense of loss or regret when we are compelled to choose one value of religious liberty over and against another value, the challenge to those who advocate a comic monistic value or set of values of religious freedom is to explain why we ought to disregard "the thoughtful testimony of millions of apparently reasonable people, including ourselves, that they, and we, often want to realize two values but the nature of these values is such that they cannot be realized together."[6]

Comic monistic accounts tend not to acknowledge that life presents us with ethical dilemmas incapable of complete resolution. The attempt to resolve those dilemmas decisively and in such a manner so that the resolution may be systematically applicable to other cases within the same domain leads to a misrepresentation of the experience of genuine moral conflict.[7] Again, this is not so much a question of feeling bad or showing empathy toward the losing side as it is the acknowledgment of the loss of different real values. In Martha Nussbaum's study of Aeschylus's *Agamemnon*, the king at first recognizes the horror and moral disaster of the choice forced on him—whether to sacrifice the life of his daughter or those of his men. And yet when he chooses, he represses the guilt of his choice:

> Once the decision is reached, the case appears soluble, the competing claim "counts as nothing." A proper response, by contrast,

would begin with the acknowledgment that this is not simply a hard case of discovering truth; it is a case where the agent will have to do wrong. Such a response would continue with a vivid imagining of both sides of the dilemma, in a conscientious attempt to see the many relevant features of the case as truly and distinctly as possible.[8]

Instead, when he acts, Agamemnon manifests the "monstrous boldness"[9] of a man who refuses to acknowledge the tragedy. The set of internal rules that guide his decision making have proved inadequate, for they have met the "recalcitrance of the contingent world,"[10] and now his own ethical sensibilities have been deadened.[11]

Of course, common experience alone may be insufficient to demonstrate the truth of the answer from loss. Someone might claim that while it is true that conflicts and the sense of loss in their resolution are ubiquitous, that is only because we are not thinking rightly about how religious liberty conflicts ought to be resolved—that we haven't solved the problem just yet.[12] Yet while that objection may be logically forceful, there is something inadequate about it. The answer from loss makes sense of the world of legal conflict in a way that monistic approaches do not.

The Supreme Court's decision in *Goldman v. Weinberger*,[13] for example, is difficult because the values in conflict there elicit the sense of loss just described whichever way the case is decided.[14] Goldman, an Orthodox Jewish military serviceman, sought a religious exemption from a generally applicable U.S. Air Force regulation against the wearing of any headgear; he argued that he ought to be permitted to wear his yarmulke while in uniform for reasons based on the Free Exercise Clause.[15] One set of values in the conflict was represented by Goldman's firm obligation to wear his yarmulke—values that include not only the external recognition that his conscience dictated it, but also the internal understanding of all that the practice expresses about his moral and cultural way of life.[16] The competing set of values included the military virtues of obedience, commitment, unity, equality of treatment, and esprit de corps. The crucial point is that these two clusters of values do not admit an election for one and against the other in this case without a sense of loss or regret that something of real value has been missed.[17]

Justice Rehnquist's opinion for the Court emphasized the deference accorded to the military about the nature of its interests: the military's judgment was that an exception-less dress code encourages "a sense of hierarchical unity by tending to eliminate outward individual distinctions" and is a vital component of the particular way of life exemplified in military service.[18] Making an exception—any exception—for the particular religious sensibilities of individuals is antithetical to the way of life that the military seeks to foster.[19]

Explaining the answer from loss is difficult, however. Refusals to evaluate or judge between options must somehow be experientially significant, since people do make trade-offs and cost-benefit comparisons all the time, particularly in legal conflicts.[20] Sometimes people are compelled to make these choices when the options are weighty and clashing, as the Court was in *Goldman*. But this confuses the fact of choice with the reasons that it was made. Even a nonarbitrary choice between two or more options—Justice Kennedy's choice in *Lee* for noncoercion as the master value of the Establishment Clause, for example[21]—does not necessarily indicate anything about the commensurability of the values in conflict.[22] It is the sense of loss—the belief that the chosen option lacks real values that the unchosen option possesses—occasioned by the choice between clashing options that is of interest here.

Another part of the explanation for the answer from loss is that in such cases the choice entails not merely having traded off one value for another—or an "all things considered" analysis, with the shoulder-shrugging insouciance that we simply cannot "cram all the adventures and treats that we might want into a single life."[23] The real difficulty is that whatever choice is made renders our concept of religious liberty—and so our theory of it—defective, incomplete, and lacking because it has injured other clashing values that we can appreciate and understand. They, too, are values we believe to be true, which carry weight, and to which we are also committed.

These attributes of the answer from loss explain why Justice Brennan's dissent in *Goldman*, however sympathetic it may have been with Goldman's free exercise rights, ultimately rings false. Justice Brennan would have adopted a "reasonableness" standard that judged dress accommodations in the military context according to "functional utility, health and safety considerations, and the goal of a polished, professional appearance."[24] Yet Justice Brennan's proposed solution is unpersuasive because the rival values advocated by Goldman and the military (a certain hard-edged neutrality that foreshadows the standard ultimately adopted in *Employment Division v. Smith*,[25] as well as values external to religious liberty such as martial discipline and esprit de corps) are clashing, and will not admit resolution by recourse to a generic "reasonableness" standard. Reason—and therefore reasonableness—admits of more than one resolution.

Justice Brennan's "polished, professional appearance" standard misses the nature of the values actually being advanced by the opposing parties. A "polished, professional appearance" has little to do with the types of values that either Goldman or the military was championing. There is little principled difference between Goldman's claim to accommodation and that of a devout Muslim who petitions to wear a long beard while in uniform,[26] but Justice Brennan's standard seems to rest on just such a distinction. And as for the military's values, it is not a "polished professional appearance" but the unity and integrity of the military way of life, as well as the equal and nonpreferential treatment of soldiers, that is at the core of its position. It is the unity of the foxhole, not of the parade.

The clash of values in *Goldman*, therefore, is a microcosm reflecting "[d]ifferent forms of life . . . animated by distinct moralities which specify discrepant virtues, or which, even if they recognize the same or similar virtues, rank them very differently."[27] One can sympathize with the Court's inclination to defer to the military as a recognition that to pronounce on the military's values and their relationship to Goldman's—to issue decrees on the respective costs and benefits in play—may be both epistemically unwarranted[28] and do violence to the military's internal, traditional structures of meaning and value.[29]

In light of the nature of the conflict, some have endorsed an "intermediate" standard to decide whether the regulation seeks to achieve "legitimate military ends" and is also "appropriate[ly]" accommodating.[30] Perhaps this is the only practical response to the reality that the values at issue here, and the ways of life that they represent, cannot both be realized. One set will be lost.[31]

Sacrifice

These last considerations point to a second, related answer to the question of what follows from the first two theses that indicates something about the nature of the loss at issue. We can call it *the sacrificial answer.* In some circumstances the comparison of values seems entirely inapt, and even though we may be compelled by circumstance to decide between clashing values, our discomfort in and resistance to doing so illuminates something about what is involved in certain kinds of relationships or commitments.[32]

The source of the discomfort may be found in the metaphor that is selected when we are compelled to choose between clashing values: are we "balancing" and "trading off" one good for another, or are we "sacrificing" one good for the sake of another?[33] Steven Lukes elaborates:

> Trade-off suggests *exchange* of valued objects at an equivalent price. . . . Sacrifice, by contrast, suggests the *forsaking* of a valued object because this is required by a sacred source of authority. . . . Trade-off suggests comparison, calculation, and estimation, bringing points of view together. . . . Sacrifice suggests precisely that we abstain from doing so: Devotion to the one exacts an uncalculated loss of the other.[34]

Lukes suggests that the experience of sacrifice, as opposed to trade-off, only arises when the comparison of values induces a sense of the monstrous or the grotesque,[35] but this need not be so. In fact, the sense of sacrifice occurs in a considerable class of conflicts other than those that elicit horror or revulsion. It arises whenever a value constitutive of or central to a particular way of life is threatened by a competing value.[36] Even so, of course, the values that will fall into this range are not infinite.[37] Moreover, the threat must be more than minimal. Not every threat will elicit the experience of sacrifice, but the threshold is low enough to include a considerable class or range of conflicts.

The range certainly includes grave threats to those values that prescribe "exceptionally solemn prohibitions" or commands such as "the taking of life, the celebration of the dead, and [commands] that govern sexual relations and family relations."[38] And the range includes less severe threats to other commitments that are part of a tradition or a practice to which "we devote ourselves . . . without calculating the loss involved, by omitting or refusing to commensurate the benefits against the costs."[39]

That an object may be sacrificed implies that it is somehow "sacred" in the first place. And what characterizes it as sacred is in part that it is entirely inappropriate and unsuitable to "trade it off" against what Émile Durkheim once called the profane object: *la chose sacrée, c'est, par excellence, celle que le profane ne doit pas, ne peut pas impunément toucher.*[40] This does not mean that sacred values are necessarily inviolable—only that their violation is uncompensable.

While sacrifices of this type need not necessarily be religious, unreasoned, or unconditional, they often do partake of these qualities.[41] Indeed, the legal historian Philip Hamburger has suggested that one of the crucial features of early Americans' conception of religious liberty was its unconditionality: religious liberty was a good incapable of being bartered away or traded off against "government interests,"[42] a position that is feasible only if the scope of religious liberty is understood comparatively narrowly. That a central quality of the commitment to religious liberty is adverbial and dispositional, rather than substantive or doctrinal, is an important idea to which I will return shortly. Here it is sufficient to note that the sacrifice of values—and especially the values of religious liberty (at least as understood at the founding)—entails loss that cannot be calculated and compared with other values without eliciting attitudes of profound loss (in the technical sense discussed earlier) and a sense of the dooming quality of choice.

One might object that the problem of sacrifice is ultimately reducible to one of "emphatic comparability,"[43] the position that certain types of intrinsic goods are "emphatically" better than, and therefore commensurable with, certain other types of instrumental goods. The sacrifice of an animal to appease a god is, at some level, regrettable, but ultimately it is well worth it if what one gains is a great deal more valuable. But this objection is not persuasive at the level of sacrificing values because the nature of the conflict that includes a sacred value is such that comparing the value is itself resisted as an inappropriate activity. In describing

Abraham's sacrifice of Isaac as a "teleological suspension of the ethical," was not de Silentio suggesting that the values of religious sacrifice cannot be commensurated on the scale of ethics?[44] Or, returning to the more prosaically ethical realm: "When one refuses to trade $1 million for $75, there is a problem of emphatic comparability; something different is at work when one refuses to trade a child or a friendship for cash."[45] The reply to the argument from emphatic comparability, as Joseph Raz has explained, is that "it leaves out of account the refusal to compare values itself."[46]

Likewise, the experience of sacrifice is not explained by the judgment that the competing values are "roughly equal."[47] In many of these conflicts, the fact that "reason allows more than one answer" does not diminish the incompatibility and incommensurability of the values at issue.[48] When one chooses to commit oneself to the life of a monk, thereby forgoing the life of a husband and father, the choices for that person may be roughly equal, but the gravity of the conflict is not thereby diminished. In fact, it matters very much which choice one makes—it is a choice of great significance—and neither option is excluded by "reason." The choice therefore can still be said to sacrifice certain values and goods for the sake of others that cannot be commensurated with them.[49] Indeed, the importance or gravity of a choice has no necessary connection at all with its commensurability with other choices.[50]

In law, it is necessary that one side win and the other lose, and yet the inevitability of loss does not preclude choice. Law operates, as Leo Katz has argued, in an uncomfortably rigid way, insisting that something is or is not the case, that the answer to the legal problem must be either *this* or *that*, without any sense of intermediacy.[51] Yet the sacrificial answer suggests that even if values must be sacrificed in the resolution of legal cases—indeed, even if it turns out that law is centrally about the sacrifices entailed by choice making—the manner in which they are sacrificed ought to make a difference. Just as in any other context, once one sees the decision to be made, this does not expunge or remove the features of a case that run contrary to the decision, and those features should affect the way in which judges render their decisions—the language that they use and the dicta that they offer.[52] The reason is not to be empathetic or kindly to the loser, but to express the genuine belief that legitimate values and ways of life were lost in the unchosen option. In this manner, even when sacrificed in a particular conflict, those values can retain some moral and legal power, whose salience may be reassessed in future controversies.

Custom

Finally, the third answer to the question of what follows from the first two theses of the method of tragedy and history involves the genre of activities often implicated in religious liberty disputes and the type of disposition of the claimants to those issues. We might call it *the disposition of custom*, and it is best explained by revisiting briefly an essay by the English political theorist Michael Oakeshott.[53]

Oakeshott's essay describes a mood or disposition rather than a set of principles or doctrines. That mood centers on the inclination "to use and to enjoy what is available rather than to wish for or to look for something else; to delight in what is present rather than what was or what may be."[54] Its crucial characteristics are the celebration of and attachment to the familiar and the particular, the suspicion of imposed innovation, and the discomfiture that attends change—principally because change always entails the deprivation of something that one has learned, often enough only with great patience and effort, to appreciate and enjoy.[55] Innovation, for the person of this temperament, "entails certain loss and possible gain": what is gained may or may not represent an improvement over what has been lost and may or may not, with time and use, be enjoyed,[56] but what has been "lost was something [that one] actually enjoyed and had learned how to enjoy and what takes its place is something to which [one] has acquired no attachment."[57]

Nevertheless, because change is inescapable,[58] this disposition entails a particular type of response to or accommodation of change. It is characterized by a keen awareness and apprehension of the threat to personal loyalties and community identity . And this is because identity, whether communal or individual, is "not a fortress into which we may retire" but ineffably fragile—"an unbroken rehearsal of contingencies, each at the mercy of circumstances and each significant in proportion to its familiarity."[59] Innovation entails not only the promise (often unfulfilled) of a specific improvement, but also "a new and complex situation of which this is only one of the components" and the "certainty that the change will be greater than was intended" or foreseen.[60] Changes that resemble growth rather than the grafting of new shoots, changes that imitate what is already existing rather than replacing it, changes that respond to some local or particular defect rather than those with more general or comprehensive aims, changes that proceed gradually with the possibility of readjustment, changes whose consequences can be reasonably anticipated—these are the types of change favored by the person disposed toward custom.

A fair number of these ideas may be said to correspond closely to the mood or disposition of those who are attached to particular conceptions of religious liberty, which are themselves often influenced and shaped by particular beliefs, practices, and traditions. The commitment to a conception of religious liberty reflects a disposition about the achievement of a particular identity—sometimes conventionally religious, sometimes not—that is simultaneously "firm" and "precariously balanced."[61] The connection to the other two components of this chapter—loss and sacrifice—is that often enough those who are committed to a conception of religious liberty would recoil at the notion of trading it off. They are *loyal* to the community and to the way of life of which it forms a part. The values inherent in the commitment to a particular conception of religious liberty could not be attained without having internalized the disposition of custom and without resisting as illegitimate the suggestion that they should be betrayed for the sake of a different and incommensurate sort of gain.[62]

For the Amish in *Yoder*, religious liberty represented, on the one hand, the freedom to affirm a long-standing tradition of belief, custom, affiliation, and practice and, on the other, a bulwark or mediating force against the inevitable incursions of externally imposed innovation directed against what they sensed was their own fragile way of life. The state imposed a choice on them: accept a significant violation of your religious liberty—one that will gravely alter your customs and traditions—or be punished. To accept the violation of their religious liberty would have meant more than simply an unwanted disruption to themselves and to their children. It would have signified a betrayal of their customs and ways of life in order to avoid the pain of punishment. And because the disposition of custom was strong in them, the Amish refused to make the sacrifice.

The same may be said of the Native Americans in *Employment Division v. Smith*[63] or *Lyng v. Northwest Indian Cemetery Protective Association*[64] in both of which the state sought to impose a change upon existing customs and traditions. It may be said of Deborah Weisman in *Lee v. Weisman* as well as of the students who graduated with her, or of Goldman in his case against the military, or of the proponents and opponents of the display of religious symbols on government property,[65] or of the religious institutions that seek independence from the state in deciding who counts as a minister for employment purposes,[66] and many others. In all of these cases, the values of religious liberty are reflected in a disposition or mood that is elicited in response to conflicts where the individual's or the group's underlying religious commitments are challenged, if not threatened, in the name of an engrafted innovation or change to those ways of life and traditions.[67] The values of religious freedom are manifested in the inclination to conserve existing patterns and structures of life—the customs of identity—in which individuals are "nested,"[68] reflecting the reality that "[e]ach generation of human beings is born into a cultured or cultivated world."[69]

Moreover, this disposition or mood may be no less in evidence for those whose religious commitments are individualistic, novel, or radical than it was for the Amish or members of other established religious traditions. It is quite possible to hold the disposition of custom in respect of one's commitment to religious liberty but to be radical in one's religious beliefs or practices. A crucial feature of the disposition of custom, then, is that it may be present in one type of activity or practice but not in another.

The existence of the customary disposition does not necessarily correspond with what many might deem traditionalist or orthodox religious views—a belief in natural law, for example, or a devout Evangelicalism, or a belief in Sabbath observance, or a rejection of interest in financial transactions (as in traditional Islam). In fact, the customary disposition does not depend on any particular substantive position. To the contrary, it is the dispositional issue of an appreciation for the monumental untidiness and conflict of people's aims, desires, and pursuits.

The reason that the person of customary disposition is attracted by this state of affairs is that he recognizes theoretical disorder and conflict to be a characteristic feature of his own projects and aspirations. These discordant features are frankly acknowledged as a real state of affairs, both in his own life and in that of others. By contrast:

> Surveying the scene, some people are provoked by the absence of order and coherence which appears to them to be its dominant feature; its wastefulness, its frustration, its dissipation of human energy, its lack not merely of a premeditated destination but even of any discernible direction of movement. . . . [T]hey have no feeling for the warmth of untidiness but only for its inconvenience. . . . They feel that there ought to be something that ought to be done to convert this so-called chaos into order. . . . Like Apollo when he saw Daphne with her hair hung carelessly about her neck, they sigh and say to themselves: "What if it were properly arranged."[70]

Some legal theorists feel this discontent when they see the wilderness of conceptions of religious liberty growing out of the unruliness of religious belief, practice, and association. They hope for something approaching order—a value, or set of principles, of religious liberty. Their dream is that of the developer: to burn the brambles and pull the weeds, turning the disorderly wilderness into a neatly trimmed garden. In this discontent, the customary disposition is conspicuously absent.

One might argue that there is nothing unique about the customary disposition in the context of religious liberty; one might feel it strongly in any number of other legal contexts. For example, one might claim that commitment to the idea of free speech is dependent on a similar orientation. There may be some truth in this, and it is likely that the customary disposition may be brought to bear on other legal fields—free speech, criminal law, legal ethics, and so on. Nevertheless, there are reasons for the customary disposition's special relevance in the area of religious liberty that involve the structural tensions and conflicts that inhere in the Free Exercise and Establishment Clauses and in the concept of "religious" liberty generally.[71]

One might also object that there is nothing especially startling in the claim that the customary disposition predominates in law, and that law has always been informed by the customary cast of mind, the common law being a primary example. In fact, however, while the customary disposition may be a feature of the law of religious liberty as well as other legal fields, there are also powerful views that oppose it and instead favor the politically and legally untested. Sometimes these views are accompanied by the optimistic presumption that change and innovation are inevitably healthy, or for the better, or necessary for the pragmatic discovery of "what works."

In the law, there has been no more potent and celebrated expression of the drive to innovate, to rethink, and to make new, usually for the purpose of imposing the better-thought-out change on others, than Oliver Wendell Holmes's thundering charge that "[i]t is revolting to have no better reason for a rule of law than that so it was laid down in the time of Henry IV. It is still more revolting if the grounds upon which it was laid down have vanished long since, and the rule simply persists from blind imitation of the past."[72] Whatever may be the case in other areas of the law, someone with the disposition of custom would not be revolted at such thoughts.[73] The belief in a particular conception of religious liberty is at its core a predisposition toward institutional attachment, where the term *institution* denotes an organized structure of social meaning and value that is itself felt to be intrinsically worthwhile and to which individuals have devoted themselves, often enough with great effort and steadfastness.[74]

Institutional associations are at once obstructive and formative. They are composed of belief systems, rituals, and practices that supply fragile scaffolding for people's ways of living.[75] Institutional associations, including religious institutions, are not merely instruments through which we learn to express ourselves or to discover our true natures. More than this, they are a deposit of contingent accretions that gradually, often imperceptibly, impart strata of meaning and value.[76]

Religious routines and rituals—to take only two institutional features of what religious liberty is enlisted to protect—are surely improvable, but one of their chief virtues is that those committed to them experience them as fixed. Rituals are enjoyed as they are familiar, as they fulfill what is expected of them, and as they have become objects of loyalty and commitment.[77]

Yet the commitment to religious liberty is not the nostalgic loyalty of the individual determined to swim against the tide come what may, or of the poor soul who refuses to acknowledge—or who simply cannot see—that he has been outflanked by the clever maneuverings of those more keenly attuned to contemporary circumstance. It is rather that religious liberty both protects and is intimately bound up with those other attachments of religious belief, association, and practice that are familiar and presently enjoyed for their own sake. "To go on changing one's butcher until one gets the meat one likes . . . is conduct not inappropriate to the relationship concerned."[78] But to discard one's religious beliefs, associations, practices, and traditions because they happen not to sate the needs of the ever-present moment, or because something newer and more practical might be more efficacious at conforming itself to one's instant desires, is an unlikely attitude to take both toward one's religion and toward one's conception of religious liberty.

Of course, that the tie is primarily one of loyalty rather than utility does not mean that conceptions of religious liberty are not the product of reflection, or that they are fixed in amber and immune from reconsideration or change (can this be said of any social practice?). This is obviously not true; indeed, we saw when considering the spheres of variation of religious liberty in Chapter 3 that change in this area is itself continuous. It does mean, however, that such reassessments are not the normal state of affairs and are usually undertaken gradually and with circumspection since the value of one's conception of religious liberty depends on its settled quality. Innovation to suit present circumstance—particularly very radical and hastily conceived rearrangement—is commonly felt, for those with the disposition of custom, to entail grave and irretrievable loss.

I do not claim that everyone must feel this way about religious freedom, or that everyone's commitment to religious freedom will adopt this orientation—only that many people actually do, and that the opposite view would be a less common attitude that might also betray a misunderstanding of the nature of the goods at stake. Indeed, the method of this book is itself much like the disposition that I am describing. That is, I am arguing against comic monistic views of religious liberty, but I am making my claims largely by describing those features of religious liberty that seem to me important or meaningful for people committed to various conceptions of religious liberty. The assumption of the method is that if readers are skeptical, describing those qualities of religious liberty that seem important to me may persuade them to my view. But I am not presenting a principle or value of religious liberty and insisting that the reader accept that it can systematically resolve concrete conflict.[79] My method does not depend on deductive arguments from first principles, but instead on taking accurate measure of an existing social practice.[80] All of this describes the customary disposition.

The Third Thesis of the Method of Tragedy and History

In sum, these are the characteristics of the third thesis of the method of tragedy and history:

- Even when conflicts of religious liberty are decided appropriately, a certain type of experientially significant loss or regret often attends the selected outcome.
- An important reason that these types of losses are often experientially significant is that they entail the sacrifice, and not merely the trade-off, of values whose loss elicits profound regret.
- In consequence, the general attitude or disposition of those committed to the idea of religious liberty is likely to be that of customary attachment.

These observations answer the question of what follows from the first two theses of the method of tragedy and history, and they conclude the description of the methodological challenges that attend the activity of theorizing about religious liberty. It remains to explain how the method of tragedy and history answers those challenges.

CHAPTER 6

The Need for Modest Movement

T he first three theses have described the tragic features of the method of tragedy and history—those that render theorizing about religious liberty particularly difficult and problematic. The last two theses respond to these features, offering an approach that best accommodates the predicaments of tragic judgment. That approach is called "historical," and the two historical theses prescribe a minimalist and incremental approach to adjudication that emphasizes doctrinal and social history.

The Predicament Restated

Before developing the fourth thesis, it is useful to take the measure of what has been said thus far. This book began by describing a predicament faced by legal scholars: the activity of theorizing is both necessary (indeed, inevitable) and yet always in danger of distorting and misunderstanding the legal phenomena that are its subject. Over the course of the first five chapters, that predicament was explained and developed by recourse to the concept of tragedy and the grave difficulties and complications that it imposes on the legal theoretical enterprise. If the condition of tragedy accurately reflects the shape of many conflicts of religious liberty—that is, if the first three theses of the method of tragedy and history are accepted as a true representation of legal conflict in religion clause cases—the question arises how adjudication should proceed. Monistic approaches have been ruled out, and while we saw in Chapter 4 that not all conceivable values have been admitted into the fray, the range of legitimate values of religious liberty (and those that may oppose them) has been expanded. But adjudication demands the conclusive saying of something; what should be said?

In order to begin to formulate an answer to this question, rather than focusing on the substantive values themselves, it is more useful to consider the structure, stylistic quality, and rhetoric of an ideal judicial opinion.[1] From there, we can work backwards toward the predicament of legal theory and the type of resolution and method of judicial decision that would reflect a tragic-historic approach.

If tragic conflict, the plurality of values of religious liberty, the sense of loss and sacrifice, and the disposition of custom are the conditions under which legal theory often operates, then they point directly toward the importance of incremental or gradualist adjudication. Judicial opinions that do not greatly disrupt the existing legal landscape and do not rely on a single and exclusive value or ideal are to be favored over their opposite. Because people rely on the continuity of their practices and traditions, including their legal practices—because they generally have adopted the disposition of custom in the context of religious liberty disputes—rapid, dramatic, and unpredictable changes in legal practice (particularly those that settle conclusively the hierarchy of one value over another for all future cases) are to be avoided.

Predictability is surely an important virtue of any properly functioning legal system, though predictability as a value cannot be allowed to overpower the reality of the tragedy of conflict. As Frederick Schauer has put it:

> As a value, predictability is neither transcendent nor free from conflict with other values. Yet predictability plainly is, *ceteris paribus*, desirable. We attain predictability, however, only by diminishing our ability to adapt to a changing future.[2]

In order to capture at least some of the value of predictability without permitting it to dominate the other values with which it conflicts, the method of tragedy and history favors modest, gradual movements, as well as decisions that are focused on factual particulars and their relationship to past decisions. This approach accommodates tragic conflict (including the conflict between the value of predictability and other rival values, such as justice and "the diversity and complexity of social reality"[3]) far better than does one that is concerned to imprint a single value across all of the disputes of religious liberty. The method of tragedy and history begins with an allegiance to precedent—a mode of legal decision making that highlights doctrinal history—for the reason that adherence to precedent stabilizes the unpredictability of tragic conflict.[4]

Baby Steps

Following from these reflections, the first of the responsive historical theses prescribes exactly this modest and incremental adjudicative approach, one that bears some similarity to the constitutional interpretative theory called "judicial minimalism."[5] Judicial minimalism as a general approach to adjudication champions decisions that are both "shallow" and "narrow."[6] A shallow decision, as distinguished from a deep one, "seek[s] to leave the foundational issues undecided," where "foundational" means philosophically ambitious as well as highly contested.[7] A narrow decision aspires to resolve the absolute minimum necessary to dispose of the case and leaves undecided other hypothetical, or future, controversies, while a wide decision forecloses in advance different decisions with respect to the same class of conflict. And decisions may be any combination of shallow, deep, narrow, or wide.

A particular form of minimalism that is useful to the inquiry here is "Burkean minimalism,"[8] a reference to the eighteenth-century Irish statesman, politician, and political theorist Edmund Burke, of whom more will be said later. Burkean minimalism's basic adjudicative orientation as to (at least) constitutional interpretation is that "courts should be closely attentive to entrenched practices, and must give deference to the judgments of public officials extending over time."[9] In addition to subscribing to the overarching minimalist positions of narrowness and shallowness, Burkean minimalists espouse three additional core beliefs about constitutional adjudication: (1) a commitment to incremental reasoning;[10] (2) careful attention to established traditions and practices; and (3) skepticism about abstract, independently premeditated moral and political arguments, particularly those of judges, as the approach likeliest to achieve the best outcomes.[11]

What are the advantages of Burkean minimalism in constitutional adjudication? First, the narrowness of incremental decisions reflects the belief that judges are frequently insufficiently aware of the range of particular situations to which a wide rule might apply. Recall the epistemic abstention of the Supreme Court in *Goldman v. Weinberger*, where the issue was whether to overturn the air force's decision to enforce its uniform rule against the wearing of headgear while in military dress.[12] The court was unwilling to impose a wide and deep rule outside its own sphere of competence.[13] Errors that result from wide rulings are more difficult to reverse because "large steps can have unintended bad consequences."[14] Shallowness is likewise advantageous for its studied modesty:

> Those who favor passive virtues, narrow decisions, and incompletely theorized agreements tend to be humble about their own capacities. . . . They know that their own attempts at theory may fail. They know that both law and life may outrun seemingly good rules and seemingly plausible theories. . . .[15]

Second, Burkean minimalism favors the use of history in adjudication in two distinct but mutually inclusive ways. On the one hand, a mindfulness of actual social and cultural practices and a respect for their bearing on judicial interpretation—we might call this "social" history. On the other hand, an emphasis on "the slow evolution of judicial doctrine over time"[16]—which we might call "doctrinal history."

While one need not necessarily favor both social history and doctrinal history and, indeed, they may at times be in tension,[17] it is certainly possible to adhere to both.[18] Social and doctrinal historians "see[] the common law as a form of customary law," and count it as an advantage of the common law that it is not explainable by or reducible to a single overarching theory.[19] For the Burkean minimalist, judicial review is a welcome institution, provided that one accepts that the core function of courts is to "protect long-standing practices against renovations based on theories, or passions."[20] Burkean minimalism is not skepticism about the desirability of judicial review. It simply envisions a specific role for the judiciary that ties it closely to considerations of social and doctrinal history.

The Fourth Thesis: Modest Movement

With these observations in mind, several features of Burkean minimalism render it a useful (even if ultimately flawed) model for the method of tragedy and history—one that may be profitably reformulated as the need for modest movement.

Free exercise claims frequently implicate disputes about whether a religious practice should receive an accommodation from an otherwise generally applicable law. While there is no longer pervasive strict scrutiny for constitutionally grounded accommodations,[21] the RFRA[22] and its state analogues[23] and the RLUIPA[24] reinstated a regime in which courts are routinely required to evaluate competing religious and state interests. Under these laws, courts must determine whether the claimant has alleged a substantial burden to religious belief or practice that can be overcome only by a compelling state interest achieved by the least restrictive means. The existing state of the legal landscape, therefore, is one in which courts are being asked to resolve tragic conflict among rival and clashing values internal and external to a broad and diverse array of conceptions of religious liberty.

Likewise, Establishment Clause cases dealing with religious displays, public education, government funding, and issues of taxation, to name only a few, are some of the most contentious and closely watched and debated on the Supreme Court's docket. Indeed, it is frequently said that one of the fundamental purposes of the religion clauses is irenic: to promote civic peace and "avoid that divisiveness based upon religion that promotes social conflict,"[25] an aim which presupposes that this area is fraught with an uncommonly high level of emotion and moral and political controversy. If "shallow rulings tend to promote social peace,"[26] then one would be hard-pressed to find an area of legal conflict better suited to theoretically modest rulings.[27]

Furthermore, the grounds or bases for adjudicating religious liberty conflicts are famously fluid, with many scholars complaining that religion clause doctrine is murky or worse, and some Justices arguing that "in respect to the First Amendment's Religion Clauses, . . . there is 'no simple and clear measure which by precise application can readily and invariably demark the permissible from the impermissible.'"[28] If broad and theoretically deep or ambitious accounts of the religion clauses were workable, it is likely that the actual conflicts of religious liberty would not have proven so persistently intractable to them. In light of the immense theoretical disagreement in this area, and the likelihood that new cases presenting different situations will confound any inflexible rules that emerged in previously confounding cases—that, in the language of moral particularism discussed in earlier chapters, the shape of the dispute will show different values to be legally salient at different moments—decisional narrowness is just as necessary as shallowness. Though Burkean minimalism may be inappropriate for certain fields in constitutional law,[29] it is a comfortable fit in the area of religious liberty.

The argument from modest historical movement might be used either as a shield or as a sword.[30] It is commonly used as a shield to stop a court from challenging long-standing social or doctrinal traditions. Chief Justice Rehnquist's concurring opinion defending the words "under God" in a case challenging the constitutionality of voluntary recitation of the Pledge of Allegiance in public schools is a distinctive example of modest movement in the social historical context.[31] There, the Chief Justice emphasized the force of historical social practice and the "mere historical fact of public acknowledgement of the existence of God" as reasons to avoid interfering with the practice.[32] Whether it is a *sufficient* reason not to hold the complained-of language unconstitutional is a different question, but the Chief Justice's point is suggestive of social historicism as a *presumptive* reason not to strike the language down.[33]

The use of both offensive and defensive modest movement appears in the well-known companion Ten Commandments cases.[34] In *Van Orden v. Perry*, a Ten Commandments monument had existed for forty years, without incident, in a park outside the Texas State Capitol and had achieved a certain permanence as part of the cultural landscape. By contrast, in *McCreary v. ACLU*, the posting of the Ten Commandments inside the courthouses of two Kentucky counties was of very recent vintage and was met almost immediately with public opposition. And the nature of the display changed rapidly several times in response to legal pressure.[35]

In *McCreary*, the argument from modest movement and evidence of social and doctrinal history was used offensively by Justice Souter to argue that by introducing the Ten Commandments into the Kentucky courthouses, the "government is dramatically altering the status quo."[36] Justice Souter rejected the counties' claim that only the last iteration, and not the history, of the display should be examined:

> [T]he world is not made brand new every morning, and the Counties are simply asking us to ignore perfectly probative evidence; they want an absent-minded objective observer, not one presumed to be familiar with the history of the government's actions and competent to learn what history has to show.[37]

Similarly, the offensive use of modest movement as well as doctrinal and social history appears in Justice Souter's attempt to distinguish another case, *McGowan v. Maryland*[38]—which involved the constitutionality of Maryland's laws prohibiting the sale of certain goods on Sundays: "*McGowan* held that religious purposes behind centuries-old predecessors of Maryland's Sunday laws were not dispositive of the purposes of modern Sunday laws. . . . But [that] conclusion . . . says nothing about the relevance of recent evidence of purpose."[39]

As for the defensive use, in the companion case (*Van Orden*), Justice Breyer observed that the passage of time bestowed a normatively wholesome aura on the Ten Commandments monument.[40] It is a testament to the power of arguments for modest movement and the importance of social and doctrinal history that Justice Breyer—no Burkean minimalist he—believed that the existence of the monument for many years, where it had achieved a permanence in the common culture and consciousness, ought to be legally relevant.

Naturally, these are all matters of degree. Even advocates of modest movement could not adopt an unchanging or frozen approach to doctrinal or social history. Nor would they want to, since any viable approach must accommodate variability in the nature of the commitment to conceptions of religious liberty described in the first thesis. But they would

nevertheless grant to existing social and doctrinal traditions and practices a presumption of validity and noninterference, while viewing the
absence of an existing custom or tradition as a reason for extra vigilance.[41]

The Instrumental and the Foundational

Yet while there are similarities between the fourth thesis of the method
of tragedy and history and Burkean minimalism, there are also substantial differences. The contemporary American scholars who urge Burkean
minimalism rather than alternative approaches "in the grip of an abstract
theory . . . that would do away with an inheritance"[42] do so because they
consider it the most reliable method of producing the best outcomes. It is
this consequentialist orientation that leads Cass Sunstein to characterize
Burkean minimalism as a type of "second-order perfectionism—that is, a
form of perfectionism that is alert to institutional weaknesses of the federal
judiciary, and that therefore refuses to pursue perfectionism directly."[43]

But Burkean minimalism *does* pursue perfection in constitutional adjudication, because constitutional ideals can only be cast in the best light
if the burdens on the judiciary of "theory-building" are minimized.[44] Of
the argument that social and doctrinal traditions are intrinsically worthwhile and have value unto themselves, even if only presumptive force
that may be overcome in appropriate circumstances, Sunstein says:

> I reject such positions for both politics and constitutional law. . . .
> Burkeanism does not rest on a belief that the past has any kind of
> inherent authority, or on a judgment that people owe some kind of
> duty to the past, or the notion that we are in some way constituted by
> our tradition. . . . Burkeanism is best justified in pragmatic terms, on
> the ground that it is likely to lead to better results than the imagin-
> able alternatives.[45]

Perhaps Burkean minimalists believe that any approach to the Constitution must of necessity be "perfectionist," if by that one means the aspiration to an interpretive approach that makes the Constitution "as good as
it possibly can be."[46] But this requires the theorist to have some foundational criterion against which to make assessments of value and by which

to give an account of adjudicative perfection. One might infer that for Burkean minimalists, first-order perfectionism—that is, a philosophically deep and wide account of the Constitution or any of its provisions—would in fact be the adjudicative ideal. The impediment is pragmatic: in certain categories of conflict (though not in all of them) judges are unfortunately just not very able theoreticians, but if they were or might become so, matters would be different.[47] Indeed, Burkean minimalism, it should be remembered, is a subspecies of minimalism itself, which depends on there not being sufficiently powerful democracy-enhancing aims that override it.[48]

Less Burkeanism, More Burke

It is here that the method of tragedy and history parts ways with Burkean minimalism. The reasons might be summed up in the aphorism "less Burkeanism, more Burke." Burkean minimalism shows insufficient appreciation for the core virtue of modest movement in the resolution of religious liberty conflicts—that is, the constitutive tragic nature of the conflicts developed in the first three theses and the foundational impossibility that comic monistic theory will ever resolve tragic conflict, no matter how clever a judge may be. Burkean minimalism *denies* just this position.[49] This difference between the method of tragedy and history and Burkean minimalism is reflected especially in the claim that the best arguments for the latter are "pragmatic" and merely contingently held, in that "respect for traditions is likely to produce better results, all things considered, than reliance on theories of one or another kind."[50] The distinction between the two is also implied in the claim that Burkean minimalists are only provisionally committed to their view, and that they might readily abandon it if a sufficiently appealing or practicable monistic theory were devised, or one that offered enough in the way of democracy-enhancing benefits. It remains for the fifth and final thesis of the tragic-historic method to explain that social and doctrinal history is not merely pragmatically useful. Rather, social and doctrinal history are the only reliable raw material we possess to construct accounts of religious liberty that can adequately conciliate the conflicts described by the tragic theses.[51]

Before developing those claims in the next chapter, however, it is worth pausing briefly over some of the writing of Edmund Burke himself, since it bears a closer connection to the method of tragedy and history than to any ersatz Burkeanism. This is not a book about Burke, and nothing like a comprehensive account of his thought will be offered here. And for a writer of Burke's range and cast of mind, even systematic treatments are unlikely to capture his ideas adequately. Instead, what is offered here is an impressionistic and selective review of Burke's beliefs, specifically with respect to the importance of particular circumstances in the resolution of political conflict, the nature of political and legal change, and the relationship between theory and practice. This review provides a useful historical analogue for the method of tragedy and history's commitment to modest movement.

A succinct and suggestive characterization of Burke's thought was offered some years ago by the eminent political theorist Harvey Mansfield:

> If there is one recurrent theme in Burke's letters, speeches, and writings, it is his emphasis on the moral and political evils that follow upon the intrusion of theory into political practice. It is theory as such that he rejects; his emphasis on the evils of intrusive theory is not balanced by a compensating reliance on a sound theory that men would need as a guide to their politics.[52]

This is a useful beginning, but a persistent confusion should be cleared up at the outset. By claiming that Burke opposed theory "as such," Mansfield cannot mean that Burke opposed thinking hard about difficult political issues; or that he disavowed serious intellectual struggle with the complicated legal questions of his day; or that he did not believe that there was any way to arrive at sound judgments in political and legal matters.[53] If "theory" is understood so broadly—as giving organized, rational thought of any kind to a particular problem, or deciding in careful fashion which concerns are important and which are less so—then surely Burke was a theorist. Indeed, Burke explained that it was never his intent to "vilify theory and speculation—no, because that would be to vilify reason itself."[54]

What is it, then, that Burke is doing in attacking theory as often incompatible with or detached from practice, or in questioning the adequacy of abstractions to cope with the world's complexity? A learned interpreter of Burke has noted that "[s]o emphatic were Burke's pronouncements that some writers concluded that because he opposed theorizing, he was without any theory of his own."[55] But we can avoid this misunderstanding by offering a friendly amendment to Mansfield's description that illustrates something important about the method of tragedy and history as well. What Burke decried was "weak, erroneous, fallacious, unfounded, or imperfect theory"[56]—that is, theory as he saw it often constructed in his intellectual circles, theory that was untrue because incapable of capturing the rich complexity of the world of practical affairs. For Burke, the evils of speculation constituted the "imperfections" of theory,[57]—which manifested themselves in abstraction from the particulars of a (usually extreme) case to devise principles of universal application. Invariably, this exercise resulted in distortion, and if it was broadly adopted as the best method to think through common political and legal problems, something worse. The danger was the "dreadful energy" of intellect liberated from custom.[58] Or, as one commenter has it: "[A] rejection of abstractions did not, for Burke, require a denial of all reasoning in politics, but was, rather, part of a turn to principles solidly based on the dictates of experience and history."[59]

Burke's view of the evils of theory extended to the law as well,[60] where he commended a highly particularized approach to decision making:

> Nothing universal can be rationally affirmed on any moral, or any political subject. Pure metaphysical abstraction does not belong to these matters. The lines of morality are not like the ideal lines of mathematics. . . . They admit of exceptions; they demand modifications. These exceptions and modifications are not made by the process of logic, but by the rules of prudence. . . . Our courts cannot be more fearful in suffering fictitious cases to be brought before them for eliciting their determination on a point of law, than prudent moralists are in putting extreme and hazardous cases of conscience upon emergencies, not existing.[61]

It is in the world of practical legal experience, and through the common-law method, that Burke believed that the tug of circumstance and the competition between rival values would find its keenest assessment:[62] "no certain laws, establishing invariable grounds of hope and fear," can substitute for the habits of mind cultivated by a jurisprudence which represents "the collected reason of ages, combining the principles of original justice with the infinite variety of human concerns."[63] That gathering pool of legal customs is more than simply pragmatically useful in reaching outcomes that are appealing from a consequentialist perspective. It is more than the somewhat vague appeal to "what works." It is constitutive of our collective legal identity.[64] Because "human culture precedes human reason,"[65] the latter is dependent on an existing reservoir of the former.

Burke writes that the nature and scope of human rights (including the right to religious liberty) are not to be identified in "extreme" generalities or abstractions but instead must be found:

> in a sort of *middle*, incapable of definition, but not impossible to be discerned. The rights of men in governments are their advantages; and these are often in balances between differences of good; in compromises sometimes between good and evil, and sometimes, between evil and evil.[66]

In this passage, Burke offers something akin to the account in the first and second thesis of the method of tragedy and history. Because judges are faced with rival claims underwritten by conflicting and incommensurable notions of the good, the hard abstractions of theory are of limited use in determining what ought to be done.[67] Discerning the "middle" corresponds to what was previously described as the particularist's capacity to discern the "shape" of any given dispute;[68] and yet the fact that we cannot define *ex ante* where the middle lies does not mean that there is no middle or that judges are not capable of predictably locating it.

It is in part for this reason that changes to existing arrangements are generally to be effected gradually and with the focus always on the particulars of the case: for the sake of stabilizing the middle, and with an eye to making it possible for judges and litigants to predict where the middle lies. For even though a "state without the means of some change is without the means of its conservation," radical changes—"harsh, crude, and unqualified reformations" to legal practice—dislodge more than is necessary or healthful.[69] Indeed, it was just such a political approach that Burke pressed upon the English Parliament in negotiating the fraying relationship with the American colonies—one that depended on adapting to the rapidly changing circumstances by making a series of prudent "concessions" in governance (a view that, for good or ill, was consistently rejected).[70]

The reason that modest movements and changes to existing legal practice are optimal is that in matters of religious liberty, people committed to various conceptions of the proper relationship of church and state are likely to display the disposition of custom: "We are so wonderfully formed, that, whilst we are creatures desirous of novelty, we are as strongly attached to habit and custom."[71] That disposition is a reflection of the broad and unruly diversity of aims and ends that people in liberal democracies are free to pursue, and the Constitution should account for and incorporate the breadth of those ends. As Burke puts it in the second of his fiery *Letters on a Regicide Peace:* "The British state is, without question, that which pursues the greatest variety of ends, and is the least disposed to sacrifice any one of them to another, or to the whole. It aims at taking in the entire cycle of human desires, and securing for them their fair enjoyment."[72] The pursuit of "the greatest variety of ends" and the unwillingness to "sacrifice any one of them to another" is an apt characterization of portions of the first and third thesis of the method of tragedy and history as well as of the pursuits of the American constitutional state.

It may be objected that a constitutional theory like Burke's is only possible in the absence of a written constitution. The "writtenness" of our own Constitution is an argument against the type of common-law constitutionalism developed by Burke. One might answer this objection purely pragmatically: if one could be certain that the writtenness of the Constitution fixed an original meaning of the religion clauses, then the objection might have force. But, as will be seen in Chapters 8 and 10, while limited core meanings do exist, many meanings are historically contested. Or one might answer it in a deeper way: the fact of our Constitution's writtenness in no way diminishes the justification of incremental evolutionary changes in legal practice which, though consistent with original meaning, are predicated on the absence of any controlling substantive constitutional vision.[73] Indeed, Burke's common-law constitutionalism presents a model for constitutional interpretation according to the method of tragedy and history—a far better model than any Burkeanism. It is a theory of law depending on the "reciprocal struggle of discordant powers" which, when brought together into conflict again and again, "draws out the harmony of the universe."[74]

To conclude, when confronted with tragic conflict in the disputes of religious liberty, modest movement is needed both for reasons of predictability of legal outcome and because of the nature of the commitments involved. Yet the need for modest movement is just as much about movement as modesty: changes in the application of core and peripheral values of religious liberty are necessary to ensure that appropriate legal reforms are made to the social practice of religious liberty with the passage of time—a view entirely in keeping with the high variability of conceptions of religious liberty that prompted the need for a tragic theory in the first place.[75] It is this conception of change—change by "insensible degrees"[76] in the social and legal practice of religious liberty, change in which the past can "be a guide to the future, and, therefore, need not be set in opposition to it"[77]—which is implicit in our own national constitutional aim of forming a "more perfect Union."[78] The Constitution is not perfect and can never be made so. It is inherently imperfect, for if it were perfect, it could not contain within itself the necessity of incremental change,[79] of modest movement, at the heart of the fourth thesis of the method of tragedy and history.

CHAPTER 7

The Conciliations of History

The final thesis of the method of tragedy and history is that history—both legal and cultural—has value because it represents the collected wisdom of the past in managing the tragic clashes of religious liberty. The history of the conflicts of religious liberty is the sum of its conciliations. The "intellectual sacrifice" required of the commitment to religious liberty demands the abandonment of the abiding certitude that a unified answer may be found to the question of why it is that religion has value and ought to be protected.[1] It requires this relinquishment because the collisions of the values of religious liberty are an essential part of what they are and what we are. It is because these clashes reflect a foundational and often ultimately irreconcilable pluralism, rather than merely the appearance of conflict, that the tragic conciliations of the past deserve particular regard.

The foundation for doctrinal historicism—for a presumption in favor of precedent in adjudication—has been well put by Anthony Kronman:

> An argument from precedent asserts that something should be done a certain way now *because* it was done that way in the past. . . . To be sure, such arguments are not always decisive. Sometimes they are overridden by arguments of other sorts (for example, that it would

be unjust to follow precedent). . . . [But] the past is, for lawyers and judges, a repository, not just of information, but of value, with the power to confer legitimacy on actions in the present.[2]

Against the background of the first three tragic theses, an acknowledgment of the wisdom of precedent represents a recognition of the multiplicity of ways in which courts have struggled with the irreconcilable conflicts of religious liberty. It is a link with the legal past. Legal precedent is the blending and accretion of "reason-in-custom"[3]—constituted by the engagements of common lawyers grappling with the common details of innumerable predicaments and particular conflicts.[4] A commitment to doctrinal history—to vertical and horizontal precedent[5]—is an associational acknowledgment of common struggle with problems often incapable of systematic resolution, for this is the only way that a core range of conflicts of religious liberty are decided. It is the method of the common law filtered through the lens of the tragic theses.[6]

Doctrinal historicism is necessary in light of what the rule of law demands in the wake of the intrinsically clashing nature of the values of religious liberty.[7] For if there were an overarching single value or set of values of religious liberty that simply had not been discovered or appreciated—perhaps due to the institutional defects of the judiciary, or to some other failing—then doctrinal historicism would lose much of its binding power on future generations of common lawyers.[8] It is the existence of just such a master value that the first three theses of the method of tragedy and history deny.

It should be emphasized that deference to doctrinal history is not uncritical or unconditional obedience. It is not hidebound opposition to change or an unyielding adherence to precedent at all costs, a position that would verge on incoherence.[9] If it were these things, it would cease to be informed by the first three theses because it would elevate a single value—unflinching devotion to precedent—as paramount. Rather, doctrinal historicism is valuable for the more modest reason that it is a guide to mediating tragedy. And a solicitude for precedent is characterized by an attitude of appreciation for an assemblage of pictures, a series of memorialized illustrations of how past judgments negotiated past tragedies—the choices that they made, the sacrifices that they suffered to be made, and the fragility of their resolutions. Precedent has authority not because obedience to it or hostility to change is a supreme legal value, but because the judgments of the past are simply, to borrow a line from Eliot, "that which we know."[10] The past lies inside us and is constitutive of who we are, and though history may be epistemically uncertain, logical certitude is hardly the point of a theory of religious liberty.[11]

This point serves as the connection to social history. If the doctrinal negotiations of the past are worthy, though imperfect, counselors for the predicaments of the present—if they are that which we know, and their memory is that which we have—then the objects of those negotiations deserve attention as well. Political communities are not atemporal or static associations. They are trans-generational enterprises that depend on the transmission of political and social histories.[12] In their classic work on "tragic choices" in law, Guido Calabresi and Philip Bobbitt write:

> A historical perspective presents a mapping of society's conflict with tragic choice—by showing how a society has dealt with the dilemma previously, we are made aware of the perimeters of future choices, most especially those adaptations which are necessary just because other attempts have preceded. . . . How tragic choices are made, how they can be made, is necessarily governed, in some measure, by earlier attempts at resolution.[13]

Just because other attempts have preceded, and not necessarily because they have met with complete success. A historically informed approach to the conflicts of religious liberty would be attuned, therefore, not only to the adjudicative bottom line but also to the peculiar social context that shaped the conflicts. As was seen in Chapter 3, the *Yoder* case was exactly the embodiment of countless value clashes internal and external to Amish and liberal democratic culture. Its imperfect reconciliation of those conflicts inevitably created tragic remainder that is at least as worthy of study as its holding.

A disclaimer at the outset: those desiring hard-edged rules fashioned by reference to abstract ideals may be frustrated by the discussion that follows. No readily applied, one-size-fits-all resolutions will be offered. What is distinctive in the method of tragedy and history is not the outcome. It is the method. Hard cases should be marked by historical nuance, by alertness to the particular circumstances, by a careful excavation and weighing of the competing interests and values at stake, by close attention to the statements and perspectives of the litigants, and by dicta that acknowledge frankly and openly the sacrifices and losses that the negotiation of conflict demands. It is that method, and not adherence to an abstract ideal, that gives the law an overarching legitimacy and maps the terrain for future litigants when, inevitably, some must win and some must lose.

A Tale of Four Crosses

To understand the historical conciliation at the root of the fifth thesis, it will be useful to consider a particular issue in which courts have acknowledged the force of social history in shaping their judgments. Many issues could be selected, but a recurrent question is whether it is permissible for a government to display a Christian cross or Roman Catholic crucifix on public property, or to designate memorials and other public displays that include crosses as national monuments. To be sure, the public display of religious symbols is only one subset of Establishment Clause doctrine, and other controversies are discussed elsewhere. Yet the method of tragedy and history is helpfully elucidated by exploring how different courts, at home and abroad, have addressed the problem of the cross— the central symbol of the historically dominant religion in the United States and all Western democracies. Courts applying something like the tragic-historic method have ultimately divided on the issue of the cross's permissibility, but some have shared a common style of analysis that represents a relatively unified jurisprudence.

Case One: The Crucifix in Italian Public Schools

To this point, this book has discussed the American law of religious liberty and the opinions of United States courts—especially the Supreme Court. But as a first case study, I propose to examine a foreign decision: the judgment of the European Court of Human Rights in a case involving the display of crucifixes in Italian public schools.[14] Many features of the case—the court's jurisdiction, the text of the rights alleged to have been violated, the applicable precedent, and the political and cultural history in issue—distinguish it from the American legal framework. A one-to-one correspondence should not be expected. Yet the methods employed by the European Court in negotiating the tensions among competing values of religious liberty—the dicta and orientation of the court, rather than its legal holding examined in isolation—serve as a rough but suggestive example of the tragic-historic method in action.

Soile Lautsi, a Finnish woman and Italian resident, an atheist, and a mother of two school-aged children, filed a complaint against the Italian Republic alleging that Italy's practice of displaying crucifixes in its public school classrooms violated the European Convention on Human Rights.[15] The convention provides that member states, including Italy, are required to provide persons within their borders with a public education that "respect[s] the right of parents to ensure such education and teaching in conformity with their own religious and philosophical convictions,"[16] and that "[e]veryone has the right to freedom of thought, conscience, and religion."[17] The court has previously held that member states must act "neutrally and impartially" in ensuring that believers and nonbelievers are able to coexist harmoniously within a democratic society.[18] In the educational context, while the convention's command to "respect" the "religious and philosophical" wishes of parents implied some "positive obligation" on the part of member states, the contours of that duty "vary considerably from case to case, given the diversity of the practices followed and the situations obtaining in the Contracting States."[19]

How, then, was the court to decide whether Italy's practice of displaying the crucifix ran afoul of the requirement that all belief systems must be treated neutrally respectfully? Like the U.S. Constitution (as well as the convention), and unlike the French Constitution, the word *laic* or *secular* does not appear in the Italian Constitution, so the difficulty could not be resolved by recourse to text.[20]

The problem was rendered with special pungency in a "parable" offered to the court at oral argument by Joseph Weiler, who represented several intervening states in the litigation.[21] Weiler told the fictional story of Marco and Leonardo, two friends about to begin school together in

Italy. Leonardo visits Marco's house, and he sees a crucifix on the wall. When Leonardo asks Marco's mother about it, she responds that display of the crucifix is an important religious tradition for their family and for many other people. Agitated, Leonardo returns home, where his mother patiently explains that believing Catholics display crucifixes, but people of other traditions do not. When Marco visits Leonardo's home, he is similarly surprised to see no crucifix; when he returns home to ask whether the family crucifix should be removed, his mother explains that while Leonardo's family is loving and worthy of respect, it would be unthinkable for their own family to remove the crucifix from the wall.

Imagine, now, that Marco and Leonardo attend school. If a crucifix is displayed, Leonardo may wonder whether it really is acceptable not to display a crucifix at home; if it is not displayed, Marco will wonder whether his family's crucifix is truly necessary as well. In either case, the state will not be able to act entirely neutrally or respectfully, at least not without some frame of reference within which the commitments to neutrality and respect can be understood in context.

But now suppose further that over a span of 150 years, the crucifix had been consistently displayed in the classroom, but that on the 151st year, it had been removed.[22] Or suppose instead that for 150 years, no crucifix had ever been part of the educational experience or displayed by the state as an ostensibly civic and educational symbol, but on the 151st, the state mandated its display in order to reaffirm its Catholic heritage and identity (perhaps in part for expressive reasons in light of increasing Muslim immigration).[23] Even still and in either case, perfect neutrality and equal respect are unachievable. Whichever course the state takes will slight some group's interests. Removal of the crucifix will indicate to Christians that their religious tradition is being disvalued; its retention will indicate to nonbelievers that their beliefs are being disvalued.[24] And yet social history now provides at least *some* context within which the various clashing values of neutrality and respect can be mediated.

It was social history that supplied that context in *Lautsi*. The court reviewed extensively the historical roots of Italy's domestic law and practice with respect to the display of the crucifix in public school classrooms.[25] The crucifix is a symbol of ancient religious, cultural, and educational importance to Italians; as one of the concurring judges noted, "[f]or many centuries, virtually the only education in Italy was provided by the Church, its religious orders and organizations—and very few besides."[26] But the practice of displaying the crucifix in public school classrooms first began in 1860 during the *Risorgimento*, by royal decree of the Kingdom of Piedmont-Sardinia.[27] Later, during the early years of Italy's national formation, the continued hanging of crucifixes in classrooms was the product of a compromise between the secular forces of Giuseppe Garibaldi's Italian Army and the Catholic Church.[28] A compromise—a religious, political, legal, and cultural conciliation—between avowedly secular and religious worldviews both of which were responsible for founding a nation composed of fragmented constituencies.[29] And still later, during Italy's fascist period beginning in the 1920s, the government again promoted the practice of displaying the crucifix. Display remained the rule in Italian public school classrooms ever since.[30]

Ultimately, the European Court concluded that while the crucifix is undoubtedly a religious symbol, and while all member states are obliged to ensure that curricular instruction is imparted in an objective, critical, and pluralistic fashion—neutrally, respectfully, and "free of any proselytism"[31]—the display of the crucifix did not violate the commitment to neutrality. The court could only reach this result, however, by contextualizing the value of neutrality in light of Italy's social history.

Moreover, recognizing the intense disagreement among the several member states as to the acceptability of religious displays in public schools,[32] the cultural meaning that Italy ascribed to the crucifix (as amply supported by Italy's particular historical circumstances) and the decision to display it in recognition of that history were accepted as within Italy's "margin of appreciation"—its individual, local discretion.[33] Italy, said the court, was at liberty to transmit its cultural and historical traditions to public school children through the "passive symbol" of the crucifix.[34]

Yet the court did not embrace Italy's cultural understanding and it acknowledged both that the crucifix is an undeniably religious symbol and that it is being accorded a "preponderant"—and therefore nonneutral—"visibility" in the classroom. The court also recognized that Lautsi and others would understandably view its continued presence as conveying a lack of respect for her interests in her own children's education.[35]

As one of the concurrences observed, the court was faced with a tragic conflict: "the right of parents to ensure their children's education and teaching in conformity with their own religious and philosophical convictions" against "the right or interest of at least a very large segment of society to display religious symbols as a manifestation of religion or belief."[36] Ultimately, the court held that Italy would not be required to disavow perhaps the most important religious and cultural symbol of its history in fulfilling its civic, educational responsibilities. Yet the court recognized the sacrifice of other values of religious liberty—an important conception of neutrality among them.[37]

Discussion of a foreign decision may elicit the suspicion that it is inapposite to the American context. Indeed, the objection appears especially forceful when directed at an approach that itself purports to foreground a particular doctrinal and social history—that of the United States. It is certainly true that the holding of *Lautsi* would not be acceptable here. Given the history—social and doctrinal—of this country, it would violate the Establishment Clause for the government to display crucifixes in American public school classrooms.[38]

But that is precisely the point. The methodology of *Lautsi* sheds light on and echoes several important themes in the American law and theory of religious liberty that the method of tragedy and history sets in high relief: the relevance of social history; the inevitability of tragic choice among conflicting values; and the interpenetration of culture and religion.

Social history is a valuable instrument through which the tragedies of religious liberty may be mediated. Naturally, it is not the only lodestar nor will it resolve the tragic clashes described in earlier chapters. The American law of religious liberty—like that of the Council of Europe— is deeply committed to many other values, including neutrality, equality, and liberty, incommensurable though these may be among and within themselves.[39] But consideration of social history is nevertheless a crucial modality of constitutional argument and decision making.[40] We have already seen that arguments from social history were profoundly important in Justice Breyer's measured concurrence in *Van Orden v. Perry* to distinguish between two very different Ten Commandments monuments:

This case also differs from *McCreary County*, where the short (and stormy) history of the courthouse Commandments displays demonstrates the substantially religious objectives of those who mounted them, and the effect of this readily apparent objective upon those who view them. That history there indicates a governmental effort substantially to promote religion, not simply an effort primarily to reflect, historically, the secular impact of a religiously inspired document.[41]

Likewise, social history figured prominently in Justice Souter's claim that in *McCreary County*, the government was altering the status quo and ignoring the relevant social history of the effort in Kentucky to erect the monument.[42] "[R]easonable observers," Justice Souter observed, "have reasonable memories."[43]

Few American cases, however, more acutely illustrate social history's role than *Elk Grove Unified School District v. Newdow*,[44] in which the Supreme Court was faced with an Establishment Clause challenge to the words "under God" in the Pledge of Allegiance, as recited voluntarily by public school students in a California public school district.[45] The Pledge was written in 1892 to commemorate the four hundredth anniversary of Christopher Columbus's discovery of America, and for the first sixty-two years of its existence, it did not contain the words "under God."[46] In 1952, Congress introduced "under God" to recognize that "[f]rom the time of our earliest history our peoples and our institutions have reflected the traditional concept that our Nation was founded on a fundamental belief in God."[47] "Under God" has remained part of the Pledge ever since.

Opponents of "under God" made arguments startlingly similar to some of the claims made in the *Lautsi* litigation. Objectors to the crucifix argued that display was solely the product of a shameful and thoroughly discredited fascist moment.[48] Yet surely this criticism was not the product of a "reasonable memory." The prior history of the practice—history that reflected the types of civic compromises vital to Italy's formation— as well as the much older and deeper connections between Christianity and Italian cultural history were not remembered. Likewise, opponents of "under God" in the Pledge often emphasized its inclusion by Congress as of a piece with the intensely anticommunist ethos of the 1950s, with its attendant promotion of civil religion and its paranoid McCarthyism.[49]

Though *Elk Grove* ultimately was dismissed on the technical ground that the plaintiff lacked standing to bring the suit, Chief Justice Rehnquist's concurrence developed more fully the social history of the phrase "under God" in civic pronouncements that are vital to the American sense of national culture and identity—because, not in spite, of their religious roots.[50] A "reasonable memory" would remember that public and "patriotic invocations of God and official acknowledgements of religion's role in our Nation's history abound"—from George Washington's acknowledgment of "Almighty God" in his first Thanksgiving Proclamation,[51] to Abraham Lincoln's famous and celebrated use of the phrase "under God" in the Gettysburg Address,[52] to the official pronouncements of Woodrow Wilson, Franklin Delano Roosevelt, Dwight D. Eisenhower, and other public figures.[53] The phrase "In God We Trust" on the coinage (first appearing during the Civil War),[54] the opening exhortation of the Supreme Court's Marshal, "God save the United States and this honorable Court"[55]—"[a]ll of these events," the Chief Justice wrote, "strongly suggest that our national culture allows public recognition of our Nation's religious history and character."[56] As time has passed, the country has become more religiously pluralistic, and public statements of this type may have taken on different coloring; but the fact that reasonable disagreement exists about the quality of these public, religiously rooted expressions does not distinguish the present America from its past.

Nevertheless, *Lautsi* and *Elk Grove* are not entirely analogous within their respective legal frameworks: *Lautsi* involved a "passive" symbol, while *Elk Grove* dealt with the active, though voluntary, speaking of the Pledge of Allegiance.[57] The values of noncoercion identified in *Lee v. Weisman* as particularly salient in the educational context are stronger in *Elk Grove* than they would be if, for example, a school district had elected to display the text of the Pledge on a classroom wall.[58] Yet both *Lautsi* and the Chief Justice's *Elk Grove* concurrence stand for the proposition that social history is its own reason for permitting a practice to endure. It is not a conclusive reason or an indefeasible reason. Considerations of noncoercion and others might in some circumstances override it. But it is a presumptive reason: social history is a modality of constitutional argument that contextualizes what would otherwise be intractable clashes of abstract values.

Social history offers more than a political or prudential reason for not striking down the phrase "under God" in the Pledge. It may well be true that the Court would have been the object of "widespread outrage and antagonism"[59] had it stricken "under God," and that civic peace would thereby have been disrupted. But that is not the primary reason for restraint. Rather, where, as in *Lautsi* and in *Elk Grove*, a legislative body has made the choice to preserve a practice with pervasive, unambiguous, and long-standing historical connections,[60] and one that, as a result of that social history, is deeply embedded in popular practice and feeling, courts should be leery (not implacably opposed but reticent) to disturb that decision in favor of the inculcation of a monistic value. The reason is not the implausible one that social histories are always inherently worth preserving, or that democracies always make correct choices—surely neither is true—but that social history, and the doctrinal history that is addressed to it, give particular color and texture to a dispute that pits clashing values of religious liberty.[61]

This suggestion may elicit the fear that courts attuned to social history would strike nothing down or that they would defer unconditionally to legislatures or popular will and condone unrestrained trenching on individual rights. Yet this objection fails to account for the actual historical experience of courts with religious liberty conflicts. While it is true that at any given point in time, a court attentive to social history might be more deferential to existing decisional and social practices than one that was concerned to instill a single value, this does not mean that any American court—today—would approve laws that would: require candidates for elected office to affirm religious or antireligious creeds; provide direct funding to religious institutions; require the teaching of creationism in public schools; require students to pray in public schools; officially promulgate particular religious doctrines as true; appropriate substantial sums of the public fisc to erect permanent religious monuments on municipal property; target a religious institution or antireligious organization for discriminatory treatment; intervene in decisions about clerical appointments or dismissals; compel attendance at religious services; or, of course, establish a national or state religion.

Many more unambiguously forbidden laws of this kind could be added to the list, but it should be sufficient at this length to show that though a court which countenances social history will be mindful of a zone of legislative prerogative, that zone is always bounded by the prior engagements of doctrinal history's struggle with social history.[62] And as for that most prominent and well-reported legal contest of our day—the battle between originalism and living constitutionalism—the method of tragedy and history surely esteems a living Constitution.[63] But it is "living" because it exists within and through the social history of its people, not detached and deracinated from it.

Case Two: The Mount Soledad Cross

Readers may at this point object that the method of tragedy and history too easily approves the display of religious symbols, that it is too "religion-friendly,"[64] and that it does not recognize the substantial costs incurred when individuals within the community are excluded. Yet a court attuned to social and doctrinal history may reach an ostensibly religion-unfriendly result. Indeed, it is not the result, but the method of argument, the attention to doctrinal and social history, the particularism of the discussion as well as its recognition of polyvalent and clashing values, and the gradualist rhetorical contours of the language used, that mark out the method of tragedy and history.

In 1913, a cross was erected atop a large hill called Mount Soledad in the city of La Jolla, California. The land on which the cross stood was at that time owned by the city, and the cross was replaced in the 1920s and then again in 1954.[65] The civic group responsible for the 1954 twenty-nine-foot cross, "The Mount Soledad Memorial Association," dedicated it "as a memorial to American service members and a tribute to God's 'promise of everlasting life,'" and it served for years as a site for Easter services.[66] In the late 1980s, perhaps in part incident to the beginning of legal trouble, a plaque was added designating the site as a war memorial and thereafter veterans' organizations began holding memorial services at the site. The war memorial, of which the cross was the centerpiece, featured six concentric walls around the cross's base and numerous stone plaques honoring the dead.[67]

In response to protracted litigation aimed at removing the cross because of its location on public land, Congress intervened to transfer the land at issue from the city to the federal government. The legislation authorized the transfer "in order to preserve a historically significant war memorial . . . as a national memorial honoring veterans of the United States Armed Forces."[68] This provoked several individual plaintiffs as well as a group called the Jewish War Veterans to file suit alleging that the cross violated the Establishment Clause.[69]

The Ninth Circuit began by refusing to apply an "absolute rule of neutrality because doing so would evince a hostility toward religion" and would lack the necessary contextual nuance.[70] After considering not only the text of the legislation, but also its extensive legislative history and the statements of four members of Congress (some of which mixed religious and secular motivations) the court concluded that Congress's purpose in acquiring the memorial was predominantly secular—the preservation of a historically significant war memorial.[71]

But it is the court's highly fact-sensitive and modulated discussion of the "primary effect"[72] of the memorial, and its focus on the historical features of this particular monument and the conflict it engendered, which most keenly evince a tragic-historic methodology:

> In our analysis, we must consider fine-grained, factually specific features of the Memorial, including the meaning or meanings of the Latin cross at the Memorial's center, the Memorial's history, its secularizing elements, its physical setting, and the way the Memorial is used.[73]

After noting that the cross has a distinct meaning as the primary symbol of Christianity,[74] the court also acknowledged that the cross can and often does acquire different meanings, though it was careful not to take the position that the cross could mean anything to anyone and that it was therefore fruitless to search for any reasonable meanings at all.[75]

The court examined the historic use of crosses as war memorials in the United States, finding that their use increased after the Civil War and that "[m]ilitary cemeteries have not, of course, remained entirely free of religious symbolism"—including the "row upon row of small white crosses" that memorialize soldiers who died in the First and Second

World Wars.[76] Nevertheless, the court distinguished the use of a cross to memorialize a single soldier from its use as a default symbol memorializing all of the war dead; it concluded that the latter use has not been a common one and even when it has been employed as a unitary symbol, other civic symbols (such as an eagle) generally have been displayed next to or in the vicinity of the cross.[77] For example, the crosses at Arlington National Cemetery—the Canadian Cross of Sacrifice, the Argonne Cross, and a cross commemorating the Mexican Civil War—are accompanied by "countless headstones of soldiers buried in Arlington and alongside a large number of other monuments that do not incorporate religious imagery."[78] The crosses at Arlington and Gettysburg National Military Park, the court found, are "non-dominant features of a much larger landscape providing a 'context of history' and memory that overwhelms the sectarian nature of the crosses themselves."[79]

The question then became how the Mount Soledad memorial fit into this complicated historical landscape—whether the cross's secular components, considered "against the background of its particular history and setting," rendered the entirety of the memorial unconstitutional.[80] Taken altogether, the court found that the cross's message of religious endorsement was strong enough to overpower its civic memorial message. For most of its history, the court observed, the memorial consisted of the cross alone, and the two earlier crosses on the site were not war memorials but the sites of Easter sunrise services.[81] There was no physical indication that the current cross was a war memorial until 1989, when, in the face of litigation, the plaque was added. Throughout its history, the cross was widely promoted and celebrated exactly as a Christian symbol by the Mount Soledad Association and used as the site of Christian religious services and other religious events. By contrast, few secular events were held at the memorial, and the majority of these occurred after the lawsuit.[82]

All of this, the court concluded, distinguished the Mount Soledad Cross from the Ten Commandments display in *Van Orden v. Perry*, because in the latter there was little overt recognition, let alone celebration, of the monument's religious quality. In *Van Orden*, the display was held constitutional because it was only one part of a series of other monuments adorning the grounds of the capital and because of the role of that particular Ten Commandments monument "in shaping civic morality."[83]

The longevity of the Mount Soledad Cross alone, the court held, could not salvage its constitutionality in this case because its early history had been pervaded by an explicitly and exclusively religious meaning.[84]

Yet the court nevertheless observed:

> [W]e do not discount the fact that the Cross was dedicated as a war memorial, as well as a tribute to God's promise of "everlasting life," when it was first erected, or that, in more recent years, the Memorial has become a site for secular events honoring veterans. We do not doubt that the present Memorial is intended, at least in part, to honor the sacrifices of our nation's soldiers.[85]

It was the Mount Soledad Cross's "short history of secular usage" by comparison with its more sustained and long-standing usage as an explicitly religious symbol, as well as its considerable size and prominence within the memorial (coupled with the fact that the cross alone was openly visible to those not physically present at the memorial),[86] that ultimately tipped the court against it.[87]

In concluding that the Mount Soledad Cross memorial either must be modified or removed,[88] the Ninth Circuit's methodology corresponds roughly to the method of tragedy and history. The court focused on the social history of both the practice of displaying crosses as war memorials and the specific historical context of *this* cross, at *this* site, within *this* city. It directed its attention backward to that history, rather than forward toward a premeditated value to which the facts must be conformed. Its holding was circumspect and limited, closely examining the Establishment Clause doctrine in this area and eschewing any uniform test or single value. It arrived at no categorical judgment about the fixed, unchanging meaning of a symbol with as complex a history as the cross. Instead, in its discussion and dicta, the court recognized the multiple and often interconnected meanings that might reasonably be attributed to this specific cross.

Yet for all of its attention to detail, its ultimate conclusion that the balance of historical and contextual factors favored a finding of unconstitutionality was neither unexpected nor unpredictable. Indeed, the Mount Soledad Cross case is likely to give future litigants as much or more guidance about the quality of analysis to expect from a court confronted with issues of this kind as would a decision that proceeded from a fixed abstract value. More to the point, however, judicial opinions like this—those which struggle in depth and in earnest with the conflict of values at issue in these cases, which include evidence of that struggle in dicta, and which treat those clashes fairly and thoughtfully—are likely to be deemed more legitimate by the litigants and the broader American public than those that do not display the virtues of the method of tragedy and history.

Case Three: The Mojave Desert Cross

Another theme that suffuses this collection of cross cases is that in certain areas of conflict, it is impossible and unprofitable to maintain the conceptual purity of the religious and the cultural, or to assess authoritatively the relative strength of a symbol's different reasonable meanings.[89]

That theme emerges in our third cross decision, where the Supreme Court was asked to declare the meaning of a five-foot white cross that had been placed in the Mojave Desert in 1934 by a group of veterans to honor the memory of American soldiers who died in World War I.[90] The cross had stood for nearly seven decades, where it "and the cause it commemorated had become entwined in the public consciousness,"[91] serving as a site for both Christian celebrations and civic and military remembrances.[92] In 2001, Frank Buono, a retired Park Service employee, complained of the cross's presence on federal land.[93] The case was complicated by the question of ownership of the land on which the cross stood, but the important issue is the capacity of a court to assess the cross's legal meaning.

One unconvincing approach is to give up on the enterprise of assigning meaning at all because context can supply an endless number of possible meanings.[94] It is one thing to say that the legal meaning of a symbol cannot be permanently or singularly fixed and quite another to leap to the view that the bounds of any symbol's meaning are limitless and therefore nonexistent.[95] The fact that a "reasonable memory" might identify more than one, but less than an infinite, number of meanings is exactly proof that context can be legally significant.

And just as context was useful in *Lautsi* and *Trunk*, so it was in *Buono* as well. Having carefully reviewed the relevant social history, Justice Alito's concurrence identified two reasonable meanings for the *Buono* cross: the original Christian meaning as a marker of the Resurrection, given contextual support in this specific case by the continued celebration of Easter before the cross by certain groups; and a civic meaning intended to commemorate the war dead, also supported by evidence as this particular cross's initial and ongoing reason for existence.[96] In dissent, Justice Stevens countered that the cross "necessarily" symbolizes an "inescapably sectarian message,"[97] and so any additional meaning is tainted.[98] He went further: "Making a plain, unadorned Latin cross a war memorial does not make the cross secular. It makes the war memorial sectarian."[99]

In this respect, at least, Justice Stevens is correct: the cross's military commemorative meaning is not simply a culturally detached meaning that happened to arise second in time. It is connected to the Christian meaning in this stronger sense: had there been no prior Christian meaning, there would not have been a tradition out of which a subsequent military commemorative meaning could have arisen. Likewise, if the crucifix had never attained its Catholic meaning, the subsequent civic, educational, and cultural uses to which it has been put in Italy would never have occurred. The centuries-long tradition of Catholicism made possible additional meanings.

We saw in Chapter 1 that some scholars have argued that symbols have an "objective social meaning," as determined by a "competent member of the community."[100] Yet these same writers are right to point out that "the preservation of religious materials over time can shift the meaning of their display."[101] In fact, with the passage of time, multiple "objective" or reasonable meanings often can and do emerge. As to the Mojave Desert Cross, the Court properly acknowledged two such meanings. Others have claimed that any nonreligious meaning ascribed to the cross is merely "derivative" of the cross's religious meaning,[102] but if "derivative" means something like "ultimately indistinguishable from," that is inaccurate. It is more precise to say that subsequent meanings, though distinct, exhibit a temporal and causal connection with the religious meaning.[103] Is this connection between a symbol's religious and other reasonable meanings sufficient categorically to forbid the state from recognizing the symbol as part of its civic and cultural life?

It hardly seems so. As Justice Stevens noted, "[c]ontext is critical to the Establishment Clause inquiry,"[104] and any assessment of the cross's meaning that assigns a monolithic, unalterable, master meaning to the cross—a meaning that, no matter the particular circumstances in which the cross appears, renders it unconstitutional—betrays an inattention to those historical circumstances in which different reasonable meanings may arise. It is also exceptionally difficult to tease out and isolate which meanings of a symbol are purely religious and which are purely secular—to know what it is precisely that the veterans intended to commemorate when they erected the cross, and what subsequent generations of onlookers have understood.

Consider several plausible meanings connected to this specific cross, all of which are variations on the cross's civic, commemorative meaning and many (though not all) of which depend to some degree on the temporal and causal priority of the Christian meaning: a remembrance of sacrifice for the greater good; a tribute to the military life; an acknowledgment of lives lived honorably or nobly; a token of civic unity; an emblem of national goodwill; a monument to the transience of life and to the world that lies beyond it; a marker of the eternal and transcendent, coming into contact with the time-bound and earthly.[105] These submeanings should not be deemed categorically illegitimate merely because they bear a temporal and causal connection with a religious meaning that, as a matter of social history, cannot be entirely disentangled from it.[106]

One might argue that these various reasonable meanings have only arisen because many people were or are sadly ignorant of the original soteriological meaning. If they had been aware of that meaning, new (civic) meanings would not have arisen. Or, if they were now made aware of the religious meaning, any subsequent meaning might be abandoned or disappear.

The first position strikes me as uncharitable; the second as unlikely. Consider the motto of Harvard University, "Veritas"—"Truth." The original (and still, for limited purposes, current) motto, adopted in 1692, is "Veritas Christo et Ecclesiae"—"Truth for Christ and the Church"— chosen, among other reasons, to honor the college's primary function of training Christian ministers.[107] That meaning is reflected in the 1780 Massachusetts constitution's language specifically describing Harvard College as an institution where "the encouragement of arts and sciences, and all good literature, tends to the honor of God, the advantage of the Christian religion, and the great benefit of this and the other United States of America."[108] At some point, the decision was made to drop the last three words of the motto, and generations since have known the motto as "Veritas." Independent, reasonable meanings have arisen as a result, though those meanings are temporally and causally connected to the motto's original, religious meaning. And meanings that have achieved widespread acceptance may well be reasonable even if those who hold to them are entirely unaware of the original religious meaning. It is highly doubtful that they would abandon the entrenched, more recent meaning if apprised of the original meaning. It is true that, unlike the original Harvard motto, the cross's original religious meaning is still vital; but the point is that reasonable subsequent meanings may arise and endure for many historical reasons that do not depend on popular ignorance or lack of learning.

Just as it is impossible to distinguish precisely where the religious ends and the artistic begins in a Bach oratorio, a Giotto fresco, or a Dantean canto,[109] so, too, is it fruitless to attempt to tweeze away the *Buono* cross's civic submeanings from an antecedent religious meaning.[110] But the fact that it is unprofitable to perform this exercise in segregation, and in quantifying the importance of this or that meaning, does not mean that permitting these various submeanings to exist is equivalent to condoning state sponsorship of religious belief. Religious and cultural meanings may and do interpenetrate across time. And meanings that emerge from that interpenetration are not ipso facto constitutionally impermissible, but invitations to historically and contextually graduated judgment.

Case Four: The September 11 Memorial Cross

The last of the cross cases is in some ways the most intriguing because it has not yet resulted in a judicial opinion (though it has prompted litigation). It therefore presents the opportunity for some speculation about how a person applying the method of tragedy and history might approach an as-yet undecided conflict.

In the immediate aftermath of the terrorist attacks of September 11, 2001, on New York City's World Trade Center, Frank Silecchia, a rescue worker, discovered a group of steel beams that had fused together in the shape of a cross amid the debris.[111] This seventeen-foot cross provided inspiration and hope to many who had lost loved ones or were grieving.[112] The cross was moved temporarily to a Roman Catholic church in the area, and when New York City later attempted to display the cross as part of the National September 11 Memorial and Museum, an organization named American Atheists sued to block its inclusion as a violation of the Establishment Clause.[113]

In the meanwhile, five members of Congress—three Democrats and two Republicans— introduced legislation to make the September 11 cross a national monument.[114] The bill recognizes that the cross's installation in the museum is intended "to tell the story of not only what happened on 9/11 but the 9-month recovery period that followed."[115] One of the sponsors of the bill, Representative Michael Grimm, offered the following statement in support of the legislation:

> This cross was a symbol of hope and freedom at a time when New Yorkers were coping with loss and destruction in the aftermath of the deadliest terrorist attack on American soil. . . . I find it reprehensible that this group [American Atheists] would disgrace the beliefs of millions of people in an effort to garner a little media attention for their cause. By establishing the 9/11 Memorial Cross as a national monument, we ensure this symbol of freedom continues to stand for all those we lost and those whose faith remains to this day.[116]

Representative Charles Meeks, another of the bill's sponsors, commented that like "any other religious symbol or object of hope that was recovered from that tragic site . . . this cross is part of the tapestry and history of that hallowed ground." Likewise, Representative Timothy Bishop noted that "it is vital to preserve the artifacts that gave so many Americans solace and hope in the dark days following" the attacks, and that the cross "is an important symbol of national unity and fortitude."[117]

No suit has yet been filed challenging this proposed legislation. But if it is, and if the judge were to approach the case by the method of tragedy and history, several things can be said. First, no single value or value set would drive the analysis. Appeals to "neutrality" or "equality" or "the separation of church and state" in the abstract are simply inadequate to arrive at a satisfying resolution, and they misrepresent the nature of the conflict. It is not "neutral" or disinterested either to forbid the government from making the cross a national monument or to dismiss the atheists' complaint as illegitimate; to the contrary, any decision is partial and interested, and it will properly be perceived that way.

Second, a distinctive feature of this particular cross is its having been occasioned not by the efforts of a particular group, but by the terrorist attacks themselves. This cross was part of—indeed, it was created incident to—the events of a national civic tragedy. Its genesis lies within the historical record of that event. Its specific history is therefore primarily a civic and secular history, not a religious history, which distinguishes it from the Mount Soledad Cross. It is true that the cross is likely to have inspired and provided comfort to grieving Christians (though surely not only to them), but an official acknowledgment of that inspiration as part of the history of the attacks is not the same as government sponsorship of Christianity. By contrast, denial or suppression of that history in the form of a judicial order preventing the cross's official state acknowledgment would give the impression that the government was actively disfavoring religion.

Third, and on the other hand, there is some indication in the congressional statements supporting the legislation (particularly those of Representative Grimm) that the motivation for declaring the cross a national monument is at least in part to communicate official condemnation of American Atheists for suing to enjoin the cross's display in the museum.[118] This is problematic, for it tinges the legislation with the objectionable color of state-sponsored disapproval of a particular organization, which is part of a distinct minority in American political life, because it is expressing its antireligious views through legal means. Indeed, it might even be inferred that part of the legislation's aim is to express that disapproval, and to counter American Atheists' lawsuit by reaffirming the importance of the cross and of Christianity. Yet this is only a part of the record—a single statement of one sponsor of the legislation[119]—and the other justifications offered by Representative Grimm, as well as the statements of the other cosponsors, emphasize the civic value of historical acknowledgment of the role that the cross played.[120]

Fourth, though it does not bear directly on the issue of making the cross a national monument, it is noteworthy that the cross is not the only religious symbol that is displayed at the museum: beside the cross will be a Star of David that was cut from the debris as well as a Bible fused to a piece of steel found during recovery efforts.[121] These other religious symbols do not appear to be part of the national memorial, however, and the singling out of the cross alone might suggest official favoritism for Christianity. But a more plausible interpretation in light of the specific history of this cross is that it was the cross alone among these symbols that had a historically important civic significance during the aftermath of the attacks. Recognizing and acknowledging the special historical importance of the cross is perfectly proper.

If a suit is eventually filed to stop this legislation, the question of the September 11 cross's constitutionality as a national memorial will be difficult. There are multiple clashing values pervading the case, values that combine religious, cultural, and historical phenomena in complex and layered ways. A much more developed record than what I have offered would be needed to understand as fully as possible the valences of the dispute. My own sense is that in light of the balance of concerns, the legislation is constitutional, but if it were shown that the legislation's overriding purposes was to express official censure for atheist views—or to indicate that such views were false—the balance might tilt in the other direction.

The Tragic-Historic Cast of Mind

To recapitulate, the method of tragedy and history affirms as its principal justification for valuing social history that the first three tragic theses are essential features of the conflicts of religious liberty. There is some precedent in American law supporting respect for the combination of doctrinal and social history in the Supreme Court's Due Process Clause jurisprudence: "Our Nation's history, legal traditions, and practices . . . provide the crucial 'guideposts for responsible decisionmaking.'"[122]

While it is not clear that the Court's doctrinal and social historical due process jurisprudence[123] has carried the day in subsequent cases,[124] legal scholar Michael McConnell writes that the underlying basis for the Due Process social historical approach is that a "longstanding national consensus" as to a particular practice is evidence that the practice represents "the will of the people."[125] Furthermore, "reliance on longstanding consensus is likely to be a more reliable means of reaching a correct result," because "if a practice is adopted by many different communities, and maintained for a considerable period of time, this provides strong evidence that the practice contributes to the common good and accords with the spirit and mores of the people."[126] McConnell concludes that "the voice of tradition is thus the voice of humility" because it is a voice of deference to social history.[127]

The tragic-historic reasons for appealing to social history in the religion clause context are related, but also somewhat different. To be sure, as was seen in Chapter 6, the method of tragedy and history is uncomfortable with wide and deep judicial decisions on controversial subjects. It is leery of superimposing untried policies in the name of unitary and beguiling abstractions.[128] But the most essential reason for appreciating social history relates not to any of these factors, but instead to the underlying nature of the clashing conflicts of values of religious liberty.

The method of tragedy and history presses just this metaphysical speculation: each value of religious liberty has independent and irreducible worth, each struggles to be recognized as legitimate in its own right, and each resists domination by or subordination to the others. Its allegiance to social history is based on the reality of tragic conflict as an indelible structural feature of the commitment to religious liberty, and a consequent presumption in favor of doctrinal and social history to guide judgment.[129] This is the reason that cognizance of social history is consistent with the first thesis of the method of tragedy and history. One might object that social history impacts the conflict of values of religious liberty by providing a fixed gauge of comparison against which the values may be measured. If that were true, the clashing values of religious liberty would in fact be commensurable along the scale of social history. But it is not true. The use of social history does not eliminate or resolve the problem of incommensurability.

Both doctrinal and social historicism are conciliations—ways to arrive at resolutions that, unlike monistic theories of religious liberty, are likely (1) not to elevate a monistic value as the scale of measurement; (2) to approach the disputes of religious liberty in an incremental and particularistic fashion, thus retaining the vivid sense of the inappropriateness that accompanies deciding between clashing values; and (3) to reflect effectively and truly—in a way that approximates current realities—the tragic nature of the dispute. Religion's proteanism helps to explain further why the method of tragedy and history is not a "second-best approach" to thinking about religious liberty, since that would presuppose that some "first-best" account is out there, somewhere, elusive, always tantalizingly just beyond the grasp of our interpretive mistakes and institutional limitations.[130] The method of tragedy and history does not purport to offer a unitary solution at all, or a second-best decision procedure. It offers instead a disposition or a cast of mind that relies on incremental adjudication and social and doctrinal history to give it shape and structure.

The past, in sum, is a beacon. It is a consolation, sometimes effective, other times not, against the ravages of conflict, incommensurability, sacrifice, and tragic loss. In part it is the ineffability of "religion" itself that demands a keen sense of the past, for religion is a unique feature of social life: ideological, personal, political, institutional, communal, a phenomenon of cultural identity and at the same time a source of trans-temporal truth—all of these things and yet irreducible to any one of them.[131]

This concludes the discussion of the five theses of the method of tragedy and history. More remains to be said about the tensions between and within social and doctrinal history in religion clause jurisprudence and how these should be resolved. And some more definite sense also is needed of how the tragic-historic method's distinctive cast of mind and its reliance on doctrinal and social history would apply to several concrete issues. It is to these subjects that we now turn.

PART III

The Method of
Tragedy and History

In this part of the book, the method of tragedy and history is applied to a selection of religious liberty disputes. The survey of issues and cases is not exhaustive, since earlier chapters have already examined how a tragic-historic theorist would decide various conflicts in both the free exercise and establishment contexts, and since the aim here is merely to give the reader a sense of the analysis that a tragic-historic approach would entail.

It is problematic to offer any single rule, value, or principle that represents the method of tragedy and history's approach to conflict resolution; indeed, one of the concepts illustrated by the tragic-historic method is that unidimensional decision procedures underwritten by monistic values and sets of values in this area are inadequate.

Instead, it may be helpful to suggest a metaphor that more or less captures the mood or ethic of the method of tragedy and history—that of judicial review as a localized rain shower in a particular microclimate. Courts will be required to intervene in religious liberty disputes, and their resolutions will be to a considerable extent predictable, but never completely so. It will be possible for lawyers and legal scholars to forecast judicial intervention in certain kinds of cases—where there are very substantial harms and values at stake at the core of the commitments to free exercise and disestablishment, for example. In these cases, where the elements are unusually propitious for rain, predictions will be possible and accurate. But there will be no iron rule or general theorem for when judicial intervention is necessary or for how a dispute ought to be decided across large swaths of legal terrain.

This may be as frustrating to lawyers and legal theorists as it is to meteorologists (and to those who rely on them), but two further points are worth emphasizing. First, a local shower does not cause permanent damage. If courts are intervening regularly, their decisions ought to be keenly attuned to the specific nature of the values in conflict and greatly limited by those factual particulars. That is, the mildness of the microclimate of religious liberty ought to influence both the analysis of the dispute and the scope of the decision. Second, someone might object that if no single rule or set of rules of judicial review is feasible, then judges ought simply to exit the scene and leave these matters to the coordinate political branches. To this, the method of tragedy and history responds that judges have a vital role to play in maintaining the social ecology of religious liberty. Indeed, they are institutionally best situated to reflect and implement a tragic-historic approach after a fashion that is sensitive to the damage that reliance on a comic monistic theory can do to the microclimates of religious liberty.

CHAPTER 8

The Challenge of Free Exercise

Before discussing specific applications of the method of tragedy and history in the following chapters, it is necessary to address a complex challenge posed by the current state of Free Exercise Clause jurisprudence. The clause bars the government from "prohibiting" religious "free exercise,"[1] and the central free exercise issue involves requests for exemptions from laws that interfere with religious freedom.[2] The issue is under what circumstances, if any, such exemptions are constitutionally required. The most important free exercise decision of the late twentieth century, *Employment Division v. Smith*,[3] held that in general they are never required. *Smith* involved the state's denial of unemployment compensation benefits to two men who had been fired from their jobs after using the hallucinogenic drug peyote as part of a Native American religious ritual.[4] The Court announced the rule that facially neutral laws of general applicability do not violate the Free Exercise Clause no matter how gravely they burden religious exercise and no matter how insubstantial the government's interest in enforcing the law against the religious claimant.[5] The value of formal neutrality reached something approaching comic monistic status in *Smith*: it is only overridden where religion has been targeted for discriminatory treatment or there is evidence that the law is not of general applicability.[6]

The challenge of free exercise is that the tragic-historic judge's commitment to doctrinal history seemingly counsels incompatible courses of action. *Smith* radically changed existing free exercise jurisprudence, which had constitutionalized an approach balancing the quality of the state's interests in implementing the law against the burden on the religious claimant in complying with it.[7] The *Smith* Court undid a doctrinal tradition regarding religious exemptions that had stood for approximately thirty years. On the other hand, one might argue that *Smith* actually restored an earlier doctrinal tradition of religious liberty, represented by *Reynolds v. United States*, where the Court held that no special religious exemption for a member of the Church of Jesus Christ of Latter Day Saints from a law against bigamy was constitutionally required.[8] The rule of *Reynolds* had been in turn subverted roughly a century later by the balancing approach of *Sherbert v. Verner* and the line of cases following it.[9] Free exercise law has always been something of "a moving target" during this period, making it difficult to discern exactly what a commitment to doctrinal history demands.[10]

Smith is now more than twenty years old. It is the mainstay of the Court's formally neutral approach to free exercise.[11] A powerful doctrinal countertradition was developed by Congress in response to *Smith*, principally in the form of the RFRA,[12] the RLUIPA,[13] and the case law interpreting those statutes, all of which reinstated the interest-balancing approach. Likewise, some states have adopted their own RFRA analogues,[14] and some offer more substantial types of constitutional protection for religious liberty.[15] That countertradition is also now more than a decade old. How does the method of tragedy and history's commitment to doctrinal history make sense of the challenge of free exercise?

In order to work through this tangle of problems, it is necessary to proceed in four steps. In step one, this chapter takes stock of the social history of free exercise—how the commitment to the free exercise of religion was understood at the founding and how it has developed since. This part includes evidence of the Free Exercise Clause's original meaning and its interpretation in early America, but it does not presuppose a commitment to originalist methodology nor does it endeavor to uncover new evidence of original meaning. For the method of tragedy and history, evidence of original meaning is probative inasmuch as it gives an interpreter insight about which values lie at the core of the commitment to free exercise, and which at the periphery, and in order to understand how the tradition of the commitment to free exercise has developed from the original period to the present.

What a perusal of history will show is that just as there have been competing interpretations of the Free Exercise Clause within the last 150 years, so, too, have there been similarly competing interpretations before that time. The meaning of free exercise has been cogently described as a "canopy of opinions—which swayed and stretched even while covering the same basic ground."[16] There is evidence that the social history of the Free Exercise Clause has reflected and sometimes oscillated between two different meanings: first, what legal historian Philip Hamburger has called "freedom from penalty on religion"[17]—that is, formal neutrality as between religions and "freedom from laws that impose constraints on the basis of religion";[18] second, the view espoused principally by Michael McConnell (which encompasses and extends the first meaning) that "exemptions on account of religious scruple should have been familiar to the framers and ratifiers of the free exercise clause" and that an interpretation of the Free Exercise Clause requiring religious exemptions in certain circumstances is "more consistent with the original understanding than is a position that leads only to the facial neutrality of legislation."[19]

Since the social history of free exercise suggests that these two meanings have always existed, competed against one another, and are each respectively consistent with our constitutional traditions, the second step is to consider which interpretation of the clause is most in keeping with a commitment to the tragic theses. Once again, there are two possibilities: that formal neutrality best comports with the tragic theses because it generally leaves the electorate to resolve the clash of values of religious liberty; or that an approach in which judges are charged to conciliate the conflicts of tragedy by reference to social and doctrinal history is more consonant with the tragic-historic method. The second of these alternatives is defended.

The third step is to examine an argument that is often made by *Smith*'s supporters, and that is likely to be made against the method of tragedy and history: that without the hard contours of the comic monistic rule of *Smith*, the decisions of courts will be entirely unpredictable. In fact, the predictability and certainty of cases applying *Smith* is greatly overstated. The rule of *Smith* is somewhat predictable but not nearly to the degree that some of its supporters may believe, and there are reasons to doubt that the rhetorical or psychological appeal to certainty is a salutary feature of the current doctrine.

Finally, the fourth step is to consider what the best approach toward *Smith* would be for someone committed to the method of tragedy and history. Rather than overruling the case outright, which would compromise the incrementalism discussed in the fourth thesis, and in light of the statutory and other incrustations that have happily grown around *Smith*, the better course is gradually to limit *Smith*'s reach.

The Social History of Free Exercise

Before getting to the content of the Free Exercise Clause—the "what" question—it may be helpful to address which organs of government are bound to obey it—the "who" question. This answer is, if not entirely free from dispute, at least more settled than the question of the clause's meaning. Though as an original matter applicable only against Congress— as a proscription against federal laws interfering with a private party's religious freedom[20]—the clause has since 1940 been held to apply to the individual states as well by its "incorporation" through the Reconstruction-era Fourteenth Amendment.[21]

The question of the clause's content depends in some measure on the distinction between, on the one hand, religious belief and expression and, on the other, religious practice. Everyone agrees that the Constitution protects a private party's religious beliefs and expressions—the "right of private judgment in matters of religion"[22]—from governmental penalty or discrimination. But the contexts in which the clause should be read to protect religious practices burdened by civil law are disputed. A proscription on performing the Catholic Mass or on acts of religious worship are easy cases, but laws that regulate public behavior and punish disturbances of the public peace, including religiously motivated behavior, are more difficult. Douglas Laycock has observed that the Free Exercise Clause "guarantees a substantive right to exercise one's religion. 'Exercise' means activity or practice, both now and in the Founders' time; it is not confined to belief or to speech."[23] And yet the extent to which the clause protects the freedom to conduct oneself according to religious precepts has proved especially thorny across its history.

Early Americans relied on numerous and varied conceptions of religious liberty and the freedom of individual conscience, drawing from Christian, medieval, Reformation, and Enlightenment sources.[24] Many have remarked on the special influence on the founding generation of John Locke's ideas about the liberty of religious conscience.[25] In his 1689 *Letter Concerning Toleration*,[26] for example, Locke challenged the claims of religious persecution on both theological and pragmatic grounds—that it was not Christian, as well as practically futile and counterproductive, to compel religious belief:

> If any one maintain, that men ought to be compelled by fire and sword to profess certain doctrines, and conform to this or that exterior worship, without any regard had to their morals; if any one endeavor to convert those that are erroneous to the faith, by forcing them to profess things that they do not believe . . . it cannot be doubted indeed that such a one is desirous to have a numerous assembly joined in the same profession with himself: but that he principally intends by those means to compose a truly Christian church, is altogether incredible.[27]

Locke's aim in the *Letter* was to "distinguish exactly the business of civil government from that of religion, and to settle the just bounds that lie between the one and the other" in a way that depended on the division between "civil interests" and the "care of souls":[28] "it is one thing to persuade, another to command: one thing to press with arguments, another with penalties."[29]

This specific meaning of the liberty of conscience—the freedom to believe in and, within limits, to practice religion on equal terms with everyone else and free from legal "penalties"[30]—was highly influential, and it reflects an important part of the social history of the Free Exercise Clause.[31] In an illuminating study about a controversy involving the Quakers in Pennsylvania, Philip Hamburger argues that the debates about two very different meanings of religious liberty—a "freedom under law, regardless of one's religion and a freedom from law on account of one's religion"—came to a head.[32] The issue was that at the time of the Revolutionary War,[33] the pacifist Quakers sought the more expansive religious freedom, refusing to support the voluntary militias on religious grounds either by direct participation or by paying an "equivalent," a sum of money in support of the war effort.[34] As resentment against the Quakers rose, the Continental Congress proposed a compromise: the Quakers were urged to "contribute liberally . . . to the relief of their distressed brethren"[35] in ways that did not offend their religious scruples— "protection money" for avoiding conscription.[36]

But this was not acceptable to the Philadelphia revolutionaries, who insisted on either direct participation or payment under "Terms of Exemption [that] may be adequate to the Dangers, Loss of Time and Expense incurred to those who shall associate under the proposed Regulations."[37] Relying in part on the 1701 Charter of Pennsylvania, which included language about not compelling anyone to do "any other Act or Thing contrary to their religious Persuasion,"[38] the Quakers petitioned the Pennsylvania legislature for the broader right. Again the Philadelphia revolutionaries demurred, remonstrating that the Quaker position was "unjust and unequal" as well as (and here the fact of war was certainly relevant) inconsistent with "the great Law of Self-preservation."[39] Ultimately, the revolutionaries' view was vindicated: the Pennsylvania Assembly "required conscientious objectors to pay an equivalent, even if under another name."[40]

Yet it is possible to characterize this outcome in somewhat grayer terms. The Quakers were, in effect, exempted from military service, but they were required to pay equivalents that were not remotely severe enough to bankrupt them.[41] Neither side in the conflict achieved everything that it wanted. A compromise was reached, suggesting some sympathy for religious exemptions, but also definite limits. Furthermore, exemptions from military service are unusual in that they present an extreme case: they pit the gravest type of burden on religious conscience—the civil injunction to kill others—against the most compelling state need— its own self-defense. In light of the extremity of the conflict, the resolution of the military exemption issue may not also "entail opposition to all exemptions" in other contexts.[42] Indeed, generalization from an extreme case like this one to create a general rule would not reflect the circumstantial orientation of the tragic-historic approach in the least.[43] Nevertheless, the Philadelphia episode offers important evidence that the narrower "no penalty" interpretation of the liberty of conscience was a powerful one in early America.

The liberty contained in the federal Constitution is not that of "conscience," of course, but of the "free exercise" of "religion." *Conscience* was a word that was proposed for inclusion by James Madison in the Bill of Rights but was ultimately rejected by the Senate for uncertain reasons.[44] Some have argued that the ultimate choice of "free exercise" as opposed to "conscience" indicates as a textual matter that protection for conduct, rather than simply belief or expression, was preferred; this might be an argument in favor of the broader interpretation of the clause.[45] Unfortunately, however, there is little evidence in the drafting history that provides much justification for reading the elimination of the "conscience" language as significant,[46] let alone adequate to discern the adoption of an exemption interpretation over a "no penalty" interpretation.

Others have argued, by contrast, that in the view of some members of the founding generation, the free exercise of religion would have been understood to entail the accommodation of religious believers gravely burdened by "facially benign laws"—a broad right not only to believe, speak, and worship, but also to act (or to refuse to act) on the basis of belief with legal protection.[47] As influential congregational minister and former Yale College president Elisha Williams put it in a 1744 political sermon entitled "The Essential Rights and Liberties of Protestants":

> If the rulers only are to judge, we may be sure they will judge in favor of their own laws: if they exceed this bound set to them by this general law; they will never judge that law of Christ to be contrary. . . . [T]o suppose [Christians] have a right of judgment for themselves, is to suppose they have a right to *act* according to their judgment: and therefore none (not the civil magistrate) can have any right to hinder them. A right that in this case is dependent on the will of another, is no right at all.[48]

Yet even if religious exemptions from general laws were known to and even favored by early Americans as a theological or prudential matter, it is a different question whether such exemptions would have been understood to carry constitutional force.

Those who support a right of constitutional exemption by recourse to historical sources do not claim that such an interpretation unambiguously reflects the content of the clause; the social history of free exercise at the founding does not support that view. Rather, they make the milder and more persuasive argument that the exemption reading is consistent with fragments of the historical record, and that—in light of deep uncertainty about the original meaning of the Free Exercise Clause—the judicial exemption reading is a plausible interpretation. Michael McConnell supports this view of the clause with several examples of pre-constitutional history, the most interesting of which is the question of oath-taking, "[b]y far the most common source of friction" with respect to the wisdom of religious exemptions.[49] The problem again involved the Quakers and other Protestant denominations whose members refused on grounds of religious conscience (grounded in the Bible) to swear oaths.[50] The conscientious refusal to swear prevented members of these groups from offering testimony, which in turn meant that they had no legal recourse to vindicate or defend themselves.[51] As McConnell notes, by the end of the eighteenth century, "virtually all of the states had enacted oath exemptions."[52]

The issue of oath-swearing provides a useful contrast with the military-conscription context considered earlier. The difference is not in the nature of the burden on religious conscience. To the contrary, oath-swearing in the eighteenth and early nineteenth century was viewed as an extremely grave affair: it was of "profound, almost covenantal significance for the framers—a significance that may be difficult for some fully to understand and appreciate today."[53] The theological seriousness of oath-swearing is reflected in the existence of a separate portion of the Constitution specifically stating that federal and state executive, legislative, and judicial officers "shall be bound by Oath or Affirmation, to support this Constitution," but that "no religious Test shall ever be required as a Qualification to any Office or public Trust under the United States."[54] It is reflected also in Alexander Hamilton's description in *The Federalist* of the "sanctity of an oath" to "support this Constitution."[55]

Rather, the difference between the oath and conscription contexts may well depend on the quality of the respective government interests at stake and the feasibility of fashioning an adequate alternative—a difference that might affect the force and persuasiveness of the exemption reading in various areas of conflict. Conscription was vital for the very preservation of the Republic:[56] in carrying out the nation's self-defense, there was little substitute for the regular supply of bodies.[57] Moreover, an exemption from military conscription, once granted, was likely to be broadly desirable and therefore all the more dangerous to the state.[58] By contrast, oath-swearing, important as it was,[59] could be feasibly substituted in appropriate circumstances with affirmations or pledges with far less deleterious effect on the state's interests. This was precisely the result reached in Article VI by the inclusion of the "affirmation" alternative.[60] More importantly, the likelihood that others would be induced to seek an exemption was much smaller in the oath context. Only a person genuinely religiously opposed to swearing an oath would find the exemption appealing. While these distinctions do not bear definitively on the persuasiveness of the exemption reading of the Free Exercise Clause, they do suggest that the receptivity of the founding generation to the issue of religious exemptions depended not on a categorical rule but on particular details and circumstantial judgments. Both interpretations of the clause, in sum, had their moments.

One way to reconcile these two different meanings of free exercise is by an appeal to an incremental evolution in intellectual history as American society became increasingly pluralistic and secular. That is, the ideas grounding the Free Exercise Clause may evince a slow and subtle shift from the no-penalty interpretation to the view that constitutionally mandated exemptions were at least a permissible, even if not a compelled, reading of the clause. Steven Smith, for example, notices a crucial conceptual development in ideas about what the right to free exercise of religion was thought to protect.[61] While in the early Republic, the principal threat to free religious belief and practice had historically been the imposition religious orthodoxy, the more contemporary threat in the late nineteenth and twentieth century was felt to come not from religious orthodoxy but from the disregard of democratically enacted secular law that has the effect of burdening religious conscience or practice.[62] "Democratic governments might try to avoid such conflicts by accommodating minority religions," writes Smith, "[b]ut then again they might not do this—because they are unaware of the burdens they are imposing on religion, or because they are aware but don't care, or because they think it impractical or objectionable to excuse religious dissenters from generally applicable laws."[63]

Similarly, in the views of Kurt Lash and Akhil Amar, when the Fourteenth Amendment was adopted in 1868, and even more so when the Free Exercise Clause was incorporated against the states via the Fourteenth Amendment in 1940, the quality of what the clause protected had altered and expanded. It now enshrined not only a right against explicit discrimination against religion, but also a right to accommodation, in appropriate circumstances, from the burdens imposed by secular laws.[64] As of the adoption of the Fourteenth Amendment, Lash says, majoritarian indifference to religious exercise became part of the core of the Free Exercise Clause's concern—a "privilege or immunity of citizens." Whatever may have been true a century before, in the "Reconstructed" Constitution, "generally applicable laws might sometimes impermissibly violate an individual's religious liberty."[65]

But the argument that Reconstruction extended the reach of the Free Exercise Clause to include exemptions from neutral laws has been persuasively contested as well. The heightening fears and antipathies toward Catholics by the Protestant majority in the late nineteenth century belies any firm or unswerving commitment to a new, thoroughgoing right of religious exemption.[66] Indeed, it was in part these very fears, directed at a different religious minority, the Mormons, only a decade after the adoption of the Fourteenth Amendment, that may explain the less than obliging language of the *Reynolds* decision.

Collecting these various threads of the story, one may conclude that the plausibility of interpreting the Free Exercise Clause to require religious exemptions from neutral, generally applicable laws under certain circumstances is not definitively answered by an examination of the social history of free exercise.[67] Neither is the plausibility of interpreting it *not* to require such exemptions. Rather, whether such exemptions were "a constitutional right or an equitable exception—the source of much scholarly contention today—the eighteenth-century sources at our disposal do not dispositively say"; and neither do any sources after that period.[68] This is in many ways a fitting verdict, since it is a true reflection of our own ongoing disagreements and conflicts about the proper interpretation of the clause.[69] These conflicts are mirrored and manifested in the swinging pendulum of Supreme Court free exercise doctrine—from *Reynolds* to *Sherbert* to *Smith*.

Combining Social History and Tragedy

Since an examination of social history leaves us with two plausible but very different meanings of constitutional free exercise, the question is how to select between them as the interpretation most in keeping with the method of tragedy and history. The answer lies in the marriage of the social history of free exercise with the first three theses of the method of tragedy and history. The method of tragedy and history distinguishes those doctrinal traditions that merit preservation from those that do not by examining the degree to which the particular doctrinal tradition is faithful to the tragic theses.

Viewed through that lens, there is little doubt that the first option— judicial withdrawal in the absence of direct targeting of religion—is not viable. The involvement of the judiciary in the protection of religious liberty is necessary because courts are institutionally best positioned to consider tragic conflicts fairly, in some degree sheltered from raw majoritarian influence,[70] and to provide a state with "a security to its justice against its power."[71]

Echoing the historical jurisprudents of the late nineteenth century and early twentieth century,[72] the constitutional theorist Alexander Bickel described the special institutional qualities of the judiciary in these terms:

> [C]ourts have certain capacities for dealing with matters of principle that legislatures and executives do not possess. Judges have, or should have, the leisure, the training, and the insulation to follow the ways of the scholar in pursuing the ends of government. This is crucial in sorting out the enduring values of a society, and it is not something that institutions can do well occasionally, while

operating for the most part with a different set of gears. It calls for a
habit of mind, and for undeviating institutional customs.[73]

For the method of tragedy and history, the "habit of mind" to be cultivated is attuned to tragic conflict in a way that other legal and political institutions are poorly suited to develop. The legislature deals only
prospectively with legal conflict, while courts are "concerned with the
flesh and blood of an actual case," a perspective that "tends to modify,
perhaps to lengthen, everyone's view. It also provides an extremely salutary proving ground for all abstractions."[74] The courts, by temperament, institutional position, and protection from political importunacy,
are best suited to apply the tragic-historic method in careful and even-
handed fashion.[75]

Exactly because the judiciary is focused on the particulars of past
disputes—because, in an important way, it faces backward in searching
for guidance in moving forward—it is the institution of government in
the most natural position to discern the social and doctrinal history that
forms the raw material of the method of tragedy and history.[76] As the late
Yale Law School dean Harry Wellington once put it:

> [T]he courts alone deliberately search the past for elements worth
> preserving. . . . By applying those elements to the often heated con-
> troversies before them—thereby reminding the polity of the values to
> which it has long adhered—the courts may be seen as the key political
> institution charged with taking account of our public traditions.[77]

The involvement of courts in discerning the nation's social and doctrinal
history is thus a core feature of the method of tragedy and history. The
path of these histories' development—analogical and gradual—is such
that "it makes sense for courts to have a prominent role."[78]

As applied to the doctrines of free exercise that have shaped the law
of religious liberty in the past fifty years, an approach which recognizes
that constitutionally required religious exemptions are sometimes necessary to protect religious liberty is preferable to one which, for the sake of
sustaining the value of formal neutrality, denies that reality. In this sense,
the substantial burden/compelling governmental interest strict scrutiny

approach of *Sherbert* and the cases following it better reflects and does justice to the plural-valued vision of the tragic theses than does the *Smith* framework, which elevates a single value to master status.[79]

This does not mean that the interest-balancing test is ideal from a tragic-historic perspective: it depends heavily on the incorrect notion that the values of religious liberty and those against which they compete can be accurately measured and commensurated on an all-encompassing scale of value.[80] Indeed, the interest-balancing regime, though in theory much more open to the possibility of constitutionally required religious exemptions, often in practice resulted in a loss for the religious claimant.[81] The method of tragedy and history resists the idea of single-gauge balancing.[82] Moreover, a judge faithful to the method of tragedy and history at times might come out differently on the question of religious exemptions than did the Supreme Court under the interest-balancing regime that preceded *Smith*.[83]

Nevertheless, the tragic-historic method does accept that comparisons of some type must be made in order to achieve a proper resolution. It relies on doctrinal and social history as presumptively valid guideposts in arriving at reasonable judgments, for reasons explained in the fourth and fifth theses. The *Sherbert* test, though not ideal or identical with the method of tragedy and history, at least lends itself in rough terms to a tragic-historic approach, in that it permits a judge who was otherwise inclined toward the method of tragedy and history to describe fully the nature of the conflicting values and the social and doctrinal context in rendering his decision. It demonstrates, in Ernest Young's apt phrase, "a faith in the ability of judges to oversee the incremental evolution of our constitutional tradition."[84] If the constitutional law of religious liberty is, indeed, "typically a response to past practices that 'We the People' have by consensus come to condemn," then it is part of the judicial role to investigate and articulate those social mores—to follow gradually and haltingly in the wake of custom.[85]

There are, indeed, two points here. First, while courts institutionally may not be reliably more solicitous of religious liberty interests than legislators or other actors, courts applying the method of tragedy and history would approach the exemption issue with attention to the specific nature of the conflicts at issue, rather than assuming that an exemption ought, or ought not, to apply to a uniform category of cases. And second, permitting the courts a second look at the exemption issue institutional-izes a judicial checking function that is more protective of religious lib-erty simply in virtue of providing another layer of government attention to free exercise claims.

Smith, by contrast, is not compatible with the tragic theses. Its hold-ing that neutral laws of general application are valid against any adverse interest, so long as the government is able to proffer a rational basis for the law, fairly well repudiates any role for judges to reflect carefully on the nature of the clashing values in free exercise disputes. Instead, it leaves the field almost entirely to legislative choice and instructs courts to con-cern themselves exclusively with the challenged law's formal neutrality. But this is precisely what the method of tragedy and history resists, for it envisions a central role for judges. The doctrinal tradition represented by *Smith* is one that the method of tragedy and history cannot accept.

The Problem of Predictability

Even if an approach permitting constitutional religious exemptions is more in keeping with the method of tragedy and history than the monism of *Smith*, an important objection remains: *Smith*'s virtue is its predict-ability. The strongest form of the objection is that the *Smith* approach is the only view consistent with the "rule of law" or the "public good."[86] A more tenable version is that by laying out a hard rule that is easily applied by courts, *Smith* offers a consistent and predictable approach to free exercise cases that also promotes equality.[87] Litigants know and can plan for what they will get from a court that applies *Smith*, and the monism of *Smith* is beneficially constraining on judges.[88] By contrast, approaches that do not rely on a single value are uncertain and unpredictable.

In earlier chapters, I noted that predictability is important, but it is only one value in any viable approach to religious liberty conflicts. Pre-dictability should not be allowed to overpower all other values.[89] Indeed, there is sometimes a quality of the defense of *Smith* as supremely pre-dictable that takes equality to be the foundational commitment around which religious liberty ought to be organized.[90] To that extent, and for reasons explained in previous chapters, the method of tragedy and history would reject *Smith*. Here I instead want to test the premise of the objection—to explore the asserted formalist virtues of *Smith*. Is it really true that *Smith* offers much more predictability of outcome than would the method of tragedy and history?

The surprising answer is: not nearly as much as many suppose. *Smith* itself contains a number of exceptions, and some lower courts have used these exceptions to reach outcomes seemingly in tension with *Smith*'s rule.[91] *Smith* created as many as three exceptions, each of which triggers an interest-balancing approach that is in theory more generous on the issue of religious exemptions: (1) where the free exercise claim is accompanied by another right (the parental right to direct education, for example, or a right to free speech), creating a "hybrid right";[92] (2) where the "state has in place a system of individual exemptions"—for example, in the administration of unemployment or other benefits—"it may not refuse to extend that system to cases of 'religious hardship' without compelling reason";[93] and (3) where the claim to exemption from laws is made by a religious institution, rather than an individual, under doctrines of church autonomy or the so-called "ministerial exception."[94] The last of these exceptions was reaffirmed and expanded in the Supreme Court's most recent religious liberty decision: *Smith* does not impact the right of religious institutions to manage and govern themselves or to control decisions about the hiring and firing of ministers.[95]

Consider next the "hybrid rights" exception: a less-than-viable free exercise claim under *Smith*, when joined with another constitutional claim of uncertain strength, will lift the case out of the *Smith* framework to require strict scrutiny of the law. While some federal circuits have concluded that this exception is merely dicta,[96] others have interpreted it as binding: some courts require that a free exercise claim be joined with an "independently viable" right,[97] while others only require a "colorable claim that an independent right has been violated."[98]

And a few courts in jurisdictions where the hybrid rights exception is treated as binding have used it to circumvent *Smith*.[99] Among other examples, public school students have used the exception successfully against facially neutral regulations impinging free exercise and free speech rights;[100] a church has used it to preserve its free exercise rights in a challenge to an otherwise religiously neutral zoning ordinance that violated its equal protection, free speech, and assembly rights;[101] parents and grandparents have used it successfully to challenge neutral public school uniform or dress policies that combine parental rights claims with otherwise insufficient free exercise claims;[102] and a church has used it to resist otherwise neutral state assertions of the power of eminent domain by combining freedom of association and free exercise claims.[103] Analysis of the hybrid rights exception, as one circuit court has noted, demands a "very fact-driven" inquiry and an examination of the particular claims "on a case-by-case basis."[104] This is especially true for those circuits that have adopted the "colorable claim" approach to the exception: that view of hybridity requires "courts reviewing free exercise claims to make difficult, qualitative, case-by-case judgments regarding the strength of companion-claim arguments."[105] Under that approach, at least part of *Smith*'s asserted predictability is diminished.

But it is the individual-assessment exception that more severely compromises *Smith*'s predictability. Two cases decided by Judge Samuel Alito before his appointment to the Supreme Court are instructive. In the first, the Newark Police Department had instituted a policy against facial hair for police officers as well as a system of individualized exemptions, and several Muslim police officers sued when their requests for religious exemptions from the policy were denied.[106] Judge Alito held that even though the policy was neutral, the police officers had a viable free exercise claim because the city had granted health-related exemptions to other officers.[107] In so doing, Judge Alito analogized the case to those to which *Smith* had applied the individual-assessment exemption.[108]

Judge Alito relied on the individual-assessment exception again a few years later, in a case where a Native American owner of black bears sued the Pennsylvania Game Commission when it refused to grant him a religious exemption from a permit fee to keep wildlife.[109] Because the government had the discretion to waive the fee "where hardship or extraordinary circumstance warrants,"[110] and because it had engaged in case-specific evaluations, the court concluded that an otherwise neutral policy implicated the individual-assessment exception.[111] It should be noted that the government will extremely infrequently impose on itself an *absolute prohibition* from granting an exemption from a law for an "extraordinary circumstance."[112] At any rate, that Justice Alito repeatedly endorsed an extension of the individual-assessment exception suggests that there may be at least one vote for expanding it should the Supreme Court have the occasion.

What renders the individual-assessment exception unpredictable is that it depends on a court's willingness to analogize from the unemployment benefits context.[113] Several courts have drawn these analogies. In one case, a parochial school student was barred from participating in extracurricular activities within a public school district because he was not enrolled within that district.[114] The district had instituted a neutral policy, but it had made a few exceptions for students enrolled in charter schools and homeschooled students. The parochial student sued on free exercise grounds, and the court held that the individualized-assessment exception applied.[115] In another case, a Christian church sued a municipality when it was denied certain permits to develop a parcel of land for its expanding ministry.[116] Merely because the municipality opined on the suitability of the parcel of land for certain purposes, rather than for others, the court concluded that it had engaged in an individual assessment, removing the case from the *Smith* rule.[117] In a third case, a court held that all zoning laws are "by their nature" individual-assessment schemes, and therefore never subject to the *Smith* rule.[118]

Other courts have declined to draw these analogies. In several cases, for example, courts have refused to apply the individual-assessment exception where a municipality had passed a neutral zoning ordinance, instituted a system for obtaining variances for secular reasons, and denied a religious institution's requests for variances.[119] In another case dealing with a state immunization statute with a health exemption, a court declined to extend the individualized-assessment exception because it believed that "the individual exemption cases have as their central concern the prospect of the government making a value judgment in favor of secular motivations but not religious motivations," and this statute did not meet that standard.[120] In still other cases, courts have taken an intermediate position, adopting highly fact-specific criteria for determining *in which circumstances* to extend the individualized-assessment exception.[121]

The difficulty with the exception, therefore, is that it is unpredictable when a court will, or will not, choose to analogize from the unemployment compensation context and what constraints it will place on drawing the analogy. The most expansive interpretation of the exception might even swallow the *Smith* rule itself.[122] Yet the more pressing concern is not that *Smith* actually ceases to be meaningful at all, but that it loses a great deal of its purported predictability by liberal use of the exception.[123] One solution, of course, might be for the government never, ever, to make any exceptions to its laws; so far, that has not seemed either practicable or the course of political prudence.

There are other issues involving the interpretation of *Smith*—internal or structural ambiguities rather than express exceptions—that also contribute to its unpredictability. First, courts generally agree that a law may run afoul of the Free Exercise Clause either by being facially nonneutral toward religion or by evincing, through legislative history, a discriminatory motivation against religion.[124] Different outcomes might follow by using motivation as the gauge of neutrality as opposed to the text itself.[125] Because few government entities are likely to pass laws that are flagrantly, facially, discriminatory against religion, an examination of legislative motivation seems desirable.[126] But legislative motivation or intent is not only difficult to pinpoint as an evidentiary matter (that is, "courts are likely to make factual errors in discerning motivation"), but also problematic conceptually.[127] There is no uniform approach to determining what ought to count as legislative motivation, "no accepted method of aggregating these diverse individual motivations into a single 'intent of the legislature.'"[128] Courts attempting to divine legislative motivation "will almost surely have a range of choices about how to construct" the existence of legislative neutrality. The point is not that these constructions of legislative motivation are fantasies or empty, but that the reasons courts might opt for one or another construction of legislative motivation are unpredictable.[129]

Second, and finally, the existence of statutory and other state frameworks that, as already noted, differ from the *Smith* framework, introduces a component of unpredictability. Litigants now must deal with at least two very different legal frameworks in pursuing their religious liberty claims rather than one. No matter how rule-like the *Smith* framework is, by its very existence it introduces unpredictability and complexity.[130]

None of this discussion is meant to suggest that the rule of *Smith* in reality provides lower courts and litigants with little or no predictability as to outcomes. Surely it does. But it does not offer the level of predictability that its proponents sometimes claim for it. And while it may be a more predictable approach than the method of tragedy and history, the comparative predictability is one of smaller, rather than larger, degrees. As Nelson Tebbe puts it: "I take it to be relatively uncontroversial that judges actually do consider a wide range of values in this area—the fighting question today is not whether they are deploying polyvalent adjudication but instead whether they should be."[131]

The counterintuitive upshot of the surprising flexibility of *Smith* for free exercise law seems to be that the announcement of a hard-edged rule may be appealing for rhetorical or psychological reasons[132]—for the surface reassurance that courts are not acting according to whim—as well as for reasons of real predictability.[133] This unexpected flexibility points to another drawback of certain comic monistic approaches: subscribing to *Smith*, particularly if one also believes the overstated claims of predictability made on its behalf, may mask the truth of what judges actually do with free exercise cases. Comic monism can blind us to the reality of particularistic assessment that actually does occur in the real world of adjudication notwithstanding the rhetoric of neutrality.[134] If the vice of pluralistic approaches is that they are predictable only to those who know how they will be applied, that is no less true of monistic approaches. And in light of the other substantial disadvantages that inhere in comic monistic methods, the reasons to opt against them are all the more powerful.

Negotiating around *Smith*

A rejection of *Smith* still leaves the question of how best to redirect free exercise jurisprudence toward a tragic-historic framework—whether to chip away at *Smith* in incremental fashion or to overrule it outright. Another possibility is simply to allow *Smith* to stand, fortified by the thought that the RFRA, the state RFRAs (for those states that have them), and other state protections for religious liberty have more-or-less reinstated the previous regime as to both the federal government and the individual states.[135] In some ways, *Smith* has been rendered irrelevant by these statutes, and the social history of legislatively enacted exemptions also represents, as Douglas Laycock has argued, "an unbroken tradition" "from the late seventeenth century to the present."[136]

While this last option might be strategically feasible, there is more than strategy at stake here. *Smith*'s elevation of a single value to overriding status represents the type of methodological approach that has attracted many contemporary scholars of the religion clauses. Though few of these writers adopt *Smith*'s value of formal neutrality, many endorse *Smith*'s underlying methodological perspective on judicial review of the religion clauses. The method of tragedy and history, by contrast, rejects that approach.

The movement toward neutrality as the unifying value of religious liberty under the Constitution is regrettable for both symbolic and practical reasons, and it suggests that some type of opposition to *Smith* itself, as well as to any parallel rule in the Establishment Clause context, is warranted. The approach most consonant with the method of tragedy and history may well be to dismantle *Smith* incrementally, perhaps by using and expanding *Smith*'s carve-out for individual assessments or church autonomy. This approach is preferable to a onetime repudiation of *Smith*, whose consequence would be too sudden, unpredictable, and unsettling to the extant doctrinal landscape of free exercise.

CHAPTER 9

Free Exercise Applications

T he current doctrine of free exercise was seen in the last chapter to
obstruct the possibility of a tragic-historic approach. This chapter
applies the method of tragedy and history to a selection of the core issues
of free exercise law. Three specific problems are considered: the conflict
between ordinary government projects and religious liberty interests;
the issue of church autonomy from secular authority; and the more specific question of whether religious institutions should be exempt from
antidiscrimination laws in hiring and firing certain employees.

Substantial Burdens and Compelling Interests

One fundamental type of free exercise problem concerns what the government ought to do when its ordinary operations and projects conflict
with an individual or group's religious beliefs and practices. In these
cases, the state is performing a specific function that clashes with a
religious liberty claim. These disputes implicated, before *Employment
Division v. Smith*,[1] the basic free exercise conflict between the law or
practice's substantial burden on the religious interest and the corresponding compelling government interest in seeing that the law or practice prevail.[2]

That was the case in *Lyng v. Northwest Indian Cemetery Protective Association*, where a group of Native Americans objected to the federal government's plan to build a road directly through the Chimney Rock Area of the Six Rivers National Forest.[3] The National Forest Service had commissioned a study which concluded that the road should not be built because it would impair the religious use of the land, but the Forest Service rejected the study's recommendations.[4] The Native Americans argued that they required a private, undisturbed, and entirely natural place for their worship, and that the land would be demolished by the logging necessary to build a highway.[5] Justice O'Connor's opinion for the Court held that the government was entitled to proceed with its road because the Native Americans had not shown that the government was prohibiting their religious practice. The road had "no tendency to coerce individuals into acting contrary to their beliefs,"[6] even if it might destroy the Native Americans' religious practice on that site. Applying the first thesis of the tragic-historic method, here is a plain case of values that are clashing at two distinct levels of conflict.

The first clash occurs *among conceptions of religious liberty*. The Court affirmed the absolute importance of one value—noncoercion—while the Native Americans emphasized a different value—piety.[7] These values are not entirely incompatible. Indeed, there often is an instrumental connection between noncoercion and piety. Unless the government valued non-coercion, religious believers often could not achieve piety within their own religious traditions. Consider a state that engaged in religious persecution.

Yet the value of noncoercion is, if treated as the monistic value of free exercise, incompatible with the particular type of piety cherished by the Native Americans. The Court admitted as much:

> Even if we assume that we should accept the Ninth Circuit's predic-
> tion, according to which the . . . road will "virtually destroy the . . .
> Indians' ability to practice their religion" . . . the Constitution sim-
> ply does not provide a principle that could justify upholding respon-
> dents' claims.[8]

The reason that the values are incompatible is that the Court takes non-coercion or noncompulsion to be the monistic value of religious liberty protected by the Free Exercise Clause.[9] The Native Americans asked the Court to recognize that their conception of religious liberty depended on the ritualized and undisturbed use of sacred lands in Chimney Rock. But noncoercion, as interpreted by the Court and when adopted as the master value of free exercise, not only does nothing to protect the Native American ritual practice, but it is also incompatible with the values of religious liberty corresponding to the Native Americans' practice.

And it is also true that the free exercise values here—noncoercion and piety—are at least partially incommensurable if either is taken monistically. Noncoercion is a valuable concept within an idea of religious liberty; piety and the achievement of a noetic state are as well;[10] and there seems to be no covering value by which we can rank order the values without misunderstanding (or without being ignorant of) what renders noncoercion and piety valuable in the first place. While it is true that the Court saw fit to privilege noncoercion over piety, one has the distinct sense that the Court did not understand and was impatient with the Native Americans' conception of religious liberty. The Court's lack of understanding of the importance of Chimney Rock to the Native Americans—to the point that the Court was prepared to "virtually destroy" their religion in order to preserve its principle of noncoercion—bespeaks a failure of what was described in Chapter 5 as "the sense of loss."[11]

Nevertheless, the Court's impatience was given expression in a persuasive retort: if the Native Americans' claim to piety was accepted, what was to distinguish that claim from one in which they sought to exclude all human use of the sacred land except their own?[12] An approach that took piety as the master value of religious liberty would overpower all other values of religious liberty, including the noncoercion or noncompulsion advocated by the Court. One can easily imagine another group whose religious beliefs required raucous, celebratory use of Chimney Rock being forcibly excluded from using those lands under the regime advocated by the Native Americans.

In sum, the Native Americans were making a claim about what piety demanded of them—a solitary, tranquil, and undisturbed holy ground in order to undertake a spiritual journey leading to an apperception of the transcendent[13]—within their overarching concept of what it is to lead a moral life.[14] Religious liberty was valuable to them precisely in order to participate in and live out that moral life.[15] The Court rejected that set of values of religious liberty, even if it might well have understood them in a different context. If the government needed to build a road through a well-known Christian church (New York City's Saint Patrick's Cathedral, for example), the very same claims of noncoercion against those of piety may have drawn greater understanding.[16] Yet what is certain is that noncoercion and piety cannot coexist if either is taken as the monistic value of religious liberty. And the values cannot be rank ordered without misunderstanding what renders them valuable to begin with.

The second clash in *Lyng* occurs *between one conception of the values of religious liberty* (the Native Americans') *and a different set of values entirely* (relating to the government's interest in the road). This conflict turns on the fact that Chimney Rock, after all, belongs to the government. A theory of religious liberty that divested the government of all rights to use its own land as it saw fit would be wholly inadequate. Kent Greenawalt has argued that the government's interest in this particular road was "slight,"[17] though there is some indication that abandoning the project entirely would have left "two existing segments of road to dead end in the middle of a National Forest,"[18] rendering the existing roads wasteful, inefficient, and aesthetically offensive. But the larger point is that the government's interest in the use and development of its own property to promote the general industrial and economic welfare is substantial. When the values underwriting that interest conflict with the Native Americans' values of religious liberty, it is easy to appreciate their clashing quality.[19] It is probably true that the state's interest in the road ought to have yielded,[20] but the reason has nothing to do with our ability to rank order the respective conflicting values in a way that could be comfortably generalized across all other situations of conflict.

In a conflict such as *Lyng*, where the question is what sorts of restraints on the government a court may demand, the method of tragedy and history takes much more careful stock of the values that both sides bring to bear than did the Court. If one accepts the objections of the Native Americans as sincere, a judge following the method of tragedy and history would find this a much closer case than did the Court, and would likely have ruled for the Native Americans because of the degree to which the road would have negatively impacted their worship. But whether or not the Court's ultimate conclusion is correct, the conciliations that a tragic-historic judge would reach would be much more limited and fact-specific than is the Court's opinion. They would eschew the rigidity with which Justice O'Connor considered the Native Americans' claims,[21] and they would have found a way to account for the quality of the spiritual harms that were being pressed as deprivations of religious liberty. They would also have taken stock of the changing meaning of free exercise[22] as well as of this country's social history of both actual persecution and official accommodation of Native American interests.

Though the Court's conclusion in *Lyng* was probably incorrect from a tragic-historic perspective, the primary point is not to disagree with that outcome. It is instead to acknowledge that in the process of fashioning a decision, the dicta of an opinion matter. A decision that followed a tragic-historic methodology would look entirely different than the Court's decision. Whether or not the outcome would change, the language of the case would augur change in the way that future cases bringing similar types of claims were received and assessed. At the very least, in a future case where the government's interest was even weaker, the language of a tragic-historic opinion would offer a much stronger foothold for a decision favoring the religious interest. Moreover, the tragic-historic approach would allow courts to speak to the losers in a different register than is possible by recourse to a single value. It would permit courts not only to acknowledge the true and actual values that had been sacrificed, but also the costs that the decision for some and against others had incurred. Finally, the use of a tragic-historic methodology in the writing of the opinion might serve as a signal to other government actors—to legislators and administrative bodies—that greater efforts at compromise and accommodation would have been desirable and will be expected in the future.

Church Autonomy

A different type of free exercise conflict involves the question of church autonomy. The issue is whether, and in what circumstances, the state is empowered to interfere with matters of church governance and management.[23] An important subcategory of church autonomy consists of cases where the state is asked to resolve church property disputes,[24] and in which the Supreme Court has historically favored a dichotomous approach depending on whether the church's internal organization is "congregationalist" or "hierarchical."[25] As a general matter, courts are highly protective of church authority, and the Supreme Court has gone so far as to suggest that courts may not adjudicate between competing views even when a church has acted inconsistently with its own internal laws.[26]

From a tragic-historic viewpoint, this position, which elevates separationism and deference to religious institutions to overriding status, was appropriately tempered in a later case which held that courts are permitted to apply "neutral principles" to interpret internal church documents so long as courts do not pronounce on any religious doctrine.[27] The issue in *Serbian Eastern Orthodox Diocese v. Milivojevich* was whether a local schismatic church or the highest institutional authority (which was located in the former Yugoslavia) had authority to control certain property in Illinois. The Supreme Court distanced itself altogether from this dispute, holding that it is inappropriate for courts to inquire into whether a hierarchical religious institution has complied with its own laws.[28] The Court later held in *Watson v. Jones* that provided a court is not being asked to inquire into religious doctrine, it can rely on authoritative statements of the religious organization to resolve intrachurch property disputes through the use of "neutral principles of law."[29] A judge following the method of tragedy and history likewise could support a limited place for the application of such neutral principles, since the state's interests in the equitable distribution of property are substantial enough to counsel against an absolute rule prohibiting court involvement. However, the more intrusive approach is sensible so long as the neutral principles were chosen by the religious institution itself—that is, so long as the institution desired to bind itself to them—and provided that "neutral principles of law" is not interpreted to implicate the formally neutral blunderbuss represented by *Smith*.[30] Elevating formal neutrality to the status of a monistic value would destroy church autonomy by requiring substantial intermeddling by courts in religious doctrine. Furthermore, it would harm another value of the "neutral principles" approach: the ability of churches to plan in anticipation of future legal disputes, so as to mitigate the possibility of tragic conflict.

The Ministerial Exception

A different issue involves the viability of a judicially created doctrine that exempts religious organizations from laws against discrimination, such as Title VII of the Civil Rights Act and other antidiscrimination laws.[31] This doctrinal problem—the so-called "ministerial exception"—is ideal both for understanding the method of tragedy and history and for assessing its merits. In fact, the Supreme Court's most recent religious freedom decision, involving the ministerial exception, is as close an approximation of the method of tragedy and history as may be found.[32]

The ministerial exception "operates to bar any claim, the resolution of which would limit a religious institution's right to select who will perform particular spiritual functions."[33] This exemption, which has roots not only in the American policy of noninterference with a church's clerical appointments,[34] but also in the more ancient tradition of partition between temporal and ecclesiastical authority,[35] embodies several values of religious liberty. First, and most obviously, institutional autonomy: the "right to decide matters of faith, doctrine, and church governance."[36] Second, the separationist concern of "excessive entanglement" that government intrusion would activate.[37] Just as the legislature may not delegate civic functions to religious bodies,[38] so, too, is it barred from appropriating functions that concern the internal operations of religious bodies. Third, the "right to choose ministers without government restriction underlies the well being of religious communit[ies],"[39] and the state has a role in promoting that well-being. Fourth, since the remedy for violations of many nondiscrimination laws is usually equitable rather than monetary, the relief in these lawsuits might empower courts to compel the religious organization to accept excluded individuals by forcibly reinstating them over the religious institution's objection—commanding the religious institution to tolerate what it otherwise could not.[40] Fifth, it may be that the government's interpretation of values such as equality is not necessarily universally applicable. Permitting other interpretations to coexist in a limited institutional context exemplifies the value of humility in the face of contested and contestable points of view. It represents a civil libertarian limit on the state's otherwise monopolistic control of the sources and interpretation of civic and moral values.[41]

The ministerial exception's viability depends, however, on the nature of the employee's job as well as on the nature of the dispute. An employee whose work does not relate to the religious institution's doctrinal or creedal positions is not precluded from suing. A church groundskeeper, for example, or an administrative assistant, may sue the religious institution for race or sex discrimination. Likewise, a plaintiff alleging a non-religious wrong is also not barred from suit: "The minister struck on the head by a falling gargoyle as he is about to enter the church may have an actionable claim."[42]

These limitations are sensible because the state, too, has cognizable interests: "[t]he government's interest flows from the central place churches have in many communities and from the way their understanding of roles can radiate into the rest of social life."[43] Contrary to the piety that secular interests are simply not activated by "matters of purely ecclesiastical concern,"[44] the state properly attends to the content of religious doctrine—not by specifying or controlling it, but by caring about its effects on citizens' behavior.[45] "It is the right of government to attend much to opinions; because, as opinions soon combine with passions, even when they do not produce them, they have much influence on actions."[46]

Hosanna-Tabor and the Method of Tragedy and History

Perhaps as much as any opinion in its history, the Supreme Court's unanimous decision involving the ministerial exception reflects an approach closely aligned with the method of tragedy and history.[47] As in other contexts, the method of tragedy and history counsels an intermediate approach that emphasizes doctrinal and social history as well as particularist and incremental adjudication. That is largely the method applied by the Supreme Court in *Hosanna-Tabor Evangelical Lutheran Church and School v. EEOC.*

Cheryl Perich worked from 1999 to 2005 for Hosanna-Tabor Evangelical Lutheran Church and School in Redford, Michigan, as an elementary school teacher. The school employed two different types of teachers—"lay" and "called." "Called" teachers, of which Perich was one, were required to complete various college-level courses in theology and other facets of Christian faith. Upon completion of this training, these teachers were designated "commissioned ministers,"[48] and they were expected "[t]o teach faithfully the Word of God, the Sacred Scriptures, in its truth and purity and as set forth in all the symbolical books of the Evangelical Lutheran Church."[49] As part of her regular job responsibilities, Perich taught a religion class and planned, led, and otherwise participated in worship services, selecting liturgical texts and appropriate hymns. These activities constituted only a fraction of her daily routine, however.[50] The school also expected Perich to act as a Christian role model for her students and to integrate faith into all subjects, though the record is unclear about how frequently Perich did this.[51]

Perich took a disability leave one autumn after falling ill and was later diagnosed with narcolepsy.[52] That winter, she informed the school that she planned to return to work in two or three months, and the school responded that it intended to amend its employee handbook to require called teachers who had been on medical leaves for more than six months to resign their "calls" in order to allow the school to fill those positions responsibly, with the possibility of reinstatement upon the unwell employee's return to health. The school was concerned that Perich would not be able to fulfill her job responsibilities, and the school's congregation passed the amendment to the handbook and replaced Perich with another teacher.[53] When Perich declined to resign her call, and when she further refused to submit to the Church's internal dispute resolution procedures, the school rescinded her call and fired her.[54] In her suit against the school, Perich claimed that the termination and threatened retaliation against her for failing to avail herself of the Church's mediation procedures violated the Americans with Disabilities Act (ADA).[55]

The case turns on the existence, nature, and scope of the ministerial exception,[56] but the Sixth Circuit's failure to consider the full range of interests implicated in the dispute made for an unsatisfactory opinion. The court decided in cursory fashion that because the average number of minutes on the clock per day that Perich devoted exclusively to religious activities was comparatively small, Perich's primary duties were not ministerial.[57] It admitted that its approach was rigid, but it followed it nonetheless.[58] And it disregarded the doctrinal and historical significance of both the ministerial exception and its application in this case.

As a result, its opinion was incapable of describing the quality of the conflict accurately.[59]

The Supreme Court reversed, but it is the Court's method even more than its result that warrants close attention. There were two issues facing the Court: whether the ministerial exception exists at all and whether it applied in this case. The Court's opinion on both questions reflected just the kind of historical, particularist, and incremental approach recommended by the method of tragedy and history.

The Social History of the Ministerial Exception

For the method of tragedy and history, any reasonable analysis must begin with the historical heritage of the ministerial exception within the tradition of religious liberty. That heritage is rich and ancient, with roots in the so-called "Papal Revolution" of the eleventh century, in which the Catholic Church, in various legal edicts including the *Dictatus Papae* issued by Pope Gregory VII,[60] separated itself decisively from the dominion of the Holy Roman emperor, King Henry IV: In 1075, "Pope Gregory VII declared the political and legal supremacy of the papacy over the entire church and the independence of the clergy from secular control."[61] Five centuries later, the Peace of Augsburg and the subsequent Treaty of Westphalia stabilized not only the issue of nation-state sovereignty over religion (*cuius regio, eius religio*), but also the power dynamics between spiritual and temporal authority.[62]

These events grounded American ideas about the freedom of "the Church,"[63] and, with time, the nature of the "separation" of church and state[64]—ideas that, at their source, have far more to do with formally recognizing the independence of distinct realms of authority than with whether the state can acknowledge the civic importance of religious traditions.[65] The institutional and jurisdictional independence of church and state as distinct loci of authority constitutes a vitally important precept of the Western—and therefore the American—political and legal tradition.[66] It explains the historical source of the American commitment both to free exercise and disestablishment that, notwithstanding the early existence of various state establishments of religion,[67] eventually came to represent the uniform position in the United States. Civil authorities ought not to use their offices to select and dismiss ministers and other employees who perform religious functions.[68] Finally, this history uncovers a fact often hidden from the modern mind: church–state independence was first sought and stimulated by *religious*, not secular, institutions. It would be a perversion of that history to strip it away with the anachronistic claim that it never even existed.[69]

The method of tragedy and history begins with this foundation of social history. It sees this historical context as an independent and presumptively valid reason to retain the ministerial exception. And it rejects any approach that would discard the ministerial exception without so much as considering, let alone grappling with, the role of social history in the development of our distinctive practice of religious liberty.[70]

The Supreme Court began with precisely this historical foundation. Chief Justice Roberts devoted an extended portion of his opinion for the Court to the history of "[c]ontroversy between church and state over religious offices," citing to the first clause of the Magna Carta in which "King John agreed that 'the English church shall be free, and shall have its right undiminished and its liberties unimpaired.'"[71] The Court proceeded with a discussion of the turbulent history of conflict between state and ecclesiastical authority in the Plantagenet and Tudor monarchies.[72] And it undertook a nuanced examination of the American colonial experience with the appointment and retention of religious authorities on the part of the state. The First Amendment, wrote the Chief Justice, was motivated in part by the desire "to ensure that the new federal government—unlike the English Crown—would have no role in filling ecclesiastical offices."[73] The Court relied on that history as a critical element in its framing of the problem of the ministerial exception. Social history was, in fact, the keystone of the Court's analysis.

The Doctrinal History of the Ministerial Exception

The doctrinal, no less than the social, history of the ministerial exception evinces a long tradition of recognizing the ministerial exception as a crucial component of religious liberty in American law. The exception was first acknowledged by the Fifth Circuit Court of Appeals over forty years ago,[74] and the overwhelming majority of federal courts of appeals have held that the doctrine exempts churches from lawsuits for discrimination in the hiring and retention of clergy,[75] though they have disagreed about the scope and application of the exception. The Supreme Court, however, is not bound by the decisions of inferior courts. It is free to go its own way. But a tragic-historic Supreme Court justice would nevertheless take notice of the fact that a flat decree that no ministerial exception exists would disrupt a mature tradition of doctrinal history. He would consider carefully the judgment of his colleagues on the bench, and he would count their accumulated wisdom as a reason—even if not a conclusive reason—in favor of recognizing the exception's viability.

Again, the Supreme Court adopted just this approach. First, the Court surveyed and reaffirmed its established church autonomy doctrine, in which it has repeatedly recognized the "spirit of freedom for religious organizations, an independence from secular control or manipulation— in short, power to decide for themselves, free from state interference, matters of church government as well as those of faith and doctrine."[76] Second, and more strikingly, the Court acknowledged the "extensive experience" of lower courts with the ministerial exception, as well as the "uniform" view of the federal courts of appeals that the ministerial exception exists, is grounded in the First Amendment, and "precludes application" of legislation such as Title VII "to claims concerning the employment relationship between a religious institution and its ministers."[77] What makes this reliance particularly noteworthy is that the Court was under no institutional obligation of stare decisis to rely so heavily on the findings of lower courts. The fact that the Court chose on two separate occasions to highlight these decisions immediately before it announced its own view of the ministerial exception suggests that the court believed in the jurisprudential importance of an existing, mature doctrinal tradition.[78]

Particularism, Incrementalism, and the Suite of Inquiries

The Court agreed that the ministerial exception exists, and it held that the exception applied in *Hosanna-Tabor*.[79] Though the details of the decision are worth exploring, it is the Court's particularist and incremental methodology that distinguishes it as one of the Court's few

tragic-historic opinions.[80] While recognizing the existence of the ministerial exception, the Court framed its discussion of the doctrine's application with these words:

> We are reluctant, however, to adopt a rigid formula for deciding when
> an employee qualifies as a minister. It is enough for us to conclude, in
> this our first case involving the ministerial exception, that the excep-
> tion covers Perich, given all the circumstances of her employment.[81]

What is important in these lines and what is reflected in the balance of
the opinion is a highly particularized set of questions about the nature
and function of Perich's duties—a suite of fact-specific inquiries—without reliance on any one of those inquiries as controlling. The Court sig-
naled that it will depend on this method, rather than any categorical rule
or monistic value, to fashion the doctrine of the ministerial exception
over time very much in the method of the common law.

This is a close cousin to the method of tragedy and history, which
is likewise guided by multiple discrete inquiries, all of which focus on
the particulars of the specific dispute at issue and illuminate the quality
of the conflict. Those individuated assessments combined to indicate
to the Court an appropriate resolution of *Hosanna-Tabor*, leaving future
controversies and difficulties undecided.

First, the tragic-historic judge would take stock of the complete panoply of clashing values. On one side, the Church's autonomy to select
teachers who perform religious functions; its freedom not to be dictated to by the state in terms that might contravene its religious beliefs
(its institutional conscience);[82] its liberty to establish a locus of moral
and institutional authority distinct from and in some measure beyond
the government's reach; and the importance of the historical heritage
and roots of the ministerial exception as one of the fundamental ideas
grounding our contemporary understanding of church–state independence. On the other side, the government's interest in seeing that its laws
are complied with uniformly and by everyone; its own interest in nonentanglement with religious entities; the civic value in promoting the well-
being of religious institutions; and the value in vindicating the state's
conception of egalitarian and other secular norms.

As to the last value, the fact that a religious institution is involved does not *diminish* the state's interest, for that would imply that other rival values are commensurable with the vindication of secular nondiscrimination. Rather, the involvement of a religious institution *complicates* that state interest, introducing other competing values of religious liberty with which that interest clashes. Moreover, at least some of the values in play are internally incompatible and incommensurable. How should the state choose between or rank order the values of nonentanglement and promoting the civic value of religious institutions? Or between nonentanglement and the equal enforcement of its laws? There is no way to select between these values systematically—choosing one that will dominate the other for all future cases—without doing violence to commitments each of which are important components of the American social practice of religious liberty. It is for this reason that a particularist and incremental approach represents the most plausible and least damaging negotiation of these conflicts.

Second, the tragic-historic judge would consider the nature of the claimant—the employee's job responsibilities. At the most obvious level, decisions about ministers or ordained clerics are different from decisions about employees who perform no religious functions at all, such as janitors or administrative aides.[83] The more difficult cases are those, like *Hosanna-Tabor*, where the employee performs both clerical and nonclerical functions. Before the Supreme Court's decision, several courts had adopted a "primary duties" test,[84] attempting to fix the respective percentages of religious and nonreligious job responsibilities. But this approach mischaracterizes the way in which a position combines together various types of work. To describe a missionary who spends 95 percent of her time building structures for potable water in an undeveloped nation and only 5 percent preaching as performing primarily nonreligious duties misunderstands the quality of her employment. That it is possible to describe "construction," "civil engineering," or "medical care" as secular activities misses the point altogether: "After all," one commenter wryly observes, "wasn't Mother Teresa's job primarily secular? Nonreligious people feed and clothe the poor all the time; no one would call those actions inherently religious."[85] The motivation of employers and employees is often difficult to discern, and the primary duties test threatens to fragment artificially the often integrated and holistic quality of a person's work.

The method of tragedy and history takes an approach more attuned to whether the employee was required to perform numerous duties and roles *that the employer* would in good faith characterize as part of its religious mission. The employer's viewpoint is most relevant because it is the employer who created and offered the position in the first place, and so it will have the clearest conception of the nature of the job. A judge following the tragic-historic method would need to be aware of the possibility of fraud on the part of the employer—for example, that the employer might attach the label "religious" to all sorts of work to make it more likely that the defense would apply. But evidence such as the employee's job description, policies issued by the employer before the onset of litigation (and consented to by the employee), or binding statements of religious doctrine setting forth the nature of a particular position within the church, is relevant to understand the employer's vision of the job and how its responsibilities relate to the religious commitments of the institution. To be sure, this inquiry requires courts to examine more evidence than is typically necessary under the primary duties test. But it would give courts a keener sense of how the position connected to the employer's religious aims without arbitrarily partitioning and quantifying job duties as religious or secular. Once again, the focus of the method of tragedy and history is on the "shallow" particulars of the case, not on the abstract and altogether too "deep" question of whether an activity is conceptually religious or secular.[86]

This was largely the approach followed by the Supreme Court, which examined the title that Perich held as well as the functions that she performed.[87] There was little question that Perich's job responsibilities, when assessed from the employer's good faith point of view, were religious. As a "called" teacher[88] and a commissioned minister of the Church,[89] Perich was required to pass a series of courses designed to educate her in Christian theology and to pass a final examination and obtain the endorsement of the Synod.[90] Her job description demanded that she include Christian themes in her regular teaching, that she teach a religion course from the perspective of a religious adherent, and that she serve as a Christian role model whenever she interacted with students.

From the Church's perspective, her job duties were integrally religious,[91] they were expressed to Perich as religious, and she agreed to perform them as such.[92]

A third inquiry concerns the nature of the claim. This is not necessarily the same issue as the nature of the employee's job responsibilities, though the two may overlap. The question here is what type of evidence a court will need to examine in order to decide whether an employer's stated reason for an adverse employment decision was sincere or pretextual. The hypothetical tort case of the "falling gargoyle" is a clear example where the nature of the claim is justiciable, irrespective of the nature of the employment.[93] Simple claims for failure to pay money on a contract might be another. Other cases may be more complex. In one, when a music director and organist of a Catholic diocese was fired, the employee alleged that he had been discriminated against on the basis of age, while the diocese claimed that the employee had failed to select and perform liturgically appropriate music.[94] Where the nature of the court's inquiry as to pretext would directly embroil it in judgments about religious doctrine—the type of music that is liturgically most appropriate, or the style of performance that best reflects the beliefs of the institution—a court is well advised to avoid the dispute.

The claim in *Hosanna-Tabor* was an allegation of retaliation by the Church for Perich's decision not to present herself to the Church's internal dispute resolution body, as required by Church doctrine. In order to decide whether the Church's termination of Perich was pretextual, a court would need to inquire into the centrality of internal mediation to the Church's religion as well as the sincerity of the Church's commitment to those practices. That commitment is theological, deriving from Saint Paul's first letter to the Corinthians admonishing them to resolve their disputes internally.[95] As the Lutheran Synod said in its amicus brief:

> These Scriptural demands, along with the authoritative church interpretations of them, are not merely good advice that the Synod is free to ignore. The Synod believes that Christians simply must resolve certain disputes within the church. Those who disobey that text disobey God, and the church that tolerates such disobedience also disobeys God.[96]

Declaring that the Church retaliated against Perich because of her unwillingness to submit to these procedures, and that the Church's dispute resolution practices are a pretext for illicit discrimination, excessively entangles the state with religion. A court would be saying that a fundamental theological practice is actually a sham.

On the other hand, churches with internal mediation procedures seem in effect to be insulating themselves from retaliation claims altogether. There is no way for a court to decide whether a particular claim is more in the nature of a simple tort or contract action or is instead a claim that will implicate religious doctrine. The internal mediation procedure neutralizes any inquiry about the nature of the claim. Though this factor favors the Church in *Hosanna-Tabor*, courts must be especially attuned to the possibility of fraud on the part of religious institutions with respect to this inquiry. It would be all too easy for a church to invoke fraudulent internal dispute resolution procedures to insulate itself from a proper evaluation of the nature of the claim. Though the Supreme Court recognized that "the point" of the ministerial exception is to ensure that religious bodies retain the authority to select their clerics,[97] it did not sufficiently account for the potential for fraud. Yet in keeping with its incrementalism, the Court did note that actions by employees sounding in tort or breach of contract were reserved for another day.[98]

A fourth inquiry involves the quality of the remedy sought. One of the values of religious liberty at stake in ministerial exception cases is the interest of the religious institution in not being compelled to accept what it otherwise could not tolerate—the forcible reinstatement of an employee, accompanied by the government's edict over the religious institution's objection that the employee is in fact a minister. That concern is less acute when the employee is not demanding reinstatement but simply seeking an award of damages. Moreover, both the state's and the religious institution's respective interests in mutual nonentanglement are implicated by the possibility of compelled reinstatement, as the state will have to monitor the day-to-day operations of the institution to ensure full compliance with its equitable order. That concern is not as salient if the employee wants nothing to do with the religious institution other than its money. At one point in the dispute, Perich sought reinstatement, but before the Supreme Court she sought only damages.[99]

Some scholars claim that the nature of the remedy is irrelevant because the government still entangles itself in ministerial control, effectively ordering the religious organization to "[a]ppoint this minister or pay a fine."[100] The Supreme Court seemed to adopt this position in *Hosanna-Tabor* as well, calling the distinction between money and reinstatement "immaterial."[101] But this way of putting the problem misstates the aim of the litigation. Perich was not seeking an either-or resolution. She was seeking money only, not money as an alternative to continued employment. And the payment of money to resolve a past conflict is less intrusive with respect to the institutional liberty of the religious organization than the compulsion to accept an intolerable minister indefinitely.

It is true that depending on the nature of the religious institution's wrongdoing, the quantity of money might be fairly substantial. Damages awards that would bankrupt a church represent a different degree of entanglement than smaller awards, because awards that would destroy an institution more closely approximate compelled reinstatement. Yet unlike the Supreme Court, a tragic-historic judge would inquire into the quantity sought and the church's ability to pay it. For nonbankrupting awards, the prospect of continuous church–state entanglement and the state's control over the identity of the church's clerics is greatly diminished. A tragic-historic judge would properly recognize that this factor—the nature of the remedy sought—should have cut in Perich's favor.

A fifth inquiry is whether the Church, in taking the employment decision that it did, is acting in accordance with its stated principles and doctrines. If the religious institution specifically indicates in an official statement of policy or in binding church documents that it does not discriminate on specific grounds, then courts might be in a stronger position to intervene. Suppose the official position of a particular church is that it is an egregious sin to discriminate on the basis of race in the selection of its ministers. Suppose further that it then rejects every single African American applicant for a clerical position over a five-year period. In a lawsuit alleging the church's violation of Title VII, a tragic-historic judge would not shield himself from evidence of the church's commitments and practices. He would not elevate church–state autonomy so high as to immunize the church absolutely from suit. Instead, if there were evidence that the church had regularly acted in ways directly contrary to its stated practices and policies, the tragic-historic judge would deem it relevant insofar as the truthfulness or sincerity of the church was concerned in making its claims to religious autonomy.

There is a thorny issue here involving discrimination on the basis of status as opposed to discrimination on the basis of particular beliefs or conduct. A religious institution might say in its official documents that it does not discriminate on the basis of sexual orientation, for example, but if it then terminated an employee who had engaged in homosexual acts, or who had taught a class of children about homosexuality in a way that directly contravened the tenets of the church, the question would arise whether the church was acting in accordance with its stated principles. In one recent case, California's Hastings Law School refused to recognize a local student chapter of the Christian Legal Society (CLS) because CLS limited membership to those who shared its beliefs, including the belief that homosexual conduct is wrong.[102] The law school denied CLS recognition because it found that CLS's limitations violated its antidiscrimination policy. The Supreme Court upheld the law school's determination and rejected CLS's claim that there was a distinction between the status of homosexuality and belief or conduct affirming the morality of homosexuality.[103]

Whatever may be said of the Court's decision in *Martinez*, when the decision-making organization is a religious institution, the situation is different. A religious institution whose documents indicate that it does not discriminate on the basis of status should be allowed to draw a distinction between status and belief/conduct. The reason goes to the historical heart of the ministerial exception: churches cannot be compelled by the state to hire clerics who disagree with the core tenets of the faith. To bar a religious institution from distinguishing between status and belief/conduct is tantamount to forcing it to hire or retain a minister who does not share its faith.

In *Hosanna-Tabor*, this factor clearly favors the Church. Perich refused to take part in the internal dispute resolution procedures plainly required by Church doctrine, even though she held herself out as a minister.[104] The Church was also selective about whom it chose as a called teacher and a commissioned minister, and the substantial responsibilities of a called teacher were clearly explained to Perich.[105] In making this inquiry, the method of tragedy and history focuses on the particular—on the Church's specific practices and procedures, on its stated aims and commitments, and on the extent to which the Church acted in a manner consistent with its beliefs—in order to achieve a complete understanding of the conflict. The Supreme Court likewise considered many, if not all, of these factors.

In sum, while not all of the factors in the suite of inquiries favor the Church, on the whole the Church's claims are stronger than Perich's on the applicability of the ministerial exception. And yet in deciding this case in favor of the Church, the tragic-historic judge would acknowledge the values sacrificed thereby—most especially the values of formal equality and nondiscrimination as conceptualized by the state—so as to ensure their viability in future cases. More generally, the suite of inquiries pursued by the method of tragedy and history in this and similar contexts illustrates the quality of ideal decision making—one that emphasizes the particularism and incrementalism that these conflicts demand.

The Method of Tragedy and History Distinguished

Various scholarly treatments of the ministerial exception demonstrate the dangers of slighting either the government's or the religious institution's interests by operation of a hard-edged and categorical rule. These views are useful for distinguishing the method of tragedy and history as a unique and intermediate approach to these issues.

Legal scholar Caroline Corbin's approach represents one side of the legal academy's often dichotomous views. Corbin repudiates the ministerial exception wholesale. She "rejects the notion that church autonomy is a distinct constitutional right," and she argues that Establishment Clause values that have been traditionally used to justify the exception "are no longer viable" after the Supreme Court's turn toward formal neutrality.[106] She also claims that the distinction between the free exercise of institutions and individuals is unconvincing because it "amounts to privileging the secondary right over the primary one."[107]

Corbin's is a comic monistic approach; all possible interests in religious liberty are reduced to a single value—neutrality. It also gets things backward from a historical perspective. The primary historical right was the freedom of the outer church—the church conceived as an external institution—from which the freedom of the inner church (the freedom of conscience) eventually developed.[108] Likewise, while it is true that the Court has recently turned toward formal neutrality in its establishment decisions, one wonders why that "necessitates" abandoning any concerns about state entanglement with religious institutions and interests.[109] In fact, it is only necessary if one agrees that the Constitution has room for one value. The method of tragedy and history denies this view. Allowing a law suit to proceed against, for example, the Catholic Church because it "discriminates" against women in the selection of its clergy does violence to all of the values underwritten by the ministerial exception. It entangles the government directly in religious doctrine,[110] and so impinges on a religious institution's autonomy. As a result, it requires the government to monitor and supervise the doings of churches and to intervene constantly to ensure that its commands are obeyed. And it displays an unseemly statist arrogance—a presumption that any competitor interpretation of values such as equality that conflicts with the state's must be stamped out wherever it exists.

On the diametric opposite end lies Paul Horwitz's expansive view of the ministerial exception. Arguing from a perspective of "sphere sovereignty," Horwitz writes that the ministerial exception is one of the most critical protections against the incursion of the state on what is unquestionably at the core of a religious organization's right to self-constitution and determination.[111] For Horwitz, this autonomy protects employment decisions based on race and sex just as it protects theological decisions. But Horwitz goes even further:

> A more robust version of institutionalism, however, would treat the question more categorically: churches qua churches are entitled to a substantial degree of decision-making autonomy with respect to membership and employment matters, regardless of the nature of the employee or the grounds of discrimination.[112]

A tragic-historic view would not subscribe to an expansion of the ministerial exception to shield any church employment decision. The state has interests in these decisions as well—values that it has a stake in vindicating—and if the church is to seek exemption, it should explain why the proscriptions of Title VII or any other law would offend its doctrines. An absolute bar on state interference as to any employment decision for the sake of preserving institutional autonomy goes too far in elevating one type of value of religious liberty above all others.[113] As Richard Garnett puts it: "it is precisely because secular, liberal, democratic governments like ours have an 'interest' in the content, and therefore in the 'development,' of religious doctrine—an interest that such governments will, if permitted, quite understandably pursue—that religious freedom is so fragile."[114]

Closer attention to the tragic clash of values would require distinguishing between situations where an act ordinarily proscribed by nondiscrimination laws is related to and justified by a religious institution's doctrines and practices and other situations in which the church appears to be acting against its stated doctrines and practices. Likewise, the type of employment position ought to make a difference, as should the nature of the claim and the quality of the remedy. Adopting an approach akin to the method of tragedy and history—as did the Court in *Hosanna-Tabor*—is likely over the long run to produce a vigorous and thriving common law of the ministerial exception and free exercise generally.

CHAPTER 10

Establishment Clause Applications

O ne serious difficulty in applying the method of tragedy and history to the Establishment Clause has been described as an innate
feature of the clause: it seems to forbid the weighing of interests.[1] This
"all-or-nothing" approach has had the regrettable effect of stunting the
natural process of examining different types of conflicting values and
practices in Establishment Clause contexts by a kind of fixation on the
"definitional stage,"[2] where the selection of a test, and the analysis of a
practice by measurement against that test, assumes cardinal importance.

Thus, for example, whether one chooses a neutrality test or a coercion
test will predetermine whether a prayer at a public event constitutes an
establishment or not. Yet once one has settled on the test, the conflict
will rarely be about whether the test is inadequate to capture the nature
of the dispute but instead simply whether a practice qualifies as an establishment under the test. Establishment Clause jurisprudence seems,
therefore, preprogrammed from its inception against a tragic-historic
approach. The method of tragedy and history dissolves this difficulty by
turning attention toward the tragic theses and by requiring that decision
making and conflict resolution conform to the historic theses.

This chapter reviews some of the social history of the meaning of
establishment in the United States, concluding that outside of a core of

settled applications, its meaning has always been a matter of contestation among clashing values. As in the discussion of free exercise, I do
not endorse an originalist methodology.[3] While the method of tragedy
and history considers evidence from the late eighteenth-century historical record as probative of contemporary meaning, its appeal to history is
attuned to the gradual changes occasioned by legal and social customs
and traditions, of which that early historical record forms an important
part. The discussion here does not uncover new evidence of the original meaning of the Establishment Clause. Instead, the reason to survey
various treatments of the Establishment Clause that focus on its early
history is to illustrate that the clash of values at the core of the method of
tragedy and history has always been a part of the ongoing effort to give
meaning to the term *establishment*. The preprogrammed, comic monistic approach to establishment is a modern innovation and is untrue to
the social history of the meaning of establishment. That meaning did
not spring fully formed and systematic, like Athena, from the minds of
James Madison and Thomas Jefferson into the 1940s-era opinions of the
Supreme Court, to be plugged in reflexively to contemporary church-
state disputes.[4] The interpretive conflicts swirling about the meaning of
establishment are an ingrained part of the clause's social history,[5] and for
the tragic-historic judge, those conflicts must influence decision making.

Several Establishment Clause issues—the state display of religious
symbols, prayer at public school graduations, and the use of religious
words in the Pledge of Allegiance, in political speeches, and on the cur-
rency, among others—have already been addressed in previous chapters. This chapter examines the contribution of the method of tragedy
and history to three other establishment issues: government funding of
religious institutions, tax exemptions for religious entities, and teaching
about religion in public schools.

The Social History of Establishment

The First Amendment forbids Congress from making any law "respecting an establishment of religion,"[6] and since 1947 the clause has been
held by the Supreme Court to apply to state governments as well.[7] And
yet with the exception of certain indisputable core meanings, most

uncontroversially the proscription against a national church,[8] the precise contours of "establishment" have always been a matter of contestation. As of the adoption of the First Amendment in 1791, roughly half of the thirteen colonies had some form of established religion,[9] a situation that continued for approximately thirty to forty years and whose undoing was a localized and gradual "state-by-state affair."[10] Complicating the process of "disestablishment" was that establishments were not grounded in a single and straightforward declarative law, but were instead "constituted by a web of legislation, common law, and longstanding practice."[11] Michael McConnell has divided this network of establishmentarian customs and traditions into six categories: control over doctrine, governance, and personnel; compulsory church attendance; financial support; prohibition on dissent; public use of churches;[12] and restrictions on political participation.[13]

Notwithstanding general consensus among early Americans that these practices constituted the core of establishmentarian regimes, however, sharp disagreements existed—and persisted—about the extent to which disestablishment required something more than the elimination of this core. Even religious dissenters from establishments were not interested in rigorous separation of church from state: as Philip Hamburger has argued, while antiestablishment dissenters such as the Baptists opposed financial benefits for particular religious institutions and championed freedom from government penalty, "these protesters typically did not reject the utterly conventional assumption that there was a necessary and valuable moral connection between religion and government."[14] And with respect to the core of disestablishment, the New England colonies' localized establishments[15] are a case study in the wildly unsettled and shifting meaning of establishment in early America,[16] exemplified in the nuanced understanding of John Adams—one in which various notions of establishment are mutually in tension:

> Commenting on Massachusetts' support for churches a few years before the Commonwealth essentially codified that approach in the 1780 constitution, Adams wrote that the "laws of Massachusetts were the most mild and equitable establishment of religion that was known in the world, if indeed they could be called an

establishment". . . . [D]espite the efforts of numerous New England
proponents of the standing order to distance themselves from the
term . . . New Englanders simply did not share one definition of
establishment, irrespective of whether they were for or against whatever it was.[17]

Formally establishment churches ceased to exist by the 1830s,[18] and yet
it was Adams's conflicted approach to the right relationship of church
and state that often held sway in the pre-1940s Supreme Court era.[19]
Likewise, numerous influential political sermons[20] of the pre- and
postrevolutionary period evince a complicated, layered, and shifting
understanding of the meaning of "establishment" in early America.[21] As
Calvinist and Harvard divinity professor David Tappan put it in a 1792
sermon entitled "A Sermon for the Day of General Election," while a
"union" between the temporal and spiritual orders was undesirable and
represented "the main pillar both of civil and religious tyranny . . . we
may consistently recommend to the two orders, a liberal and patriotick
combination for the general good. There is indeed, in many respects, a
natural alliance between intelligent, virtuous magistrates and ministers,
in a free and christian state."[22] The substantial differences among members of the founding generation over the proper relationship between
religion and government—and the flexibility of the text of the Establishment Clause itself—suggest that no thick, let alone uniform, consensus
understanding was either needed or achievable by the founders at the
time of the drafting of the Bill of Rights.[23] Indeed, it was exactly *because*
the founders did not take themselves to be cementing in the Constitution a single principle or value of religion–state relations—because they
believed that they were constitutionalizing something unremarkable—
that the Establishment Clause was accepted.

Direct religious tax assessments of the type favored in the New England colonies were largely abandoned by the first few decades of the
nineteenth century,[24] but many other controversies about the meaning
of establishment continued. As early as the 1830s, for example, there was
disagreement about the extent to which disestablishment and complete
church–state separation were synonymous. President Andrew Jackson
justified his decision not to declare a national day of fasting (as an official

observance of the ravages of a cholera outbreak) on the basis of a conception of proper church–state relations that most Americans would not have recognized as implicating any establishmentarian concerns.[25]

Such conflicting understandings are little different than the disputes that rage today about the constitutionality of a federal law creating a "National Day of Prayer,"[26] or a state statute setting aside a "period of silence for 'meditation or voluntary prayer'" at the beginning of each public school day,[27] or the permissibility of prayers at the beginning of legislative sessions.[28] These conflicts are perennial in large measure because they instantiate tragic clashes of the values of religious liberty across the centuries that have never been soluble by recourse to a single principle or interpretive master rule.[29] Indeed, the early social history of establishment makes plain that few practices rest on more solid ground than the legislative association of American government with Providence: "God and country were linked in the legislative mind, and public recognition of that fact via chaplains and prayers was an element of Congress's ordinary course of business, a practice that continues, in one form or another, to the present day."[30] From the perspective of the method of tragedy and history, the long-standing and unbroken quality of this particular social practice creates a powerful presumption—in the absence of extremely strong countervailing values—against disruption by courts.[31]

Contestation outside the core about the meaning of establishment continued during the ratification of the Fourteenth Amendment in the mid-nineteenth century as well. Debates about the meaning of establishment developed in a different direction from the founding during the nineteenth century, focusing on the rights of the individual as against the state, rather than the rights of the state against the federal government.[32] Moreover, notions of disestablishment as strict separation assumed, first, a nativist and virulently anti-Catholic valence and, second, an openly secularist cast. The anti-Catholic calls for separation served as a cohesive political and cultural agent for an increasingly fragmented Protestant majority.[33] Yet ideas of total separation and disestablishment were neither identical nor coextensive in the nineteenth century, as there was sizable agreement that some contact and "mutual cooperation" between religious and state institutions were salutary for both.[34] Thereafter, late nineteenth-century liberals advocated an identity between religious liberty and secularist ideas of separation, appealing for strategic reasons to a single, unambiguous, unified historical principle of constitutional disestablishment.[35] It was this separationist value that made its way into the opinions of the 1940s Supreme Court, but that ideal was deeply contested in the late nineteenth century. As noted by the author of a retrospective titled "Religion in America, 1776–1876": "At the close of a century, we seem to have made no advance whatever in harmonizing the relations of religious sects among themselves, or in defining their relation to the civil power."[36] Just as it did in the eighteenth and nineteenth centuries, the clash of values evinced by the conflicts of religious liberty—and by pervasive disagreement about the proper relationship of religion and state—continues to reassert itself in case after case to the present day.[37]

All of this social history of conflict and disagreement about the meaning of establishment should not be surprising. Excepting the core of disestablishment, we have ourselves been unable to agree on a single, unified, and unchanging value or principle of antiestablishment; our forebears were no different.[38] That the religion clauses have been incorporated against the states is a settled question in constitutional law at this point in our legal history. Notwithstanding the view that courts ought to wipe away decades of precedent for originalist reasons, there is little prospect of turning back the clock to a preincorporated view of establishment. More importantly, a tragic-historic approach, with its preference for incremental change and its presumption in favor of existing decisional and social patterns, would (for rule-of-law reasons, among others) recoil from undoing generations of legal practice and custom.

Yet if the Supreme Court and federal courts generally are to remain substantially involved in religion clause conflicts at the state and local levels, then they ought to recapture the ethic animating efforts to resolve these controversies which predated the Supreme Court church–state opinions of the 1940s—one that did not purport to announce any general law or iron rule of American church–state relations, but that instead recognized the clashing values and the particular and local character of these disputes in mediating them.[39] Just as early Americans "did not share a uniform understanding of the proper relationship between church and state,"[40] so, too, do contemporary Americans lack such a systematic understanding—let alone a single value or set of values that embodies a consensus view about establishment's meaning.

This is not to say that there is no body of doctrinal or social custom that gives any shape at all to the meaning of establishment, nor is it to relegate the Establishment Clause to a kind of nihilistic postmodern emptiness. Just as "it is possible to narrow the range of historically supportable usages within the entire set of possible links between religion and government" in early America, so, too, is it possible today.[41] First, as discussed in the preceding, there is the settled core of disestablishment that delimits its meaning. Federal and state-established churches are forbidden. Direct financial aid to religious organizations—even if distributed equally among religious groups—is forbidden. Government cannot control the makeup, membership, or doctrine of religious groups; it cannot issue religious doctrine; it cannot compel religious belief, practice, or participation; and it cannot punish religious dissent (together, these limits combine to form the liberty of conscience). Government cannot delegate official civic functions to religious institutions.[42] And it cannot condition political participation of any kind on membership in a religious group.[43] Second, government favoritism or preferential treatment for one religion over other religions is impermissible if the reason for such preferential treatment is that the favored religion is true and the others are false.[44] Third, government favoritism for religion generally over nonreligion is not permitted if the reason for that favoritism is that religion is true and nonreligion is false.[45] Fourth, government cannot target religious or nonreligious groups for discriminatory treatment.

This body of categorical proscriptions on federal and state power does not exhaust the range of cases in which a court might find that the government violated the Establishment Clause. As discussed in Chapter 7, a court following the method of tragedy and history could conclude that, for example, the government's decision to display a religious symbol violates the Establishment Clause under the specific facts of the case. The point is simply that, outside the context of propounding religious truth, government displays of religious symbols are not part of the Establishment Clause's categorical prohibitions. More generally, outside the limits of the core of disestablishment, many legitimate and constitutionally viable competing values clash. When those conflicts arise, they should be recognized as falling outside the core and within a zone of reasonable contestation. Outside the core, comic monistic theories of disestablishment should be resisted.[46] Conflicts outside the core should not be resolved by recourse to an overarching principle or value of religious liberty. Courts should instead consider the landscape of current case law and the particular clashing values at stake and make decisions that proceed in incremental fashion by the light of existing doctrinal and social history.

The Establishment Clause largely preserved the widespread disagreement, conflict, and contestation existing in the early Republic about the proper relationship between religion and government. That was its function, and that is its most lasting and strikingly contemporary legacy. Courts that decide Establishment Clause conflicts should proceed with this social history foremost in mind.

Government Subsidies and Tax Exemptions

The government's direct financial support of churches has always represented a clear example of impermissible establishment.[47] The objection to direct government subsidy of religious organizations—principally churches—was one of the primary considerations leading to universal disestablishment in the states.[48] In contemporary religion clause jurisprudence, the most prominent and heavily litigated type of funding conflict concerns not aid to churches themselves but to parochial private schools.[49]

And yet, religious tax exemptions of various kinds—for property, income, unemployment, and sales taxes—generally have not raised any constitutional problems.[50] Several justifications relying on a panoply of values of religious liberty have been offered to explain the distinction between direct government funding and tax exemptions. The difference might be justified in separationist terms: because the "power to tax involves, necessarily, a power to destroy,"[51] a negative decision by the state with respect to the imposition of a tax is conceptually different from a positive decision to provide financial assistance. The decision not to tax fosters the autonomy of church from state, whereas the decision to subsidize intermingles the two.[52] A different explanation accepts the long-standing historical practice of tax exemptions for religious institutions as an exception to the general rule,[53] the abrogation of which could destroy them and consequently damage the state.[54] Churches are given tax exemptions because historically they have been deemed beneficent from a civic point of view,[55] because they have undertaken civically useful activities, and because the alternative might be to lose them.[56] A third type of justification concerns the difficulty of valuing church property and whether the process of undertaking such a valuation is both unfeasible (how to put a cash value on spiritual worth?) and poses unacceptable risks of state entanglement. Justice John Marshall Harlan offered a fourth explanation: tax exemptions are justified because of the "cultural and moral improvement" that is part of many religious organizations' core missions, provided that the state exempts other organizations with similar functions.[57] Finally, tax exemption comes at a price: the state forgoes taxes from religious institutions only on the condition that the latter not "participate" or "intervene in" political campaigns or otherwise devote a large part of their activities to influencing legislation.[58]

Some writers take the view that all tax exemptions for religious entities are constitutionally impermissible. Noah Feldman, for example, would eliminate all state funding of religious organizations, including tax exemptions,[59] as inconsistent with the proposition that "the core separation of church and state in the American experiment . . . has historically been *institutional:* keeping government and religious entities apart."[60] Feldman's view, which is deeply informed by early American historical practice, is that "the reason for such separation is straightforward: to prevent churches and other religious organizations from entering into the fight for public resources, where taxes would go to support religion."[61] Though Feldman does not emphasize tax exemptions, his general approach does not distinguish between indirect aid to private religious schools in the form of vouchers, direct state aid to religious charities, and tax exemptions for religious entities. All, in his view, are unconstitutional.

The method of tragedy and history is more attuned to the differences between various financial arrangements as filtered through the lens of the social history of establishment. One of the primary arguments that Feldman raises in favor of an "absolutely no aid" principle is the stock justification that the government's financial support of religious institutions has been especially divisive:

> [S]tate funding actually undercuts, rather than promotes . . . cohesive national identity. . . . Even when filtered through vouchers distributed by the government and directed by individual choice, state financial aid for religious institutions like schools or charities does not encourage common values; it creates conflict and division.[62]

The fear of civic divisiveness is an important component of Feldman's particular institutional separationist concerns, and it is the value that dominates his policy recommendations.

Yet from a historical perspective, overlooking the specific type of funding involved is curious. The no-aid absolutist is on firmest ground historically with respect to government funding of religious schools. Indeed, Feldman recounts effectively the nineteenth-century struggle of American Catholics to obtain funding for their schools, just as did the nominally "nonsectarian" public schools of the Protestant majority.[63] It was the desire to seal off Catholic schools from public revenue that inspired the effort of Congressman James G. Blaine of Maine to introduce a federal constitutional amendment in 1875 that would have absolutely prohibited any state money from being used to benefit "any religious sect"—a tacit reference to Catholicism.[64] Later nineteenth-century liberal secularists went further, insisting that religious institutions should be barred from receiving government "benefits distributed on purely secular grounds,"[65] though this stricture did not succeed legally at the time.[66]

Direct government subsidies for religious schools, let alone religious tax assessments of the type proscribed by the core of disestablishment,[67] are not the same as support through voucher programs or other forms of indirect assistance.[68] Vouchers for religious schools within a neutral program of distribution would not have been understood to violate the Establishment Clause as an original matter.[69] Nevertheless, the disconnection between the core proscription against compelled assessments and subsidies for religious schools that emerged in the nineteenth and twentieth centuries may be overstated.[70] Both involve compelled financing and both present the same family of concerns that lie at the core of the social history of establishment. The social history of compelled financing merits careful attention in the context of the school-funding debate, and it is an additional reason in support of the method of tragedy and history's cautious and intermediate approach to this issue.

The most important school-funding case of the last generation is *Zelman v. Simmons-Harris*,[71] which dealt with the constitutionality of a city program permitting parents to send their children to religious (many of them Catholic) schools at partial government expense. *Zelman* implicates numerous clashing values of religious liberty: neutrality against autonomy; neutrality against separationism; and conflicting understandings of equality—the unequal impact of religious schools disproportionately benefiting from government voucher subsidies against the unequal impact inherent in the government's overall favoritism of secular public schools over religious schools. There are other values at stake as well. Indirect government aid to parochial schools in the form of vouchers makes it possible for poorer students to obtain a better education. Vouchers provide at least some educational choice to those who otherwise might have no other option at all than to attend dismally performing public schools, thereby mitigating at least to some extent the problems of pervasive educational inequality in America.[72]

Both doctrinal and social history counsel caution in this area. Cases such as *Zelman* and *Mitchell v. Helms* augured a major shift in the Supreme Court's doctrinal approach to the question of school funding,[73] though not one that was entirely unexpected given the Court's school aid decisions in the last two decades.[74] Moreover, public schools have long represented a cornerstone of civic and moral education in the United States.[75] Many people, including several Supreme Court justices,[76] have long viewed public schools as vital vehicles for teaching social equality and tolerance: "[T]he twentieth-century state school is designed to serve a function very similar to that of the eighteenth-century state church: imparting community values and promoting moral conduct among ordinary citizens, upon whose virtue republican government ultimately rests."[77]

Social historical concerns are therefore especially acute—indeed, not only values, but the American institutions in which they are instantiated, seem to clash—and a judge applying the method of tragedy and history would regard with suspicion a radical departure from a long-standing practice that might well threaten the institution of the public school for the sake of vindicating an abstract theory of "differential impact." A full embrace of school vouchers, even if administered on a neutral basis, does not properly account for unforeseeable dangers to the institution of public school education (which can ill afford further degradation) that a broad and untested regime of systematic public aid to religious schools might bring. Indeed, were financial support of private and religious schools to reach extensive proportions, it is probable that public schooling would lose any capacity to offer a diverse atmosphere, bringing with it the specter that "students might be sorted out on lines of religion, ethnicity, and class more than they now are."[78] In light of the social history of the core of establishment, which demonstrates that fiscal support of religious institutions is one of the paramount concerns of disestablishment, the method of tragedy and history would opt for a more reticent view of school-funding questions.

Nevertheless, given the arguments brought to bear by proponents of vouchers—which also rest on powerful values including educational equality of opportunity, formal neutrality as between religion and non-religion, and nondiscrimination against religious education—condemnation of all school-funding arrangements is inappropriate as well. A tragic-historic judge would regard the program in *Zelman* as constitutional given its comparatively small size and limited scope, but a larger program or one that gave exclusive support to religious schools would be constitutionally problematic.[79] Larger or more extensive programs—particularly any that are national in scope—would increase the competition for government funds. The greater and more pervasive the competition for money, the greater the likelihood of triggering the core concerns animating the social history of disestablishment discussed earlier.[80] The Court's current and near-exclusive focus on neutrality with respect to the school voucher question entirely ignores the issue of scope:

> [T]he government funding cases leading up to and including *Zelman* articulate an approach to the question of government funding that eliminates consideration of the scale of government support, the

> local balancing of religious and secular interests, and the dangers of
> a centralized monopoly.... The doctrinal logic of the new neutrality
> is categorical.[81]

The categoricity of the "new neutrality" is as much conceptually at odds with the tragic theses as it is inconsistent with the social history of establishment. *National* establishment sits at the very core of the social historical understanding of disestablishment concerns. A system of nationalized subsidies to religious organizations, even if indirect and filtered through the autonomous choices of parents, is more constitutionally concerning than a local voucher program—in part because of the exponentially greater potential for competition for money and the consequent friction it would engender.

But by comparison with the school context, the evidence for civic divisiveness in the context of state aid to religious charities is considerably weaker. In describing the proliferation of Roman Catholic orphanages in the early to mid-nineteenth century, Feldman acknowledges this historical difference: "These Catholic institutions received direct state support no differently than their nonsectarian Protestant equivalents, without generating the sort of controversy associated with the schools."[82] Indeed, the state support offered to religious charitable organizations was motivated by the hard realities of the "urbanization and industrialization of the post–Civil War years, and the growing poverty that accompanied them,"[83] a clear example of the values of religious liberty clashing with values both internal and external to them.

Yet even if one accepts the view that civic divisiveness is an evil that the Establishment Clause is intended to mitigate, that cannot be the end of the story. To the extent that "open political debate about which religious institutions deserve[] funding and which d[o] not" is divisive,[84] it is *also* divisive to issue a constitutional edict that religious charities and parochial schools are to receive no money at all.

Moreover, the question of tax exemptions for religious organizations— a practice of even older vintage than the issue of direct funding—is not even directly implicated by the social history of establishment. There is little evidence that tax exemptions for religious organizations historically have been excessively divisive. Indeed, given the historical practice of granting tax exemptions to religious charities in recognition of their civic contributions, an argument might well be made that *greater* civic divisiveness might well ensue if those tax exemptions were now made unconstitutional for the sake of conformity to the sort of global compromise between "secularists" and "values evangelicals" that Feldman advocates.

More importantly, there are many other values to be considered in the tax exemption context, including the value of equality of treatment. Admittedly, these are values that implicate free exercise more than establishment concerns, and the *Smith* decision seems to foreclose most such arguments. Nevertheless, equality is implicated: religious organizations "have a substantial claim of justice to be treated like other private organizations."[85] If nonreligious organizations receive government support—either directly or through the mechanism of tax exemption—a certain understanding of the value of equality is damaged if religious organizations are not eligible for similar assistance.

Indeed, these conflicts often reflect the structural patterns described in the first thesis. In *Bob Jones University v. United States*, for example, where the federal government's decision to withdraw tax exempt status from a university that prohibited interracial dating was upheld by the Supreme Court,[86] two understandings of equality contended against one another: equality of institutional treatment by the government (or equality of access to a benefit) against a more substantive notion of racial equality. And intersecting these two values are numerous other values of religious liberty—entanglement worries (does a state that wields the taxing power bend church teaching to its will?), concerns about individual and institutional autonomy, and the degree to which Bob Jones University promotes "cultural and moral improvement" apart from its racially discriminatory policies[87]—all of which judges must attempt to describe accurately if the tragic quality of the conflicts are to be managed adequately. And there is finally the overarching structural tension between permissible accommodation—a free exercise value—and impermissible sponsorship—an establishment value—that tax exemption cases bring into high relief.

For these reasons, a simplistic solution prohibiting financial support of any kind—irrespective of its historical roots and the specific values it instantiates—is inadvisable. Systematic answers offered in the spirit of Kulturkampf resolution are not up to the task of negotiating the perpetual conflicts of values in religion clause disputes.[88]

In the context of tax exemptions for religious organizations—a practice with an ancient pedigree[89] that is deeply entrenched in American doctrinal and social history[90]—the best approach accepts a strong presumption in favor of tax exemptions and yet is attentive to the ways in which exemptions may conflict with other deeply held values both internal and external to religious liberty. *Bob Jones* may have been properly decided, but if it was, the reason is *not* that government funding of religious organizations—direct or indirect—is categorically anathema.[91]

Public Schooling and Religious Learning

The relationship between the Establishment Clause and teaching about religion in public schools appears to be a problem only imperfectly handled by the method of tragedy and history. In part, this is due to the dichotomous terms in which the Supreme Court has traditionally addressed this question—as one of "sponsorship" versus "non-promotion,"[92] or the "secular" versus the "sectarian."[93] Constitutional assessment in these types of cases seems to depend on an initial conclusion about whether religion is being taught as true, or instead as a historical, cultural, and intellectual phenomenon.[94]

This simple binary view of the issue does resolve some conflicts: mandatory daily devotional prayers in public schools[95] are an example of the type of coerced worship that violates the core of disestablishment.[96] Likewise, the teaching of creationism in a biology course to the exclusion of evolutionary theory represents unambiguous government sponsorship of certain religious beliefs as true,[97] as of course would the teaching of any religious belief as the exclusive and unchallengeable truth. A graduation prayer presents a more complex question from a tragic-historic point of view,[98] but the sponsorship/nonsponsorship approach is adequate for religious liberty conflicts that are generally a part of the comparatively distant past.

The difficulty is that the disputes about religious learning in public schools today are rarely amenable to this type of analysis. Part of the reason is the difficulty of neatly separating those aspects of teaching about religion that contribute to a student's educational growth and those that relate exclusively to matters of religious creed and practice and that have no civic educational component. Justice Robert Jackson once wrote that "for good or for ill, nearly everything in our culture worth transmitting, everything which gives meaning to life, is saturated with religious influences."[99] More modestly, religious learning can contribute to students' educational growth and cultivation, and knowing how and in what measure to make religious learning a part of the public school curriculum is a complicated educational issue.

But it is not, in the main, a constitutional issue, and so there is some truth to the view that the method of tragedy and history is largely inapplicable in this context—not because it is incompetent to manage these particular questions, but because they are not generally constitutional questions at all.

A relatively recent case decided by the Third Circuit Court of Appeals illustrates the point. In *Stratechuk v. Board of Education*, New Jersey's South Orange-Maplewood School District enacted a policy prohibiting the singing of "celebratory" religious music at school-sponsored events.[100] The school district's recognition that "[m]usic, art, literature, dance and drama along with religious customs and traditions . . . may be used to broaden our students' awareness of the many elements that comprise our diverse American culture," and its belief that religious music was properly part of the curricular experience if it was "presented objectively" and "neither inhibit[ed] nor advance[d] any religious point of view," led the district to some bizarre decisions.[101] For example, the district prohibited the Martin Luther King Gospel Choir from performing at any December concerts and likewise prohibited the performance of traditional fare such as "Joy to the World" and "Silent Night"; but it allowed the performance of Antonio Vivaldi's "Gloria in Excelsio (Cum sancto spiritu)" ("Glory in the Highest [With the holy spirit]") "because '[t]he program does not have a religious orientation and it does not refer to a holiday.'"[102] Other music that was permitted included "Concerto VIII Fatto per la notte di natale" ("Concerto VIII Made for Christmas Eve")[103] and "Agnus Dei/Cum Sanctis."[104]

The father of two students who attended public school in the district sued the district for violation of the Establishment Clause, and the court rejected the claim. Although the Establishment Clause does not prohibit a public school from performing religious music, neither does it require it to perform such music.[105] Moreover, not all religious music was banned from the December concerts: religious music was permitted, apparently so long as its references to religion were unlikely to be understood. The policy also satisfied the endorsement test because it conveyed a message neither favoring nor disfavoring religion.[106]

From the perspective of the method of tragedy and history, *Stratechuk* was properly decided. The values at issue—the enjoyment of certain specific kinds of Christmas or religious music at a concert or the sense in which inclusion of some types of religious music and not others might be perceived to exclude certain people—are simply not substantial enough to ground a constitutional challenge. They are extremely distant from the core of the social history of disestablishment, implicating none of those fundamental concerns. In these types of situations, the method of tragedy and history refrains from intervening.

Had the facts in *Stratechuk* been different, however, the plaintiff might have had a colorable claim under a tragic-historic view. For example, had the district banned the performance of all religious music at any time of year, including during the holiday season, on the ground that it wanted to maintain an ostensibly "neutral" or "secular" ambience, that type of policy would have rightly been perceived as specifically targeting religious expression for unequal treatment.[107] Not all "actions taken to avoid potential Establishment Clause violations" are whitewashed simply because they "have a valid secular purpose."[108] Moreover, because religious expression in public settings—including in schools—was never part of the core social history of disestablishment, a policy banning it entirely simply does not represent any part of the customs and practices constitutive of disestablishment. The fact that a school district wishes to present itself as "secular" is not a disestablishmentarian concern. Likewise, if the district had *required* that religious music, along with other music, be sung by all students during the December concert month, objecting students or their parents would have had a colorable establishment claim because of the compelled participation in religious activity (again, a core disestablishment concern). Or, had the district required the performance of *exclusively* religious music during the December concert and banned all music that did not explicitly reference, say, Christmas or the birth of Jesus Christ, that would have violated the Establishment Clause under a tragic-historic approach, as it would implicate several values at the core of disestablishment.

Under the actual facts of *Stratechuk*, however, the method of tragedy and history would reach the same outcome as did the Third Circuit. While one might sympathize with the plaintiff and believe that the district's policy and its implementation were churlish and ignorant, there is no basis for constitutional intervention. As much of a shame as it may be for public school students who enjoy certain music to be barred from performing it in public schools, the Constitution is not implicated when a school district allows "Frosty the Snowman" but prohibits "Silent Night." The method of tragedy and history adopts a pluralistic orientation that counsels abstention when the alleged violations are insufficiently powerful. This does not necessarily distinguish it from rival approaches. The point is merely that a judge applying the method of tragedy and history is also capable of knowing when *not* to intervene.

CHAPTER 11

Objections and Replies

Having seen how the method of tragedy and history might operate in several free exercise and establishment contexts, some concluding observations about its potential weaknesses are in order. Perhaps unsurprisingly, many of the qualities that render the method of tragedy and history appealing might also be deemed deficiencies.

The Objection of Lawlessness

The most powerful objection is that the method of tragedy and history is not sufficiently organized as a theory to provide any guidance to judges or litigants, and that it threatens to unravel into judicial lawlessness. Indeed, the method of tragedy and history may not be a "theory" at all, but only a mood or outlook that might inform a different, more structured theory of the religion clauses. This objection mirrors the genre of critique voiced by legal scholar Thomas Berg in his incisive article on religion clause "anti-theories": "[T]here is a fairly widespread view . . . that if judges cannot find a coherent single principle—or at least a rather small and manageable set of principles—on a subject, they should exit entirely and let the politically accountable branches decide such questions prudentially."[1] Part of the objection's force derives from the argument that to ask so much of the judiciary invites a dangerous and lawless triumphalism that imperils the rule of law and even democratic government itself. Because of the non-rule-like quality of the method of tragedy and history, judges applying it are free to decide cases unpredictably, unequally, and in whatever way they like. A related criticism is that judges simply will not be very good at, or will not have the time for, the type of particularistic, consuming, and historically sensitive inquiries demanded by the method of tragedy and history. The method is overly ambitious and unrealistic in light of the responsibilities of courts to decide cases promptly.

It is true that the method of tragedy and history does not offer a straightforward rule, and it is also true that its aspirations are ambitious. Indeed, this objection goes to the very heart of the tragic-historic project. Several responses are therefore warranted.

First, it is precisely the notion that only a monistic rule-based legal theory can satisfactorily resolve questions of religious liberty that the method of tragedy and history is meant to challenge. Predictability is an important value in adjudication, but it is only one value, so that even if it were true that monistic accounts are much more predictable than their pluralistic counterparts, that should not be a decisive or even a presumptive reason for selecting them. It has been this book's burden to demonstrate that there are many reasons to be skeptical about what rule- or value-delimiting theories can offer.

Second, courts themselves are similarly skeptical, a view that has emerged in the common-law refusal to accede to academic demands for theoretical systems that champion master values. This was seen in Chapter 8, where the ostensibly hard-edged formal neutrality of *Employment Division v. Smith* has been consistently massaged by courts—at times using the stated exceptions within *Smith* itself, at times trading on ambiguities internal to *Smith*'s logic—to account for and accommodate factual nuance. The point is not that courts are nefariously manipulating the purity of *Smith*. To the contrary, some of the doctrines that they are using were explicitly contemplated by the *Smith* Court. Rather, what that discussion demonstrates is that an approach like the method of tragedy and history is, in some sense, inevitable. *It is what courts do, and what they will do, irrespective of the theoretical regime imposed on them.* The Supreme Court's recent decision involving the ministerial exception makes that plain enough: the Court explicitly adopted the historical and particularist features of the tragic-historic method.

Third, and related to this point: monistic theories offer the illusion of certainty and predictability. They provide conceptual cover for what is always in some measure a plural-valued assessment by courts. The method of tragedy and history is more honest about the realities of adjudication, and so it is also more legitimate in a liberal democratic polity—more candid and more transparent. It confronts the inevitably particularistic assessments that courts undertake even when they work from an ostensibly hard-edged rule. A judge applying the method of tragedy and history is therefore able to use doctrine to communicate more clearly and directly with other government actors.

Indeed, the "incoherence" in Establishment Clause jurisprudence that religion clause scholars bemoan is, in fact, a healthful symptom of many courts' profound reluctance to impose comic monistic rules on enormously different types of cases. And for all its flaws, the current Establishment Clause regime is neither lawless nor antidemocratic. In many cases, it simply represents judges' struggles with the tragic theses—a kind of unspoken and unacknowledged method of tragedy and history at work in the law. It is this gradual, halting, and evolutionary development—one that is "often messy. It is not like solving a math problem; it is not algorithmic"[2]—which characterizes the "progress" (if such it can be called) of the law of religious liberty.

Fourth, if actually compelled to choose between a simple and predictable rule that mutilates the conflicts of religious liberty in the service of theoretical cohesion and a complicated approach that allows a judge to aspire to analyze the conflicts on the terms that they merit, the choice for the latter seems straightforward. But in fact, to worry about such either-or compulsions is pointless. It is a fabrication of those who imagine that perfect theoretical coherence is ever possible, let alone desirable, in law. There is nothing qualitatively more lawless in the method of tragedy and history than exists already in several of the standards or approaches that are, or have been, in use by courts throughout the history of religion clause conflict.

Fifth, the objection overlooks the highly constrained quality of the method of tragedy and history—its deep reliance on incremental adjudication and doctrinal and social history. Cognizant that the tragic theses have the potential to injure the rule of law values of predictability and equality of application, the historical theses emphasize gradualism, contextualism, and the normative force of precedent in resolving these disputes. Contrast this with the approach of, for example, Justice Thomas in *Van Orden v. Perry*, which would have overturned decades of precedent with a sudden coup de grâce, all for the sake of elevating a single,[3] rather unassuming, value of religious liberty to overriding status—a result that would have destabilized profoundly the procedural values of the rule of law and that would have made the same reductive mistake of which many legal theorists are guilty.

Sixth, with respect to the issue of ambition, it is sensible to concede that the method of tragedy and history is an ideal—an aspiration—that judges might more or less nearly achieve. There should be no illusion that attaining the ideal is easy or simple. And it may well be that some courts will be less capable—for reasons of heavy caseloads, differential expertise, or other institutional pressures—of applying the method of tragedy and history than others. But not all courts are so overworked that the approach is altogether infeasible. It is also true that certain religion clause tests and judicial approaches have achieved the tragic-historic ideal in greater degree than others, so there is at least some reason to believe that courts might, with time and experience, more nearly approximate it. Some have already done so.

In the free exercise domain, there is no closer model than the Court's decision in *Hosanna-Tabor*.[4] In the Establishment Clause context, the approach adopted by Justice Breyer toward government religious displays in *Van Orden*,[5] or by the Ninth Circuit in the Mount Soledad cross display case,[6] or by Justice Alito in the Mojave Desert Cross case,[7] is more in keeping with the method of tragedy and history than the approach of Justice Thomas in *Van Orden*, which would "abandon" all precedent in favor of the conclusion that the Establishment Clause has no application against the states at all, or that if it does, the only evil against which it protects is "legal coercion,"[8] or than Justice Stevens's view in the Mojave Desert Cross case, which would conclusively decide the cross's indelible, monolithic, legal meaning for all conceivable cases to come.[9]

It might be that the real root of the objection of lawlessness is that the method of tragedy and history enables a court unrestrainedly to imprint those values on society that it deems best. Indeed, perhaps readers may feel that way about the results that, throughout this book, I have indicated that I favor—that I have smuggled overarching commitments into the discussion that have not been given full expression or that have not been adequately defended.[10] Because of the unpredictability of the method of tragedy and history—and because of its presumptive preference for social and doctrinal historical settlements as well as the modesty of doctrinal movement that it prescribes—I am able to reaffirm other deeper commitments that lie below the surface of the method.

The objection is, on its face, a fair one. It is true that the method of tragedy and history provides less predictability of outcome than might be optimal, and that distinctive value choices lie embedded in the methods that it favors. Indeed, it may be some answer to say that it provides less of *every* value than might be optimal. But the objection risks becoming quite unfair if it goes on to claim that other approaches are immune from these difficulties.[11] They are not. All theories, of religious liberty no less than of any other legal discipline, reflect deep political and ethical commitments. And no theory—or at least no theory worth defending—can promise an optimal degree of predictability without sacrificing the substantive values at its core. If the objection is really that without an increase in predictability there is no reason to make any change at all in our approach to religious liberty, let alone to opt for the method of tragedy and history, then it sorely misapprehends the fundamental reason to engage in the activity of legal theory at all: so that we may think well—accurately, truly, and in a way that best captures the world's complexity—about the law.

The Objection of Nonexclusivity

A second objection is that there is nothing in the method of tragedy and history that is applicable exclusively to the law of religious liberty. The method of tragedy and history, in this view, is in reality an approach either to constitutional law or a view about the limits of legal theory generally, but it is not about religious liberty specifically. The weak version of the objection is that the tragic-historic method need not be solely a theory of religious liberty; it might have application to various other legal fields. The strong version of the objection is that the method is no more applicable to the jurisprudence of religious liberty than to any other area, and even perhaps less applicable.

The weak version of the objection has merit, but it does not upset any of this book's arguments. It may well be that the insights of the tragic-historic method are applicable to other legal fields. I have suggested elsewhere that criminal law is one possibility,[12] constitutional interpretation another,[13] and surely there are more. Indeed, the disposition of the method of tragedy and history might be a corrective to comic methodological assumptions in many legal fields. Be that as it may, and whether or not the approach may have broader implications for legal thought, the specific subject of this book is the capacity of the method of tragedy and history to explain and understand the idea of religious liberty in constitutional law. The weak version of the objection does not disturb that project.

The strong version of the objection, by contrast, is in error, because it overlooks certain crucial merits of the tragic-historic method as it relates specifically to the law of religious liberty. One of these is that the tragic quality of religious liberty disputes is dealt with not incompetently by deference to doctrinal and social history. Because of its deference to existing social and decisional patterns, the tragic-historic method is well equipped to manage the fundamental challenge facing the law of religious liberty—the jumble of religious pluralism and the innumerable conflicts that it engenders—without creating significant disruption. The qualities of the tragic-historic method—humility, caution, and theoretical diffidence—are particularly valuable in this context.

This may strike some as rather faint praise. Why, after all, should we set our aspirations as low as a modestly competent constitutional interpretive practice for a subject as consequential as religious liberty? In fact, in light of the conflicts that were described in the first three theses, the drawbacks of more ambitious approaches are so substantial that the method of tragedy and history is promising enough. It also has the advantage of avoiding large-scale and unsettling departures from existing constitutional practice in an area that is particularly volatile, shifting, and resistant to theoretical reduction.

A second virtue of the tragic-historic method in this specific context relates to the unique structural tensions between the religion clauses of the First Amendment. The Free Exercise Clause protects the right to religious belief and practice by prohibiting government interference.[14] The Establishment Clause proscribes government privileging or sponsorship of religious belief and practice.[15] One need not go so far as to claim that the clauses are antithetical to recognize that tension and conflict inhere within the textual structure[16]—an internal, intrinsic, and ineradicable pressure that the Supreme Court has repeatedly acknowledged.[17]

There is at the very least an association between protecting religion and privileging it that renders sharp qualitative distinctions between the two clauses untenable unless one is able to distinguish between features of religion that deserve constitutional protection and others that should not be privileged.[18] The distinction between permissible protection and forbidden privilege may be elusive. The tension between the clauses suggests that an approach which is attuned to conflict—indeed, which foregrounds conflict—may negotiate that tension with greater success than its rivals.

A third advantage of the method of tragedy and history concerns the problem of religion's constitutional definition. The subject matter of the religion clauses is itself contested, as is the subject matter against which religion is differentiated. These are unique difficulties in constitutional law.[19] The tragic-historic method seems particularly apt because the very subject matter of what can be regulated, and in which ways, is itself highly—perhaps even essentially[20]—contested, thus rendering it not at all amenable to any theoretical abstraction, single value, or value set. This is the reason that the most persuasive studies of what religion ought to mean for constitutional purposes are oriented toward social history. The "family resemblance" approach, for example, in which courts decide what qualifies as religious by "comparison with the indisputably religious, in light of the particular legal problem involved," drawing from established religious traditions to ground such evaluations but without "prejudging whether some conditions are absolutely necessary or usually crucial,"[21] has strong affinities with the tragic-historic method. That approach uses as its raw analogical material neither any particular substantive view of what ought to qualify as religious nor any specific function that religious belief might perform, but instead the social histories and "manifested practices of institutions" that all agree are religious.[22] This type of approach—which considers the social history and customs of particular cultures—is entirely sensible in light of the instability of the category "religion." More importantly, recourse to doctrinal and social history is crucial in an area given to so much conflict and contestation.

The Objection of Pragmatism

A third objection to the method of tragedy and history is that it is too negative. It does not give sufficient credit to legal theory's meliorative powers. Theory not only orders, but it also expresses our highest aspirations for the ways in which we hope and expect society to progress. Stated in this strong form—as a bald assumption that the more systematic and tightly structured a theory is, the more likely it is to bring about moral progress and improvement—the objection seems to overlook the very arguments against such organized theories that were made in Part One. One kind of counterargument might simply borrow from Stuart Hampshire's response, when confronted with similar claims about the inevitable improvements that would be wrought by consequentialist theories of moral progress:

> [H]ope of continuing improvement, if it survives at all now, is now largely without evidence. Lowering the barriers of prohibition, and making rational calculation of consequences the sole foundation of public policies, have so far favoured, and are still favouring, a new callousness in policy, a dullness of sensibility, and sometimes moral despair, at least in respect of public affairs.[23]

A more tenable version of this objection would posit that in order for the method of tragedy and history to be viable as a theory of religious liberty, it must take a more positive view of what it can accomplish for the political order. It must aim at the best all-things-considered outcome— that is, at something very much like legal pragmatism.

As with the first objection, there is indeed some truth to this critique. The historical orientation of the method of tragedy and history points toward a comparatively pessimistic view of legal theory's role as an agent of moral progress. The method of tragedy and history is pessimistic not in the usual sense of the word—its adherents are not necessarily personally morose or unhappy people. Instead, the method of tragedy and history is pessimistic in virtue of its tragic view of the business of legal theory—that legal theory ought not to aspire to be a vehicle through which to solve the problems of religious liberty systematically, or without the acknowledgment of loss and regret. But this does not mean that the method of tragedy and history posits a theory of decline, dissolution, or thick skepticism about the possibility of constitutionally protected religious liberty. The method of tragedy and history is a negation, not the opposite, of comic theories of religious liberty.[24]

An adherent of the tragic-historic method also need not deny that there has been progress in thinking about the social practices of religious liberty, or that in many ways the freedom of religion has become firmer, more capacious, and more substantial in contemporary liberal democracies than it once was or than it remains elsewhere in the world. But tragic-historic theorists also believe that progress in ideas of religious liberty have incurred significant costs—costs that often enough are uncompensable and go unperceived. Advances and progress in conceptions of religious liberty have been both beneficial and harmful.

As a result, the method of tragedy and history adopts the disposition of custom described in Chapter 5 when faced with religious liberty disputes, and it dissents from theories of religious liberty that proceed from comic monistic abstractions because they are methodologically committed to denying or marginalizing the costs that attend change. An exclusive focus on equality, or autonomy, or neutrality, or the separation of church and state—however understood—as the master value of religious liberty obscures the reality of the other clashing values of religious liberty, and the extent to which these theories must sacrifice them in the service of their respective overriding ideals.

Yet the pessimism of the method of tragedy and history is not a debilitating despair of the possibility of religious liberty, or a retreat from the practice of judicial review in favor of purely political resolutions. It is judges, primarily because of their institutional roles, obligations, and internal norms, who are best able to adopt the tragic-historic cast of mind and apply it to the conflicts of religious liberty.

In fact, one way of thinking about the tragic-historic method's pessimism is as a rejection of legal pragmatism as a theory of constitutional adjudication.[25] The method of tragedy and history does not celebrate the serenity that is said to follow from the pragmatic relinquishment of the aspiration to any "master theory,"[26] and it does not subscribe to an all-things-considered approach that "weigh[s] text and history, precedent and policy, principle and consequences" until the result somehow reflects "a blend of statesmanship and workmanlike lawyering."[27]

The method of tragedy and history is not pragmatically antifoundationalist, in the sense of disclaiming any explanation for its approach beyond the desire to reach the best all-things-considered result with any available tool.[28] Its foundation is the tragic one developed in the first three theses. Moreover, it rejects, as in the fourth and fifth thesis, the pragmatic idea of "second-order perfectionism" in constitutional adjudication,[29] which is linked to the notion that "there *must be* an answer to our fundamental questions, even if we have not found it yet, and that this answer will deliver us from suffering."[30] It is pessimistic, and antipragmatic, in its insistence that the conflicts of religious liberty are not riddles waiting to be solved or consequentialist cost-balancing puzzles but very often the product of disputes where there is not one correct ranking of values, and where any given ranking will result in actual sacrifice.

Lastly, and on a more positive note, the method of tragedy and history is not as antiprogressive as it might appear, since it aims to awaken and open the minds of decision makers to the values that underwrite the ways of life that come into conflict in legal disputes. As Martha Nussbaum puts it:

> [H]ard cases like these, if one allows oneself really to see and to experience them, may bring progress along with their sorrow, a progress that comes from an increase in self-knowledge and knowledge of the world. An honest effort to do justice to all aspects of a hard case, seeing and feeling it in all its conflicting many-sidedness, could enrich future deliberative efforts.[31]

That increased receptivity to the multifaceted quality of conflict will issue in improvement of its own—not progress toward a comically unified system of legal valuation, but progress in the layered acuity with which judges confront and cope with the tragedies of judgment.

Conclusion

Legal theory's misapprehensions have had a distorting influence. There has been too little thought for the predicaments and irreconcilable conflicts faced by law. There has been too much for constructing systems that solve problems conclusively and without tragic remainder. We would do better to cast a colder eye on the sanguine pieties of legal theory. We may find that our theories, when composed in minor keys, are less negative than we had supposed. Legal theory, stripped of its pretensions, has the power to understand the world, to imagine why it is the way that it is, and, in the end, both to change and to be changed accordingly. It is through a sense of the conciliating force of social and doctrinal history—a presumptive willingness to be guided by history as a negotiating power—that legal theory offers its most promising possibilities, for to "feel the past as part of oneself is to know that it is alive, ever-changing in relation to the self that necessarily alters as it passes through time."[1]

The method of tragedy and history, in contrast with its rivals, is a fragile theory. Some may see this as a disqualifying characteristic but they are wrong to do so. Theorizing about religious liberty is a precarious and byzantine activity fraught with the possibility of oversimplification and dogmatic entrenchment. Yet fragility in one's theories—as in most of life—is not often admired. To be fragile is to be ill at ease, disquieted, and unsteady. As a psychological quality, fragility is easily mistaken for weakness, but it may have more in common with a kind of melancholy moderation. Still, the reasons for fragility's low esteem are not hard to guess. To be fragile is to be confronted with the discomfiting facts of impermanence and contingency.

Yet such is the condition of the elusive social practices of religious liberty. In response, the fragile often seek refuge from their anxiety in reassuring narratives of invulnerability or comprehensive mastery. Eventually, if the truth of their fragility is successfully suppressed, they may even come to forget it and to develop the sense that they are sturdier than they had supposed. When the test comes, the surprise of its coming is all the more acute. It seems that those who are fragile profit from attending to their condition, perhaps even loving it a little, but at all events never showing it anything less than a circumspect and probing concern. That is the cast of mind that the method of tragedy and history brings to its subject.

In his masterpiece, *Pensées*, Pascal penetrates both the glories and follies of the intellectual enterprise:

> All the dignity of man consists in thought. Thought is therefore by
> its nature a wonderful and incomparable thing. It must have strange
> defects to be contemptible. But it has such, so that nothing is more
> ridiculous. How great it is in its nature! How vile it is in its defects![2]

The wonder of theory is that it has the power to illuminate our understanding of the world. Those who create it can so sharpen our sight that each snowflake is crisply identifiable in its microcosmic uniqueness. But such keen vision can distort our view of the storm—blinding us to the ways in which inconsistency, conflict, the mundane dissonances of lived oppositions, loss, and regret permeate and are constitutive of common experience, in law and elsewhere. Theory can obscure the loyalties and dispositions of custom that those committed to the social practices of religious liberty hold dear. Sharp vision—like sharp thought—is in the end valuable only if it does not distort the complexity of the world. Today's legal intellectuals may feel themselves "[i]solated and divided by the tangled forest of a society impenetrable to rational organization,"[3] but their prescriptions are unlikely to pierce through the barriers behind which the world hides itself without a keener sense of the place of tragedy and history.

The law is no seamless web, no comic dream. It is a tradition, a historical practice engaged in across time to manage the unsolvable predicaments of life's unceasing conflicts. No sphere of law manifests these struggles more richly than the constitutional commitment to religious liberty. The particularism of the common law—"a merry road, a mazy road,"[4] whose crookedness will not be straightened by the abstractions of theoretical system—is the most fruitful avenue through which to approach the tragedies of judgment. The procession of legal theories designed to disguise conflict by rendering it a problem about which we have not yet thought hard enough have amplified it. Theory and the world in which it is claimed to apply have grown further and further apart "till the explanation has become so complete as not to interfere with the thing explained."[5] The storms of conflict—the values that vie violently against one another in perpetuity—demand an intellectual scaffolding supple enough to withstand the buffeting. These clashes may be conciliated only. They will never be resolved.

It has been the aim of this book to offer a theory that does justice to conflict; that attempts to understand it before pronouncing what should be done; and that adopts a cautious, tentative, and abidingly historical attitude toward the decisions that it reaches. Its fragility is a strength; its reticence a defense. But it is its genial openness to the world's values, past and present, and its struggle to grasp the tragedies of what is sacrificed when those values are lost, that is its distinctive mark.

Conflict there will be. But even in times of strife and acrimony, wisdom marinates in the broth of tragedy and history. And it endures.

Notes

INTRODUCTION

1. See, e.g., Steven D. Smith, "Discourse in the Dusk: The Twilight of Religious Freedom?," 122 *Harv. L. Rev.* 1869, 1871 (2009) (reviewing 2 Kent Greenawalt, *Religion
   and the Constitution: Establishment and Fairness* (2008)) ("Probably the most common adjective used in descriptions of the contemporary jurisprudence of religious
   freedom is 'incoherent.'") (quoting Steven G. Gey, "Vestiges of the Establishment
   Clause," 5 *First Amendment L. Rev.* 1, 4 (2006)).
2. 494 U.S. 872 (1990). In *Smith*, the Court ruled that the Native American religious
   practice of smoking peyote need not be exempted from an Oregon criminal law
   against drug possession. Id. at 890. In doing so, the Court fundamentally reshaped
   the existing constitutional law of religious accommodations.
3. See, e.g., Douglas Laycock, "The Supreme Court's Assault on Free Exercise, and
   the Amicus Brief that Was Never Filed," 8 *J.L. & Religion* 99, 102 (1990) (*Smith*
   was "inconsistent with the original intent, inconsistent with the constitutional text,
   inconsistent with doctrine under other constitutional clauses, and inconsistent with
   precedent"); Michael W. McConnell, "Free Exercise Revisionism and the *Smith*
   Decision," 57 *U. Chi. L. Rev.* 1109 (1990); Ira C. Lupu, "Employment Division v.
   Smith and the Decline of Supreme Court Centrism," 1993 *BYU L. Rev.* 259, 260
   ("*Smith* is substantively wrong and institutionally irresponsible"); John Witte, Jr. &
   Joel A. Nichols, *Religion and the American Constitutional Experiment* 138 (3d ed.
   2011) ("The *Smith* case was widely denounced as a travesty to religious liberty").
4. See, e.g., Alan Brownstein, *Introduction to the First Amendment: The Establishment of
   Religion Clause* 15 (Alan Brownstein ed., 2008) ("There are few areas of constitutional
   law that are as controversial and unsettled as the interpretation of the Establishment

Clause of the First Amendment. The case law interpreting and applying the Establishment Clause is routinely condemned as arbitrary, incoherent, and inconsistent"); Daniel O. Conkle, "The Establishment Clause and Religious Expression in Governmental Settings: Four Variables in Search of a Standard," 110 *W. Va. L. Rev.* 315, 315 (2007) ("Establishment Clause doctrine is a muddled mess, at least as it relates to religious expression in governmental settings"). The point is also ably noted in Paul Horwitz, *The Agnostic Age: Law, Religion, and the Constitution* (2011).

5. Isaiah Berlin, "Political Ideas in the Twentieth Century," in *Liberty* 55, 56 (Henry Hardy ed., 2002).

6. See "Commedia," in *The Encyclopedia of Dante* 181, 185 (Richard Lansing ed., 2000) ("[S]tandard medieval definitions . . . associate comedy with fraught beginnings and happy endings . . ."); compare Jack M. Balkin, *Constitutional Redemption: Political Faith in an Unjust World* 81–82 (2011) ("If the Constitution is a tragedy, it is not a tidy story where only those at fault suffer. On the other hand, if the Constitution is a comedy, then like a comedy it has a happy ending").

7. Dante refers to the *Inferno* as a "comedy" in at least two places. See Dante Alighieri, *Inferno*, cantos XVI, XXI (Robert Pinsky trans., 1994) (1472); see also "Commedia," *Encyclopedia of Dante*, 185–186 (discussing the reasons for Dante's decision to designate the work a comedy).

8. Dante Alighieri, *Paradiso*, canto XXX (John D. Sinclair trans., 2d prtg. 1962) (1472); see also Giuseppe Mazzotta, *Dante's Vision and the Circle of Knowledge* 240–241 (1993) ("But the poet knows what his comic vision means. He knows, through his musings on play and his own imaginative effort, that tragedy, with its all too solid horrors, may not be real").

9. See Dante, *Inferno*, canto I, at 4–5.

10. See Dante, *Paradiso*, canto XXX, at 434–435.

11. Aristotle, *Poetics* 47–49 § 1449b (Stephen Halliwell ed. & trans., Loeb Classical Library ed. 1995).

12. Martha C. Nussbaum, *The Fragility of Goodness: Luck and Ethics in Greek Tragedy and Philosophy* 5 (rev. ed. 2001).

13. 2 G. W. F. Hegel, *Aesthetics: Lectures on Fine Art* 1196 (T. M. Knox trans., 1975).

14. Ronald M. Dworkin, *Freedom's Law: The Moral Reading of the American Constitution* 38 (1996).

15. By monism, I intend the view that all values can be systematized according to a single scale or formula of worth, in order to resolve (or dissolve) legal disputes that implicate the religion clauses. See George Crowder, "Two Concepts of Liberal Pluralism," 35 *Pol. Theory* 121, 125 (2007).

16. Ronald M. Dworkin, *Justice for Hedgehogs* 1, 7 (2011) ("This book defends a large and old philosophical thesis: the unity of value"); compare Isaiah Berlin, *The Hedgehog and the Fox: An Essay on Tolstoy's View of History* (1993).

17. An account of these theories is offered in Chapter 1. It should by this point be clear that the term *comic* is employed throughout this book not in the ordinary sense of humorous or insubstantial, but as a term of art that contrasts with my own approach. Indeed, far from being silly or frivolous, some of the most interesting, thoughtful, and powerful theories of religious liberty are comic in the sense used here.

18. See Lyng v. Northwest Indian Cemetery Protective Ass'n, 485 U.S. 439 (1987).

19. As we will see in Chapter 1, a monistic account of religious liberty need not be egalitarian, though some of the most influential versions are.

20. See Hanoch Dagan, "Pluralism and Perfectionism in Private Law," 112 *Colum. L. Rev.* 1409 (2012).

21. Stuart Hampshire, *Justice Is Conflict* 38–39 (1999).

22. Arthur O. Lovejoy, *The Great Chain of Being* 312 (1960).

23. See, e.g., Antonin Scalia, "The Rule of Law as a Law of Rules," 59 *U. Chi. L. Rev.* 1175 (1989).

24. John Finnis, *Natural Law & Natural Rights* 279–280 (2d ed. 2011) ("Lawyers are likely to become impatient when they hear that social arrangements can be more or less legal, that legal systems and the rule of law exist as a matter of degree . . . and so on"). For a sympathetic description of law's reduction of conflicts to "bivalent" possibilities, see Timothy A. O. Endicott, *Vagueness in Law* 72–74 (2001) ("It is a consistent feature of legal systems that legal institutions treat legal standards as if their application were bivalent. . . . Juridical bivalence radically simplifies some of the law's most difficult tasks").

PART I. RELIGIOUS LIBERTY AND THE COMEDY OF LEGAL THEORY

1. James Fitzjames Stephen, "Liberty, Equality, Fraternity," in *Liberty, Equality, Fraternity, and Three Brief Essays* 23, 54 (1991) (1873).

2. See Sanford Levinson, "Is It Possible to Have a Serious Discussion about Religious Commitment and Judicial Responsibilities?," 4 *U. St. Thomas L.J.* 280, 283 (2006); see also Sanford Levinson, *Wrestling with Diversity* 26 (2003); Jack Balkin & Sanford Levinson, "Thirteen Ways of Looking at *Dred Scott*," 82 *Chi.-Kent L. Rev.* 49, 79 (2007) ("One of us ([Sanford] Levinson) has suggested that most constitutional theorists are almost inevitably addicted to 'happy endings' in constitutional interpretation").

3. Thomas C. Berg, "Religion Clause Anti-Theories," 72 *Notre Dame L. Rev.* 693, 694 (1997).

4. See, e.g., William James, "The Sentiment of Rationality," in *The Will to Believe and Other Essays in Popular Philosophy* 63, 63–66 (1956) (1897) (describing the "sentiment of rationality" as the need for order in disorder and for reconciling the evident and distressing diversity of the world around us in comfortably simple theory); see also Isaiah Berlin "Two Concepts of Liberty," in *Liberty* 166, 216 (Henry Hardy ed., 2002) ("There is little need to stress the fact that monism, and faith in a single criterion, has always proved a deep source of satisfaction both to the intellect and to the emotions").

1. THE MONISTS

1. Some egalitarian arrangements may be instrumentally valuable, in that they secure some other good or avoid some other evils. But the egalitarian accounts of religious

liberty discussed here make the more ambitious claim that equality is the crucial, if not the sole, reason that religious liberty ought to be protected.

2. There would be no value in the equal distribution of nonvaluable objects (a perfectly equal distribution of particles of gravel on all of the gravel driveways in the country, for example), so that the comic egalitarian must attach value both to the fact of equal distribution and to some conception of the value of what is distributed.

3. Martha C. Nussbaum, *Liberty of Conscience: In Defense of America's Tradition of Religious Equality* 21–22 (2008). It may come as a surprise to see Nussbaum's account of religious liberty characterized as a comic egalitarian view, since she is well known for her substantial contributions to pluralist political theory. See generally Martha Nussbaum, *The Fragility of Goodness: Luck and Ethics in Greek Tragedy and Philosophy* (updated ed. 2001). Nevertheless, in her work on religious liberty, Nussbaum is clear that equality is the master value—not only the master political value, but also the master moral value.

4. Id. at 21.

5. Id. at 2 ("Liberty of conscience is worth nothing if it is not equal liberty").

6. Id. at 21.

7. Id. at 22.

8. Id. at 22, 24.

9. Id. at 12, 25. Elsewhere, I have criticized Nussbaum's position at length. See generally Marc O. DeGirolami, "No Tears for Creon," 15 *Legal Theory* 245 (2009).

10. Id. at 229; see also Martha C. Nussbaum, *Women and Human Development: The Capabilities Approach* 86 (2001) ("A focus on capabilities as social goals is closely related to a *focus on human equality* . . .").

11. Christopher L. Eisgruber & Lawrence G. Sager, *Religious Freedom and the Constitution* (2007); see also Christopher L. Eisgruber & Lawrence G. Sager, "The Vulnerability of Conscience: The Constitutional Basis for Protecting Religious Conduct," 61 *U. Chi. L. Rev.* 1245 (1994).

12. Eisgruber & Sager, *Religious Freedom*, 9.

13. Id. at 14.

14. Id. at 53.

15. Id. at 13, 15, 54.

16. Id.; see also id. at 52 ("Equal Liberty insists that aside from this deep and important concern with discrimination, we have no constitutional reason to treat religion as deserving special benefits or as subject to special disabilities").

17. Id. at 264.

18. Id. at 59, 264. E&S's broad sense of discrimination might have assisted the Native American plaintiff in *Employment Division v. Smith*, however. Their approach is echoed in Martha Fineman's claim that "vulnerability" is the strongest foundation for the value of human equality. See Martha Fineman, "The Vulnerable Subject: Anchoring Equality in the Human Condition," 20 *Yale J. L. & Feminism* 1, 10 (2008).

19. Eisgruber & Sager, *Religious Freedom*, 59, 264.

20. Id. at 17–18.

21. Id. at 19.

22. Id. at 19–20. "Disparagement" seems for the authors to be the establishmentarian equivalent of what "discrimination" is for free exercise.

23. Id. at 166, 173. Nevertheless, E&S see an "asymmetry" between secular meditation and religious prayer: because references to religion present particularly acute disparagement concerns, E&S argue that courts must be especially sensitive when religious language is used by public school teachers and administrators. Id. at 174.

24. Id. at 134, 136.

25. Lynch v. Donnelly, 465 U.S. 668, 688 (1984) (O'Connor, J., concurring); County of Allegheny v. ACLU, 492 U.S. 573, 595 (1989); Eisgruber & Sager, *Religious Freedom*, 130. E&S often disagree with Justice O'Connor's application of the endorsement test, however.

26. Id. at 131–132.

27. Id.

28. Id.

29. Id. at 132–133.

30. Id. at 135–136.

31. See Stratechuk v. Bd. of Educ., 587 F.3d 597, 601, 605 (3d Cir. 2009) (opining that the decision of a public school to exclude a gospel choir from a holiday concert was reasonably related to a concern about violating the Establishment Clause).

32. See Lee v. Weisman, 505 U.S. 577, 633–635 (1992) (Scalia, J., dissenting) (discussing inaugural prayers and Thanksgiving proclamations); Marsh v. Chambers, 463 U.S. 783 (1983) (holding that a chaplain offering a prayer at the beginning of each session of the Nebraska legislature does not violate the Establishment Clause).

33. Eisgruber & Sager, *Religious Freedom*, 132.

34. See Jaroslav Pelikan, *The Vindication of Tradition* 79–80 (1984). Pelikan describes trenchantly the inextricability of religious tradition from aesthetic experience. Listen only, he says, "to two or three settings of the Mass, to hear how the composer has been able to find . . . a vehicle for an utterly personal and subjective voice. . . . So idiosyncratic is each of them that some superficial interpreters have been tempted to dismiss the common element in all of them, which is the text of the Mass, as no more than a pretext which allowed the composers to say what they would have said anyway, since, after all, the text was 'merely traditional.' But tradition is not so 'mere' as all that, even when the Mass is composed by Mozart the Catholic Freemason or Bach the orthodox Lutheran or Beethoven the believer/unbeliever."

35. See Marc O. DeGirolami, "The Problem of Religious Learning," 49 *B.C. L. Rev.* 1213, 1221 (2008) (quoting Bd. of Educ. v. Allen, 392 U.S. 236, 260 (1968) (Douglas, J., dissenting)).

36. See Ira C. Lupu & Robert W. Tuttle, "The Limits of Equal Liberty as a Theory of Religious Freedom," 85 *Tex. L. Rev.* 1247, 1259 (2007) ("The social meanings of displays are occasionally simple and obvious, but they are frequently complex and multi-faceted, and we have no confidence that Equal Libertarians can make them less so").

37. Eisgruber & Sager, *Religious Freedom*, 135.

38. Id. at 133, 136.

39. Id. at 135.

40. Id. at 136–137.

41. Id.

42. 465 U.S. 668, 671 (1985).

43. Id. On the other hand, the *Lynch* display was temporary, perhaps decreasing the disparagement quotient.

44. Id.

45. Eisgruber & Sager, *Religious Freedom*, 143.

46. See Van Orden v. Perry, 545 U.S. 677, 737–747 (2005) (Souter, J., dissenting).

47. Id. at 681 & n.1.

48. Id. at 742–743 (Souter, J., dissenting).

49. Id.

50. Id. at 743.

51. In a recent controversy, an atheist group and several others have sued New York City to exclude the so-called "Ground Zero Cross" from a Memorial and Museum commemorating the terrorist attacks of September 11, 2001. See Complaint, American Atheists, Inc. v. Port Authority of New York and New Jersey, No. 1108670 (N.Y. Sup. Ct. July 26, 2011), *available at* http://atheists.org/upload/WTC_Complaint.pdf. The cross is a group of steel beams found amid the debris of the World Trade Center after the attack whose proportions resemble a Christian cross. The precise reasons for the cross's planned inclusion at the Memorial and Museum—its inspirational, historical, aesthetic, cultural, and religious value—are extremely difficult to keep conceptually pure.

52. Eisgruber & Sager, *Religious Freedom*, 147.

53. See Gurinder Singh Mann et al., *Buddhists, Hindus & Sikhs in America* 102 (2002).

54. For related discussion, see Lupu & Tuttle, "Limits," 1254.

55. See 2 Kent Greenawalt, *Religion and the Constitution: Establishment and Fairness* 188–190 (2008).

56. 437 F.3d 1 (2d Cir. 2006).

57. Id. at 3–4.

58. Id. at 25.

59. Skoros was Roman Catholic. Id. at 54.

60. Eisgruber & Sager, *Religious Freedom*, 197.

61. See Lupu & Tuttle, "Limits," 1259.

62. County of Allegheny v. ACLU, 492 U.S. 573, 677 (1989) (Kennedy, J., concurring and dissenting in part).

63. Eisgruber & Sager, *Religious Freedom*, 173, 269–270.

64. See Thomas C. Berg, "Can Religious Liberty Be Protected as Equality," 85 *Tex. L. Rev.* 1185, 1207 (2007).

65. Id. at 1205–1206.

66. Eisgruber & Sager, *Religious Freedom*, 63.

67. See Lupu & Tuttle, "Limits," 1269 ("It is very difficult to imagine that any other form of employer could successfully insulate itself from the civil rights laws with respect to its leaders").

68. Greenawalt, *Establishment*, 63.
69. Id. at 125–126.
70. Berg, "Can Religious Liberty," 1206.
71. Eisgruber & Sager, *Religious Freedom*, 161.
72. Id. at 201–221 (arguing that if the government offers private school choice options, the state has a "valid, nondiscriminatory reason for wishing to retain control over how public funds are spent").
73. Id. at 11–12 ("The variety of possible conflicts is as vast as the variety of religious obligations in America—which is to say, about as vast as one can imagine").
74. Id. at 21.
75. Id. at 102.
76. Id.
77. Charles E. Larmore, *Patterns of Moral Complexity* 42–43 (1987); see also id. at 53 (discussing neutrality as a strategy for either resolving or bypassing disagreement).
78. See generally Symposium, "The Supreme Court's Hands-Off Approach to Religious Doctrine," 84 *Notre Dame L. Rev.* 793 (2009).
79. Neutrality might approach the separationist-sounding view that the state ought to have as little influence on religion as possible. See Mark DeWolfe Howe, *The Garden and the Wilderness: Religion and Government in American Constitutional History* 149 (1965) (describing Roger Williams's view that "government must have nothing to do with religion lest in its clumsy desire to favor the churches or its savage effort to injure religion it bring the corruptions of the wilderness into the holiness of the garden").
80. See Steven D. Smith, *Foreordained Failure: The Quest for a Constitutional Principle of Religious Freedom* 77 (1995) ("Perhaps the most pervasive theme in modern judicial and academic discourse on the subject of religious freedom is 'neutrality'"); see generally Ira C. Lupu, "The Lingering Death of Separationism," 62 *Geo. Wash. L. Rev.* 230 (1994).
81. See Daniel O. Conkle, "The Path of American Religious Liberty: From the Original Theology to Formal Neutrality and an Uncertain Future," 75 *Ind. L. J.* 1, 11 (2000) ("In the 1980s, the Supreme Court continued to apply the doctrinal framework of *Sherbert* and *Yoder*, but, at least in hindsight, the Court's rejection of a series of religious-exemption claims pointed toward a shift from substantive neutrality to formal neutrality . . .").
82. See Zelman v. Simmons-Harris, 536 U.S. 639, 662–663 (2002) (upholding a school voucher program on the basis that public funds were neutrally distributed and left decisions about how they were to be spent to private choice); Mitchell v. Helms, 530 U.S. 793, 801 (2000) (plurality decision permitting government to lend state materials to religious as well as secular schools on the basis of school enrollment); Agostini v. Felton, 521 U.S. 203, 231 (1997) (upholding a program for funding teachers to teach secular, remedial courses at religious schools because "[public] aid is allocated on the basis of neutral, secular criteria that neither favor nor disfavor religion, and is made available to both religious and secular beneficiaries on a nondiscriminatory basis"); Rosenberger v. Rector & Visitors of Univ. of Va., 515 U.S. 819, 845–846 (1995) (holding that the Constitution required public funding for a

religious publication if such funding was extended by a university in an otherwise neutral way to other student publications and organizations); Zobrest v. Catalina Foothills Sch. Dist., 509 U.S. 1, 8 (1993) (upholding government funding for a sign language interpreter at a religious school because "government[al] programs that neutrally provide benefits to a broad class of citizens defined without reference to religion are not readily subject to an Establishment Clause challenge").

83. Douglas Laycock, "Formal, Substantive, and Disaggregated Neutrality toward Religion," 39 *DePaul L. Rev.* 993, 1001 (1990).

84. Id. at 1002. Other prominent advocates of theories that bear a family resemblance to Laycock's are Thomas Berg and Michael McConnell. See, e.g., Thomas C. Berg, Response, "Religious Choice and Exclusions of Religion," 157 *U. Pa. L. Rev. PENNumbra* 100, 103 (2008); Michael W. McConnell, "Religious Freedom at a Crossroads," 59 *U. Chi. L. Rev.* 115, 169 (1992).

85. Douglas Laycock, "Substantive Neutrality Revisited," 110 *W. Va. L. Rev.* 51, 54 (2007).

86. Id.

87. Id. at 55.

88. Id.

89. Id. at 65.

90. Id. ("Minimizing government influence leaves religion maximally subject to private choice . . .").

91. Douglas Laycock, "The Underlying Unity of Separation and Neutrality," 46 *Emory L.J.* 43, 45 (1997).

92. See Nussbaum, *Liberty of Conscience*, 229.

93. Berg, "Can Religious Liberty," 1211.

94. Laycock, "Substantive Neutrality," 64–65.

95. Conkle, "Path," 10.

96. See Smith, *Foreordained Failure*, 81.

97. See, e.g., Douglas Laycock, "Conceptual Gulfs in *City of Boerne v. Flores*," 39 *Wm. & Mary L. Rev.* 743, 745 (1998); Douglas Laycock, "Free Exercise and the Religious Freedom Restoration Act," 62 *Fordham L. Rev.* 883, 895–897 (1994); Douglas Laycock, "The Supreme Court's Assault on Free Exercise, and the Amicus Brief that Was Never Filed," 8 *J.L. & Religion* 99, 102 (1990); Douglas Laycock, "Theology Scholarships, The Pledge of Allegiance, and Religious Liberty: Avoiding the Extremes but Missing the Liberty," 118 *Harv. L. Rev.* 155, 210–213 (2004).

98. See 1 Kent Greenawalt, *Religion and the Constitution: Free Exercise and Fairness* 49 (2006).

99. See, e.g., Welsh v. U.S., 398 U.S. 333, 335 (1970).

100. Id. at 342.

101. Michael W. McConnell, "Accommodation of Religion," 1985 *Sup. Ct. Rev.* 1, 10–11.

102. Douglas Laycock, "Religious Liberty as Liberty," 7 *J. Contemp. Legal Issues* 313, 334–335 (1996).

103. Id. at 336.

104. Paul Tillich, *Dynamics of Faith* 1 (1957).

105. For criticisms of the ultimate concern standard, see Greenawalt, *Free Exercise*, 132–134.

106. Laycock, "Religious Liberty as Liberty," 336 ("An individual's religious beliefs may evolve from theism to deism to modernism to resymbolized Christianity to humanism to agnosticism to atheism. This evolution is itself an exercise of religion. . . . The state should not draw a line across this evolutionary path; it should not decree that anyone who crosses the line forfeits his right to conscientious objection and loses protection for his deepest moral commitments").

107. Id. In other work, Laycock has described this as the "second-best solution." 1 Douglas Laycock, *Religious Liberty: Overviews & History* 755 (2010) ("The second-best solution is to protect at least the great majority of conscientious objectors who are traditionally religious . . .").

108. See Andrew Koppelman, "Is It Fair to Give Religion Special Treatment?," 2006 *U. Ill. L. Rev.* 571, 586.

109. Smith, *Foreordained Failure*, 96.

110. The discussion in this paragraph draws on certain points made in Greenawalt, *Establishment*, 454–456.

111. Greenawalt raises the case of religions in which snake-handling is practiced, arguing that the state might still refrain from religious influence while discouraging the practice of snake-handling for reasons of public safety. Id. at 454–455. I am doubtful whether it is possible to make this type of separation for more extreme examples— Satanism, for example, or religions that advocate racial hatred.

112. Id. at 455–456 ("[T]he caution about 'no effect of influence' can only be one side of the balance, telling us whether or not something is being sacrificed in terms of the government's relation to religion, but not whether a law overall is justified. . . . [T]he 'no influence' view does not purport to say when its injunction may be overridden . . .").

113. Marci A. Hamilton, *God vs. the Gavel: Religion and the Rule of Law* (2005).

114. Id. at 280.

115. At times Hamilton claims that the approach of *Smith* is the best course for constitutional adjudication, which suggests an endorsement of permissive formal neutrality. At others, however, Hamilton makes the stronger claim that only accommodations that impose "de minimis" harm to others will pass constitutional muster. Id. at 280. And at yet still others, she argues that it is appropriate to deny all exemptions to religious claimants "unless they can prove that exempting them will cause no harm to others." Id. at 5.

116. Id. at 78–110.

117. Id. at 80.

118. Id.

119. Id. at 100–101.

120. Id. at 97–98.

121. 42 U.S.C. § 2000cc(a)(1).

122. Hamilton, *God vs. the Gavel*, 97.

123. Id. at 106–107.

124. Id. at 107.
125. Id. at 110.
126. Id. at 103.
127. The quality of the advantage will depend on an individual state's religious accommodation laws. Many states have zoning laws favorable to religious entities. See generally Donald A. Giannella, "Religious Liberty, Nonestablishment, and Doctrinal Development Part II. The Nonestablishment Principle," 81 *Harv. L. Rev.* 513, 539 (1968) ("The greatest number of zoning ordinances grant special exemptions for churches in residential areas provided they do not cause traffic hazards, congestion, or excessive and untimely noise"). Furthermore, Hamilton herself points out that various states have enacted their own individual RFRAs. Hamilton, *God vs. the Gavel*, 182–184.
128. Id. at 96.
129. Id. at 89.
130. Id. at 106, 110, 213–224.
131. Id. at 94.
132. See id. at 273–305.
133. I have limited my discussion to two neutralists, ignoring many other theories of neutrality, including an important new defense by Andrew Koppelman. Andrew Koppelman, *Defending American Religious Neutrality* (2013).

2. THE SKEPTICS

1. See, e.g., Winnifred Fallers Sullivan, *The Impossibility of Religious Freedom* (2005).
2. Steven D. Smith, *Foreordained Failure: The Quest for a Constitutional Principle of Religious Liberty* (1995).
3. Id. at 11.
4. Id. at 58.
5. Id. at 63, 67.
6. Id. at 68.
7. See id. at 70, 71–75. For an attempt to reconcile a commitment to neutrality with the nonneutral favoring of a "baseline" position, see Andrew Koppelman, *Defending American Religious Neutrality* (2013).
8. Smith, *Foreordained Failure*, 71–72.
9. Id. at 59–60.
10. See Steven D. Smith, *Getting over Equality: A Critical Diagnosis of Religious Freedom in America* (2001).
11. Id. at 10–26.
12. Id. at 27–44.
13. Id. at 45–46.
14. Id. at 67–68.
15. Id. at 61.
16. Id. at 96–97 (quoting Lee C. Bollinger, *The Tolerant Society: Freedom of Speech and Extremist Speech in America* 182 (1986)).

17. Id. at 97.

18. Steven D. Smith, "Is a Coherent Theory of Religious Freedom Possible?," 15 *Const. Comment.* 73, 73 (1998).

19. See Steven D. Smith, "Discourse in the Dusk: The Twilight of Religious Freedom?," 122 *Harv. L. Rev.* 1869 (2009) (reviewing Kent Greenawalt, 2 *Religion and the Constitution: Establishment and Fairness* (2008)).

20. Id. at 1907.

21. Alasdair MacIntyre, *After Virtue: A Study in Moral Theory* 263 (2d ed. 1984) ("If my account of our moral condition is correct, we ought also to conclude that for some time now we too have reached that turning point. What matters at this stage is the construction of local forms of community within which civility and the intellectual and moral life can be sustained through the new dark ages which are already upon us").

22. Talal Asad, *Genealogies of Religion: Discipline and Reasons of Power in Christianity and Islam* 29 (1993).

23. See generally John Locke, *A Letter Concerning Toleration* (Patrick Romanell ed., 1950).

24. See Noah Feldman, "The Intellectual Origins of the Establishment Clause," 77 *N.Y.U. L. Rev.* 346 (2002); Philip Hamburger, *Separation of Church and State* 53–55 (2002).

25. Asad, *Genealogies*, 206.

26. Jonathan Z. Smith, *Imagining Religion: From Babylon to Jonestown* xi (1982).

27. One way to reimagine religious liberty from a constitutional standpoint is to render it entirely dependent on some other provision of the Constitution for protection— the Equal Protection Clause, for example, which prescribes that "no state shall . . . deny to any person within its jurisdiction the equal protection of the laws." U.S. Const. amend. XIV, § 1. The projects of comic egalitarians might be described as such an effort.

28. Tomoko Masuzawa, *The Invention of World Religions: Or, How European Universalism Was Preserved in the Language of Pluralism* xi (2005).

29. Id. at 20.

30. Timothy Fitzgerald, *The Ideology of Religious Studies* 7 (2000).

31. Masuzawa, *Invention*, 328.

32. See Nelson Tebbe, "Nonbelievers," 97 *Va. L. Rev.* 1111, 1131 (2011) (describing the religious studies literature on the question of religion's definition as "of little use in law").

33. See generally Stephen Breyer, *Active Liberty: Interpreting Our Democratic Constitution* (2005); Bruce Ackerman, "The Living Constitution," 120 *Harv. L. Rev.* 1737 (2007).

34. To be sure, some constituents of the Bill of Rights are more dormant than others— the Third and Ninth Amendments, for example—but none has been read out of the Constitution.

35. For example, Martin Riesebrodt, *The Promise of Salvation: A Theory of Religion* 72–75 (2010) (favoring a "content-based" definition of religion).

36. See, e.g., Émile Durkheim, *The Elementary Forms of Religious Life* 9 (Karen E. Fields trans. 1995) (describing religion as an "eminently social" activity that functions to represent and express "collective" beliefs).

37. See Kent Greenawalt, "Religion as a Concept in Constitutional Law," 72 *Cal. L. Rev.* 753, 753–754 (1984).

38. The critical legal studies movement of the 1970s and 1980s offered something of an analogue, but it has not remained as influential as it once was. See generally Roberto Mangabeira Unger, *Knowledge and Politics* (1975); Stephen M. Feldman, *American Legal Thought from Premodernism to Postmodernism: An Intellectual Voyage* 130–133 (2000) (summarizing the contribution of the "crits").

39. Sullivan, *Impossibility*, 8.

40. Id. at 154–155.

41. Winnifred F. Sullivan, "Requiem for the Establishment Clause," 25 *Const. Comment.* 309, 315 (2008).

42. Id.

43. In a forthcoming essay, Smith argues that the religion clauses are best interpreted, as a historical matter, as protecting the "freedom of the Church," rather than "religious" liberty; yet he himself genially admits that such an interpretation is unlikely to be adopted today. Steven D. Smith, "Freedom of Religion or Freedom of the Church?" (University of San Diego Legal Studies Research Paper, Paper No, 11–061, 2011), *available at* http://papers.ssrn.com/sol3/papers.cfm?abstract_id=1911412&download=yes.

44. See Michael W. McConnell, "Why Is Religious Liberty the 'First Freedom'?," 21 *Cardozo L. Rev.* 1243 (2000); Thomas J. Curry, *The First Freedoms: Church and State in America to the Passage of the First Amendment* (1986); see also Douglas Laycock, "Religious Liberty as Liberty," 7 *J. Contemp. Legal Issues* 313, 317 (1996) ("[I]n history that was recent to the American Founders, governmental attempts to suppress disapproved religious views had caused vast human suffering in Europe and in England and similar suffering on a smaller scale in the colonies that became the United States").

45. Steven D. Smith, "The Pluralist Predicament: Contemporary Theorizing in the Law of Religious Freedom," 10 *Legal Theory* 51, 52 (2004).

46. Thomas C. Berg, "Religion Clause Anti-Theories," 72 *Notre Dame L. Rev.* 693, 694 (1997).

47. Id. at 698.

48. See Smith, *Foreordained Failure*, 58.

49. See Richard W. Garnett, "Judicial Enforcement of the Establishment Clause," 25 *Const. Comment.* 273, 276 (2008) ("These questions [of religious liberty] are hard, answering them requires balancing and trade-offs, there are many values at stake, and sometimes in tension, and so the best way to answer these questions—with a few exceptions—is through politics"). Smith is more equivocal. While he supports greater judicial reticence than do most scholars, he is open to the possibility that courts may continue to have an important role to play. See Steven D. Smith, "*Wisconsin v. Yoder* and the Unprincipled Approach to Religious Freedom," 25 *Cap. U. L. Rev.* 805, 813 (1996).

50. These norms may be of greater and lesser strength among judges, to be sure, but as compared with other governmental actors and the general public, judges are more

likely to treat legal precedent with greater care and respect. See generally Marc O. DeGirolami, "Faith in the Rule of Law," 82 *St. John's L. Rev.* 573 (2008). For a provocative discussion of the possibility that the judicial oath may be an effective method for reinforcing the concept of judicial duty and respect for precedent, see Paul Horwitz, "Judicial Character (and Does It Matter?)," 26 *Const. Comment.* 97 (2009) (reviewing H. Jefferson Powell, *Constitutional Conscience: The Moral Dimension of Judicial Decision* (2008), Richard A. Posner, *How Judges Think* (2008), Daniel A. Farber & Suzanna Sherry, *Judgment Calls: Principle and Politics in Constitutional Law* (2009)).

51. See Brian Leiter, "Why Tolerate Religion?," 25 *Const. Comment.* 1 (2008).

52. See Bernard Williams, "Tolerating the Intolerable," in *Philosophy as a Humanistic Discipline* 127 (A. W. Moore ed., 2006) ("If we are asking people to be tolerant . . . [t]hey will indeed have to lose something, their desire to suppress or drive out the rival belief; but they will also keep something, their commitment to their own beliefs, which is what gave them that desire in the first place. There is a tension here between one's own commitments and the acceptance that other people may have other and perhaps quite distasteful commitments").

53. The concept of a hybrid or mixed theory has not yet become influential in religion clause scholarship, though it has deeply affected other legal disciplines, including criminal law. See, e.g., Paul H. Robinson, "Hybrid Principles for the Distribution of Criminal Sanctions," 82 *Nw. U. L. Rev.* 19 (1987); Michael T. Cahill, "Punishment Pluralism," in *Retributivism: Essays on Theory and Policy* 25–48 (Mark D. White ed., 2011).

54. Steven H. Shiffrin, *The Religious Left and Church–State Relations* 13 (2009). Shiffrin identifies seven free exercise values and a corresponding seven establishment values. He has previously offered a defense of an "eclectic," case-by-case methodology for the First Amendment, using a "Kantian heuristic" to describe its opposite, though that account tends to focus more on the Free Speech Clause. See Steven H. Shiffrin, *The First Amendment, Democracy, and Romance* 110–139 (1990).

55. Greenawalt's views are drawn from his two-volume treatment of religion and the Constitution. See Greenawalt, *Free Exercise*, and Greenawalt, *Establishment*.

56. Greenawalt, *Free Exercise*, 1.

57. Id. at 2, 5–6.

58. Id. at 5–6.

59. Both comic egalitarians and neutralists rely on the idea of "fairness" as synonymous with distributive egalitarianism and formal neutrality.

60. Id. at 4; see also id. at 443.

61. Greenawalt, *Establishment*, 446–447; see also id. at 480 for a different type of union between fairness and equality. The locus classicus for an egalitarian statement of justice as fairness is John Rawls, *Justice as Fairness: A Restatement* (2001).

62. Id. at 451.

63. Id. at 446–447, 449. At still other times, Greenawalt intends fairness to mean a more general idea of justice or perhaps even truth-telling. See, e.g., id. at 449, n.55.

64. This is not how Greenawalt has generally been interpreted by his interlocutors. See generally "Symposium: Establishment and Fairness," 25 *Const. Comment.* 241–320

(2008). Critics have been misled by the fact that Greenawalt is one of the few scholars of the religion clauses who takes seriously the conflict of values of religious liberty. In consequence, they ascribe a position to him that does not properly reflect his approach.

65. Greenawalt, *Establishment*, 100.
66. Elk Grove Unified Sch. Dist. v. Newdow, 542 U.S. 1, 36–37 (2004) (O'Connor, J., concurring).
67. See Noah Feldman, *Divided by God: America's Church–State Problem—And What We Should Do about It* 242 (2005) ("In some instances, pluralistic public religion even holds out the possibility of enabling new religious minorities to participate fully in the American public sphere").
68. See Sherman v. Cmty Consol. Sch. Dist. 21, 980 F.2d 437, 445 (7th Cir. 1992) (Easterbrook, J.).
69. Greenawalt, *Establishment*, 101.
70. Id. at 102.
71. Id. at 92.
72. Id. at 540.
73. Id. at 190.
74. Steven Smith offers the following about Greenawalt's commitment to cultural history as a guide for constitutional decision making: "Greenawalt never actually attempts to show how his views and prescriptions flow from any deliberate or developed interpretation of the American political tradition. Nor could he, I suspect. That is because, by and large, Greenawalt's commitments run strongly contrary to well-entrenched American traditions." Smith, "Discourse," 1900–1901.
75. 536 U.S. 639 (2002).
76. Id. at 646.
77. Id. at 649, 653.
78. Greenawalt, *Establishment*, 541.
79. See Chapter 1. For thoughtful discussion of *Zelman*, see Thomas C. Berg, "Vouchers and Religious Schools: The New Constitutional Questions," 72 *U. Cin. L. Rev.* 151 (2003).
80. Greenawalt, *Establishment*, 418.
81. Id. at 423. Approximately 18 percent of the institutions partaking of the voucher program in Zelman were nonreligious.
82. Lemon v. Kurtzman, 403 U.S. 602 (1971).
83. Berg, "Vouchers," 158; Eugene Volokh, "Equal Treatment Is Not Establishment," 13 *Notre Dame J.L. Ethics & Pub. Pol'y* 341, 348 (1999).
84. This is not to deny that there are areas of overlap between Greenawalt's quasi-tragic approach and the method of tragedy and history—particularly in the area of government funding of religious institutions. For further discussion, see Chapter 10.
85. Shiffrin, *Religious Left*, 16–41; see also Marc O. DeGirolami, "The Handmaid of Politics," 26 *J. L. & Religion* 641 (2010–2011) (reviewing Steven H. Shiffrin, *The Religious Left and Church–State Relations* (2009)).
86. Paul Horwitz, *The Agnostic Age: Law, Religion, and the Constitution* (2011).

87. Id. at 200–201, 300–308.
88. Id. at 150–154.
89. Id. at 71–121.
90. Id. at 307.
91. See Philip Hamburger's excellent study for the dubious roots of this conception of religious liberty. Hamburger, *Separation*.
92. Horwitz, *Agnostic Age*, 59.
93. Lemon, 403 U.S. at 612–613.
94. The excessive entanglement component of the *Lemon* test at times seems to have been abandoned as an independent prong. See Agostini v. Felton, 521 U.S. 203, 232–233 (1997). Nevertheless, separationism understood in this fashion surely remains an important value of religious liberty.
95. Consider Christ's admonition in the Sermon on the Mount: "All things whatsoever you would that men should do to you, do you also to them. For this is the law and the prophets." Matthew 7:12. A state might be quite confident that this statement is "true," or at the very least a wise rule of thumb, but still reticent to entangle itself in the truth-telling and truth-seeking affairs of Christian churches.
96. Wong Sun v. U.S., 371 U.S. 471, 488 (1963).
97. Trammell v. U.S., 445 U.S. 40, 53 (1980).
98. Id. at 51.
99. U.S. Const. amend. V.
100. Herrera v. Collins, 506 U.S. 390 (1993).

PART II. TRAGEDY AND HISTORY

1. The first three theses are substantially influenced by the philosophical view known as value pluralism. In addition to the work of Isaiah Berlin and Michael Oakeshott, which always hovers in the background, of crucial importance are Stuart Hampshire, *Morality and Conflict* (1983); John Kekes, *The Morality of Pluralism* (1993); Joseph Raz, *The Morality of Freedom* (1986); and Bernard Williams, *Ethics and the Limits of Philosophy* (1985). Also influential are George Crowder, *Liberalism and Value Pluralism* (2002); William A. Galston, *Liberal Pluralism: The Implications of Value Pluralism for Political Theory and Practice* (2002); John Gray, *Isaiah Berlin* (1995); John Gray, *Two Faces of Liberalism* (2000); Stuart Hampshire, *Justice Is Conflict* (1999); Bernard Williams, *Moral Luck* (1981); and the essays in *Incommensurability, Incomparability, and Practical Reason* (Ruth Chang ed., 1997).
2. Frederick Beiser, "Historicism," in *The Oxford Handbook of Continental Philosophy* 155, 156 (Brian Leiter & Michael Rosen eds., 2007); see also Frederick Beiser, *The German Historicist Tradition* (2012).
3. Beiser, "Historicism," 156–157.
4. Id. at 158, 160–161.
5. Among these may be the historicists' belief in the "radical *context-dependency* of all social-historical phenomena," though Beiser is clear that this doctrine need not

imply a complete relativism: "Although *specific* laws and policies will differ, they could still be variations upon more general principles." Id. at 158, 168.

6. See generally 1 Frederick Pollock & Frederic William Maitland, *The History of English Law before the Time of Edward I* xciii (2d ed. 1968) (1898).

7. James C. Carter, *Law: Its Origin, Growth, and Function* 327, 334 (1974) (1907); see also Lewis A. Grossman, "Langdell Upside Down: James Coolidge Carter and the Anti-Classical Jurisprudence of Anti-Codification," 19 *Yale J. L. & Human.* 149, 156–159 (2007).

The influence of German historicists such as Friedrich Savigny and English historicists such as Sir Henry Maine on American jurisprudence is disputed. Compare Roscoe Pound, Book Review, 24 *Pol. Sci. Q.* 317, 319 (1909) (reviewing James C. Carter, *Law: Its Origin, Growth, and Function* (1907)) (linking Carter with Savigny), and James E. Herget, *American Jurisprudence, 1870–1970: A History* 22–30, 130 (1990) (same), with Lewis A. Grossman, "'From Savigny through Sir Henry Maine': Roscoe Pound's Flawed Portrait of James Coolidge Carter's Historical Jurisprudence" (American University Washington College of Law, Working Paper No. 2009-2021, 2009), *available at* http://papers.ssrn.com/sol3/papers.cfm?abstract_id=1407623 (downplaying the influence).

8. A critical historicism has also played an important role in more recent constitutional theory. Jack M. Balkin & Sanford Levinson, "Legal Historicism and Legal Academics: The Roles of Law Professors in the Wake of *Bush v. Gore*," 90 *Geo. L.J.* 173, 181 (2001); see also Jack M. Balkin, *Constitutional Redemption: Political Faith in an Unjust World* 177–186 (2011).

9. Michael Oakeshott, "Historical Change," in *On History and Other Essays* 105, 106 (Liberty Fund ed. 1999) (1983).

3. The Clash of Values of Religious Liberty

1. See, e.g., Van Orden v. Perry, 545 U.S. 677, 698 (2005) (Breyer, J., concurring) (observing that the freedom of religion is intended "to avoid that divisiveness based upon religion that promotes social conflict, sapping the strength of government and religion alike"); Lemon v. Kurtzman, 403 U.S. 602, 622 (1971) (discussing "the divisive political potential" of establishmentarian practices).

2. Jeremy Waldron attributes this view to Locke. See Jeremy Waldron, "Locke: Toleration and the Rationality of Persecution," in *Justifying Toleration: Conceptual and Historical Perspectives* 61, 66 (Susan Mendus ed., 1988).

3. See John H. Garvey, *What Are Freedoms For?* 42–57 (2000).

4. See John H. Garvey, "An Anti-Liberal Argument for Religious Freedom," 7 *J. Contemp. Legal Issues* 275, 284–287 (1996) (discussing the performance of rituals, the desire "to acquire and spread knowledge about the esoterica of [religious] belief[s]," and the obligation of particular moral duties, as three reasons that religious believers might care deeply about religious liberty).

5. See Paul Horwitz, "Churches as First Amendment Institutions: Of Sovereignty and Spheres," 44 *Harv. C.R.-C.L. L. Rev.* 79, 86 (2009) ("[T]he government

is not the only protagonist in First Amendment doctrine"); Richard W. Garnett, "Do Churches Matter? Towards an Institutional Understanding of the Religion Clauses," 53 *Vill. L. Rev.* 273, 291 (2008) ("It is not new to observe that American judicial decisions and public conversations about religious freedom tend to focus on matters of individuals' rights, beliefs, consciences and practices").

6. One might claim that it is irrelevant why religious people value religious liberty; "we"—the citizens of a liberal democratic polity—might justifiably value religious liberty for reasons that religious believers reject. Yet it seems perverse to exclude the concerns of the very people whose beliefs and practices our theories of religious liberty are designed to protect. See Garvey, "Anti-Liberal Argument," 279.

7. See People v. Woody, 394 P. 2d 813, 817 (Cal. 1964) ("Although peyote serves as a sacramental symbol similar to bread and wine in certain Christian churches, it is more than a sacrament. Peyote constitutes in itself an object of worship; prayers are directed to it much as prayers are devoted to the Holy Ghost. On the other hand, to use peyote for nonreligious purposes is sacrilegious"); see also 1 Kent Greenawalt, *Religion and the Constitution: Free Exercise and Fairness* 68–69 (2006).

8. On "moral significance," see Stuart Hampshire, *Morality & Conflict* 24, 97 (1983).

9. The values of autonomy, strife avoidance, futility, or a handful of others may motivate the state to protect wine sipping or peyote smoking, but because the attachment of the state to these practices as intrinsically worthwhile is nonexistent and politically motivated, that protection is not likely to be secure.

10. The Federalist No. 10, at 73 (James Madison) (Clinton Rossiter ed., 2003).

11. The "Magisterium" is the "teaching office and authority of the Catholic Church; also the hierarchy as holding this office." *The HarperCollins Encyclopedia of Catholicism* 805 (Richard P. McBrien et al. eds., 1995).

12. See, e.g., Michael J. Perry, "Catholics, the Magisterium, and Moral Controversy: An Argument for Independent Judgment (with Particular Reference to Catholic Schools)," 26 *U. Dayton L. Rev.* 293, 317 (2001).

13. For example, dissent on the issues of abortion and capital punishment implicates different degrees of divergence with the Catholic Church's core teachings. Gregory C. Sisk & Charles J. Reid, Jr., "Abortion, Bishops, Eucharist, and Politicians: A Question of Communion," 43 *Cath. Law.* 255, 262–263 (2004).

14. Perry, "Catholics," 322.

15. See Imad ad-Dean Ahmad, "American and Muslim Perspectives on Freedom of Religion," 8 *U. Pa. J. Const. L.* 355, 362 (2006).

16. Id.

17. Id. at 363. The enforceability of Islamic law on the citizens of a polity raises what are Establishment Clause concerns in the United States.

18. See Philip Hamburger, *Separation of Church and State* 484–485 (2002) ("That American majorities used the separation of church and state to impose their vision of their religion and their Americanism upon religious minorities is a sober reminder that as religious liberty becomes more individualistic, it does not necessarily increase individual liberty").

19. See Anver M. Emon, "On the Pope, Cartoons, and Apostates: Shari'a 2006," 22 *J.L. & Religion* 303, 312–313 (2006–2007).

20. See Hamburger, *Separation,* 157–159, 163–180 ("These Baptists, like so many of their predecessors, argued that the power of government did not extend to religion. . . . Apparently, separation was not what the Baptists wanted"). Compare this view with the position of the First Baptist Church in the early twentieth century: "Led by the virulently anti-Catholic pastor of the First Baptist Church . . . the True Americans backed a Baptist candidate [who advocated] '1. The complete separation of church and state, to the extent that no Catholic or friend of a Catholic shall hold any elective or appointive position under any city, county, state, or national government.'" Id. at 404–405. That view may be contrasted again with contemporary Baptist understandings of religious freedom.

21. See Jean Bethke Elshtain, "The Dignity of the Human Person and the Idea of Human Rights: Four Inquiries," 14 *J.L. & Religion* 53, 61–62 (1999–2000) (*"Dignitatis [Humanae]* proclaims religious freedom a 'civil right' that is in accordance with the dignity of persons, being lodged in a very principle of our natures"); see also John Courtney Murray, *Religious Liberty: Catholic Struggles with Pluralism* 189–190 (J. Leon Hooper ed., 1993) ("Today, religious freedom, as a human and civil right, personal and corporate, which requires the protection of a legal institution, has emerged as an exigence of the personal and political reason").

22. See Murray, *Religious Liberty,* 184. Murray describes the "first" view of religious liberty—which was dominant as late as the nineteenth century—as championing (1) "the establishment of Catholicism by law as the single religion of the state," and (2) "intolerance of other religions."

23. Interstate variation in ideas of religious liberty (as among the governments of the United States, France, and Iran, for example), intrastate variation (Texas and Massachusetts have different laws dealing with religious liberty), and temporal variation—for example, the cyclical development in understanding of the free exercise of religion instantiated in Reynolds v. United States, 98 U.S. 145 (1878), Sherbert v. Verner, 374 U.S. 398 (1963), and Employment Division v. Smith, 494 U.S 872 (1990).

24. Title VII immunizes religious organizations from civil suits "with respect to the employment of individuals of a particular religion to perform work connected with the carrying on by such corporation, association, educational institution, or society of its activities." 42 U.S.C. § 2000e-1(a) (2006).

25. John Kekes, *The Morality of Pluralism* 59 (1993).

26. See Steven Lukes, "Comparing the Incomparable: Trade-Offs and Sacrifices," in *Incommensurability, Incomparability, and Practical Reason* 184, 192 (Ruth Chang ed., 1997). Liberal traditions are likewise intramurally at odds in their interpretations of the value of equality. See id.; see also Marc O. DeGirolami, "The Problem of Religious Learning," 49 *B.C. L. Rev.* 1213,1247 (2008) ("'Human equality' is not an obvious and self-applying ideal; it invites individual interpretation and is likely to be the subject of vigorous disagreement").

27. Bernard Williams, *Moral Luck* 72 (1981).

28. See Kekes, *Pluralism,* 24 ("[T]he vast majority of conflicts we encounter occur within particular traditions or within particular people").

29. John Gray, *Isaiah Berlin* 43 (1996); see also Jonathan Wolff, "Fairness, Respect, and the Egalitarian Ethos," 27 *Phil. & Pub. Aff.* 97, 97 (1998) (arguing that the egalitarian values of "fairness" and "respect" often can conflict).

30. Kekes, *Pluralism*, 63 ("These conflicts . . . will be due to individuals' having committed themselves to the conventions of their tradition").

31. See Charles Taylor, "Leading a Life," in *Incommensurability*, 170.

32. Lukes, "Comparing," 185 (describing a covering value as the notion that "something can be better than, or equal to, another only in some respect, in virtue of some value, explicit or implicit").

33. See Lyng v. Nw. Indian Cemetery Protective Ass'n, 485 U.S. 439, 442 (1988) (the Native Americans claimed that the government's proposed road would impair their religious practice by depriving them of needed "privacy, silence, and an undisturbed natural setting"). This is one of several levels at which the state's and the Native American's conceptions of religious liberty conflicted. See Chapter 9 for further discussion.

34. See Wayne Proudfoot, *Religious Experience* 183–184 (1985) (describing an experience as being religious by reference to "its significance for the truth of religious beliefs"). See People v. Woody, 394 P. 2d 813, 817–818 (Cal. 1964) ("Members of the church regard peyote also as a 'teacher' because . . . it enables the participant to experience the Deity").

35. Brian Bix, "Dealing with Incommensurability for Dessert and Desert: Comments on Chapman and Katz," 146 *U. Pa. L. Rev.* 1651, 1651 (1998).

36. See Ruth Chang, "Introduction," in *Incommensurability*, 1; Lukes, "Comparing," 184–185 ("Thus we want to know whether, with respect to the goodness of places to live, an economically poor community with breathtaking landscapes is better than a moderately prosperous community blanketed with unsightly features and smokestacks—not whether, with respect to the value, goodness of places to live, the value of beauty is better than the value of prosperity"); Joseph Raz, "Value Incommensurability: Some Preliminaries," 86 *Proc. of the Aristotelian Soc'y* 117, 118 (1985).

37. See Raz, "Value Incommensurability," 118 ("It makes no sense to talk of choosing between perfect liberty and absolute equality . . .").

38. See Cass R. Sunstein, "Incommensurability and Kinds of Valuation: Some Applications in Law," in *Incommensurability*, 234, 240.

39. Lukes, "Comparing," 185.

40. See Joseph Raz, *The Morality of Freedom* 323 (1986) ("[J]udgments of incommensurability deny the truth and not the meaningfulness of judgments of commensurability").

41. Whether the values are incommensurable again will depend on the reason for the exclusion. It is at least theoretically possible that a church might believe in full racial equality and integration in the civic sphere while at the same believing that a divinity commands its members to remain racially pure within the church body. That view might be compatible and commensurable with the polity's view that racial harmony is a paramount *civic* value, whatever people may choose in their private lives.

42. Kekes, *Pluralism*, 61.

43. 406 U.S. 205 (1972).

44. Id. at 207 (citing Wis. Stat. § 118.15 (1969)).

45. Id.

46. There are differences between the Old Order Amish and the Mennonite Church, but for simplicity the *Yoder* plaintiffs are here referred to as "the Amish."

47. Id. at 209.

48. Id. The state rejected a possible compromise that would have required the children to attend an Amish vocational program three days a week, in which they would have been taught English, mathematics, health, and social studies, as well as agriculture and homemaking, by an Amish teacher. The state felt that this program would not offer the Amish children "substantially equivalent education" to that provided in public or private school. Id. at 209, n.3.

49. Id. at 210.

50. Id. at 210–212.

51. Id. at 211–212. Public school education through the eighth grade was not objectionable to the Amish because it enabled their children to "read the Bible, to be good farmers and citizens, and to be able to deal with non-Amish people when necessary in the course of their daily affairs." Id. at 212.

52. See Greenawalt, *Free Exercise*, 93–98.

53. Yoder, 406 U.S. at 212–213.

54. Id. at 212.

55. Pierce v. Soc'y of Sisters, 268 U.S. 510, 535 (1925).

56. Yoder, 406 U.S. at 216.

57. Id. at 245 (Douglas, J., dissenting).

58. Id. at 244.

59. Id. at 217.

60. See DeGirolami, "Problem," 1224.

61. See Greenawalt, *Free Exercise*, 91–92.

62. Id. ("Education assists people to enjoy forms of culture; cutting their education short restricts development of that capacity in students").

63. See Josh Chafetz, "Social Reproduction and Religious Reproduction: A Democratic-Communitarian Analysis of the *Yoder* Problem," 15 *Wm. & Mary Bill Rts. J.* 263, 264 (2006) (describing the state's interest as one of "social reproduction").

64. Yoder, 406 U.S. at 217 (describing both "symbolic and practical" value in the Amish rejection of technological comforts); see also Kent Greenawalt, *Private Consciences and Public Reasons* 3 (1995) ("In cultures pervaded by a concern for material welfare and the pursuit of advantage for oneself and one's family, the sense of belonging to a community is weak").

65. To say this is not to say, as Justice Douglas does in his dissent, that "[r]eligion is an individual experience." Yoder, 406 U.S. at 243 (Douglas, J., dissenting). Whatever this statement might mean, it cannot mean that for any person, let alone for a child, one's view of the worth of religion and one's own religious traditions are capable of being understood in a vacuum, deracinated from the influences (positive or negative) of family, culture, and community. This is not to deny that the feelings of the

children, Vernon Yutzy and Barbara Miller, about their religion may have been complicated and worth exploring within the overall context of the opposing claims.

66. Richard W. Garnett, "The Story of Henry Adams's Soul: Education and the Expression of Associations," 85 *Minn. L. Rev.* 1841, 1846–1847 (2001).

67. It is noteworthy that the Amish view of higher education was not altogether negative. Rather, the Amish were opposed to certain values that higher education may have a tendency to develop—pride or an inflated sense of the self and the importance of its contributions. Yoder, 406 U.S. at 212.

68. For an expanded discussion of *Yoder*, see Marc O. DeGirolami, "No Tears for Creon," 15 *Legal Theory* 245 (2009).

69. Compare this with the virtue of tolerance championed by some skeptics in Chapter 2.

70. Not all will agree with each of the values, and some may utterly reject one or more of them. See, e.g., James Dwyer, "Parents' Religion and Children's Welfare: Debunking the Doctrine of Parents' Rights," 82 *Calif. L. Rev.* 1371, 1375, 1447 (1994) (arguing that a parent's "privilege" to direct a child's education can never measure up to the state's right of intervention on behalf of the child). Yet even those staunch critics of *Yoder* who dispute one of the values asserted by the Amish plaintiffs may be open—perhaps even sympathetic—to one or more other such values.

71. See Yoder, 406 U.S. at 216 (observing that the Amish are deeply committed to Saint Paul's admonition to the Romans: "be not conformed to this world . . .").

72. A child's meaningful chance at exit—at rejecting his or her own history—is certainly needed. See George Crowder, "Two Concepts of Liberal Pluralism," 35 *Pol. Theory* 121, 128 (2007).

73. Stephen Macedo, "Liberal Civic Education and Religious Fundamentalism: The Case of God v. John Rawls?," 105 *Ethics* 468, 488–489 (1995).

74. 494 U.S. 872 (1990).

75. Yoder, 406 U.S. at 220.

76. Id.

77. Id. at 221 (quoting Walz v. Tax Comm'n, 397 U.S. 664, 672 (1970)).

78. Id. at 216.

79. Steven D. Smith, "*Wisconsin v. Yoder* and the Unprincipled Approach to Religious Freedom," 25 *Cap. U.L. Rev.* 805, 805 (1996).

80. Laura S. Underkuffler-Freund, "*Yoder* and the Question of Equality," 25 *Cap. U.L. Rev.* 789, 790 (1996).

81. Id. at 793.

82. Id. at 803.

83. Id. at 801.

84. Id. at 802.

85. Id. at 795.

86. Id. at 803.

87. It is here that a community's history of law-abidingness may matter. If the state is to grant an exemption from the last two years of compulsory schooling—a time period in which young people are particularly susceptible to unhealthy influences—it is

only reasonable to take notice of the extent to which the exempted community is law-abiding and advocates values that are not entirely inconsistent with the state's.

88. 505 U.S. 577 (1992).

89. Id. at 580.

90. Id.

91. Id.

92. Id. at 587–588.

93. Id. at 595. Any distinction between a high school and a middle school graduation in the context of the "coercion" argument was not addressed.

94. Id. at 593.

95. Id. at 629 (Souter, J., concurring).

96. Id. at 606–607, 629 (Blackmun, J., concurring).

97. Id. at 617–618.

98. Id. at 630 ("One may fairly say, as one commentator has suggested, that the government brought prayer into the ceremony 'precisely because some people want a symbolic affirmation that government approves and endorses their religion, and because many of the people who want this affirmation place little or no value on the costs to religious minorities.'") (quoting Douglas Laycock, "Summary and Synthesis: The Crisis in Religious Liberty," 60 *Geo. Wash. L. Rev.* 841, 844 (1992)).

99. 2 Kent Greenawalt, *Religion and the Constitution: Establishment and Fairness* 113, n.40 (2008).

100. Id. at 115.

101. One might interpret this as an expression of human humility juxtaposed against a particular religion's divine superiority, but that strikes me as uncharitable. There was no suggestion in the *Lee* invocation or benediction that the God of monotheism was appealed to or acknowledged as the one true divinity.

102. The point was not lost on Justice Kennedy. See Lee, 505 U.S. at 595 ("Their contention, one of considerable force were it not for the constitutional constraints applied to state action, is that the prayers are an essential part of these ceremonies because for many persons an occasion of this significance lacks meaning if there is no recognition, however brief, that human achievements cannot be understood apart from their spiritual essence").

103. See McCreary County v. ACLU, 545 U.S. 844, 900 (2005) (Scalia, J., dissenting) (recognizing the "legitimate competing interests" of the minority in not feeling excluded and the majority of religious believers in "being able to give God thanks and supplication as a people, and with respect to our national endeavors").

104. Ira C. Lupu & Robert W. Tuttle, "The Cross at College: Accommodation and Acknowledgement of Religion at Public Universities," 16 *Wm. & Mary Bill Rts. J.* 939, 981 (2008).

105. Id. at 989; see also Lynch v. Donnelly, 465 U.S. 668, 674 (1984) ("There is an unbroken history of official acknowledgment by all three branches of government of the role of religion in American life from at least 1789").

106. Lupu & Tuttle, "The Cross."

107. Lee, 505 U.S. at 646 (Scalia, J., dissenting).

108. See McGowan v. Maryland, 366 U.S. 420, 449 (1961).

109. See Angela C. Carmella, "Religion as Public Resource," 27 *Seton Hall L. Rev.* 1225, 1225–1226 (1997).

110. Grace Davie, *The Sociology of Religion* 12 (2007). Davie describes this orientation toward religion as more European than American; for America, she uses the metaphor of "competing firms in a religious market" and an approach drawn from economics—rational choice theory. See also id. at 67–88 ("Europeans, as a consequence of the state church system . . . regard their churches as public utilities rather than competing firms"). Nevertheless, and provided that the idea of religion is taken at a fairly high level of abstraction, the "public utility" metaphor resonates distinctively in the American context as well. See Andrew Koppelman, "Secular Purpose," 88 *Va. L. Rev.* 87, 126–128 (2002).

111. Carmella, "Public Resource," 1226. For similar points about the "public" nature of religious learning, see DeGirolami, "Problem."

112. Funerals may represent occasions where the communal use of religious resources and artifacts serves these public ends. See Peter Berger et al., *Religious America, Secular Europe?: A Theme and Variations* 35 (2008) ("[Churches] are useful social institutions, which the great majority in the population are likely to need at one time or another in their lives"). One might object that no one going to the funeral of a friend would have cause to complain if the friend's family members had a religious ceremony before the burial, but the situation is different for graduates because each of them has an "ownership" interest (for lack of a better phrase) in the graduation ceremony. That is true, but I am dubious that friends or distant family members of the deceased have *no* "ownership" stake in the funeral, in the sense intended here. It is precisely their connection with the deceased and their wish to honor and remember him or her that provide such a stake, although admittedly not one that supersedes the ownership interest of more intimate connections. And any graduate's interest in the graduation ceremony is precisely equal to that of any other, so it is unclear why one should assume that Deborah Weisman's interest *must* overpower other interests.

113. Marsh v. Chambers, 463 U.S. 783, 787–789 (1983).

114. Lee, 505 U.S. at 635 (Scalia, J., dissenting).

115. See, e.g., County of Allegheny v. ACLU, 492 U.S. 573, 616 (1989); Lynch v. Donnelly, 465 U.S. 668, 680–681 (1984) (acknowledging the independent, secular significance of celebrating the Christmas holiday).

116. Lee, 505 U.S. at 628–629 (Souter, J., concurring).

117. Id. at 629.

118. See Chapters 6 through 10.

4. THE INADEQUACY OF SKEPTICISM

1. Christopher L. Eisgruber & Lawrence G. Sager, *Religious Freedom and the Constitution* 75 (2007). The authors do not endorse this view.

2. See Winnifred F. Sullivan, *The Impossibility of Religious Freedom* 159 (2005) (arguing that constitutional law should abandon the search for any distinct protection for religious liberty and should instead rely entirely on "laws guaranteeing equality").

Compare Steven D. Smith, *Foreordained Failure: The Quest for a Constitutional Principle of Religious Freedom* 11 (1995) ("In acknowledging a variety of versions of religious freedom, we can still insist that some opinions about the proper scope of religious freedom are more attractive, or more rationally defensible, than others") with Steven D. Smith, *"Wisconsin v. Yoder* and the Unprincipled Approach to Religious Freedom," 25 *Cap. U.L. Rev.* 805, 811 (1996) (arguing that "principled" approaches to religious liberty are "pernicious"); Steven D. Smith, "Is a Coherent Theory of Religious Freedom Possible?," 15 *Const. Comment.* 74–85 (1998) (explaining "[w]hy there can be no theory of religious freedom").

3. See Bernard Williams, *Ethics and the Limits of Philosophy* 72 (1985) ("An ethical theory is a theoretical account of what ethical thought and practice are, which account either implies a general test for the correctness of basic ethical beliefs and principles or else implies that there cannot be such a test"). More ambitious accounts of theories—those that insist, for example, that theories, to be theories, *must* systematize, or *must* provide general principles, or *must* prioritize values for all future cases—take an unduly narrow view of what theory is and might be. See Martha Nussbaum, "Why Practice Needs Ethical Theory: Particularism, Principle, and Bad Behaviour," in *Moral Particularism* 233–236 (Brad Hooker & Margaret Little eds., 2000).

4. John Kekes, *Against Liberalism* 162–163 (1997).

5. Stuart Hampshire, *Morality & Conflict* 87 (1983).

6. Id. at 89; see also William A. Galston, "What Value Pluralism Means for Legal-Constitutional Orders," 46 *San Diego L. Rev.* 803, 804 (2009) ("Some goods are basic in the sense that they form part of any choiceworthy conception of a human life. To be deprived of such goods is to be forced to endure the great evils of existence").

7. Hampshire, *Morality & Conflict*, 91; see also George Crowder, "Two Concepts of Liberal Pluralism," 35 *Political Theory* 121, 126 (2007) ("There are objective goods, but these may conflict, and such conflicts cannot be resolved by simple monist formulas").

8. Hampshire, *Morality & Conflict*, 91–92.

9. See Kent Greenawalt, *Private Consciences and Public Reasons* 29 (1995) ("People in any society lack the self-transcendence to understand which arguments are grounded only in shared assumptions and which are grounded in the nature of things and are true, independent of what people at that time and place happen to think is right. Most of what is accepted by consensus will seem to be true on realist grounds").

10. Hampshire, *Morality & Conflict*, 98.

11. Id.

12. John Kekes, *The Morality of Pluralism* 41–42 (1993).

13. Joseph Raz, *The Practice of Value* 16 (2003).

14. Kekes, *Pluralism*, 48.

15. I am packing a considerable amount into the terms *good* and *worthwhile for human beings*, leaving them perhaps frustratingly undertheorized. This is largely because I wish to avoid delving too deeply into enormously complex issues—the nature of

the good and the plausibility of moral realism—that are not necessary to resolve here. The argument is in part dependent on accepting the earlier point that there is a significant domain of commonality among the plurality of values between cultures, at least as to certain basic moral prohibitions and injunctions. Even if one disputes the idea of a commonality amid plurality, the more important claim is that it is far easier to achieve agreement about values in the abstract and about whether they ought *somehow* to apply in particular cases of conflict, than to decide with precision beforehand which of those values ought (always, or normally) to be the most powerful in those same circumstances of conflict.

16. See Kekes, *Pluralism*, 171.

17. William A. Galston, *Liberal Pluralism: The Implications of Value Pluralism for Political Theory and Practice* 37 (2002) (emphasis added).

18. I owe the form of this example to Kent Greenawalt, "Fundamental Questions about the Religion Clauses: Reflections on Some Critiques," 47 *San Diego L. Rev.* 1131, 1135–1136 (2010), though the lessons I draw are different.

19. On the notion of moral salience and the "shape" of a situation as to which one needs to make a decision, see Jonathan Dancy, *Moral Reasons* 112–113 (1993) (noting that when we are faced with making a decision, "[w]hat we are doing is telling the story of the situation, and our narrative has to follow the shape that the situation has. By the time that we have mentioned every salient property, we have said enough to show how we see the situation and hence the reasons we find here for the action we do").

20. Jonathan Dancy, *Ethics without Principles* 7 (2004). Other useful treatments of moral particularism include John McDowell, *Mind, Value, and Reality* (1998); *Moral Particularism* (Brad Hooker & Margaret Little eds., 2000); *Challenging Moral Particularism* (Mark Norris Lance et al. eds., 2008); Walter Sinnott-Armstrong, "Some Varieties of Particularism," 30 *Metaphilosophy* 1 (1999); Joseph Raz, "The Trouble with Particularism (Dancy's Version)," 115 *Mind* 99 (2006) (reviewing Jonathan Dancy, *Ethics without Principles* (2004)).

21. See Jonathan Dancy, "The Particularist's Progress," in *Moral Particularism*, 30.

22. Dancy, *Ethics without Principles*, 10.

23. See State Rubbish Collectors Ass'n v. Siliznoff, 240 P.2d 282, 284 (Cal. 1952) (Traynor, J.); see generally Daniel Givelber, "The Right to Minimum Social Decency and the Limits of Evenhandedness: Intentional Infliction of Emotional Distress by Outrageous Conduct," 82 *Colum. L. Rev.* 42 (1982).

24. See Michael T. Cahill, "Punishment Pluralism," in *Retributivism: Essays on Theory and Policy* 28–31 (Mark D. White ed., 2011). To say this is of course *not* to say that the infliction of pain on another human being in the context of punishment is morally insignificant or unconcerning.

25. See Galston, "What Value Pluralism Means," 805–806 (linking value pluralism and moral particularism); David Bakhurst, "Ethical Particularism in Context," in *Moral Particularism*, 164. As Bakhurst notes, there are important connections in particularist thought to Alasdair MacIntyre's thesis of "situatedness" within particular social practices and traditions. See generally Alasdair MacIntyre, *After Virtue: A Study in Moral Theory* (2d ed. 1984).

26. See Lawrence B. Solum, "Natural Justice," 51 *Am. J. Juris.* 65, 98–101 (2006) (embracing in law the "modest" particularism that "our judgments about particular cases play a more powerful role in moral deliberation than do abstract principles and general rules"); Frederick Schauer, "Rules and the Rule of Law," 14 *Harv. J. L. Pub. Pol'y* 645, 649–650 (1991) (discussing "rule-sensitive" particularism); R. George Wright, "Dreams and Formulas: The Roles of Particularism and Principlism in the Law," 37 *Hofstra L. Rev.* 195 (2008) (arguing for a "symbiotic relationship" between particularism and principle).

    Joseph Raz has observed: "One may be attracted by [particularism's] rejection of absolute, non-overridable moral principles, by its rejection of codifiable morality, or by its denial that in practical reflection we should reason from principles to cases.... These are sound motives—morality cannot be codified, and many decisions call for contextually sensitive judgement—but they do not require particularism to vindicate them." Raz, "The Trouble with Particularism," 118. It is not necessary for me to take a stand on moral particularism's merits; the point is merely that a modest species of particularism is a suggestive model to conceptualize legal decision making.

27. See H. Jefferson Powell, *The Moral Tradition of American Constitutionalism: A Theological Interpretation* 3–4 (1993) ("Moral and political questions in America finally *are* legal questions, whether they concern the authority of the national government to wage war or the authority of a comatose person's family to command the attending physicians to cease their efforts to sustain his or her life").

28. See Dancy, *Moral Reasons*, 60.

29. Here I disagree with the anthropologist Clifford Geertz's view that "the defining feature of legal process" is "the skeletonization of fact so as to narrow moral issues to the point where determinate rules can be employed to decide them." Clifford Geertz, *Local Knowledge: Further Essays in Interpretive Anthropology* 170 (3d ed. 2000). There is no defining feature either of the legal process or of constitutional interpretation, and attempts to locate such phantoms are destined to end in failure. But if there were such a defining feature, it certainly would not be the willful distortion of facts so as to warp moral vision for the sake of developing hard rules. If it were, it would hardly be worth having a legal system in the first place.

30. Greenawalt, "Fundamental Questions," 1137.

31. The differences are ones of degree, not of kind. An ethics that was completely unpredictable and treated people inconsistently would be flawed.

32. See especially Chapters 6 and 7.

33. See Bakhurst, "Ethical Particularism," 170. Bakhurst has observed that "[p]articularism is crying out for an infusion of the kind of historical selfconsciousness which informs MacIntyre's approach." Id. at 176–177. I advance such a historically self-conscious approach in Chapters 6 and 7.

34. See Dancy, *Moral Reasons*, 113 ("The persuasiveness here is the persuasiveness of narrative: an internal coherence in the account which compels assent"); McDowell, *Mind, Value, and Reality*, 50 ("A conception of right conduct is grasped, as it were, from the inside out"). This internal coherence can be found in constitutional law no less than in other legal contexts.

35. For similar reflections, see Michael Stocker, *Plural and Conflicting Values* 87 (1990).

36. One can engage in *reductio ad absurdum*-style arguments to make the experiential point more vivid. Someone asked me once whether the value of the pleasure of clicking one's tongue should count, or the value of looking at a pebble. It seems to me that the claim from experiential significance is capable of dealing with many kinds of trivial values. It just is not the case, historically and culturally, that these values matter all that much. See Joseph Raz, *The Morality of Freedom* 328–329 (1986) (noting that "[t]here are plenty of insignificant incommensurabilities").

37. Williams, *Ethics*, 161.

38. Andrew Koppelman, *Defending American Religious Neutrality* 51, 53 (2013); see also Raz, *Morality of Freedom*, 121–124 ("A second argument designed to show that neutrality is chimerical claims that whether or not a person acts neutrally depends on the base line relative to which his behavior is judged, and that there are always different base lines leading to conflicting judgments and no rational grounds to prefer one to the others").

39. Koppelman, *Defending*, 197.

40. See Martha C. Nussbaum, *The Fragility of Goodness: Luck and Ethics in Greek Tragedy and Philosophy* 25 (rev. ed. 2001) ("[T]ragedies also show us, and dwell upon, another more intractable sort of case—one which has come to be called, as a result, the situation of 'tragic conflict.' . . . The constraint comes from the presence of circumstances that prevent the adequate fulfillment of two valid *ethical* claims") (emphasis added).

41. Id. at 27.

42. Lord Byron's conflicted young Don Juan—"[s]ilent and pensive, idle, restless, slow . . . [t]ormented with a wound he could not know"—is perhaps more fitting for these purposes than Lorenzo Da Ponte and Mozart's brash lothario. Lord Byron, *Don Juan*, Canto I, Verse 87, in *The Poetical Works of Lord Byron* 542 (Frederick Warne Co. ed. 1819).

43. Gustave Flaubert, *Madame Bovary* (Penguin Classics ed. 2003).

44. Nussbaum, *Fragility*, 29.

45. Thanks to Paul Horwitz for this point.

46. Nussbaum, *Fragility*, 29.

47. Dancy, *Moral Reasons*, 136.

48. Theocracies—governments in which the clergy rules, or in which religious law applies to civil affairs—may be founded on both experientially significant and morally salient values.

49. I set to the side arguments that the Establishment Clause was a *purely* jurisdictional provision protecting the right of states to retain or abandon their religious establishments as they saw fit. See Akhil Reed Amar, *The Bill of Rights: Creation and Reconstruction* 33–34 (1998). For criticism, see Donald L. Drakeman, *Church, State, and Original Intent* (2010).

50. Wisconsin v. Yoder, 406 U.S. 205 (1972).

51. Lee v. Weisman, 505 U.S. 577 (1992).

52. Eisgruber & Sager, *Religious Freedom*, 75.

5. Loss, Sacrifice, and the Disposition of Custom

1. Michael Stocker, "Abstract and Concrete Value: Plurality, Conflict, and Maximization," in *Incommensurability, Incomparability, and Practical Reason* 196, 198 (Ruth Chang ed., 1997).

2. See Stuart Hampshire, *Morality & Conflict* 93 (1984) ("[F]rom the fact that a man thinks that there is nothing other than X which he can decently do in a particular situation it does not follow that it is intuitively obvious to him that he must do X"); see also Joseph Raz, "Value Incommensurability: Some Preliminaries," 86 *Proc. of the Aristotelian Society* 117, 132–133 (1985) ("Rational action is action for (what the agent takes to be) an undefeated reason. It is not necessarily action for a reason which defeats all others").

3. On empathy in adjudication, see Paul Horwitz, *The Agnostic Age: Law, Religion, and the Constitution* 71–121 (2011).

4. For discussion of this specific sense of regret as distinguished from empathy, see Jonathan Dancy, *Moral Reasons* 120–121 (1993).

5. Horwitz dwells instead on the idea of "regret" in its more ordinary sense—of experiencing "lost sleep" or a feeling of "worry" or as "an appreciation of the moral seriousness of a decision"—and he connects it to his discussion of the importance of empathy in constitutional adjudication. Horwitz, *Agnostic Age*, 214–215. In a similar vein, Thomas Colby discusses "judicial empathy" as involving "the emotional capacity to understand and feel [another] person's emotions . . . ." Thomas B. Colby, "In Defense of Judicial Empathy," 96 *Minn. L. Rev.* 1944, 1958 (2012). This is different than the sense of loss and regret that interests me here. Whether judges feel bad or emotionally pained that there was a loser is not the issue; only their belief (reflected in their opinions) that their decisions lack the values of the unchosen options.

6. John Kekes, *The Morality of Pluralism* 65 (1993).

7. Compare Rosalind Hursthouse, *On Virtue Ethics* 67 (1999).

8. Martha C. Nussbaum, *The Fragility of Goodness: Luck and Ethics in Greek Tragedy and Philosophy* 42 (rev. ed. 2001).

9. Id. at 44.

10. Id. at 49.

11. See also Dancy, *Moral Reasons*, 116–119.

12. See Joseph Raz, *The Morality of Freedom* 327 (1986) ("There is a strong temptation to think of incommensurability as an imperfection, an incompleteness. Why don't we develop the function from the different features to the overall valuation until it is complete and eliminate thereby all incommensurability? The mistake in this thought is that it assumes that there is a true value behind the ranking of options, and that the ranking is a kind of technique for measuring this value").

13. 475 U.S. 503 (1986).

14. For Horwitz, by contrast, *Goldman* is an easy case. See Horwitz, *Agnostic Age*, 215. This discrepancy may be attributable to the different meanings of "loss" and "regret" that are reflected in our respective approaches. For Horwitz, *Goldman* should be decided in favor of the religious claimant because a judge should not feel any empathy toward

the military when it is merely advocating "interests in convenience and administrability." Id. A judge applying the method of tragedy and history, and therefore relying on a different concept of loss and regret, would regard *Goldman* as a difficult case and would account in different ways for the military's interests.

15. Goldman, 475 U.S. at 504.

16. For related discussion, see Chapter 3.

17. Goldman, 475 U.S. at 507.

18. Id. at 508.

19. To be sure, as Justice Brennan pointed out in dissent, the military's own regulations did not require absolute uniformity of appearance. Id. at 518 (Brennan, J., dissenting). Nevertheless, the fact that very minor exceptions have been made to a particular custom or tradition does not necessarily diminish the importance or the power of the tradition.

20. See Raz, "Value Incommensurability," 130 ("[W]hile people reject the thought of comparing the value of various options when the question is raised in the abstract, they do make decisions about trade-offs when the issue is forced on them by the circumstances of their lives").

21. Lee v. Weisman, 505 U.S. 557, 587–588 (1992).

22. See Raz, "Value Incommensurability," 131–132 ("The choice is not arbitrary . . . [because] it may be based on a reason. Though the reason is incommensurate with the reason for the alternative it shows the value of that option and when that option is chosen it is chosen because of its value. . . . Saying that two options are incommensurate does not preclude choice"); see also William A. Galston, *Liberal Pluralism: The Implications of Value Pluralism for Political Theory and Practice* 35 (2002) ("Value pluralism does not rule out the possibility of compelling (if non-algorithmic) arguments for right answers in specific situations").

23. Ronald Dworkin, "Do Liberal Values Conflict?," in *The Legacy of Isaiah Berlin* 73, 79 (Ronald Dworkin et al. eds., 2001). Dworkin criticizes this view in the remainder of his essay.

24. Goldman, 475 U.S. at 519 (Brennan, J., dissenting).

25. 494 U.S. 872 (1990).

26. Goldman, 475 U.S. at 521 (Brennan, J., dissenting).

27. John Gray, *Isaiah Berlin* 45 (1997).

28. See Paul Horwitz, "Three Faces of Deference," 83 *Notre Dame L. Rev.* 1061, 1087 (2008) (describing the Supreme Court's epistemic deference to the military as grounded in the military's expertise in matters of its own "composition, training, equipping, and control" and in the Court's lack of competence in this area).

29. See id. at 1122 ("[T]he military deference doctrine is most applicable in cases that involve internal matters of military discipline and order").

30. 1 Kent Greenawalt, *Religion and the Constitution: Free Exercise and Fairness* 164 (2006).

31. The Court's decision in *Goldman* was superseded and effectively reversed by statute. See National Defense Authorization Act for Fiscal Years 1988 and 1989, Pub. L. No. 100–180, Div. A., Tit. V, § 508(a)(2), 101 Stat. 1019 (1987).

32. See Raz, *Morality of Freedom*, 345–357.

33. Steven Lukes, "Comparing the Incomparable: Trade-Offs and Sacrifices," in *Incommensurability, Incomparability*, 187–190.

34. Id. at 187–188.

35. Id. at 189.

36. See Hampshire, *Morality & Conflict*, 89; see also Nussbaum, *Fragility*, 41 (distinguishing between an "economic loss and the loss of a life").

37. See Chapter 4 for discussion.

38. Hampshire, *Morality & Conflict*, 95.

39. Lukes, "Comparing," 188–189.

40. Émile Durkheim, *Les Formes Élémentaires de la Vie Religiuese* 55 (Quadrige/PUF ed. 2005) ("The sacred object is *par excellence* that which the profane object must not, cannot, touch with impunity").

41. See Hampshire, *Morality & Conflict*, 89 ("Evidently these ideas have often been associated with impiety, and with a belief that God, or the Gods, have been defied, and with a fear of divine anger"); Lukes, "Comparing," 188 ("[Sacredness] may apply to interpersonal and civic commitments, and it spans the spectrum of worldviews and ideologies").

42. Philip Hamburger, "More is Less," 90 *Va. L. Rev.* 835, 858 (2004). For Hamburger, the absence of contingency on civic interests fits hand in glove with the relatively narrow interpretation of religious liberty favored in the late eighteenth century—as a "freedom from penalties on religion" or from "laws imposing constraints on Americans on the basis of their religion." Id. at 855, 873.

43. See Ruth Chang, "Introduction," in *Incommensurability, Incomparability*, 1, 21.

44. Søren Kierkegaard, "Fear and Trembling," in *Fear and Trembling and the Book on Adler* 3, 45–57 (Walter Lowrie trans., 1994). Abraham is prepared to sacrifice Isaac even though "[i]n Abraham's life there is no higher expression for the ethical than this, that the father shall love his son. Of the ethical in the sense of morality there can be no question in this instance. In so far as the universal was present, it was indeed cryptically present in Isaac, hidden as it were in Isaac's loins, and must therefore cry out with Isaac's mouth, 'Do it not!'" Id. at 50.

45. Cass R. Sunstein, "Incommensurability and Kinds of Valuation: Some Applications in Law," in *Incommensurability, Incomparability*, 234, 242.

46. Raz, *Morality of Freedom*, 337.

47. Raz, "Value Incommensurability," 126.

48. Kekes, *Morality of Pluralism*, 167.

49. See Raz, "Value Incommensurability," 128 ("The choice between looking after an aged parent and getting married in order to have a family of one's own is momentous in its consequences. It should be informed by knowledge of these consequences. And yet they may well fail to yield a determined outcome, a definite right or wrong, wise or foolish decision").

50. Raz, *Morality of Freedom*, 333.

51. Leo Katz, *Why the Law Is So Perverse* 139–156 (2011); see also John Finnis, *Natural Law and Natural Rights* 279 (2d ed. 2011).

52. There is an analogy, once again, to moral particularism here. Consider an example given by Jonathan Dancy: "For instance, I have to break some bad news to my sister. The distress I shall cause her is not sufficient reason for me to keep silent; as a reason against, it is defeated. But it still makes a difference to how I should break the news to her, when and where I should do it and so on. So it remains in the picture as a practically relevant consideration, even though it does not count among those features of the action which reveal why I do it. It is not a reason for doing it, but it is a reason for doing it this way rather than that." See Dancy, *Moral Reasons,* 116–117.

53. Michael Oakeshott, "On Being Conservative," in *Rationalism in Politics and Other Essays* 407 (1991) (1961). "Conservative," of course, is not to be understood in Oakeshott's work in its conventional American political sense, as the ideological counterpoint to "liberal," to be promptly sent, as Conor Cruise O'Brien once put it, "crabwalking down history in a narrow and jealous dialectic of change and resistance." Conor Cruise O'Brien, *The Great Melody: A Thematic Biography of Edmund Burke* lxiv (1992). Indeed, Oakeshott himself has sometimes been described as a political "liberal"—see Paul Franco, "Michael Oakeshott as Liberal Theorist," 18 *Pol. Theory* 411 (1990)—or even "post-liberal." See John Gray, *Post-Liberalism: Studies in Political Thought* 40–46 (1993). The eminent philosopher Richard Rorty deemed Oakeshott a kind of proto-post-modernist. See Richard Rorty, *Philosophy and the Mirror of Nature* 389–394 (1979). At any rate, the use of Oakeshott's essay is not meant to identify a specific set of policies, on the political left or right, so much as a methodological orientation to certain questions.

54. Oakeshott, "On Being," 408.

55. Id. at 408–410.

56. In fact, the innovation may generate not only an improvement, but also "a new and complex situation of which this is only one of the components. The total change is always more extensive than the change designed; and the whole of what is entailed can neither be foreseen nor circumscribed." Id. at 411.

57. Id.

58. Id. at 413.

59. Id. at 410.

60. Id. at 411.

61. Id. at 413.

62. See Raz, *Morality of Freedom,* 356 ("Being engaged in a pursuit or a relationship includes belief that certain options are not comparable in value. Abandoning such beliefs is therefore one way of abandoning the pursuit. . . . Regarding a class of relationships as comparable in value with other options with which they are by their constitutive conventions incomparable, makes one unfit for, incapable of having, relations of that kind"). Raz uses the term *conventions* in this passage in a manner analogous to my use of the term *customs.*

63. 494 U.S. 872 (1990).

64. 485 U.S. 439 (1988). In *Lyng,* the Court ruled against a group of Native Americans who objected on free exercise grounds to the federal government's plan to build a road through lands sacred to the group. *Lyng* is taken up in Chapter 9.

65. For discussion of cases, see Chapter 7.

66. The so-called "ministerial exception" is discussed in Chapter 9.

67. One might argue that Deborah Weisman was reacting not to an innovation but to the entrenched practice of graduation prayers. But this is a superficial description. Ms. Weisman had been raised all her life with certain views about the role of religious belief, views powerful enough that they compelled her father to engage in years of protracted litigation to vindicate them. In that sense, the imposition of a graduation prayer was very much a new and unwelcome change to the Weismans' way of life. One could say more: it was exactly because of the power and hold of custom on the Weismans that they were so committed to opposing the school prayer policy.

68. Richard W. Garnett, "The Story of Henry Adams's Soul: Education and the Expression of Associations," 85 *Minn. L. Rev.* 1841, 1849 (2001).

69. Anthony T. Kronman, "Precedent and Tradition," 99 *Yale L.J.* 1029, 1051 (1990).

70. Oakeshott, "On Being," 425–426.

71. These reasons are discussed in Chapter 6.

72. Oliver Wendell Holmes, Jr., "The Path of the Law," 10 *Harv. L. Rev.* 457, 469 (1897).

73. A better expression of the disposition of custom may be found in a very different Holmesian aphorism: "If a thing has been practiced for two hundred years by common consent, it will need a strong case for the Fourteenth Amendment to affect it." Jackman v. Rosenbaum Co., 260 U.S. 22, 31 (1922); see also Lochner v. New York, 198 U.S. 45, 76 (1905) (Holmes, J., dissenting) (arguing that the Due Process Clause is offended only where "a rational and fair man necessarily would admit that the statute proposed would infringe fundamental principles as they have been understood by the traditions of our people and our law").

74. For a superb study of the institutional features of the First Amendment, see Paul Horwitz, *First Amendment Institutions* (2013).

75. Garnett, "Story," 1853–1854.

76. See id. at 1856.

77. This point may appear to be in tension with the observation that in America, religious "brand loyalty" is "surprisingly low." See Robert D. Putnam & David E. Campbell, *American Grace: How Religion Divides and Unites Us* 148 (2010). But the tension is illusory. It is true that Americans are less frequently "born" into a religion than are Europeans, for example, though Putnam and Campbell find that the majority of Americans retain the same religious identities as their parents. See id. at 136. Nevertheless, even if loyalty toward an inherited religion is less common in America than in Europe, loyalty to religious traditions and institutions, once chosen (the fact of *choosing* is particularly important in Putnam and Campbell's account), is strong. See id. at 148.

78. Oakeshott, "On Being," 416.

79. See Steven H. Shiffrin, *The First Amendment, Democracy, and Romance* 122 (1990) ("By contrast, the eclectic believes that there are too many principles that interact in too many complicated ways in too many concrete contexts to warrant any realistic hope that any general theorist's project could succeed. The eclectic could not claim an ability to 'prove' this negative assertion. The best the eclectic can do is to point to

the ways in which the general theorist's project encounters difficulties and to refute specific principles as they are proposed").

80. For similar reflections, see Dancy, *Moral Reasons*, 114.

6. The Need for Modest Movement

1. See Steven H. Shiffrin, *The First Amendment, Democracy, and Romance* 111 (1990) ("If we are concerned about the kind of people the first amendment tends to encourage, we need to be as concerned with the rhetoric of first amendment discourse as with the details of its decisions").

2. Frederick Schauer, "Precedent," 39 *Stan. L. Rev.* 571, 597 (1987).

3. Shiffrin, *First Amendment*, 113 (describing the methodological values supporting "eclecticism" in First Amendment thought).

4. Schauer, "Precedent," 571 ("The previous treatment of occurrence X in manner Y constitutes, solely because of its historical pedigree, a reason for treating X in manner Y if and when X occurs again"). It will be seen in later chapters that the adoption of a single-value test does not necessarily increase the predictability with which that test is administered.

5. The theory is primarily Cass Sunstein's. See generally Cass R. Sunstein, *Radicals in Robes: Why Extreme Right-Wing Courts Are Wrong for America* (2005); Cass R. Sunstein, *One Case at a Time: Judicial Minimalism on the Supreme Court* (1999); Cass R. Sunstein, "Second-Order Perfectionism," 75 *Fordham L. Rev.* 2867 (2007); Cass. R. Sunstein, "Problems with Minimalism," 58 *Stan. L. Rev.* 1899 (2006); Cass R. Sunstein, "Testing Minimalism: A Reply," 104 *Mich. L. Rev.* 123 (2005); Cass R. Sunstein, "Minimalism at War," 2004 *S. Ct. Rev.* 47 (2004); Cass R. Sunstein, "Foreword: Leaving Things Undecided," 110 *Harv. L. Rev.* 4 (1996). It is not exclusively Sunstein's, however. Alexander Bickel, for example, wrote approvingly of a limited and constrained vision of adjudication in which the scope of courts' powers was curbed by "devices of not doing, or passive virtues." Alexander M. Bickel, *The Least Dangerous Branch: The Supreme Court at the Bar of Politics* 201 (1962).

6. Sunstein, *One Case*, 10–14.

7. See Cass R. Sunstein, "Trimming," 122 *Harv. L. Rev.* 1049, 1081 (2009).

8. Cass R. Sunstein, "Burkean Minimalism," 105 *Mich. L. Rev.* 353 (2006).

9. Id. at 356.

10. Id. at 356–359. Technically, incrementalism does not distinguish Burkean minimalists from other minimalists, but the reasons for Burkean minimalists' incrementalism are distinctive.

11. Id.

12. 475 U.S. 503 (1986).

13. The Court might have resolved the case on the narrow and shallow grounds that Goldberg should have been granted an exemption in this specific context, but it declined to do so.

14. Sunstein, "Burkean Minimalism," 363–364. Narrow rules also reduce decisional costs, since they will be more likely to garner agreement. Id.

15. Sunstein, *One Case*, 40.

16. Sunstein, "Burkean Minimalism," 368.

17. See the discussion of *Employment Division v. Smith* in Chapter 8.

18. Sunstein, "Burkean Minimalism," 368–369 ("For Burkeans who emphasize practices, it is not legitimate for judges to build constitutional law through small steps that reflect the Court's own judgment over time. But for those who see the case-by-case evolution of judge-made constitutional law as an acceptably Burkean project, judicial steps deserve respect, in part because those steps are unlikely to depart radically from public convictions").

19. Id. at 371–372; see also Adrian Vermeule, "Common Law Constitutionalism and the Limits of Reason," 107 *Colum. L. Rev.* 1482, 1486 (2007) ("Common law constitutionalism represents an explicitly Burkean strain in constitutional theory").

20. Sunstein, "Burkean Minimalism," 373.

21. 494 U.S. 872 (1990).

22. 42 U.S.C. §§ 2000bb–bb-4 (2006).

23. Some states have interpreted their state constitutions to require strict scrutiny. These include Arkansas, Indiana, Massachusetts, Maine, Michigan, Minnesota, Montana, North Carolina, Ohio, Washington, and Wisconsin. Other states have adopted religious freedom restoration statutes in the wake of *Smith* and *City of Boerne v. Flores*, which held that the RFRA was inapplicable against the states. These include Alabama (by state constitutional amendment), Arizona, Connecticut, Florida, Idaho, Illinois, Louisiana, Missouri, New Mexico, Oklahoma, Pennsylvania, Rhode Island, South Carolina, Tennessee, Texas, and Virginia. The remaining states (1) do not apply strict scrutiny and have no state religious freedom statute; (2) apply weak intermediate scrutiny (New York); or (3) have not yet decided.

24. 42 U.S.C. §§ 2000cc–2000cc-5 (2006).

25. Van Orden v. Perry, 545 U.S. 677, 698 (2005) (Breyer, J., concurring); Lemon v. Kurtzman, 403 U.S. 602, 622 (1971) (discussing the "divisive political potential" of state-sponsored religious institutions and activities). Even those scholars who argue that religious liberty disputes are no more "divisive" than many others might nevertheless agree that these issues do represent a category of legal conflict that is comparatively contentious. See generally Richard W. Garnett, "Religion, Division, and the First Amendment," 94 *Geo. L.J.* 1667 (2006).

26. Sunstein, "Burkean Minimalism," 365; see also Nelson Tebbe & Robert L. Tsai, "Constitutional Borrowing," 108 *Mich. L. Rev.* 459, 516 (2010) ("Minimalism is also designed to reduce the risk of political backlash against controversial decisions").

27. I am not suggesting that the "divisiveness" of religious liberty conflicts demands anything more than a narrow and shallow ruling; by itself, it does not point toward any substantive result.

28. Van Orden, 545 U.S. at 698 (Breyer, J., concurring) (quoting School Dist. of Abington Twp. v. Schempp, 374 U.S. 203, 306 (1963) (Goldberg & Harlan, JJ., concurring)). Justice Thomas's recent dissent from the denial of certiorari in a religious display case

complains about this quality of Establishment Clause law. See Utah Highway Patrol Ass'n v. American Atheists, 132 S. Ct. 12, 19–20 (2011) (Thomas, J., dissenting) (railing against the "context[ual]" standard used in religious display cases).

29. Perhaps the clearest example is racial segregation, though matters may become more complex if the issue of the remedy is included. See Sunstein, "Burkean Minimalism," 361.

30. Id. at 374–376.

31. Elk Grove Unified Sch. Dist. v. Newdow, 542 U.S. 1, 26–33 (2004) (Rehnquist, C. J., concurring).

32. Id. at 28.

33. For more on *Elk Grove*, see Chapter 7. At times Sunstein describes Chief Justice Rehnquist as a judicial maximalist, but at least in the area of religion clause jurisprudence, this is contestable. See Robert Anderson IV, "Measuring Meta-Doctrine: An Empirical Assessment of Judicial Minimalism in the Supreme Court," 32 *Harv. J. L. Pub. Pol'y* 1045, 1050, 1067–1068, 1077 (2009) (conducting an empirical study indicating that "Chief Justice Rehnquist may have been, in fact, one of the most minimalist members of the Court").

34. Van Orden v. Perry, 545 U.S. 677 (2005); McCreary Cty. v. ACLU, 545 U.S. 844, 851–855 (2005).

35. McCreary, 545 U.S. at 852–858.

36. Sunstein, "Burkean Minimalism," 376.

37. McCreary, 545 U.S. at 866.

38. 366 U.S. 420 (1961).

39. McCreary, 545 U.S. at 873, n.22.

40. Van Orden, 545 U.S. at 703–704 (Breyer, J., concurring).

41. Sunstein, "Burkean Minimalism," 377.

42. Id. at 389.

43. Id. at 395.

44. Id.

45. Id. at 387, 404.

46. Sunstein, "Second-Order Perfectionism," 2869; see also Ronald Dworkin, *Law's Empire* 343 (1986).

47. Sunstein, "Burkean Minimalism," 395–396 ("It should be obvious that the argument for theoretical ambition from the federal judiciary would be strengthened if there was a reason to trust not only the good will but also the capacities of theoretically ambitious judges. It is here, of course, that Burkean minimalists break from perfectionists"). In more recent writing, the weakness and contingency of Sunstein's allegiance to minimalism (including to Burkean minimalism) is apparent. See, e.g., Cass R. Sunstein, "Beyond Judicial Minimalism," 43 *Tulsa L. Rev.* 825, 835 (2008).

48. Sunstein, *One Case*, 57 (describing a preference for judicial maximalism when it "will promote democratic goals"). Of course, the method of tragedy and history is not opposed to enhancing or promoting democratic deliberation, and it takes democracy-enhancing resolutions to be valuable; indeed, it will be seen that social practices with strong and sustained support by the people who are committed to

them counts as an important consideration for the method of tragedy and history. But the tragic-historic method does not see that value as primary.

49. See Sunstein, "Burkean Minimalism," 387.

50. Id. at 359. Sunstein is alert to this difficulty. Id. at 404–405. But he assiduously side-steps "foundational" issues, instead suggesting that "[f]or purposes of evaluating Burkean minimalism in constitutional law, the need for commitment to any kind of foundational approach is diminished if we attend to the theory-building weaknesses of the federal judiciary." Id. at 405. Sunstein thus aligns himself with those interpreters of Burke who mistakenly believe that he was unequivocally a hard utilitarian. See, e.g., John Morley, *Edmund Burke: A Historical Study* 150–152 (1867); William Lecky, 5 *A History of England in the Eighteenth Century* 476 (1891). James Fitzjames Stephen—a complex figure to pin down in his own right—had a more nuanced and, I believe, accurate sense of the complexity of Burke's views. See James Fitzjames Stephen, "Burke on the French Revolution," in 3 *Horae Sabbaticae* 140–144 (noting that a "notion of a justice antecedent to, and by right formative of, all law, and made binding on all men by an immutable divine decree, lies at the root of every part of Burke's political theories").

51. Hence a key difference from Burkean minimalism, which, as noted earlier, denies that "we are in some way constituted by our traditions." David Strauss has also claimed the "Burkean" mantle as part of his theory of living constitutionalism, but his Burkeanism also seems thin and pragmatic, inquiring into "what has worked in practice" and rejecting the view that social customs are constitutive. See David A. Strauss, *The Living Constitution* 41–48 (2010).

52. Harvey C. Mansfield, Jr., "Introduction" to *Selected Letters of Edmund Burke* 4 (1984).

53. See Ernest Young, "Rediscovering Conservatism: Burkean Political Theory and Constitutional Interpretation," 72 *N.C. L. Rev.* 619, 687 (1994) ("It is critical, however, to remember that Burke abhorred general theories. . . . And yet, Burke devoted a great deal of time and energy to theory").

54. 3 *The Speeches of the Right Honourable Edmund Burke* 48 (1816); see also Edmund Burke, "Speech on the Petition of the Unitarians" (May 11, 1792), in 5 *The Works of Edmund Burke* 367 (Little & Brown ed. 1839) ("I do not put abstract ideas wholly out of any question, because I well know that under that name I should dismiss principles; and that without the guide and light of sound well-understood principles, all reasoning in politics, as in every thing else, would be only a confused jumble of particular facts and details, without the means of drawing out any sort of theoretical or practical conclusion"). Indeed, it would hardly do for someone so opposed to theory "as such" to write a treatise entitled "A Philosophical Inquiry into the Origin of Our Ideas of the Sublime and the Beautiful," and to describe his effort as exactly a "theory." 1 *Works*, 65.

55. Joseph Hamburger, "Edmund Burke and the Natural Law," 68 *Yale L.J.* 831 (1959) (book review).

56. Burke, *Speeches*, 48.

57. Mansfield, "Introduction," 5.

58. J.G.A. Pocock, "Introduction," in Edmund Burke, *Reflections on the Revolution in France* xxxvi (Hackett Pub. Co. 1987) (1790).

59. James Conniff, *The Useful Cobbler: Edmund Burke and the Politics of Progress* 8 (1994).

60. Though not a lawyer himself, Burke had studied law before turning his attention elsewhere, and he held the law in high esteem throughout his life. See Edmund Burke, "Speech on American Taxation," in 1 *Select Works of Edmund Burke* 185 (Liberty Fund ed. 1999) ("The law, which is, in my opinion, one of the first and noblest of human sciences; a science which does more to quicken and invigorate the understanding than all the other kinds of learning put together").

61. Edmund Burke, "Appeal from the New to the Old Whigs," in 3 *Works*, 348–349. The reference to "fictitious cases" evokes the proscription against the rendering of "advisory" opinions in federal constitutional law, opinions about hypothetical cases. See U.S. Const. art. III, § 2, cl. 1.

    The reason that judgment may be had only in actual "cases" or "controversies" is not merely that the Constitution has been interpreted to require it, or that it would be an inefficient use of the judiciary to rule on hypothetical issues, but because without the anchor of real facts and real conflicts, courts might feel unconstrained to construct abstract, broad, and deep principles in response to fictitious controversies that they might later (when confronted with a real case) regret. See *The Correspondence and Public Papers of John Jay* 488–489 (1891), quoted in *The Constitution of the United States* (Michael Stokes Paulsen et al. eds., 2010) (reprinting the letter of Chief Justice John Jay declining the request of Secretary of State Thomas Jefferson for advisory opinions arising out of America's relationship with France); see also Young, "Rediscovering," 680 ("The 'case and controversy' requirement encourages judges to make decisions in the way that Burke would prefer legislators to make them: incrementally, and in response to particular problems").

62. Edmund Burke, "Reflections on the Revolution in France," in 3 *Works*, 25 ("Circumstances (which with some gentlemen pass for nothing) give in reality to every political principle its distinguishing color and discriminating effect. The circumstances are what render every civil and political scheme beneficial or noxious to mankind"); Edmund Burke, "Speech on the Petition of the Unitarians," in 5 *Works*, 367 ("Circumstances are infinite, are infinitely combined, are variable and transient; he who does not take them into consideration is not erroneous, but stark mad"); see generally Conor Cruise O'Brien, *The Great Melody: A Thematic Biography of Edmund Burke* 25, 403–404 (1992), who notes that the concept of "circumstances" is crucial for Burke's thought: "Burke had immense respect for circumstances, and observed them with proportionate attentiveness"; Conniff, *Useful Cobbler*, 8 ("The complexity and variety of politics is so great, according to Burke, that little can be said without reference to particular circumstances").

63. 3 *Works*, 118–119. Burke's well-known remarks on the virtues of "prejudice"—meaning roughly customary dispositions of long duration and pervasive influence—are to like effect. See id. at 109–110; see also David Bromwich, *A Choice of Inheritance: Self and Community from Edmund Burke to Robert Frost* 44–45 (1989) ("A prejudice

may of course lead to bigotry (which gives the word its pejorative modern sense), but it is itself merely a disposition of judgment. . . . All those habits, customs, and local superstitions you complain of (he says to the party of improvers), just *are* human nature. They are what we are").

64. Ernest Young seems at times to side with the purely pragmatic interpretation of Burke, but he also correctly notes that Burke's suspicion of abstract theory is grounded in the view that it "can never adequately capture the complexity of real life." Young, "Rediscovering," 683. If "absolutist positions" can *never* capture the world's complexity, then there is more than merely a pragmatic reason for avoiding them.

65. Pocock, "Introduction," xlix.

66. Burke, "Reflections," in 3 *Works*, 83. This is also the reason that so far as constitutional interpretation is concerned, Burke cannot be classed as an "originalist," since for him "[t]he parts of our constitution have gradually, and almost insensibly, in a long course of time, accommodated themselves to each other, and to their common, as well as to their separate, purposes. But this adaptation of contending parts . . . [is not] the effect of a single instantaneous regulation, and no sound heads could ever think of doing it in that manner. . . . [The constitution] grew out of the habitual conditions, relations, and reciprocal claims of men. It grew out of the circumstances of the country." Id. at 324–325; see also Mansfield, "Introduction," 13 ("He praises the British constitution to the skies, but never its founders. The old Whigs, to whom he appeals against new Whigs favorable to the French Revolution, set a good example but did not lay down principles that new Whigs must follow"); Young, "Rediscovering," 664 ("If Edmund Burke were a judge in modern America, there is good reason to believe that he would not be an originalist").

67. There is an interesting exchange of letters in the appendix of Conor Cruise O'Brien's treatment of Burke between O'Brien and Isaiah Berlin, in which O'Brien is sanguine about describing Burke as a value pluralist, while Berlin is more hesitant (though not entirely opposed). See O'Brien, *The Great Melody*, 605–618.

68. See Chapter 4; see also Kent Greenawalt, "Justice Harlan's Conservatism and Alternative Possibilities," 36 *N.Y. L. Sch. L. Rev.* 53, 64 (1991) ("Skepticism about abstract ideas and rapid change, and concentration on particular context, does incline one toward balancing approaches to the resolution of social problems"). The method of tragedy and history is not a "balancing approach" because it often denies that the values of religious liberty and those against which they compete are capable of being traded off. Nevertheless, the particularism of Greenawalt's observation is in keeping with the method of tragedy and history.

69. 3 *Works*, 40, 54.

70. See Edmund Burke, "Speech on Conciliation with America," in 2 *Works*, 23 ("Because after all our struggle, whether we will or not, we must govern America, according to . . . circumstances; and not according to our own imaginations; not according to abstract ideas of right; by no means according to mere general theories of government. . . . I shall therefore endeavor, with your leave, to lay before you some of the most material of these circumstances in as full and as clear a manner as I am able to state them"); Edmund Burke, "Speech on American Taxation," in *Select*

Works, 213 ("If you apprehend that on a concession you shall be pushed by meta-physical process to the extreme lines . . . my advice is this; when you have recovered your old, your strong, your tenable position, then face about—stop short—do nothing more—reason not at all—oppose the ancient policy and practice of the Empire as a rampart against the speculations of innovators on both sides of the question"); see also O'Brien, *The Great Melody*, 91, 602 ("[Burke] was trying, during the early phases of the pre-revolutionary process, to persuade the English not to provoke Americans into rebellion; during the later pre-revolutionary phases, he was trying to dissuade the English from using force against the Americans; during the actual revolutionary war he was trying . . . to persuade the English to concede independence to the Americans; *de facto* independence up to 1778; *de jure* independence from then on"); Pocock, "Introduction," xiv ("Burke had been parliamentary agent for the colony of New York and, in his speeches and actions during the American crisis, had attacked the ministry of Lord North for actions which drove the colonists to rebellion").

71. Burke, "Philosophical Inquiry," in 1 *Works*, 139; see also Burke, "Reflections," in 3 *Works*, 111 ("This people refused to change their law in remote ages, from respect to the infallibility of popes; and they will not now alter it from a pious implicit faith in the dogmatism of philosophers; though the former was armed with the anathema and crusade, and though the latter should act with the libel and the lamp iron").

72. Edmund Burke, "Letters on a Regicide Peace," in 4 *Works*, 444.

73. James Stoner has astutely pointed out that "[n]ot only the original intention of the Constitution but also the value of recourse to original intention is oblique if common law is overlooked, for the great document and the Bill of Rights that soon joined it were written in the idiom of the common law. . . . Besides, for a century or more, American constitutional development took place in a legal context that took its bearings from common law, and even today our law is replete with precepts and institutions of common-law descent." James R. Stoner, Jr., *Common-Law Liberty: Rethinking American Constitutionalism* 10 (2003).

74. Burke, "Reflections," in 3 *Works*, 54.

75. Burke was not opposed to legal and political reform. See, e.g., Burke, "Reflections," in 3 *Works*, 237–238 ("These venerable bodies, like the rest of the old government, stood in need of reform. . . . They required several more alterations to adapt them to the system of a free constitution. But they had particulars in their constitution, and those not a few, which deserved approbation from the wise"); Edmund Burke, "Speech on the Economical Reform," in 2 *Works*, 163–164 ("But as it is the interest of government that reformation should be early, it is the interest of the people that it should be temperate. It is their interest, because a temperate reform is permanent; and because it has a principle of growth. Whenever we improve, it is right to leave room for a further improvement"); see also Conniff, *The Useful Cobbler*, 3 ("Burke sought to reconcile a generally conservative outlook with an acceptance of the need for change through reform"); Young, "Rediscovering," 653–656 ("Burke's theory of reform is thus grounded in the common-law tradition of evolutionary change").

76. Edmund Burke, "A Letter to Sir Hercules Langrishe, M.P., on the Subject of the Roman Catholics of Ireland," in 3 *Works*, 527 ("We must all obey the great law of change. It is the most powerful law of nature, and the means perhaps of its conservation. All we can do, and that human wisdom can do, is to provide that the change shall proceed by insensible degrees").

77. Conniff, *The Useful Cobbler*, 3.

78. U.S. Const. pmbl.

79. See J. G. A. Pocock, *Politics, Language, and Time: Essays on Political Thought and History* 203 (1971) (describing the "inner life of growth and adaptation" at the heart of Burke's account).

7. The Concilations of History

1. See Anthony T. Kronman, "Precedent and Tradition," 99 *Yale L.J.* 1029, 1031 (1990) (quoting Max Weber, "Science as a Vocation," in *From Max Weber* 129, 155 (H. H. Gerth & C. Wright Mills eds., 1946)).

2. Id. at 1032–1033 (emphasis added).

3. Steven D. Smith, "Stare Decisis in a Classical and Constitutional Setting: A Comment on the Symposium," 5 *Ave Maria L. Rev.* 153, 161 (2007).

4. See Edmund Burke, "Reflections on the Revolution in France," in 3 *The Works of Edmund Burke* 19, 167 (Charles C. Little & James Brown eds., 1839) ("In history a great volume is unrolled for our instruction, drawing the materials of future wisdom from the past errors and infirmities of mankind").

5. Vertical precedent describes the obligation of inferior courts to follow the judgment of superior courts. Horizontal precedent is the practice of following the holding of an earlier decision simply because it came earlier—temporal priority as an independently authoritative reason. Most of the discussion in this chapter concerns horizontal precedent.

6. For a thoughtful study of common-law constitutionalism, see James R. Stoner, Jr., *Common Law Liberty: Rethinking American Constitutionalism* (2003).

7. See, e.g., Frederick Schauer, "Precedent," 39 *Stan. L. Rev.* 571, 595–597 (1987). Rule of law arguments from "fairness" and "predictability" in defense of precedent are powerful in their own right, but they are secondary to the primary point about the need for doctrinal historicism given the tragic conflicts of religious liberty.

8. On the bindingness of precedent, see Lawrence B. Solum, "The Supreme Court in Bondage: Constitutional Stare Decisis, Legal Formalism, and the Future of Unenumerated Rights," 9 *U. Pa. J. Const. L.* 155 (2006).

9. See Steven D. Smith, "Separation as a Tradition," 18 *J.L. & Pol.* 215, 242 (2002) ("Deference, to be sure, is not veneration, much less abject submission").

10. T. S. Eliot, "Tradition and the Individual Talent," in *Selected Essays* 6 (1960) ("Some one said: 'The dead writers are remote from us because we *know* so much more than they did.' Precisely, and they are that which we know"); see also Harold J. Berman, "The Historical Foundations of Law," 54 *Emory L.J.* 13, 17 (2005) ("[T]he doctrine of

precedent is . . . primarily an expression of the historicity of law—the theory that the past decisions of courts have a normative significance in the determination of what the law is, and further, that the decision of the court in a given case has normative significance—is a precedent for the decision of analogous cases in the future").

11. See Frederick Beiser, *The German Historicist Tradition* 17–18 (2012).

12. See Michael W. McConnell, "Tradition and Constitutionalism before the Constitution," 1998 *U. Ill. L. Rev.* 173, 174 (1998) ("Like originalism, the [traditionalist] approach is historical; but instead of viewing authoritative history as a snapshot of a particular moment, it views as authoritative the gradually evolving moral principles of the nation"). McConnell's traditionalism is an important and understudied approach, though as will become clear, the tragic-historic method's reasons for reliance on social and doctrinal historicism diverge from it in certain respects.

13. Guido Calabresi & Philip Bobbitt, *Tragic Choices* 157–158 (1978).

14. Lautsi v. Italy, App, No. 30814/06, Eur. Ct. H.R. (2011), *available at* http://echr. coe.int/echr/en/hudoc.

15. The convention is formally part of the law of all member states, and it supersedes the states' domestic laws on human rights issues. See Andrew Drzemczewski, "The Sui Generis Nature of the European Convention on Human Rights," 29 *Int'l & Comp. L.Q.* 54 (1980).

16. Protocol to the Convention for the Protection of Human Rights and Fundamental Freedoms art. 2, Mar. 20, 1952, 213 U.N.T.S. 262.

17. Convention for the Protection of Human Rights and Fundamental Freedoms art. 9, Nov. 4, 1950, 213 U.N.T.S. 221.

18. See Sahin v. Turkey, App. No. 44774/98, Eur. Ct. H.R., para. 107 (2004), *available at* http://echr.coe.int/echr/en/hudoc; Metro. Church of Bessarabia v. Moldova, App. No. 45701/99, Eur. Ct. H.R., para 116 (2001), *available at* http://echr.coe.int/ echr/en/hudoc.

19. Lautsi, para. 61.

20. See Steven D. Smith, "Our Agnostic Constitution," 83 *NYU L. Rev.* 120, 129 (2008) ("The document does not affirm theism, but neither does it say anything that could be construed as an affirmation of atheism. Nor does it say—not explicitly, anyway— that governments in this country must be secular; such a requirement, if there is one, would have to be inferred from the Constitution's silence on the subject"). Italy's constitutional court has interpreted the Italian Constitution to demand both "laicità" and "neutrality." See Italian Constitutional Court, judgment no. 508/2000.

21. See Joseph Weiler, Testimony before the European Court of Human Rights, DOTSUB (June 30, 2010), *available at* http://dotsub.com/view/65bc5332-aa10-4b8c-bc50-d051e8f4fcc7.

22. This variation on the problem is similar to that which the U.S. Supreme Court faced in Salazar v. Buono, 130 S.Ct. 1803, 1817 (2010) (plurality opinion) ("The 2002 injunction thus presented the Government with a dilemma. It could not maintain the cross without violating the injunction, but it could not remove the cross without conveying disrespect for those the cross was seen as honoring"); id. at 1823 (Alito, J., concurring) ("The demolition of this venerable . . . monument would also have been

262 ~ Notes to Pages 126–127

interpreted by some as an arresting symbol of a Government that is not neutral but hostile on matters of religion and is bent on eliminating from all public places and symbols any trace of our country's religious heritage"). The *Buono* case is discussed in the following.

23. Marcella Delle Donne and Umberto Melotti have noted that the Italian history of semicontinuous domination by foreign peoples (beginning in 309 BC with the invasion of Italy by the Carthaginians) has rendered Italians particularly sensitive to the issue of immigration. Marcella Delle Donne & Umberto Melotti, *Immigrazione in Europa: Strategie Di Inclusione-Esclusione* (2004).

24. See Joseph Raz, *The Morality of Freedom* 121–124 (1986) (describing a case where in a conflict between parties A and B, where one has formerly been supplying aid to A, one acts nonneutrally whether one continues or discontinues the aid). For incisive discussion of baselines, see Andrew Koppelman, *Defending American Religious Neutrality* (2013).

25. Lautsi, paras. 15–25.

26. Id. at para. 1.3 (Bonello, J., concurring).

27. Id. at para. 17; see also Silvio Ferrari, "Civil Religions: Models and Perspectives," 41 *Geo. Wash. Int'l L. Rev.* 749, 754, n.23 (2010). The Italy that we know today is a comparatively late political development. As a nation (originally, a kingdom), Italy was born in 1861; it is younger than the United States.

28. Lautsi, para. 18.

29. See Alessandro Ferrari, "Civil Religion in Italy: A 'Mission Impossible'?," 41 *Geo. Wash. Int'l L. Rev.* 839, 841 (2010) ("Italian unity had a fortuitous character, achieved in two steps by the Kingdom of Piedmont: the proclamation of the Kingdom of Italy in 1861 and the capture of Rome in 1870. Since nothing connected the other Italian territories to the Savoy monarchy . . . Catholicism—the religion of most of the population—was the only cement binding the new country together").

For a small selection of commentary on the fragile quality of the Italian national character and the difficulties of national unity that Italy faces, see Manlio Graziano, *The Failure of Italian Nationhood: The Geopolitics of a Troubled Identity* (2010); Aldo Schiavone, *Italiani Senza Italia: Storia e Identità* (1998) [Italians without Italy: History and Identity]; G. E. Rusconi, *Se Cessiamo Di Essere Una Nazione* (1993) [If We Cease to Be a Nation]; Sergio Romano, *Finis Italiae* (1994) [The End of Italy].

30. Lautsi, paras. 19–21. Italy adopted its republican constitution in 1948, Article 7 of which states that the state and the Catholic Church "shall be independent and sovereign."

31. Id. at para. 62. For discussion of the European view of neutrality as the absence of proselytism, see Mark L. Movsesian, "Crosses and Culture: State-Sponsored Religious Displays in the U.S. and Europe," 1 *Oxford J.L. and Religion* 338 (2012).

32. In a detailed portion of the opinion, the court discussed the great variety of views among the member states. Lautsi, paras. 26–28. The majority of states have no regulations with respect to the display of religious symbols in public schools. The former Yugoslav Republic of Macedonia, France (with the exception of Alsace and the Moselle), and Georgia forbid all such symbols. Like Italy, Austria, Poland, and

certain sections of Germany and Switzerland require display. In Spain, Greece, Ireland, Malta, San Marino, and Romania, though display is not controlled by any regulation, religious symbols are frequently found in public schools. The constitutional courts of Germany and Switzerland each found the presence of the crucifix in primary or elementary school classrooms to violate their respective constitutions, but a variety of compromise solutions were reached. See Classroom Crucifix II Case (1995), 93 BVwerfGE 1 (translated in Donald P. Kommers, *The Constitutional Jurisprudence of the Federal Republic of Germany* 472–482 (2d ed. 1997)).

33. Lautsi, para. 70.
34. Id. at para. 72.
35. Id. at para. 68.
36. Id. (Rozakis, J., concurring).
37. See id. ("It is, I think, indisputable that the display of crucifixes in Italian State schools has a religious symbolism that has an impact on the obligation of neutrality and impartiality of the State"); see also Ferrari, "Civil Religions," 754 (noting that Italian courts have often stated that the crucifix "manifests the historical and cultural tradition of Italy and is a sign of a value system based on freedom, equality, human dignity, and religious tolerance").
38. See Winnifred Fallers Sullivan, "Why Are We Talking about Civil Religion Now?: Comments on 'Civil Religion in Italy: A "Mission Impossible"?' by Alessandro Ferrari," 41 *Geo. Wash. Int'l L. Rev.* 877, 885 (2010).
39. See Chapter 3.
40. On the modalities, or forms, of constitutional argument, see Philip Bobbitt, *Constitutional Interpretation* 12–13 (1991). The argument here is different from Bobbitt's historical modality; while doctrinal history is on Bobbitt's list, social history is not.
41. Van Orden v. Perry, 545 U.S. 677, 703 (2005) (Breyer, J., concurring).
42. McCreary County v. ACLU of Ky., 545 U.S. 844, 866 (2005).
43. Id.
44. 542 U.S. 1 (2004).
45. Though recitation of the Pledge in *Elk Grove* was teacher led and part of the regular morning exercises in the district, there was no claim that public school students were compelled to recite the Pledge, as compelled speech of that sort has long been held unconstitutional. W. Va. Bd. of Educ. v. Barnette, 319 U.S. 624 (1943).
46. Elk Grove, 542 U.S. at 6–7.
47. Id. at 7.
48. Lautsi v. Italy (Malinverni, J., dissenting), para. 1; see also Susanna Mancini, "The Crucifix Rage: Supranational Constitutionalism Bumps against the Counter-Majoritarian Difficulty," 6 *Eur. Const. L. Rev.* 6, 9 (2010) ("The display of the crucifix is mandated by two royal decrees that date back to the 1920s. These decrees had been enacted by the fascist government before the current Constitution came into force (1948), with the aim of introducing a confessional system").
49. See Newdow v. U.S. Cong., 292 F.3d 597, 610 (9th Cir. 2002) (stating that the 1954 act's "*sole* purpose was to advance religion, in order to differentiate the United States from nations under communist rule"); Bill Broadway, "How 'Under God' Got in There,"

Wash. Post, July 6, 2002, at B9; see also Alan K. Chen, "Forced Patriot Acts," 81 *Denv. U. L. Rev.* 703, 716 (2004) (linking the language of "under God" with McCarthyism). On civil religion in public schools generally, see Thomas C. Berg, "The Story of the School Prayer Decisions: Civil Religion Under Assault," in *First Amendment Stories* 191–226 (Richard W. Garnett & Andrew Koppelman eds., 2011). Congress had expressly disclaimed, in the text of the 1954 act, a purpose to establish religion, but that disclaimer was disbelieved by the Ninth Circuit. See H.R. Rep. No. 83-1693, at 3 (1954), reprinted in 1954 U.S.C.C.A.N. 2339, 2341–2342.

50. Elk Grove, 542 U.S. at 25–32 (Rehnquist, C. J., concurring). I am not certain what Justice O'Connor's description of the phrase "under God" as a species of "ceremonial deism" contributes. See id. at 33–45 (O'Connor, J., concurring). In the first place, it perhaps unintentionally suggests that public recognition of religious ideas and practices in the distant past violated the Establishment Clause. Second, if it refers to a particular country's entrenched social history of public acknowledgment, then there does not seem to be any need for the dismissive description, "ceremonial," or the reference to a very particular philosophy of religion, "deism."

    Some commentators claim that "ceremonial deism" is a "term of art" referring to "nonsectarian" invocations of God whose "religious impact is minimal," but in that case the term is more likely to confuse than clarify. Caroline Mala Corbin, "Ceremonial Deism and the Reasonable Religious Outsider," 57 *UCLA L. Rev.* 1545, 1549, 1552 (2010) (noting that the phrase was first used in a lecture by Yale Law School dean Eugene Rostow); see also Stephen B. Epstein, "Rethinking the Constitutionality of Ceremonial Deism," 96 *Colum. L. Rev.* 2083 (1996).

51. See Lee v. Weisman, 505 U.S. 577, 635 (1992) (Scalia, J., dissenting).

52. The last sentence of the address reads: "It is rather for us to be here dedicated to the great task remaining before us—that from these honored dead we take increased devotion to that cause for which they gave the last full measure of devotion—that we here highly resolve that these dead shall not have died in vain—that this nation, under God, shall have a new birth of freedom—and that government of the people, by the people, for the people, shall not perish from the earth." Abraham Lincoln, "Gettysburg Address," in 1 *Documents of American History* 429 (H. Commager ed., 8th ed. 1968). For further reflections, see Michael J. Perry, *Under God? Religious Faith and Liberal Democracy* 124–126 (2003).

53. Elk Grove, 542 U.S. at 26–28.

54. See Akhil Reed Amar, *The Bill of Rights: Creation and Reconstruction* 252 (1998).

55. See Myers v. Loudoun Cnty. Pub. Schs., 418 F.3d 395, 404 (4th Cir. 2005) ("Our own court, since its infancy in 1891, has opened sessions with the same refrain").

56. Elk Grove, 542 U.S. at 30.

57. *Elk Grove* is also not entirely analogous to *Lee v. Weisman*, however, as the latter dealt with a prayer while the Pledge does not. See id. at 31 (contrasting the "explicit religious exercise" and "formal religious exercise" of the *Lee* prayer with the Pledge of Allegiance).

58. Compare Stone v. Graham, 449 U.S. 39, 39–40 (1980) (invalidating a Kentucky statute requiring the posting of the Ten Commandments in every public school classroom).

59. 2 Kent Greenawalt, *Religion and the Constitution: Establishment and Fairness* 102 (2008).

60. Under California law at the time *Elk Grove* was decided, every public elementary school was required to begin the morning with "appropriate patriotic exercises," and the law further stated that "[t]he giving of the Pledge of Allegiance to the Flag of the United States of America shall satisfy" the requirement. See Elk Grove, 542 U.S. at 7 (quoting Cal Educ. Code § 52720 (West 1989)).

61. In a case involving a New Hampshire statute requiring public schools to provide a moment during the school day for voluntary, teacher-led recitation of the Pledge, one circuit court of appeals used both contextual and historical factors in upholding the statute. See Freedom From Religion Found. v. Hanover Sch. Dist., 626 F.3d 1, 7–10 (1st Cir. 2010) (Lynch, J.) (recognizing the phrase's religious, as well as its civic and patriotic, content); see also Croft v. Perry, 624 F.3d 157, 167 (5th Cir. 2010) ("Acknowledgment of religious heritage, although religiously oriented, 'is no less secular simply because it is infused with a religious element.'") (citation omitted); Myers v. Loudoun Cnty. Pub. Schs., 418 F.3d 395, 405 (4th Cir. 2005) (noting an "unbroken history" of "official acknowledgment" of religion in public pronouncements).

62. For further reflections on values that are excluded by the method of tragedy and history, see Chapter 4.

63. See David A. Strauss, *The Living Constitution* 3 (2010) ("Our constitutional system . . . has become a common law system, one in which precedent and past practices are, in their own way, as important as the written U.S. Constitution itself").

64. Any suggestion that an emphasis on social history would necessarily benefit or promote religion is belied by classic arguments that strict separation of church and state is necessary to preserve religion's zestful purity, and that interaction with the state inevitably corrupts it. See, e.g., Zelman v. Simmons-Harris, 536 U.S. 639, 711–712 (2002) (Souter, J., dissenting); see also Andrew Koppelman, "Corruption of Religion and the Establishment Clause," 50 *Wm. & Mary L. Rev.* 1831 (2009) (offering a contemporary defense of the "corruption rationale").

65. Trunk v. City of San Diego, 629 F.3d 1099, 1101–1102 (9th Cir. 2011).

66. Id. at 1102–1103.

67. Id. at 1103.

68. Id. at 1104 (quoting 152 Cong. Rec. H5422 (2006)). The act also stated: "The United States has a long history and tradition of memorializing members of the Armed Forces who die in battle with a cross or other religious emblem of their faith, and a memorial cross is fully integrated as the centerpiece of the multi-faceted Mt. Soledad Veterans Memorial that is replete with secular symbols." Id. at 1104–1105.

69. Id. at 1105.

70. Id. at 1106.

71. Id. at 1108–1109.

72. The "primary effects" test represents both the second prong of the *Lemon* test and the practical effect of the endorsement test. See Greenawalt, *Establishment*, 174.

73. Trunk, 629 F.3d at 1110.

74. See id. at 1110–1111. On the specific issue of the cross's primary Christian meaning, several courts are in agreement. See Robinson v. City of Edmond, 68 F.3d 1226, 1232 (10th Cir. 1995); Murray v. City of Austin, 947 F.2d 147, 149 (1991); Gonzalez v. North Township, 4 F.3d 1412 (7th Cir. 1993).

75. Trunk, 629 F.3d at 1111 ("This principle that the cross represents Christianity is not an absolute one. In certain circumstances, even a quintessentially sectarian symbol can acquire an alternate, non-religious meaning. . . . The cross can also have localized secular meanings. . . . The cross can even be forced to serve non-religious ends by a small group").

76. Id. at 1113.

77. Id.

78. Id. at 1114.

79. Id.

80. Id. at 1118.

81. Id. at 1119.

82. Id.

83. Id. at 1120 (quoting Van Orden, 545 U.S. at 701) (Breyer, J., concurring).

84. Id. at 1122.

85. Id. at 1118.

86. Id. at 1121, 1123–1124.

87. The court also noted that the cross has "become a flashpoint of secular and religious divisiveness" and that this divisiveness told against the cross's constitutionality. Id. at 1122. Yet to the extent that the "divisiveness" of religious symbols remains a significant issue, it does not seem to point in the direction either of retaining or taking down the symbol; the state will exacerbate civic "divisiveness" by engaging in either course of action.

88. Id. at 1125 ("This result does not mean that the Memorial could not be modified to pass constitutional muster nor does it mean that no cross can be part of this veterans' memorial. We take no position on those issues").

89. In *Lautsi*, the European Court held that the crucifix was undeniably a religious symbol, but it acknowledged that the crucifix was also, in Italy's view, a historically important cultural symbol. The *Lautsi* court did not presume to announce which meaning was paramount in all times and places, or by what degree, or for what reason. Neither, however, did it accept uncritically the meaning that Italy ascribed to the crucifix, nor did it simply throw up its hands and say that the crucifix might mean anything to anyone and was therefore devoid of meaning.

  Instead, the court accepted two interconnected meanings: it rightly held that the crucifix has a foundational, temporally primary religious meaning and it also recognized, in light of the historical evidence that Italy proffered, that the crucifix has taken on a particular and widely understood cultural meaning. It is this cultural meaning that united Italians of all ideological perspectives—from socialists to those on the far right—to oppose any measure that would mandate removal of the crucifix. See, e.g., John Hooper, "Human Rights Ruling against Classroom Crucifixes Angers Italy," *Guardian*, Nov. 3, 2009, *available at* http://www.guardian.

co.uk/world/2009/nov/03/italy-classroom-crucifixes-human-rights (reporting that an earlier order to remove the crucifix was met with condemnation by a broad spectrum of political groups, from Italy's right wing to the "new, ex-communist leader of Italy's biggest opposition group, the Democratic party, Pierluigi Bersani, [who] protested: 'An ancient tradition like the crucifix cannot be offensive to anyone.'"); see also John Witte, Jr., & Nina-Louisa Arnold, "Lift High the Cross?: Contrasting the New European and American Cases on Religious Symbols on Government Property," 25 *Emory Int'l L. Rev.* 5, 6 (2011) (noting the "intense lobbying pressure" applied by both sides in the *Lautsi* litigation).

90. Salazar v. Buono, 130 S.Ct. 1803, 1811 (2010) (plurality opinion).
91. Id. at 1817.
92. Id.
93. Id. at 1812. Originally, Buono had petitioned the government to put a stupa (a Buddhist structure) in the same place as the cross, but this request was denied.
94. See Pleasant Grove City v. Summum, 129 S.Ct. 1125, 1135–1136 (2009) (suggesting that because it is often impossible to identify a "single" meaning, and that because the meanings of symbols can and do change over time, symbols are likely to have a great many meanings). For insightful treatment of the difficulty of divining the legal meaning of religious symbols, but that goes too far in abandoning the effort to contextualize meaning, see B. Jessie Hill, "Putting Religious Symbolism in Context: A Linguistic Critique of the Endorsement Test," 104 *Mich. L. Rev.* 491, 515–516 (2005) (espousing the position that "context is boundless" and therefore too fluid to serve as a touchstone for legal meaning). For effective criticism of Justice Alito's view in *Summum*, see Mary Jean Dolan, "Government Identity Speech and Religion: Establishment Clause Limits after *Summum*," 19 *Wm. & Mary Bill Rts.* J. 1, 48–50 (2010).
95. Mary Jean Dolan likewise observes that "[t]o say that a given symbol sends more than one message is not equivalent to saying that it conveys an infinite number of messages, and thus effectively none." Mary Jean Dolan, "*Salazar v. Buono:* The Cross between Endorsement and History," 105 *Nw. U. L. Rev. Colloquy* 42, 52–53 (2010).
96. Buono, 130 S. Ct., at 1822 (Alito, J., concurring).
97. Id. at 1834–1835 (Stevens, J., dissenting).
98. Id. at 1828.
99. Id. at 1835. Justice Stevens also cited approvingly the lower court's statement that the cross is "exclusively a Christian symbol." Id. (quoting Buono v. Norton, 212 F. Supp. 2d 1202, 1205 (C.D. Cal. 2002)).
100. Christopher L. Eisgruber & Lawrence G. Sager, *Religious Freedom and the Constitution* 134–136 (2007). The authors later qualify these assertions with the observation that "[u]sually the social meaning of religious displays will be more or less the same as the meaning of the object displayed." Id. at 139. But this qualification seems either to restate the problem of determining meaning or to diminish the relevance of context.
101. Id. at 137.

102. Christopher Lund, "*Salazar v. Buono* and the Future of the Establishment Clause," 105 *Nw. U. L. Rev. Colloquy* 60, 64–65 (2010). Lund says that the cross is different from Ten Commandments monuments and other displays with verbal content because "[t]he cross is pure symbol; it has no words, no linguistic meaning." Id. at 65. But why should wordlessness imply unity of meaning? Artistic renderings of religious subjects are likewise wordless, as are instrumental musical compositions that deal with religious themes (sacred organ music, for example); yet these are no less susceptible than symbols with verbal content of being imbued with a variety of meanings. Michelangelo's *Crucifixion of St. Peter* and El Greco's *Christ on the Cross* are as wordless as the *Buono* cross but their wordlessness does not necessarily imply a single meaning.

103. See Richard A. Posner, "The Supreme Court, 2004 Term—Foreword: A Political Court," 119 *Harv. L. Rev.* 31, 101 (2005) (commenting on the "dual religious-secular character of the Ten Commandments, which resembles the dual religious-secular character of Christmas").

104. Buono, 130 S.Ct. at 1835 n.7.

105. Justice Kennedy's plurality opinion similarly noted that a Latin cross may be "a symbol often used to honor and respect those whose heroic acts, noble contributions, and patient striving help secure an honored place in history for this Nation and its people." Id. at 1820.

106. I focus on this specific cross because other crosses, in other contexts, may have very different reasonable meanings. The Court's analysis would look quite different in a case involving the meaning that the Ku Klux Klan attaches to a cross, for example. See Capitol Square Review and Advisory Bd. v. Pinette, 515 U.S. 753, 770 (1995) (Thomas, J., concurring) ("[T]he fact that the legal issue before us involves the Establishment Clause should not lead anyone to think that a cross erected by the Ku Klux Klan is a purely religious symbol. The erection of such a cross is a political act, not a Christian one . . . . In Klan ceremony, the cross is a symbol of white supremacy and a tool for the intimidation and harassment of racial minorities, Catholics, Jews, Communists, and any other groups hated by the Klan").

107. See "About Our Shield and Logo," *Harvard GSAS Christian Community, available at* http://www.hcs.harvard.edu/~gsascf/shield.html.

108. Mass. Const. of 1780, pt. II, ch. V, § 1, art. 1.

109. Marc O. DeGirolami, "The Problem of Religious Learning," 49 *B.C. L. Rev.* 1213, 1222 (2008).

110. Some may object that artistic renderings of religious subjects have redeeming aesthetic merit, whereas the *Buono* cross—apparently a somewhat ramshackle artifact—does not. But the claim is not that the *Buono* cross has independent artistic value, but that (like many great works of art and literature) it has a reasonable meaning distinct from the religious meaning—in this case a cultural meaning—that is nevertheless temporally and causally connected to the religious meaning.

111. Rod Dreher, "Holy Symbols of Hope amid Rubble," *N.Y. Post* (Sep. 23, 2001), *available at* http://webarchive.loc.gov/lcwa0001/20010926073216/http://www .nypost.com/commentary/4613.htm.

112. Elissa Gootman, "Atheists Sue to Block Display of Cross-Shaped Beam in 9/11 Museum," *N.Y. Times* (July 28, 2011), *available at* http://www.nytimes.com/2011/07/29/nyregion/atheists-sue-to-ban-display-of-cross-shaped-beam-in-911-museum.html.

113. Complaint at paras. 44–46, Am. Atheists, Inc. v. Port Auth. of N.Y. and N.J., No. 1108670 (N.Y. Sup. Ct. July 26, 2011), *available at* http://www.atheists.org/upload/WTC_Complaint.pdf. See H.R. 2865, 112th Cong. (2011).

114. Id. § 2.

115. Press Release, Reps. Grimm, Rangel, King, Meeks Introduce Bill Making 9/11 Cross a National Monument (Sept. 8, 2011), *available at* http://grimm.house.gov/press-release/reps-grimm-rangel-king-meeks-bishop-introduce-bill-making-911-cross-national-monument.

116. Id.

117. Id.

118. See id.

119. The Court has sometimes suggested that a single statement like this, standing alone, would be enough to declare a piece of legislation unconstitutional, irrespective of any other contrary or differing statements. See McCreary County, 545 U.S. at 866. Yet that approach is not optimal, because it does not give adequate consideration to the quantity and quality of the evidence of government purpose supporting the legislation.

120. Representative Bishop's view that the cross represents "a symbol of national unity" is suggestive of the use of religion as a public utility discussed in Chapter 3.

121. See Press Release. The nature of these other symbols *is* relevant to the action filed by American Atheists.

122. Washington v. Glucksberg, 521 U.S. 702, 721 (1997) (quoting Collins v. Harker Heights, 503 U.S. 115, 125 (1992)). *Glucksberg* answered in the negative whether physician-assisted suicide was an unenumerated constitutional right.

123. See Michael W. McConnell, "The Right to Die and the Jurisprudence of Tradition," 1997 *Utah L. Rev.* 665, 665–666 (1997).

124. See Cass R. Sunstein, "Due Process Traditionalism," 106 *Mich. L. Rev.* 1543, 1545 (2008) ("A decade after *Glucksberg*, it is clear that the Court's decision failed to entrench due process traditionalism. In striking down bans on same-sex relations, *Lawrence v. Texas* explicitly relies on evolving judgments, rather than long-standing practices. . . . Notwithstanding *Lawrence*, due process traditionalism often has a firm hold on reasoning within the courts of appeals") (citing Lawrence v. Texas, 539 U.S 558, 571–572 (2003)).

125. McConnell, "The Right," 682.

126. Id. at 683.

127. Id. at 684.

128. See Chapters 4, 5, and 6.

129. Compare Sunstein, "Due Process," 1546–1547.

130. Compare Cass R. Sunstein & Adrian Vermeule, "Interpretation and Institutions," 101 *Mich. L. Rev.* 885, 914 (2003).

131. Michael W. McConnell, "The Problem of Singling Out Religion," 50 *DePaul L. Rev.* 1, 42 (2000).

8. The Challenge of Free Exercise

1. U.S. Const. amend. I.
2. See 1 Kent Greenawalt, *Religion and the Constitution: Free Exercise and Fairness* 15 (2006).
3. 494 U.S. 872 (1990).
4. Id.
5. See Daniel O. Conkle, "Religious Truth, Pluralism, and Secularization: The Shaking Foundations of American Religious Liberty," 32 *Cardozo L. Rev.* 1755, 1755–1756 (2011).
6. See Church of the Lukumi Babalu Aye v. City of Hialeah, 508 U.S. 520 (1993) (invalidating local ordinances specifically prohibiting the ritual slaughter of animals as practiced by the Santeria religion, and that did not regulate any other type of animal slaughter). The conclusion that the City of Hialeah specifically targeted the Santeria religion only received two votes; it was the greater protection of nonreligious animal killings than of religiously motivated animal sacrifice that garnered a majority. See id. at 533–540, 540–542 (Kennedy & Stevens, JJ.).
7. Sherbert v. Verner, 374 U.S. 398 (1963). *Sherbert* dealt with a Seventh-Day Adventist who was fired because of her refusal to work on Saturdays and then denied unemployment compensation benefits by the government. Id. at 399–401. Because the denial of benefits constituted a "substantial burden" on the claimant's religious beliefs, Justice Brennan, writing for the Court, held that the government's denial must be supported by a "compelling state interest." Id. at 406.
8. 98 U.S. 145 (1878). In *Reynolds*, the Court upheld the conviction of a member of the Mormon Church under the law for a bigamous marriage, which was still Church practice at the time. It rejected the free exercise challenge on the ground that "it is within the legitimate scope of the power of every civil government to determine whether polygamy or monogamy shall be the law of social life under its dominion." Id. at 166.
9. For cases following *Sherbert*'s approach, see Wisconsin v. Yoder, 406 U.S. 205 (1972); United States v. Lee, 455 U.S. 252 (1980); Thomas v. Review Bd., 450 U.S. 707 (1981); Bob Jones Univ. v. United States, 461 U.S. 574 (1983); Bowen v. Roy, 476 U.S. 693 (1986); Hobbie v. Unemployment Appeals Comm'n, 480 U.S. 136 (1987); Frazee v. Ill. Dep't of Emp't Sec., 489 U.S. 829 (1989); Jimmy Swaggart Ministries v. Bd. of Equalization, 493 U.S. 378 (1990); Hernandez v. Comm'r, 490 U.S. 680 (1990). In a fair number of these cases, the religious claimant lost, but it remains true that the approach was that of interest balancing.
10. Paul Horwitz, *The Agnostic Age: Law, Religion, and the Constitution* 173 (2011); see also id. at 183 ("The Free Exercise Clause, as the courts understand it, has swung back and forth between more and less protective versions").
11. It is sufficiently settled to have inspired a generational retrospective symposium in its honor. See generally, Symposium, "Twenty Years after *Employment Division v.*

Smith: Assessing the Twentieth Century's Landmark Case on the Free Exercise of Religion and How It Changed History," 32 *Cardozo L. Rev.* 1655 (2011).

12. Religious Freedom Restoration Act of 1993, Pub. L. No. 103-141, 107 Stat. 1488 (codified at 42 U.S.C. §§ 2000bb-1 to 4 (2006)).

13. 42 U.S.C. §§ 2000cc to cc-5 (2000).

14. In City of Boerne v. Flores, 521 U.S. 507, 536 (1997), the Supreme Court held that RFRA was invalid as exceeding Congress's power over the states under section 5 of the Fourteenth Amendment.

15. See Eugene Volokh, *The First Amendment and Related Statutes: Problems, Cases, and Policy Arguments* 965–975 (3d ed. 2008).

16. John Witte, Jr., & Joel A. Nichols, *Religion and the American Constitutional Experiment* 22 (3d ed. 2011).

17. Philip Hamburger, "Religious Freedom in Philadelphia," 54 *Emory L.J.* 1603, 1604 (2005).

18. Philip Hamburger, "More Is Less," 90 *Va. L. Rev.* 835, 836 (2004). See generally Philip Hamburger, "A Constitutional Right of Religious Exemption: An Historical Perspective," 60 *Geo. Wash. L. Rev.* 915 (1992); Ellis M. West, "The Right to Religion-Based Exemptions in Early America: The Case of the Conscientious Objectors to Conscription," 10 *J.L. Religion* 367 (1993–1994); see also Vincent Phillip Muñoz, "The Original Meaning of the Free Exercise Clause: The Evidence from the First Congress," 31 *Harv. J.L. Pub. Pol'y* 1083 (2008). Justice Scalia defended this view in his *City of Boerne* concurrence. Boerne, 521 U.S. at 537 (Scalia, J., concurring).

19. Michael W. McConnell, "The Origins and Historical Understanding of Free Exercise of Religion," 103 *Harv. L. Rev.* 1409, 1511–1512 (1990). Douglas Laycock is also guardedly sympathetic to this position. Douglas Laycock, 1 *Religious Liberty: Overviews and History* 611–613 (2010). Justice O'Connor took this view in her *City of Boerne* dissent. Boerne, 521 U.S. at 548 (O'Connor, J., dissenting).

20. Cantwell v. Connecticut, 310 U.S. 296, 303 (1940); Akhil Reed Amar, *The Bill of Rights: Creation and Reconstruction* 42 (1998). James Madison had proposed an amendment protecting the rights of individual conscience applicable against the states, but though the House approved it, the Senate did not. 1 Annals of Cong. 452, 784 (Joseph Gales ed., 1834). There is greater scholarly and judicial disagreement about the incorporation of the Establishment Clause. See Chapter 10 for further discussion.

21. Amar, *Bill of Rights*, 255–257.

22. Witte & Nichols, *Experiment*, 42.

23. Laycock, *Overviews*, 81.

24. Witte & Nichols, *Experiment*, 1–2.

25. See Noah Feldman, "The Intellectual Origins of the Establishment Clause," 77 *N.Y.U. L. Rev.* 346 (2002); McConnell, "Origins," 1431–1435; Conkle, "Religious Truth," 1757–1763; Greenawalt, *Free Exercise*, 21 ("In the colonies, the most influential Enlightenment writing on religion was John Locke's 1689 Letter Concerning Toleration"); Gerard V. Bradley, "Beguiled: Free Exercise Exemptions and the Siren Song of Liberalism," 20 *Hofstra L. Rev.* 245, 264 (1991).

26. John Locke, *A Letter Concerning Toleration* (1796) (1689).

27. Id. at 9; see also id. at 9–10 ("The toleration of those that differ from others in matters of religion, is so agreeable to the gospel of Jesus Christ, and to the genuine reason of mankind, that it seems monstrous for men to be so blind as not to perceive the necessity and advantage of it in so clear a light"). On Locke's argument from futility with respect to compelling religious belief, as well as the Christian sources of his views of religious liberty and equality, see Jeremy Waldron, *God, Locke, and Equality: Christian Foundations in Locke's Political Thought* 208–233 (2002). For incisive questions about whether the argument from futility is persuasive, see Brian Leiter, "Why Tolerate Religion," 25 *Const. Comment.* 1, 4 (2008) ("Locke, it is fair to say, did not fully appreciate the extent to which states and—in capitalist societies—private entities can employ sophisticated means to effectively coerce belief, means that are both more subtle and more effective than he imagined").

28. Locke, *Letter*, 10–13.

29. Id. at 13. McConnell notes the establishmentarian quality of these comments. See McConnell, "Origins," 1433; see also Joseph Story, *Commentaries on the Constitution* Sec. 1870 (1833) (citing Locke for the proposition that "the duty of supporting religion, and especially the Christian religion, is very different than the right to force the consciences of other men, or to punish them for worshiping God in the manner which, they believe, their accountability to him requires").

30. The protection of religious "belief" alone can strike modern sensibilities as insubstantial—how could government compel anyone to believe anything on pain of punishment?—but "centuries prior to the adoption of the Constitution, governments had done just that." Steven D. Smith, "Religious Freedom and Its Enemies, or Why the *Smith* Decision May Be a Greater Loss Now than It Was Then," 32 *Cardozo L. Rev.* 2033, 2036 (2011). Indeed, early Americans took the liberty of religious belief to be the most fundamental of freedoms. Hamburger, "More is Less," 842 ("More generally, religious dissenters and their supporters argued that religious liberty was inalienable, and to establish this inalienability, they focused on belief").

31. Amar, *Bill of Rights*, 255 ("The original free-exercise clause merely barred laws targeted at religious exercise as such; its letter and spirit allowed Congress to make genuinely secular laws, even though those laws might obstruct particular religious practices").

32. Hamburger, "Philadelphia," 1604.

33. War, as the religious historian Richard MacMaster has argued, may bring out the conflicts in conceptions of religious liberty especially acutely, because in wartime the state is apt to make more onerous demands of its citizens. Richard K. MacMaster, "Neither Whig nor Tory: The Peace Churches in the American Revolution," 9 *Fides et Historia* 8, 21 (1973).

34. Hamburger, "Philadelphia," 1609.

35. Resolutions (July 18, 1775), in 2 *Journals of the Continental Congress* 189.

36. Hamburger, "Philadelphia," 1610.

37. Petition from the Committee of the City and Liberties of Philadelphia (Oct. 20, 1775) (cited in Hamburger, "Philadelphia," 1611).

38. A Committee of Ten Friends, from the Meeting for Sufferings, . . . The Address of the People Called Quakers 1, 2 (Oct. 27, 1775) (cited in Hamburger, "Philadelphia," 1614).

39. Petition of the Committee of Privates of the Association Belonging to the City of Philadelphia and Its Districts (Oct. 31, 1775) (cited in Hamburger, "Philadelphia," 1618–1619). Laycock notes that the tone of these and similar arguments was more in the nature of a policy dispute rather than an establishmentarian claim: "Defense was a necessity, so Quaker peace principles were bad policy, and the whole colony was stuck with this bad policy because of the religious scruples of those in political power." Laycock, *Overviews*, 728.

40. Hamburger, "Philadelphia," 1621.

41. See Laycock, *Overviews*, 735–737.

42. Id. at 737. Vincent Phillip Muñoz makes an analogous argument that because there is evidence that exemptions from the Second Amendment—which provides: "A well regulated Militia, being necessary to the security of a free State, the right of the people to keep and bear Arms, shall not be infringed"—were conclusively rejected, that constitutes strong evidence that they were similarly rejected for the First Amendment. Muñoz, "Original Meaning," 1110–1119. But this view assumes an equivalence between exemptions from military service that may or may not be grounded in religious conscience and religious exemptions of other kinds.

43. See Chapter 6.

44. 1 Annals of Cong. 451 (Joseph Gales ed., 1834). The final text of the draft amendment sent to the Senate read: "Congress shall make no law establishing religion, or prohibiting the free exercise thereof, nor shall the rights of conscience be infringed." S. Journal, 1st Cong., 1st Sess., at 63 (Aug. 25, 1789) reprinted in 1 *The Documentary History of the First Federal Congress of the United States of America, 1789–1791* 136 (De Pauw ed., 1972).

45. McConnell, "Origins," 1488–1489; see also id. at 1425 (quoting William Thomas Russell, *Maryland: The Land of Sanctuary* 130 (2d ed. 1908) ("The term 'free exercise' first appeared in an American legal document in 1648, when Lord Baltimore required his new Protestant governor and councilors in Maryland to promise not to disturb Christians ('and in particular no Roman Catholic') in the 'free exercise' of their religion"). In other early writing, "conscience" was felt to entail "free exercise." See William Penn, "The Great Case of Liberty of Conscience," in *The Political Writings of William Penn* 81–82 (Andrew R. Murphy ed., 2002) (1670) (quoted in Witte & Nichols, *Experiment*, 45) (connecting "Liberty of the Mind" with "the free and uninterrupted exercise of our consciences, in that way of worship").

46. Muñoz, "Original Meaning," 1108 (noting the interchangeability of "conscience" and free exercise and suggesting that the "Senate may have kept 'free exercise' for no better reason than that 'rights of conscience' came at the end of the amendment and thus was more convenient to remove").

47. Witte & Nichols, *Experiment*, 43. Ellis West argues that exemptions from military service were indeed granted, but generally as a policy accommodation or a matter of legislative "sympathy." West, "Right," 375.

48. Elisha Williams, "The Essential Rights and Liberties of Protestants," in 1 *Political Sermons of the American Founding Era* 81 (Ellis Sandoz ed., 1991) (1740) (emphasis added). More well known today is Madison's statement that religion "must be left to the convictions and conscience of every man; and it is the right of man to exercise it as these may dictate." James Madison, "A Memorial and Remonstrance against Religious Assessments" (1785). On the importance and influence of political sermons for the founding generation, see Michael W. McConnell, "Establishment and Disestablishment at the Founding, Part I: Establishment of Religion," 44 *Wm. & Mary L. Rev.* 2105, 2183–2184 (2003).

49. McConnell, "Origins," 1467–1468.

50. Id. at 1467; see Matthew 5:33–37 ("But I say unto you, swear not at all; neither by heaven; for it is God's throne: Nor by the earth; for it is his footstool . . .").

51. McConnell, "Origins," 1467.

52. Id. at 1468.

53. Michael Stokes Paulsen, "The Most Dangerous Branch: Executive Power to Say What the Law Is," 83 *Geo. L.J.* 217, 257 (1994).

54. U.S. Const. art. VI. For superb treatments of the Religious Test Clause, see Paul Horwitz, "Religious Tests in the Mirror: The Constitutional Law and Constitutional Etiquette of Religion in Judicial Nominations," 15 *Wm. & Mary Bill Rts. J.* 75 (2006); Gerard V. Bradley, "The No Religious Test Clause and the Constitution of Religious Liberty: a Machine That Has Gone of Itself," 37 *Case Wes. Res. L. Rev.* 674 (1986–1987); Daniel L. Dreisbach, "The Constitution's Forgotten Religion Clause: Reflections on the Article VI Religious Test Ban," 38 *J. Church & State* 261 (1996).

55. *The Federalist* 27, at 177 (Alexander Hamilton) (Clinton Rossiter ed., 1961).

56. See Hamburger, "Philadelphia," 1618–1619.

57. Even in comparatively tolerant Georgia, as Joel Nichols has shown, exemption from military service was eschewed, principally because of the need for defense against incursions by the Spanish and French from the south. See Joel Nichols, "Religious Liberty in the Thirteenth Colony: Church–State Relations in Colonial and Early National Georgia," 80 *N.Y.U. L. Rev.* 1693, 1705 (2005).

58. See Hamburger, "Philadelphia," 1611–1612. In response to the Quakers' request for exemptions, the Philadelphia Revolutionaries argued "that if there were to be any exemption from military service, it should be generally available" to all those "who are willing to hazard their Lives and Fortunes in Defense of their Country." Id. (quoting Petition from the Committee of the Privates of the Association of the City of Philadelphia, and Its Districts (Oct. 21, 1775)).

59. McConnell, "Origins," 1467. For an argument about the function of constitutional oaths in linking loyalty to the Constitution to government officials' "punctilious" sense of personal honor, see Akhil Reed Amar, *America's Constitution: A Biography* 62–63 (2005).

60. All of this may bear on what one can infer from what Muñoz describes as the adamant opposition by the first Congress to any constitutional right of exemption from military service in the Second Amendment debates. See Muñoz, "Original Meaning," 1110–1119. That opposition does not necessarily reflect generalized opposition

to exemptions across constitutional provisions; it may only reflect a context-specific settlement.

61. Smith, "Religious Freedom," 2036.
62. Id. at 2039.
63. Id.
64. See Kurt T. Lash, "The Second Adoption of the Free Exercise Clause: Religious Exemptions under the Fourteenth Amendment," 88 *Nw. U.L. Rev.* 1106, 1151–1155 (1994); Amar, *Bill of Rights*, 255–256.
65. Lash, "Second Adoption," 1149.
66. Philip Hamburger, *Separation of Church and State* 436, n.112 (2002) ("To the extent Americans generally changed their views about religious liberty, they responded to their fears of ecclesiastical and particularly Catholic authority, and they thereby became increasingly suspicious of any religious challenge to American laws").
67. See Laycock, *Overviews*, 709–758. Laycock does note that it is unlikely that the mandatory exemption interpretation would have been understood as violating the Establishment Clause. Id. at 712 ("There is much originalist debate about whether the founding generation understood regulatory exemptions to be constitutionally required. But there is virtually no evidence that anyone thought they were constitutionally prohibited or that they were part of an establishment of religion").
68. Witte & Nichols, *Experiment*, 44.
69. This is not to say that because there was no monolithic "understanding" of the scope of the free exercise protection that it is pointless to examine the shape of the social history of the clause. It is, to the contrary, quite possible to discern the core and peripheral values that have been protected.
70. Inherent in this claim is the view that judges have a proper role to play in mixed governments such as ours, and that they are not "interloper[s] in a presumptively majoritarian system." Ernest Young, "Rediscovering Conservatism: Burkean Political Theory and Constitutional Interpretation," 72 *N.C. L. Rev.* 619, 686 (1994).
71. See Edmund Burke, "Reflections on the Revolution in France," in 3 *The Works of Edmund Burke* 238 (Little & Brown ed., 1839) ("Whatever is supreme in a state, ought to have, as much as possible, its judicial authority so constituted as not only to depend upon it, but in some sort to balance it"); see also Young, "Rediscovering," 677 ("Burke's argument for retaining a form of judicial review in France was thus threefold: such review was an 'ancient' or traditional practice, it counteracted the power of the majoritarian legislature, and it utilized the distinctive institutional capacity of courts to integrate statutes into a coherent, developing body of law").
72. James C. Carter, *The Ideal and the Actual in the Law* 224 (1890) (observing that judges examine the legal and social "habits, customs, business and manners of the people, and those previously declared rules which have sprung out of previous similar inquiries into habits, customs, business and manner"); see generally Lewis A. Grossman, "Langdell Upside-Down: James Coolidge Carter and the Anticlassical Jurisprudence of Anticodification," 19 *Yale J.L. & Human.* 149, 190 (2007).
73. Alexander Bickel, *The Least Dangerous Branch: The Supreme Court at the Bar of Politics* 25–26 (1962); see also Young, "Rediscovering," 678–680.

74. Bickel, *Least Dangerous Branch*, 26.

75. See Young, "Rediscovering," 680.

76. In some ways, the argument offered here is directly opposed to Marci Hamilton's claim that judges are incompetent to weigh factual particulars against one another. See Marci A. Hamilton, *God vs. the Gavel: Religion and the Rule of Law* 295–298 (2005). Hamilton writes that "the legislature has unlimited latitude to frame the issues over which it has power, and to take a position," unlike the courts, which "may only consider the claims of the parties before them, and only their arguments." Id. at 296–297. That is precisely the reason that the judiciary, unlike the legislature, is best suited to implement the method of tragedy and history.

77. Harry H. Wellington, "The Nature of Judicial Review," 91 *Yale L.J.* 486, 493–494 (1982).

78. Young, "Rediscovering," 681.

79. *Smith* carved out certain exceptions for unemployment compensation cases, for "hybrid" cases in which a free exercise interest is asserted "in conjunction with other constitutional protections," and for matters of church autonomy. 494 U.S. at 881.

80. In this sense, the inalienable, noncontingent quality of the narrower understanding of free exercise—a quality that resists trading off or balancing against other values—captures something true about the nature of the commitment to religious liberty. See Hamburger, "More is Less," 837. For more on this issue, see Chapter 5.

81. See James E. Ryan, "*Smith* and the Religious Freedom Restoration Act: An Iconoclastic Assessment," 78 *Va. L. Rev.* 1407, 1412 (1992) ("A survey of the decisions in the United States courts of appeals over the ten years preceding *Smith* reveals that, despite the apparent protection afforded claimants by the language of the compelling interest test, courts overwhelmingly sided with the government when applying that test"); Bradley, "Beguiled," 246–247 (noting that in the pre-*Smith* regime "plaintiffs almost always lose"); Michael W. McConnell, "Free Exercise Revisionism and the *Smith* Decision," 57 *U. Chi. L. Rev.* 1109, 1110 (1990) ("[T]he free exercise doctrine was more talk than substance. In its language, it was highly protective of religious liberty. . . . In practice, however, the Supreme Court only rarely sided with the free exercise claimant, despite some very powerful claims. . . . In fact, after the last major free exercise victory in 1972, the Court rejected every claim requesting exemption from burdensome laws or policies to come before it except for those claims involving unemployment compensation, which were governed by clear precedent").

82. Steven Smith has written that the Court's pre-1990 approach was, in fact, not really one of balancing at all, but "a motley assortment of rhetoric and rationales." Steven D. Smith, *Getting over Equality: A Critical Diagnosis of Religious Freedom in America* 93 (2001).

83. The concerns about the majoritarianism of the pre-*Smith* regime, for example, would be greatly mitigated by the method of tragedy and history. On the former, see William P. Marshall, "In Defense of *Smith* and Free Exercise Revisionism," 58 *U. Chi. L. Rev.* 308, 310–311 (1991).

84. Young, "Rediscovering," 686.

85. Smith, "Religious Freedom," 2038.

86. See generally Hamilton, *God vs. the Gavel*. Hamilton is not clear, however, about what the "rule of law" and the "public good" actually mean. For criticism, see Marc O. DeGirolami, "Recoiling from Religion," 43 *San Diego L. Rev.* 619 (2006).

87. Marshall, "In Defense," 311–312 (criticizing the balancing approach for its "unpredictability" and "inconsistency"); Ronald J. Krotoszynski, Jr., "If Judges Were Angels: Religious Equality, Free Exercise, and the (Underappreciated) Merits of *Smith*," 102 *Nw. U.L. Rev.* 1189 (2008).

88. Bradley, "Beguiled," 307–308 (identifying the pre-*Smith* regime with the "activism" of the Warren Court); see also Antonin Scalia, "The Rule of Law as a Law of Rules," 56 *U. Chi. L. Rev.* 1175 (1989); Eugene Volokh, "A Common-Law Model for Religious Exemptions," 46 *UCLA L. Rev.* 1465 (1999).

89. See Frederick Schauer, "Precedent," 39 *Stan. L. Rev.* 571, 597 (1987); Steven H. Shiffrin, *The First Amendment, Democracy, and Romance* 113 (1990).

90. Marshall, "In Defense," 318–323 (emphasizing the egalitarianism of *Smith*); Krotoszynski, "If Judges," 1260–1262 (same); see also Smith, "Religious Freedom," 2045–2050 (speculating about "imposed secular egalitarianism" as a new threat to religious liberty). Christopher Eisgruber and Lawrence Sager approve of the *Smith* method on egalitarian grounds, though they would modify it to represent a "more articulate and robust principle of equality." Christopher L. Eisgruber & Lawrence G. Sager, *Religious Freedom and the Constitution* 96 (2007).

91. Nelson Tebbe, "*Smith* in Theory and Practice," 32 *Cardozo L. Rev.* 2055, 2057 (2011) ("Courts have been able to use these exceptions as workarounds").

92. 494 U.S. at 881 (noting that in cases involving the "Free Exercise Clause in conjunction with other constitutional protections, such as . . . the right of parents . . . to direct the education of their children," the balancing approach applies). This exception was crafted at least in part to account for Wisconsin v. Yoder, 406 U.S. 205 (1972). For more on Yoder, see Chapter 3.

93. Id. at 884. Cases in this category of exception include Frazee v. Ill. Dep't of Employment Sec., 489 U.S. 829 (1989); Hobbie v. Unemployment Appeals Comm'n, 480 U.S. 136 (1987); and Thomas v. Review Bd., 450 U.S. 707 (1981).

94. Tebbe, "*Smith* in Theory," 2060.

95. See Hosanna-Tabor Evangelical Lutheran Church and School v. EEOC, 132 S.Ct. 694 (2012). For extensive discussion of the church autonomy doctrine and the ministerial exception, see Chapter 9.

96. See Combs v. Homer-Center Sch. Dist., 540 F.3d 231, 247 (3d. Cir. 2008); Leebaert v. Harrington, 332 F.3d 134, 143 (2d. Cir. 2004); Kissinger v. Bd. of Trs. of Ohio St. Univ., Coll. of Veterinary Med., 5 F.3d 177, 180 (6th Cir. 1993).

97. EEOC v. Catholic Univ. of Am., 83 F.3d 455, 467 (D.C. Cir. 1996); Brown v. Hot, Sexy, & Safer Prods., 68 F.3d 525, 539 (1st Cir. 1995).

98. San Jose Christian Coll. v. City of Morgan Hill, 360 F.3d 1024, 1032 (9th Cir. 2004); Swanson v. Guthrie Indep. Sch. Dist. No. I-L, 135 F.3d 694, 700 (10th Cir. 1998); Cornerstone Christian Schools v. University Interscholastic League, 563 F.3d 127, 136 n.8 (5th Cir. 2009). The Eighth Circuit also recognizes the hybrid rights exception, though it has not adopted any definitive approach. See Cornerstone Bible Church v. City of Hastings, 948 F.2d 464 (8th Cir. 1991).

99. I do not mean to suggest that *Smith* did not contemplate the hybrid rights exception, and that courts are illicitly manipulating doctrine. Nor do I claim that the hybrid rights exception has been used frequently to circumvent the core rule. The point is merely that some of the exceptions within *Smith* complicate the claims to predictability that some say is its primary virtue.

100. A.A. ex rel. Betenbaugh v. Needville Indep. Sch. Dist., 701 F. Supp. 2d 863, 881 (S.D. Tex. 2009); Alabama and Coushatta Tribes of Texas v. Big Sandy Mountain Indep. Sch. Dist., 817 F. Supp. 1319, 1332 (E.D. Tex. 1993)

101. Vineyard Christian Fellowship of Evanston, Inc. v. City of Evanston, 250 F. Supp. 2d 961 (N.D. Ill. 2003).

102. Hicks ex rel. Hicks v. Halifax County Bd. of Educ., 93 F. Supp. 2d 649, 662–663 (E.D.N.C. 1999); Chalifoux v. New Caney Indep. Sch. Dist., 976 F. Supp. 659, 671 (S.D. Tex 1997).

103. City Chapel Evangelical Free, Inc. v. City of South Bend ex rel. Dept. of Redevelopment, 744 N.E.2d 443, 453–454 (Ind. 2001).

104. Axson-Flynn v. Johnson, 356 F.3d 1277, 1297 (10th Cir. 2004).

105. Thomas v. Anchorage Equal Rights Comm'n, 165 F.3d 692, 705 (9th Cir. 1999), vacated on other grounds, 220 F.3d 1134 (9th Cir. 2000).

106. Fraternal Order of Police Newark Lodge No. 12 v. City of Newark, 170 F.3d 359, 360 (3d Cir. 1999).

107. Id. at 365–367.

108. Id. at 365.

109. Blackhawk v. Pennsylvania, 381 F.3d 202, 204 (3d Cir. 2004) ("Lakota Indians believe that black bears protect the Earth, sanctify religious ceremonies, and imbue worshipers with spiritual strength").

110. Id. at 205.

111. Id. at 209.

112. A piece of legislation cannot bind future generations of lawmakers from making exceptions to it.

113. See Michael W. McConnell et al., *Religion and the Constitution* 171 (2d ed. 2006) ("How many exceptions must there be to a policy to make it less than neutral and generally applicable? One?").

114. Trefelner ex rel. Trefelner v. Burrell Sch. Dist., 655 F. Supp. 2d 581, 585 (W.D. Pa. 2009).

115. Id. at 594.

116. Cottonwood Christian Center v. Cypress Redevelopment Agency, 218 F. Supp. 2d 1203 (C.D. Cal. 2003).

117. Id. at 1222–1223.

118. Freedom Baptist Church of Delaware Cty. v. Tp. of Middletown, 204 F. Supp. 2d 857, 868 (E.D. Pa. 2002).

119. See Cornerstone Bible Church, 948 F.2d at 472; Civil Liberties for Urban Believers v. City of Chicago, 342 F.3d 752, 764–65 (7th Cir. 2003) (applying fact-specific inquiry to determine whether the zoning rule was applied in a discriminatory fashion).

120. Brock v. Boozman, 2002 WL 1972086, *6–8 (E.D. Ark. Aug. 12, 2002). The case is unreported, but no less real for all that.

121. See Axson-Flynn, 356 F.3d at 1297 (holding that the context in which the exception would operate "is one in which case-by-case inquiries are routinely made"). There are two categories of cases in which the individualized-assessment exception might apply: categorical exemption cases (where the government enacts an exemption right in the law that undermines the purpose of the general rule) and case-specific exemption cases (where the government has no exemption in the law itself but evaluates requests for exemptions on a case-by-case basis). Some cases involve both kinds of exemptions. See, e.g., Blackhawk, 381 F.3d at 204.

122. See Richard A. Duncan, "Free Exercise Is Dead, Long Live Free Exercise: *Smith, Lukumi*, and the General Applicability Requirement," 3 *U. Pa. J. Const. L.* 850, 884 (2001) (noting that almost all laws are "underinclusive").

123. Lawyers involved in these disputes are using the individualized-assessment exception more and more frequently. See email of Eric Rassbach, The Becket Fund, to the author (December 5, 2011) ("As religious liberty litigators, we make individual-assessments arguments all the time"). It may also be that adhering to the exception too strictly would severely impair facial challenges, or perhaps even class actions, thereby making the Free Exercise Clause an underenforced right.

124. St. John's United Church of Christ v. City of Chicago, 502 F.3d 616, 633 (7th Cir. 2007); Wirzburger v. Galvin, 412 F.3d 271, 281 (1st Cir. 2005); Prater v. City of Burnside, 289 F.3d 417, 429 (6th Cir. 2002); Shrum v. City of Coweta, 449 F.3d 1132, 1144–1145 (10th Cir. 2006) (McConnell, J.); Midrash Sephardi, Inc. v. Town of Surfside, 366 F.3d 1214, 1234 n.16 (11th Cir. 2004). But see Stormans, Inc. v. Salecky, 586 F.3d 1109, 1132–1133 (9th Cir. 2009) (expressing uncertainty about whether courts "may examine legislative history in determining whether a challenged law violates the Free Exercise Clause's neutrality requirement). Recall that the conclusion in *Lukumi* that the City had explicitly targeted the Santeria religion for discriminatory treatment only received two votes. Lukumi, 508 U.S. at 540–542. Reliance on non-neutral effects seems foreclosed by *Smith*.

125. Philip Kurland once argued for the textual option. See Philip Kurland, "Of Church, State, and the Supreme Court," 29 *U. Chi. L. Rev.* 1, 96 (1961); see also Mark Tushnet, "Of Church and State and the Supreme Court: Kurland Revisited," 1989 *Sup. Ct. Rev.* 373.

126. Justice Scalia, the author of *Smith*, would not inquire into legislative motivation exactly because of the difficulties in ascertaining it. See Lukumi, 508 U.S. at 558 (Scalia, J., concurring).

127. Smith, *Getting over Equality*, 112.

128. Id.

129. Id. at 113 ("So a court engaging in motive analysis will have a choice. It can choose to be charitable, and thus in effect to defer to the legislature by fashioning a fiction in which the legislative motivation is respectable. Or the court can be ungenerous; it can highlight the unfavorable evidence, thus painting a picture of illicit motivation").

130. One way in which unpredictability can crop up is that courts can resolve cases on a statutory theory while leaving the constitutional theory undecided. See Merced v. Kasson, 577 F.3d 578, 587–590 (5th Cir. 2009).

131. Nelson Tebbe, "Nonbelievers," 97 *Va. L. Rev.* 1111, 1129 (2011).

132. See Jamal Green, "Giving the Constitution to the Courts," 117 *Yale L.J.* 886, 915 (2008) (noting both the "psychologically attractive" and practical features of predictability).

133. It may also be that *Smith* provides predictability in a somewhat different way—as a sign does that says, "Swim at your own risk," inasmuch as it discourages people from planning their lives so as to depend on nonexistent or uncertain legal protections. For an elegant argument in favor of preannounced, as opposed to tailored, remedies for civil wrongs, see Samuel L. Bray, "Announcing Remedies," 97 *Cornell L. Rev.* 753 (2012). Much more systematic study of the social effects of *Smith*, over the course of several decades, would be required to know whether it impacts behavior in this way.

134. Someone might argue that even if Smith is less predictable than optimal, that is simply evidence that we should construct an even harder rule. Yet as Chapter 1 demonstrated, even scholars who champion some form of comic monism make exceptions.

135. City of Boerne, 521 U.S. 507; Gonzalez v. O Centro Espirita Beneficiente Uniao do Vegetal, 546 U.S. 418 (2006).

136. Laycock, *Overviews*, 753.

9. Free Exercise Applications

1. 494 U.S. 872 (1990).

2. The issue here is not quite the same as the question of religious exemptions from generally applicable laws, because in these cases no one else is being affected by the complained-of law.

3. 485 U.S. 439 (1988).

4. Id. at 442.

5. Id. at 453.

6. Id. at 450.

7. I have interpreted the Native Americans' claim with respect to the value of religious liberty associated with the land—that disruption of the land would diminish the "sacredness" of the area and would interfere with "training and ongoing religious experience of individuals using [sites within] the area . . . as integrated parts of a system of religious belief"—as a particular type of piety: reverence and devotion to an integrated way of life in which purity and solitude are instrumental values. Id. at 448.

8. Lyng, 485 U.S. at 451–452 (quoting Northwest Indian Protective Ass'n v. Peterson, 795 F.2d 688, 693 (1986)).

9. Id. at 448, 450 (quoting Bowen v. Roy, 476 U.S. 693, 699–700 (1986)).

10. See Wayne Proudfoot, *Religious Experience* 136–137 (1985) (describing noetic experiences as "revelatory, productive of insight into the true nature of reality," rather

than as "artifacts or projections of [one's] own subjective mental states. . . . The experience must be perceived by the subject as providing access to some reality beyond himself").

11. See 1 Kent Greenawalt, *Religion and the Constitution: Free Exercise and Fairness* 196 (2006) ("An outsider is inclined to say, 'Look, the road may make the high places used for religious rituals a little less private, quiet, and serene, and that may disturb participants at first; but everyone will adjust and things won't change very much.' But an outsider is poorly placed to evaluate just how severely religious exercise will be impaired when a site's quality is somewhat diminished. . . . [G]rasping the belief that the welfare of tribes, or even of mankind, depends on ceremonies being performed at specific undisturbed sites is [difficult]").

12. Lyng, 485 U.S. at 452–453. In truth, the Native Americans had not objected to limited public use of the sacred land.

13. Id.

14. "Individual practitioners use this area for personal spiritual development; some of their activities are believed to be crucially important in advancing the welfare of the Tribe, and indeed, of mankind itself." Id. at 451.

15. Id.

16. Even this analogy, however, probably does not do justice to the power of the claim being made by the Native Americans in *Lyng*, because destroying Saint Patrick's Cathedral, dreadful as that would be, would not destroy or even severely impair Roman Catholicism. See Paul Horwitz, *The Agnostic Age: Law, Religion, and the Constitution* 177 (2011).

17. Greenawalt, *Free Exercise*, 199.

18. Lyng, 485 U.S. at 454.

19. Indeed, this category of conflict is expanding, not only because the regulatory state is becoming larger, but also because of the increasing importance of "government speech." See generally Summum v. Pleasant Grove City, 555 U.S. 460 (2009).

20. Greenawalt, *Free Exercise*, 197–199.

21. This is surprising for a justice known for contextual sensitivity. It is perhaps less surprising that all of the justices in the *Lyng* majority (Chief Justice Rehnquist, Justice White, Justice Scalia, and Justice Stevens) except Justice O'Connor also joined the majority opinion in *Employment Division v. Smith*.

22. See Chapter 8.

23. See 2 Douglas Laycock, *Religious Liberty: The Free Exercise Clause* 308 (2011) ("The essence of church autonomy is that the Catholic Church should be run by duly constituted Catholic authorities and not by legislators, administrative agencies, labor unions, disgruntled lay people, or other actors lacking authority under church law").

24. The Court's earliest church property dispute case was Watson v. Jones, 80 U.S. 679 (1871), where it was asked to intervene in a property conflict between branches of the Presbyterian Church in Louisville, Kentucky. In Kedroff v. St. Nicholas Cathedral, 344 U.S. 94, 115–116 (1954) (holding unconstitutional a statute which transferred property belonging to the Russian Orthodox Church), the Supreme Court held that the principle of institutional autonomy—derived from the common law

and expounded in *Watson*—is also rooted in the First Amendment. See Richard W. Garnett, "'The Things That Are Not Caesar's': The Story of *Kedroff v. St. Nicholas Cathedral*," in *First Amendment Stories* (Richard W. Garnett & Andrew Koppelman eds., 2011).

25. Watson, 80 U.S. at 724–727.
26. Serbian Eastern Orthodox Diocese v. Milivojevich, 426 U.S. 696 (1976).
27. Jones v. Wolf, 443 U.S. 595 (1979).
28. 426 U.S. at 709.
29. 443 U.S. at 613. The case dealt with a dispute about control over a Church building when a Presbyterian Church split into two factions.
30. See Perry Dane, "'Omalous' Autonomy," 2004 *BYU L. Rev.* 1715, 1744 ("To treat the neutral principles idea . . . as a sort of mini-*Smith* doctrine—to confuse neutral principles of law with *Smith*'s invocation of neutral, generally applicable law and, therefore, to employ it to reject claims of autonomy in the face of any secular and neutral regulatory regime—is just flat wrong"); Paul Horwitz, "Churches as First Amendment Institutions: Of Sovereignty and Spheres," 44 *Harv. CR-CL L. Rev.* 79, 117 (2009). For discussion of the "congregationalizing" direction in which various courts have taken the neutral principles approach, in the process neglecting church autonomy, see Laycock, *Free Exercise*, 312–313.
31. Title VII permits religious organizations to discriminate on religious grounds in employment decisions, but not on any other forbidden ground (race, color, national origin, or sex). 42 U.S.C. § 2000e-1(a). Other federal nondiscrimination statutes, including those forbidding discrimination against age, disability, and pregnancy, also contain similar provisions.
32. Hosanna-Tabor Evangelical Lutheran Church and School v. EEOC, 132 S.Ct. 694 (2012).
33. Petruska v. Gannon Univ., 462 F.3d 294, 307 (3d Cir. 2006).
34. Rweyemamu v. Cote, 520 F.3d 198, 204–205 (2d Cir. 2008).
35. See generally Harold Berman, *Law and Revolution: The Formation of the Western Legal Tradition* (1983).
36. Petruska, 462 F.3d at 306.
37. Rweyemamu, 520 F.3d at 205.
38. See Larkin v. Grendel's Den, Inc., 459 U.S. 116 (1982) (holding unconstitutional a Massachusetts statute that empowered churches or schools to prevent the issuance of liquor licenses to businesses within five hundred feet of the churches or schools).
39. Rayburn v. Gen'l Conf. of Seventh-Day Adventists, 772 F.2d 1164, 1167–1168 (4th Cir. 1985).
40. See Horwitz, "Churches," 119; Christopher C. Lund, "In Defense of the Ministerial Exception," 90 *N.C. L. Rev.* 1, 5 (2011) ("The conscience component [of the ministerial exception] protects [churches] from having to break their religious obligations to adhere to the government's commands").
41. Brian Tierney, *The Crisis of Church & State 1050–1300* 2 (1964) ("The very existence of two power structures competing for men's allegiance instead of only one compelling obedience greatly enhanced the possibilities for human freedom").

42. Rweyemamu, 520 F.3d at 208.
43. Greenawalt, *Free Exercise*, 379.
44. Presbyterian Church in the United States v. Mary Elizabeth Blue Hull Mem'l Presbyterian Church, 393 U.S. 440, 449 (1969).
45. See Richard W. Garnett, "Assimilation, Toleration, and the State's Interest in the Development of Religious Doctrine," 51 *UCLA L. Rev.* 1645 (2004).
46. Edmund Burke, "Speech on the Petition of the Unitarian Society", in *Edmund Burke: Selected Writings and Speeches* 315 (Peter J. Stanlis ed., 1963) (1792).
47. Hosanna-Tabor, 132 S.Ct. 694; see also EEOC v. Hosanna-Tabor Evangelical Lutheran Church and School, 597 F.3d 769, 772 (6th Cir. 2010).
48. Hosanna-Tabor, 132 S.Ct. at 699–700.
49. Brief for the Petitioner, Hosanna-Tabor Evangelical Lutheran Church and School v. EEOC, 2011 WL 2414707, at 37 (June 13, 2010).
50. Id. at 37–38; Hosanna-Tabor, 132 S.Ct. at 708 ("[H]er religious duties consumed only 45 minutes of each workday, and . . . the rest of her day was devoted to teaching secular subjects").
51. Petitioner's Brief, 42–43; 132 S.Ct. at 707–708.
52. 132 S.Ct. at 700. Narcolepsy is a neurological condition characterized by "frequent attacks of irresistible sleepiness" during the daytime. *Adams and Victor's Principles of Neurology* 391 (9th ed., Allan H. Ropper & Martin A. Samuels eds., 2009).
53. 132 S.Ct. at 700.
54. Id.
55. Id. at 701. The ADA "prohibits an employer from discriminating against a qualified individual on the basis of disability" and from retaliating "against any individual because such individual has opposed any act or practice made unlawful by [the ADA]." Id. Under the ADA, religious entities are not compelled to hire or retain nonbelievers, but the ministerial exception is considerably broader than this. See 42 U.S.C. § 12113(d).
56. The other component of the test—whether the organization qualifies as "religious"—is satisfied in the case of a religious school. Hosanna-Tabor, 597 F.3d at 778.
57. Id. at 779.
58. Id. at 778.
59. See Lund, "In Defense," 67 ("[T]he Court resolves the issue [of Perich's primary duties] by dividing up Perich's work duties between the religious and nonreligious in terms of time, as if Perich were a lawyer billing her work to two different clients").
60. Berman, *Law and Revolution*, 94–96. On the importance of the Papal Revolution and the so-called "Investiture Crisis" to the formation of Western civilization, see Philippe Nemo, *What Is the West?* (Kenneth Casler trans., 2006). The *Dictatus Papae*—the Papal Dictate—contained twenty-seven statements establishing the independence of the Church from temporal power (as well as its supremacy over that power).
61. Berman, *Law and Revolution*, 87. For a nuanced account of the political complexities and interconnections of power very much in the minds of both pope and emperor, see Gerd Tellenbach, *The Church in Western Europe From the Tenth to the*

Early Twelfth Century 242-243 (1993) ("[W]as the option of refusal really open to Gregory? Could he deny the demonstratively penitent king forgiveness and absolution? Would he not, had he refused, have struck at the roots of his own office as supreme shepherd . . . .?"). For a highly critical discussion of the pontificate of Gregory VII, taking the view that "[w]hat betrayed his papacy was that perennial scourge of the Church, 'the priest in politics,'" see F. Donald Logan, *A History of the Church in the Middle Ages* 112 (2002).

62. Michael W. McConnell, "Establishment and Disestablishment at the Founding, Part I: Establishment of Religion," 44 *Wm. & Mary L. Rev.* 2105, 2190-2191 (2003) ("The idea of civil control over the Church was difficult to maintain during the days of a single universal Catholic Church with its headquarters in Rome. Church–state relations in those days almost inevitably consisted of conflict and negotiation between two institutionally separate authorities: the Church in Rome and the civil power, usually the monarch, in various nations of Europe. Neither could completely control the other. With the outbreak of the Protestant Reformation, however, governmental power over each national church became more feasible").

63. John Courtney Murray, S. J., *We Hold These Truths: Catholic Reflections on the American Proposition* 204 (1960) ("Instinctively and by natural inclination the common man knows that he cannot be free if his basic human things are not sacredly immune from profanation by the power of the state and by other secular powers. The question has always been that of identifying the limiting norm that will check the encroachments of secular power and preserve these sacred immunities. Western civilization first found this norm in the pregnant principle, the freedom of the Church"). For an excellent treatment of the liberty of "the church" as historically and conceptually prior to the liberty of individual conscience, see Steven D. Smith, "Freedom of Religion or Freedom of the Church?," at 23 (San Diego Legal Studies Research Paper Series No. 11-061, 2011), *available at* http://papers.ssrn.com/sol3/papers.cfm?abstract_id=1911412.

64. Since the time of the conversion of the emperor Constantine, church and state had been united in the Western tradition. See Tierney, *Crisis*, 8. For the influence of the experience of early Christianity on the founding American generation, see John Witte, Jr., & Joel A. Nichols, *Religion and the American Constitutional Experiment* 3-6 (3d ed. 2011).

65. See McConnell, "Establishment," 2131 ("Modern constitutional doctrine stresses the "advancement of religion" as the key element of establishment, but in the Anglican establishments of America the central feature was control rather than advancement").

66. Berman, *Law and Revolution*, 99 ("The separation, concurrence, and interaction of the spiritual and secular jurisdictions was a principal source of the Western legal tradition").

67. See generally, Donald L. Drakeman, *Church, State, and Original Intent* 216-229 (2009).

68. See McConnell, "Establishment," 2136-2137 ("The power to appoint and remove ministers and other church officials is the power to control the church. During the eighteenth century in England, the appointment of the ecclesiastical hierarchy became

exceptionally political. . . . As a result, loyalty to the Whig party exceeded spirituality as a qualification for preferment, a circumstance that did not enhance the standing or reputation of the [Anglican] Church during this crucial epoch"); Tomic v. Catholic Diocese of Peoria, 442 F.3d 1036, 1038 (7th Cir. 2006) (Posner, J.) ("Since the United States was not to have a national church, the federal judicial power was not envisaged as extending to the resolution of ecclesiastical controversies").

69. In response to assertions of imperial power over Church offices, Saint Ambrose, bishop of Milan in the fourth century AD, is said to have replied, "Palaces belong to the emperor, churches to the priesthood." Tierney, *Crisis*, 9.

70. A strikingly ahistorical view of the ministerial exception—which the Supreme Court called "untenable" and "extreme"—may be found in the amicus brief filed in the case by the Department of Justice, as representative of the federal government. Hosanna-Tabor, 132 S.Ct. at 706, 709; Brief for the Federal Respondent, Hosanna-Tabor Evangelical Lutheran Church and School v. EEOC, 2011 WL 291132 (Jan. 26, 2011). The position of the government was that whatever the Church's interests in autonomy, they could be protected adequately by a different constitutional doctrine, the "freedom of association." One of the Supreme Court's seminal associational freedom cases involved an allegation by a former assistant scoutmaster that the Boy Scouts had terminated his employment because he was gay, thereby violating New Jersey's public accommodation laws. Boy Scouts of America v. Dale, 530 U.S. 640 (2000). The Court held that application of these laws to force the Boy Scouts to retain Dale would violate their expressive associational rights under the First Amendment, though associational rights are subject to an interest-balancing approach against the state's claims. Id. The difficulty with this resolution of the ministerial exception is not so much the interest-balancing test itself but the fact that the entrenched and ancient social history of religious liberty and autonomy— one that is reflected in the Religion Clauses of the Constitution—is wiped away. For insightful criticisms of the Court's approach to associational freedom, see generally John D. Inazu, "The Unsettling 'Well-Settled' Law of Freedom of Association," 43 *Conn. L. Rev.* 149 (2010).

71. Hosanna-Tabor, 132 S.Ct. at 702 (quoting J. Holt, Magna Carta App. IV, p. 317, cl. 1 (1965)).

72. Id.

73. Id. at 703.

74. McClure v. Salvation Army, 460 F.2d 553 (5th Cir. 1972).

75. See, e.g., Alcazar v. Corp. of the Catholic Archbishop of Seattle, 627 F.3d 1288 (9th Cir. 2010); Rweyemamu v. Cote, 520 F.3d 198 (2d Cir. 2008); Hollins v. Methodist Healthcare, Inc., 474 F.3d 223 (6th Cir.), cert. denied, 128 S. Ct. 134 (2007); Petruska v. Gannon Univ., 462 F.3d 294 (3d Cir. 2006); Tomic v. Catholic Diocese of Peoria, 442 F.3d 1086 (7th Cir. 2006); Alicea-Hernandez v. Catholic Bishop of Chicago, 320 F.3d 698 (7th Cir. 2003); EEOC v. Catholic Univ. of Am., 83 F.3d 455 (D.C. Cir. 1996); Rayburn v. Gen'l Conf. of Seventh Day Adventists, 772 F.2d 1164 (4th Cir. 1985); McClure v. Salvation Army, 460 F.2d 553 (5th Cir. 1972).

76. Hosanna-Tabor, 132 S.Ct. at 704 (quoting Kedroff, 344 U.S. at 116).

77. Id. at 705.
78. Id. at 707.
79. Id. at 706.
80. This does not mean that the decision was perfect from a tragic-historic standpoint—only that its general method is similar to the one described in this book.
81. Id. at 707.
82. See Braunfeld v. Brown, 366 U.S. 599, 605 (1961) (describing the "particularly delicate task" of balancing the state's authority with the religious institution's independence).
83. See Corp. of the Presiding Bishop of the Church of Latter-Day Saints v. Amos, 483 U.S. 327 (1987). The issue in *Amos* was whether a janitor could be fired pursuant to Title VII's statutory exception because he did not qualify for a certification of good standing in the church. Had the church defended its decision on the basis of the ministerial exception, it should have lost; this was not a situation in which, to give an extravagant example, the Pope was washing feet and the state claimed that he was acting as a pedicurist. Thanks to Paul Horwitz for discussion on this point.
84. See, e.g., Rweyemamu, 520 F.3d at 198; Petruska, 462 F.3d at 294; Catholic Univ., 83 F.3d at 455.
85. Lund, "In Defense," 69.
86. See Chapter 6 for discussion of "shallow" and "deep" decisions.
87. 132 S.Ct. at 707–708.
88. "Called," in the Lutheran Church's view, by God. See Brief of the Lutheran Church—Missouri Synod—as Amicus Curiae, Hosanna-Tabor Evangelical Lutheran Church and School v. EEOC, 2011 WL 2470848, at 3 (June 20, 2011).
89. The Church recognizes "ordained" and "commissioned" ministers, though women are only permitted to attain to the latter position. Id. at 4–5.
90. Id. at 7.
91. Id. at 10 ("[T]he Synod has placed great emphasis on the religious education of its children and on introducing the Gospel to other children whose parents choose a Lutheran education. Religious education is integrated into every part of school life").
92. 132 S.Ct. at 708 ("In light of these considerations—the formal title given Perich by the Church, the substance reflected in that title, her own use of that title, and the important religious functions she performed for the Church—we conclude that Perich was a minister covered by the ministerial exception").
93. Rweyemamu, 520 F.3d at 208.
94. Tomic, 442 F.3d at 1040–1041.
95. Lutherans' Brief, 16–17 (quoting 1 Corinthians 6:1–8).
96. Id. at 17–18.
97. Hosanna-Tabor, 132 S.Ct. at 709.
98. Id. at 710.
99. Id. at 709.
100. Lund, "In Defense," 40.
101. Hosanna-Tabor, 132 S.Ct. at 709.

102. Christian Legal Society v. Martinez, 130 S.Ct. 2971 (2010). Recognition would have allowed the student group to use the law school's resources for its gatherings and to receive an amount of money from the law school's fund for student activities.

103. Id. at 2990; cf. Lawrence v. Texas, 539 U.S. 558, 575 (2003) ("When homosexual conduct is made criminal by the law of the State, that declaration in and of itself is an invitation to subject homosexual persons to discrimination").

104. Hosanna-Tabor, 132 S.Ct. at 707–708.

105. Id.

106. Caroline Mala Corbin, "Above the Law? The Constitutionality of the Ministerial Exception," 75 *Fordham L. Rev.* 1965, 2006 (2007).

107. Id. at 1989.

108. See Smith, "Freedom of Religion," 22–23.

109. Corbin, "Above," 2007.

110. On Corbin's view, state entanglement is "direct" only in those situations when the state actually decrees religious doctrine. Id.

111. Horwitz, "Churches," 119.

112. Id. at 120.

113. In a recent piece on the ministerial exception, Horwitz takes a more intermediate view, emphasizing the costs of both a muscular and enfeebled version of the doctrine. See Paul Horwitz, "Act III of the Ministerial Exemption," 106 *Nw. U.L. Rev. Colloq.* 156 (2011).

114. Garnett, "Assimilation," 1650.

10. ESTABLISHMENT CLAUSE APPLICATIONS

1. See Ira C. Lupu & Robert W. Tuttle, "The Limits of Equal Liberty as a Theory of Religious Freedom," 85 *Tex. L. Rev.* 1247, 1251 (2007) (reviewing Christopher L. Eisgruber & Lawrence G. Sager, *Religious Freedom and the Constitution* (2007)).

2. Id.

3. See Chapter 8.

4. See Steven D. Smith, "Freedom of Religion or Freedom of the Church?" (San Diego Legal Studies Research Paper Series No. 11–061, 2011), *available at* http://papers. ssrn.com/sol3/papers.cfm?abstract_id=1911412. Thomas Jefferson's famous Letter to the Danbury Baptist Association and his Bill for Establishing Religious Freedom during the Virginia religious assessment controversy of 1785—documents that, though important and interesting in their own right, had nothing to do with the Establishment Clause at the time of their writing—are disproportionately prominent in religion clause decisions of the Supreme Court in the late 1940s as representative of "the" early American position on the meaning of establishment. See Everson v. Bd. of Educ., 330 U.S. 1, 13 (1947); Illinois ex rel. McCollum v. Bd. of Educ. of Ewing, 333 U.S. 203, 231 (1948).

   As for James Madison, it is his famous *Memorial and Remonstrance against Religious Assessments* of 1785 that figures most prominently in twentieth-century

Supreme Court opinions as a kind of paradigm position about establishment's meaning, though again, that document had little to do with the Establishment Clause at the time of its writing. For only a handful of citations, see Everson, 330 U.S. at 11–12 (Justice Rutledge in dissent saw fit to reproduce the entire document as an appendix); McGowan v. Maryland, 366 U.S. 420, 430 n.7 (1961); Engel v. Vitale, 370 U.S. 421, 431 n.13, 432 n.15 (1962); Wallace v. Jaffree, 472 U.S. 38, 53 n.38 (1985); Lee v. Weisman, 505 U.S. 577, 590 (1992); Locke v. Davey, 540 U.S. 712, 722 (2004); and Ariz. Christian Sch. Tuition Org. v. Winn, 131 S. Ct. 1436, 1446–1447 (2011).

5. John Witte and Joel Nichols's elegant metaphor—the "canopy of opinions" about the nature of religious liberty during the founding period—is again useful. John Witte, Jr., & Joel A. Nichols, *Religion and the American Constitutional Experiment* 22 (3d ed. 2011).

6. U.S. Const. amend. I. The rejection of a national establishment (as in England) reflected a restraint on the President as well as Congress. See Akhil Reed Amar, *America's Constitution: A Biography* 178 (2005) (quoting Federalist Tench Coxe as explaining that "The British king is the great bishop or supreme head of an established church, with an immense patronage annexed. . . . In America, our president will . . . be without these influencing advantages").

7. Everson v. Bd. of Educ. of Ewing, 330 U.S. 1, 14–15 (1947) (Black, J.). Interestingly, not a single justice in *Everson* resisted the majority's conclusion that the Establishment Clause should be incorporated against the states. One distinguished scholar has observed that the "special pinprick" of the Establishment Clause is that to incorporate it destroys the very right it was meant to protect—the power of the states to establish religion (though he ultimately favors incorporation). Akhil Reed Amar, *The Bill of Rights: Creation and Reconstruction* 33–34, 256–257 (1998). On today's Supreme Court, Justice Thomas alone has argued that the Establishment Clause only forbids a national establishment of religion. See Elk Grove Unified Sch. Dist. v. Newdow, 542 U.S. 1, 45 (2004) (Thomas, J., concurring) ("I would acknowledge that the Establishment Clause is a federalism provision which, for this reason, resists incorporation").

8. See Vincent Phillip Muñoz, "The Original Meaning of the Establishment Clause and the Impossibility of Its Incorporation," 8 *U. Pa. J. Const. L.* 585, 604 (2006) (noting the concerns of Anti-Federalists about the possibility that "the new Congress would impose one form of church-state relations throughout the nation").

9. Amar, *Bill of Rights,* 32–33; Michael W. McConnell, "Establishment and Disestablishment at the Founding, Part I: Establishment of Religion," 44 *Wm. & Mary L. Rev.* 2105, 2107 (2003). At the founding, no state required disestablishment in its constitution.

10. Carl H. Esbeck, "Dissent and Disestablishment: The Church–State Settlement in the Early American Republic," 2004 *BYU L. Rev.* 1385, 1450 (2004); see also Donald L. Drakeman, *Church, State, and Original Intent* 203–205 (2009) (noting that the principal debate in the First Congress dealt with the "redundan[cy]" of the Establishment Clause in light of Congress's powerlessness to intermeddle with religion in the states).

11. McConnell, "Establishment," 2111.

12. Interestingly, religious use of public buildings was never deemed constitutionally concerning as a historical matter. Compare the modern case law, in which this issue has been deemed problematic. See Good News Club v. Milford Cent. Sch., 533 U.S. 98 (2001); Widmar v. Vincent, 454 U.S. 263 (1981); Bronx Household of Faith v. Bd. of Educ. of N.Y.C., 650 F.3d 30 (2d Cir. 2011).

13. McConnell, "Establishment," 2131.

14. Philip Hamburger, *Separation of Church and State* 480 (2002); see also id. at 97–107.

15. The 1780 Massachusetts constitution was representative of the New England approach in this respect: "As the happiness of a people and the good order and preservation of civil government essentially depend upon piety, religion, and morality, and as these cannot be generally diffused through a community but by the institution of the public worship of God and of public instructions in piety, religion, and morality: Therefore, To promote their happiness and to secure the good order and preservation of their government, the people of this commonwealth have a right to invest their legislature with power to authorize and require . . . the several towns, parishes, precincts, and other bodies-politic or religious societies to make suitable provision, at their own expense, for the institution of the public worship of God and for the support and maintenance of public Protestant teachers of piety, religion, and morality. . . ." Mass. Const. of 1780, pt. I, art. III, reprinted in 5 *The Founder's Constitution* 77–78 (Philip B. Kurland & Ralph Lerner eds., 1987).

16. Massachusetts, Connecticut, New Hampshire, and Vermont all instituted local establishments; Rhode Island, founded by Roger Williams as a haven for religious dissenters, did not. McConnell, "Establishment," 2110–2111, 2121–2126. Congregationalism was the predominant established religion in the local New England towns.

17. Drakeman, *Original Intent*, 226–227 (quoting Thomas J. Curry, *The First Freedoms: Church and State in America to the Passage of the First Amendment* 131 (1986)). For an excellent treatment of John Adams's views of religious liberty, see John Witte, Jr., "'A Most Mild and Equitable Establishment of Religion': John Adams and the Massachusetts Experiment," 41 *J. Church & State* 213 (1999).

18. Without any pressure, one may observe, from the Supreme Court. See Steven D. Smith, "Religious Freedom and Its Enemies, or Why the *Smith* Decision May Be a Greater Loss Now than It Was Then," 32 *Cardozo L. Rev.* 2033, 2037 (2011).

19. John Witte, Jr., *God's Joust, God's Justice: Law and Religion in the Western Tradition* 244 (2006).

20. As McConnell notes: "In late-eighteenth-century America . . . churches were the foremost institutions for the formation and dissemination of opinion. It is estimated that about eighty percent of the published political pamphlets in the 1770s were reprints of sermons." McConnell, "Establishment," 2183–2184.

21. Compare Elisha Williams, "The Essential Rights and Liberties of Protestants" (1744), reprinted in 1 *Political Sermons of the American Founding Era* 73 (Ellis Sandoz ed., 1991) ("This I shall endeavour fairly to consider when I have observed, that if by the word *establish* be meant only an approbation of certain articles of faith and

modes of worship, of government, or recommendation of them to their subjects; I am not arguing against it. But to carry the notion of a religious establishment so far as to make it a rule binding to the subjects, or on any penalties whatsoever, seems to me to be oppressive of Christianity, to break in upon the sacred rights of conscience, and the common rights and priviledges of all good subjects") with John Leland, "The Rights of Conscience Inalienable" (1791), reprinted in 2 *Political Sermons of the American Founding Era* 55–56 (Ellis Sandoz ed., 1991) (listing the "evils of establishment" as "[t]he love of importance," "[a]n over-fondness for a particular system or sect," and "uniformity in religion").

22. David Tappan, "A Sermon for the Day of General Election" (1792), reprinted in 2 *Political Sermons*, 72. Drakeman examines the opinions of two judges in an 1807 Massachusetts case, Avery v. Tyringham, 3 Mass. 160 (1807), suggesting that a general liberty of conscience and the town-by-town establishment of Protestantism in Massachusetts were thought to be consistent. On the other hand, in New Hampshire, a court in 1803 found that town-based tax assessments did not constitute an establishment because that term was reserved for situations "where the State prescribes a formulary of faith and worship for the rule and governance of all the subjects." Drakeman, *Original Intent*, 218–223.

23. Drakeman, *Original Intent*, 213–214 ("[W]e need to realize that the circumstances giving rise to the Bill of Rights did not require James Madison or any of his congressional compatriots either to define their terms or to agree on any substantive church-state policy. Had they tried to do so, they may well have failed").

24. See Michael W. McConnell, "The Origins and Historical Understanding of Free Exercise of Religion," 103 *Harv. L. Rev.* 1409, 1469–1471 (1990); Kurt T. Lash, "The Second Adoption of the Establishment Clause: The Rise of the Nonestablishment Principle," 27 *Ariz. St. L.J.* 1085, 1101 (1995).

25. See Hamburger, *Separation*, 185–186.

26. See Freedom from Religion Foundation, Inc. v. Obama, 641 F.3d 803 (7th Cir. 2011) (dismissing action alleging a violation of the Establishment Clause on the basis of the plaintiffs' lack of standing because "a feeling of alienation cannot suffice as injury in fact"). Madison's views on national days of prayer evince his own internal conflict on the question: he initially embraced and eventually came to oppose the practice of declaring national days of prayer. Drakeman, *Original Intent*, 17. Likewise, Jefferson seems to have followed a federalism principle on the day-of-Thanksgiving issue: as governor of Virginia, he agreed to declare such a day, but as president he did not. Amar, *Bill of Rights*, 35. For some of the Supreme Court's internal debates about the views of Washington, Adams, Jefferson, and Madison with respect to the propriety of presidential declarations of national days of prayer and thanksgiving, see the contrasting opinions of Chief Justice Rehnquist in Wallace v. Jaffree, 472 U.S. 38 (1985) (dissenting), and Justice Souter in Lee v. Weisman, 505 U.S. 577 (1992) (concurring).

27. Wallace v. Jaffree, 472 U.S. 38 (1985) (striking down such an Alabama law as a violation of the Establishment Clause).

28. Compare Marsh v. Chambers, 463 U.S. 783 (1983) (holding that funding of chaplains who lead opening sessions of the Nebraska legislature with prayers is constitutional

in part because "[legislative] prayer is deeply embedded in the history and tradition of this country") with Joyner v. Forsyth County, N.C., 653 F.3d 341 (4th Cir. 2011) (holding unconstitutional a state county practice of opening legislative sessions with "sectarian" prayers) and Galloway v. Town of Greece, 681 F.3d 20, 31-32 (2d Cir. 2012) (striking down town practice of legislative prayer but commenting that sectarian legislative prayers are acceptable).

For a skeptical view of legislative prayer—which, in my view, overemphasizes the value of neutrality as nonendorsement—see Christopher C. Lund, "Legislative Prayer and the Secret Costs of Religious Endorsements," 94 *Minn. L. Rev.* 972 (2010). Lund writes that legislative prayer is the only "official" exception to an antiendorsement conception of the Establishment Clause. "Official" or not, however, there continue to be numerous practices—from the use of religious imagery in government speech and debate, to the display of religious symbols, to the inclusion of the words "In God We Trust" on our money, to the issue of tax exemptions for religious institutions discussed in this chapter—which, though they may well be felt by some observers to "endorse" religion, have thus far withstood constitutional scrutiny. Lund also seems to favor the "divisiveness" rationale for prohibiting legislative prayer. He writes that "legislative prayer has grown into a fissure that now divides county boards, state legislatures, and city councils across the country." Id. at 974. But claims of divisiveness are not arguments against the practice of legislative prayer, any more than they are arguments in favor of it. Conflict is an endemic feature of religion clause law, and it is just as likely that stifling embedded social practices through blanket constitutional proscriptions will exacerbate as relieve cultural strife.

29. The Fourth Circuit's discussion of incommensurable values with respect to the practice of legislative prayers is instructive. On the one hand, "invocations at the start of legislative sessions can solemnize those occasions; encourage participants to act on their noblest instincts; and foster the humility that recognition of a higher hand in human affairs can bring." Joyner, 653 F.3d at 347. On the other, "[t]he proximity of prayer to official government business can create an environment in which the government prefers—or appears to prefer—particular sects or creeds at the expense of others." Id.

30. Drakeman, *Original Intent*, 258; see id. at 264-268 for similar thoughts on the issue of days of prayer and thanksgiving.

31. The disposition of custom described in the third thesis appears in the issuing of presidential Thanksgiving proclamations, in which presidents routinely raise the importance of the customary, largely unbroken, and cherished popular observance of giving thanks as a nation to God. For a complete collection of presidential Thanksgiving proclamations, see *Presidential Thanksgiving Proclamations*, Pilgrim Hall Museum, http://www.pilgrimhall.org/ThanxProc1880.htm (last visited Nov. 24, 2011).

32. See Lash, "Second Adoption," 1117. Lash argues that the historical evidence points to a "second adoption" of the Establishment Clause as of the passage of the Fourteenth Amendment as a limitation on the states' powers. See also Amar, *Bill of Rights*, 246-257. For evidence to the contrary, see Hamburger, *Separation*, 436-437.

33. Hamburger, *Separation*, 213–215 ("Yet dissensions over liberal theology and innumerable other issues flourished at the same time as the evangelical dream of unity, and as different denominations increasingly indulged in internal quarrels, they found anti-Catholicism all the more important for its capacity to bind them together"); see also Drakeman, *Original Intent*, 314–321 (noting the inconsistency of President Ulysses S. Grant's commitment to "separation"—he was against it when it came to "Christianizing" the Native Americans; and he was for it when it came to opposing the funding of Catholic parochial schools); John C. Jeffries, Jr., & James E. Ryan, "A Political History of the Establishment Clause," 100 *Mich. L. Rev.* 279, 297 (2001) ("The immediate reality faced by the Supreme Court in the mid-twentieth century was the collapse of the Protestant establishment"); Steven K. Green, *The Bible, the School, and the Constitution: The Clash that Shaped Modern Church–State Doctrine* (2012) (describing "nonsectarian" public school education in the mid-nineteenth century as a way to acculturate minorities to Protestantism).

34. Hamburger, *Separation*, 230 ("[M]any ministers still spoke about the 'connection' between religion and government that they hoped would flourish . . . in the absence of an establishment").

35. Id. at 342–359.

36. J. L. Diman, "Religion in America, 1776–1876," 122 *North American Rev.* 1 (1876) (quoted in Drakeman, *Original Intent*, 322).

37. Perhaps even more so today than in the 1940s, though this is probably attributable not so much to the fact of greater social consensus about secularism in the 1940s as to the comparative absence of commentary at that time critical of the Supreme Court's approach.

38. See Steven D. Smith, *Foreordained Failure: The Quest for a Principle of Religious Freedom* 34 (1995); Drakeman, *Original Intent*, 228–229 ("That we, through the course of the past two hundred years, have yet to settle on a single understanding of what 'an establishment of religion' means is perhaps one small additional piece of evidence supporting a verdict that the concept could have meant different things to different people during the Founding Era as well").

39. Drakeman, *Original Intent*, 75–76 ("When they arose, church–state issues were debated and determined by cities, towns, and states throughout the nation, and their outcomes varied from one locale to another").

40. Muñoz, "Original Meaning," 604.

41. Drakeman, *Original Intent*, 229, n.120.

42. See Larkin v. Grendel's Den, Inc., 459 U.S. 116 (1982).

43. See Torcaso v. Watkins, 367 U.S. 488 (1961) (holding that a state cannot bar an atheist from public office). Compare McConnell, "Establishment," 2178 (observing that religious restrictions on the right to vote were imposed in almost every colony and that "[e]ven after Independence, every state other than Virginia restricted the right to hold office on religious grounds").

44. See Kent Greenawalt, 2 *Religion and the Constitution: Establishment and Fairness* 54 (2008). This is the value of neutrality conceived as a principle of "nonsectarianism." See Mark L. Movsesian, "Crosses and Culture: State-Sponsored Religious Displays in the US and Europe," 1 *Oxford J.L. and Religion* 338, 342–43 (2012).

45. See Andrew Koppelman, "Secular Purpose," 88 *Va. L. Rev.* 87, 89 (2002) (calling the proposition that the "government may not declare religious truth" one of the "core" meanings of the Establishment Clause). Though I disagree with Koppelman that the Supreme Court's prohibition on government "endorsements" of religion is necessarily the same as a prohibition on the government's declaration of religious truth, I agree that it would be impermissible for the government to declare, for example, Christianity to be true and another religion or nonbelief false.

46. See Greenawalt, *Establishment*, 52 ("Justices can resolve cases under the religion clauses, and they can do so according to some coherent pattern, but whether that pattern can be verbalized into a coherent set of tests and standards is debatable").

47. See Ira C. Lupu, "Government Messages and Government Money: *Santa Fe, Mitchell v. Helms*, and the Arc of the Establishment Clause," 42 *Wm. & Mary L. Rev.* 771, 777 (2001) ("What the Virginians and others did fight about, and what then became the primary focus in our legacy of nonestablishment, was not government speech. It was government money. More precisely, it was coercive taxation of the populace to raise money that would be redistributed to the benefit of the established Anglican church, or a state-approved set of Christian churches").

48. McConnell, "Establishment," 2146–2159.

49. For a selection of cases from only the last two decades, see Ariz. Christian Sch. Tuition v. Winn, 131 S. Ct. 1436 (2011); Zelman v. Simmons-Harris, 536 U.S. 639 (2002); Mitchell v. Helms, 530 U.S. 793 (2000); Agostini v. Felton, 521 U.S. 203 (1997); Zobrest v. Catalina Foothills Sch. Dist., 509 U.S. 1 (1993). The concern about government funding of religious schools dates from the 1840s, when New York Archbishop John Hughes urged the state to support Catholic schools just as it supported ostensibly "nondenominational" Protestant schools. Jeffries & Ryan, "Political History," 299–301.

50. Greenawalt, *Establishment*, 279.

51. McCullough v. Maryland, 17 U.S. (4 Wheat.) 316, 327 (1819).

52. See generally Edward A. Zelinksy, "Are Tax 'Benefits' Constitutionally Equivalent to Direct Expenditures?," 112 *Harv. L. Rev.* 379 (1998). Zelinsky challenges the idea that this difference between a benefit and a direct expenditure is always present, but it is nevertheless often an accurate way to characterize the distinction between an exemption and a subsidy.

53. Walz v. Tax Comm'n of N.Y.C., 397 U.S. 664, 676, 680 (1970) (noting that the practice of tax exemptions for religious institutions is "deeply embedded in the fabric of our national life"); see also Witte, *God's Joust*, 257 ("Tradition has become one strong vector in some of the Court's more recent First Amendment cases. The Court ha[s] used arguments from tradition . . . as part of broader rationales for upholding religious tax exemptions and Sabbath Day laws").

54. Justice Brennan deemed this a particularly important reason for tax exemptions in *Walz*, 397 U.S. at 684–685 (Brennan, J., concurring) ("Thomas Jefferson was President when tax exemption was first given Washington churches, and James Madison sat in sessions of the Virginia General Assembly that voted exemptions for churches in that Commonwealth. . . . The exemptions have continued uninterrupted to the present day. They are in force in all 50 States. No judicial decision, state or federal, has ever held that they violate the Establishment Clause").

55. This is the "Erastian" point that some types of support—particularly public prayer—were a benefit not so much to religion but to the state. See Weldon S. Crowley, "Erastianism in England to 1640," 32 *J. Church & State* 549, 557 (1990) (noting that the Swiss theologian Thomas Erastus favored an established church that exercised moral suasion but left all powers of coercion to the civil authority); see also Erik J. Ablin, "The Price of Not Rendering to Caesar: Restrictions on Church Participation in Political Campaigns," 13 *Notre Dame J.L. Ethics & Pub. Pol'y* 541, 549 (1999) ("The first premise for exempting religious organizations from taxation is that they contribute value to the community in nonreligious ways, thus partially relieving the government from supporting those activities").

56. See Greenawalt, *Establishment*, 283.

57. Walz, 397 U.S. at 696–697 (Harlan, J., concurring).

58. See 26 U.S.C.A. 501(c)(3) (West 2011). For an incisive critique of this condition see Richard W. Garnett, "A Quiet Faith? Taxes, Politics, and the Privatization of Religion," 42 *B.C. L. Rev.* 771 (2001).

59. Feldman has suggested that while there may be a conceptual difference between imposing mandatory taxes to fund religious enterprises and the "indirect funding" of the tax exemption, there is no practical difference between the two. Noah Feldman, "The Intellectual Origins of the Establishment Clause," 77 *N.Y.U. L. Rev.* 346, 418, n.365 (2002).

60. Noah Feldman, *Divided by God: America's Church–State Problem—and What We Should Do about It* 15 (2005).

61. Id.

62. Id. at 244–245.

63. Id. at 65–92.

64. See Hamburger, *Separation*, 297–298; see also Jay S. Bybee & David W. Newton, "Of Orphans and Vouchers: Nevada's 'Little Blaine Amendment' and the Future of Religious Participation in Public Programs," 2 *Nev. L.J.* 551, 552, 557, n.31 (2002) (summarizing this history). Though the federal amendment failed, many states passed analogous provisions. Jeffries & Ryan, "Political History," 305 ("By 1890, twenty-nine of the forty-five States had strongly worded constitutional prohibitions on the use of public money to support sectarian schools"); see also Green, *The Bible, The School*, 179–223.

65. Hamburger, *Separation*, 305.

66. See Kyle Duncan, "Secularism's Laws: State Blaine Amendments and Religious Persecution," 72 *Fordham L. Rev.* 493, 512 (2003).

67. With the exception of subsidies for specifically religious purposes, taxation to support government programs with which a religious or nonreligious taxpayer might disagree is constitutional. See McConnell, "Establishment," 2203.

68. See Vincent Blasi, "School Vouchers and Religious Liberty: Seven Questions from Madison's Memorial and Remonstrance," 87 *Cornell L. Rev.* 783, 790 (2002) (describing the distinction as resting on the fact that the state cannot have "a stake in the religious beliefs of its citizens").

69. See Jeffries & Ryan, "Political History," 293–294.

70. See id. at 294 (arguing that the issue of school funding would not have existed for the founders because public schools themselves did not exist).

71. 536 U.S. 639 (2002). See Chapter 2 for further discussion.

72. See generally Joseph P. Viteritti, *Choosing Equality: School Choice, the Constitution, and Civil Society* (1999) (suggesting a program of vouchers limited to low-income and minority children in order to offer the underprivileged greater educational possibilities, as well as to stimulate improvement in underperforming public schools).

73. 530 U.S. 793 (2000). In *Helms*, the Court (in a plurality decision authored by Justice Thomas) held that federal subsidies for the loan of educational materials to private schools, including religious schools, were constitutional.

74. See Agostini v. Felton, 521 U.S. 203 (1997). In *Agostini*, the Court held that New York City's program permitting public school teachers to provide remedial instruction at religious schools under a "shared time" arrangement was constitutional, provided that the subjects of instruction were secular. The Court overruled *Aguilar v. Felton*, which had held the opposite twelve years before. 473 U.S. 402 (1985).

75. See Marc O. DeGirolami, "The Problem of Religious Learning," 49 *B.C. L. Rev.* 1213, 1216 (2008).

76. The Supreme Court has repeatedly emphasized the foundational character and historically central function of public schools in cultivating civic values. See, e.g., Brown v. Bd. of Ed., 347 U.S. 483, 493 (1954); Pierce v. Soc'y of Sisters, 268 U.S. 510, 534 (1925); Wis. v. Yoder, 406 U.S. 205, 221(1972); Bethel Sch. Dist. No. 403 v. Fraser, 478 U.S. 675, 681 (1986); Ambach v. Norwick, 441 U.S. 68, 76–77 (1979); Edwards v. Aguillard, 482 U.S. 578, 584 (1987) (quoting McCollum, 333 U.S. at 231).

77. Amar, *Bill of Rights*, 44.

78. Greenawalt, *Establishment*, 389; see also Sharon K. Russo, "Vouchers for Religious Schools: The Death of Public Education?," 13 *S. Cal. Interdisc. L.J.* 49, 68, 73–74 (2003) (noting the process of resegregation and the draining of resources away from public schools to which vouchers contribute).

79. In the Cleveland program at issue in *Zelman*, 18 percent of the schools receiving support through vouchers were secular.

80. See Richard C. Schragger, "The Role of the Local in the Doctrine and Discourse of Religious Liberty," 117 *Harv. L. Rev.* 1810, 1854–1855 (2004).

81. Id. at 1855.

82. Feldman, *Divided*, 93.

83. Id.

84. Id.

85. Greenawalt, *Establishment*, 461.

86. 461 U.S. 574 (1983).

87. Compare Texas Monthly, Inc. v. Bullock, 489 U.S. 1, 12 & n.2 (1989) (noting that the tax exemption in *Walz* "possessed the legitimate secular purpose and effect of contributing to the community's moral and intellectual diversity and encouraging private groups to undertake projects that advanced the community's well-being and that would otherwise have to be funded by tax revenues or left undone").

88. Justice Douglas's dissent in *Walz*, in which he says that social history is completely irrelevant when deciding the tax exemption issue, is about as far from the method of tragedy and history as is possible. See Walz, 397 U.S. at 703 (Douglas, J., dissenting) ("Hence the question in the present case makes irrelevant the 'two centuries of uninterrupted freedom from taxation,' referred to by the Court. If history be our guide, then tax exemption of church property in this country is indeed highly suspect, as it arose in the early days when the church was an agency of the state. . . . The question here, though, concerns the meaning of the Establishment Clause and the Free Exercise Clause made applicable to the States for only a few decades at best").

89. See, e.g., Robert E. Rodes, "The Last Days of Erastianism—Forms in the American Church–State Nexus," 62 *Harv. Theological Rev.* 301, 317 (1969) (quoted in Garnett, "Quiet Faith," 773, n.9) ("Churches have been wholly or partially exempt from secular taxes since the time of Constantine at least; only the most rigorous ideologues feel that such exemption violates state or federal constitutional provisions").

90. Walz, 397 U.S. at 676 ("All of the 50 States provide for tax exemption of places of worship, most of them doing so by constitutional guarantees. For so long as federal income taxes have had any potential impact on churches—over 75 years—religious organizations have been expressly exempt from the tax").

91. In Texas v. Bullock, 489 U.S. 1 (1989), the Court held in a plurality opinion that a Texas state statute exempting religious periodicals from sales and use taxes violated the Establishment Clause. In one of the more considered statements in religion clause jurisprudence, Justice Blackmun wrote: "I find it . . . difficult to reconcile in this case the Free Exercise and Establishment Clause values. The Free Exercise Clause suggests that a special exemption for religious books is required. The Establishment Clause suggests that a special exemption for religious books is forbidden. This tension between mandated and prohibited religious exemptions is well recognized. . . . Perhaps it is a vain desire, but I would like to decide the present case without necessarily sacrificing either the Free Exercise Clause value or the Establishment Clause value. . . ." Id. at 27–28 (Blackmun, J., concurring). Whether Justice Blackmun succeeded in avoiding the tensions of religious liberty in this case—whether the outcome he reached achieves the coherence he desired—is a separate issue from his alertness to the tragic burdens of judgment.

92. Sch. Dist. of Abington Twp. v. Schempp, 374 U.S. 203, 225 (1963) (Douglas, J., concurring).

93. Lemon v. Kurtzman, 403 U.S. 602, 612 (1971); Bd. of Educ. v. Allen, 392 U.S. 236, 243 (1968).

94. For more extensive discussion of these issues, see DeGirolami, "Problem."

95. See Schempp, 374 U.S. at 205.

96. See Douglas Laycock, 1 *Religious Liberty: Overviews & History* 37 (2010) ("Coerced worship is one way to understand school prayer: all the students are required to participate . . .").

97. See Epperson v. Arkansas, 393 U.S. 97 (1968).

98. See Chapter 3. The same, incidentally, would be true of a policy that permitted students to pray voluntarily before sporting events. See Santa Fe Indep. Sch. Dist. v. Doe, 530 U.S. 290 (2000).

99. McCollum, 333 U.S. at 236 (Jackson, J., concurring).

100. 587 F.3d 597 (3d Cir. 2009).

101. Id. at 599–600.

102. Id. at 600–601.

103. Brief of the American Jewish Congress Anti-Defamation League, National Council of Jewish Women American Jewish Committee and the Jewish Council for Public Affairs as Amici Curiae in Support of Appellees, Stratechuk, 587 F.3d 598 (No. 08-3826), 2009 WL 601333, *14.

104. Id. at 602.

105. Id. at 605–606.

106. Id. at 608–609.

107. See Clever v. Cherry Hill Twp. Bd. of Educ., 838 F. Supp. 929, 940–941 (D.N.J. 1993) (observing that a school district policy that suppressed all references to religious symbols during the holiday season for the purpose of creating a neutral environment would violate the Establishment Clause).

108. Stratechuk v. Bd. of Educ., 577 F. Supp. 2d 731, 743 (D.N.J. 2008).

11. Objections and Replies

1. Thomas C. Berg, "Religion Clause Anti-Theories," 72 *Notre Dame L. Rev.* 693, 702 (1997).

2. David A. Strauss, *The Living Constitution* 35 (2010).

3. 545 U.S. 677, 693 (2005) (Thomas, J., concurring).

4. 132 S. Ct. 694 (2012).

5. 545 U.S. at 701 (Breyer, J., concurring).

6. Trunk v. City of San Diego, 629 F.3d 1099 (9th Cir. 2011).

7. Salazar v. Buono, 130 S. Ct. 1803, 1822 (2010) (Alito, J., concurring).

8. Van Orden, 545 U.S. at 692–693 (Thomas, J., concurring).

9. Buono, 130 S.Ct. at 1834–1835 (Stevens, J., dissenting).

10. See Steven D. Smith, *The Disenchantment of Secular Discourse* 26–33 (2010).

11. Thanks to Paul Horwitz for discussion about these issues.

12. Marc O. DeGirolami, "The Choice of Evils and the Collisions of Theory," in *Retributivism: Essays on Theory and Policy* (Mark D. White ed., 2011); Marc O. DeGirolami, "Against Theories of Punishment: The Thought of Sir James Fitzjames Stephen," 9 *Ohio St. J. Crim. L.* 699 (2012).

   The philosopher Jeffrie Murphy comes close to the ethic animating this book when he writes that "[n]eat, formal theories . . . generally produce not illumination but rather (in Herbert Hart's fine phrase) uniformity at the price of distortion." Jeffrie G. Murphy, *Getting Even: Forgiveness and Its Limits* 6 (2003).

13. See Marc O. DeGirolami, "The Vanity of Dogmatizing," 27 *Const. Comment.* 101 (2010).

14. U.S. Const. amend. 1.

15. Id.

16. See, e.g., John Hart Ely, *Democracy and Distrust: A Theory of Judicial Review* 94 (1980) (describing the commands of the religion clauses as "cross-cutting").

17. Cutter v. Wilkinson, 544 U.S. 709, 719 (2005); see also Locke v. Davey, 540 U.S. 712, 718 (2004) ("These two clauses . . . are frequently in tension"); Walz v. Tax Comm'n of N.Y.C., 397 U.S. 664, 668–669 (1970) ("The Court has struggled to find a neutral course between the two Religion Clauses, both of which are cast in absolute terms, and either of which, if expanded to a logical extreme, would tend to clash with the other").

18. See Andrew Koppelman, "Is It Fair to Give Religion Special Treatment?," 2006 *U. Ill. L. Rev.* 571, 582.

19. One is hard-pressed to think of any constitutional right whose core subject matter is the object of as much contestation. The establishment and free exercise of religion are qualitatively different from the "freedom of speech," "the right of the people to keep and bear arms," or even the "equal protection of the laws." Though there may well be disagreement about what "speech," "keep and bear arms," and "equal protection" ought to include at the margins, there is little disagreement about the core of what is protected, or whether these rights ought to be protected at all.

20. See W. B. Gallie, "Essentially Contested Concepts," in W. B. Gallie, *Philosophy and the Historical Understanding* 157–191 (1964); see also Jeremy Waldron, "Is the Rule of Law an Essentially Contest Concept (in Florida)?" 21 *L. & Phil.* 137, 151 (2002) (defining an essentially contested concept as one that is "present to us only in the form of contestation about what the ideal really is").

21. Kent Greenawalt, "Religion as a Concept in Constitutional Law," 72 *Calif. L. Rev.* 753, 753–754 (1984); 1 Kent Greenawalt, *Religion and the Constitution: Free Exercise and Fairness* 139 (2006).

22. Greenawalt, *Free Exercise*, 139 ("No one in our society doubts that Roman Catholicism, Greek Orthodoxy, Lutheranism, Orthodox Judaism, Islam, Hinduism, and Buddhism (at least in many forms) are religions").

23. Stuart Hampshire, *Morality & Conflict* 95 (1983).

24. See Joshua Foa Dienstag, *Pessimism: Philosophy, Ethic, Spirit* 18 (2006).

25. The difficulty of pinning down what characterizes pragmatism is notorious— indeed, obscurity may be one of pragmatism's constitutive qualities. Arthur Lovejoy famously identified no less than thirteen different types of pragmatism, and scores more have accumulated in legal theory alone since he wrote. See Arthur O. Lovejoy, *The Thirteen Pragmatisms* (1963). For a small sampling of legal pragmatism as a theory of adjudication, see Richard A. Posner, *Law, Pragmatism, and Democracy* (2003); Daniel A. Farber & Suzanna Sherry, *Desperately Seeking Certainty: The Misguided Quest for Constitutional Foundations* (2002); Symposium, "The Renaissance of Pragmatism in American Legal Thought," 63 *S. Cal. L. Rev.* (1990); Symposium, "The Revival of Pragmatism," 18 *Cardozo L. Rev.* 1 (1996).

26. Farber & Sherry, *Desperately*, 140.

27. Id. at 3.

28. See R. George Wright, "Dependence and Hierarchy among Constitutional Theories," 70 *Brook. L. Rev.* 141, 148–149 (2004) ("Professor Farber[] . . . seeks to add to the appeal of constitutional pragmatism by relying on, among other considerations, precedent, the relevant legal texts, original intent, philosophy, legal rights, and first

amendment values, presumably including democracy, autonomy, self-realization, tolerance, and the pursuit of truth").

29. Cass R. Sunstein, "Second-Order Perfectionism," 75 *Fordham L. Rev.* 2867 (2007).
30. Dienstag, *Pessimism*, 34.
31. Martha C. Nussbaum, *The Fragility of Goodness: Luck and Ethics in Greek Tragedy and Philosophy* 45 (rev. ed. 2001).

Conclusion

1. Joshua Foa Dienstag, *Pessimism: Philosophy, Ethic, Spirit* 263 (2006).
2. Blaise Pascal, *Pensées* 100 (E. P. Dutton & Co. ed., 1958).
3. Isaiah Berlin, "The Role of the Intelligentsia," in Isaiah Berlin, *The Power of Ideas* 104–105 (Henry Hardy ed., 2000).
4. G. K. Chesterton, "The Rolling English Road," in 10 G. K. Chesterton, *The Collected Works of G. K. Chesterton* 467 (1994).
5. 2 James Fitzjames Stephen, *A History of the Criminal Law of England* 84 (1883).

Acknowledgments

I have incurred many debts in the writing of this book, and it is a pleasure to acknowledge them. My own institution, Saint John's University School of Law, and its dean, Michael Simons, as well as my wonderful faculty colleagues and students, have been unfailingly supportive of my work. Some of the ideas in the book germinated during a fellowship at Columbia Law School and at the Catholic University of America, Columbus School of Law, where I was fortunate to visit for a year. Other ideas appeared in articles in the *Boston College Law Review*, the *San Diego Law Review*, the *Journal of Law and Religion*, and *Legal Theory*.

Many colleagues have offered learned and improving comments on sections of the book: Ittai Bar-Siman-Tov, Thomas Berg, Vincent Blasi, Samuel Bray, Nathan Chapman, Mary Jean Dolan, Donald Drakeman, W. Cole Durham, Christopher Eisgruber, Chad Flanders, Richard Garnett, Frederick Gedicks, Jamal Greene, David Gregory, Paul Horwitz, John Inazu, Cathleen Kaveny, Paul Kirgis, Andrew Koppelman, Joseph Landau, Christopher Lund, Dana Remus, Adam Samaha, Brett Scharffs, Micah Schwartzman, Steven Shiffrin, Steven Smith, Brian Tamanaha, Nelson Tebbe, Robert Vischer, and William Wagner. Two anonymous readers for the Harvard University Press deserve special thanks for their useful criticisms and suggestions. My colleague and dear friend, Mark Movsesian, has my deepest gratitude for reading the entire manuscript and for our many talks together. Yosefa Englard and Ourania Sdogos provided excellent and careful research assistance and prepared the index, and my secretary, Christine Patrizzo, helped in many ways. For his patience and wisdom, I also thank my editor, Michael Aronson. Portions of the manuscript benefited greatly from presentations at Brigham Young University School of Law, Brooklyn Law School, Columbia University School of Law, Northwestern University School of Law, Pepperdine University School of Law, Seton Hall University School of Law, and the University of Saint Thomas School of Law.

Two men—Kent Greenawalt and Philip Hamburger—have been intellectually and personally generous with me in ways large and small. They are my academic fathers, and this book would not exist without the constancy of their guidance.

This book is dedicated to my wife, Lisa, and our son, Thomas, who have sustained me with love. And it is dedicated to my father, Umberto DeGirolami, to whom I am indebted in every way that a son may be, as a small token of my affection and gratitude.

Index